THE SIERRA CLUB
GUIDE TO
THE NATURAL
AREAS OF
NEW ENGLAND

Other Natural Areas Guides

Guide to the Natural Areas of
California

Guide to the Natural Areas of
Oregon and Washington

Guide to the Natural Areas of New
Mexico, Arizona, and Nevada

Guide to the Natural Areas of
Colorado and Utah

Guide to the Natural Areas of
Idaho, Montana, and Wyoming

Guide to the Natural Areas of New
England

The Sierra Club Guide to the Natural Areas of

New England

John Perry

and

Jane Greverus Perry

with revisions by Roger Rapoport
and Nancy Madway

SIERRA CLUB BOOKS   SAN FRANCISCO

The Sierra Club, founded in 1892 by John Muir, has devoted itself to the study and protection of the earth's scenic and ecological resources—mountains, wetlands, woodlands, wild shores and rivers, deserts and plains. The publishing program of the Sierra Club offers books to the public as a nonprofit educational service in the hope that they may enlarge the public's understanding of the Club's basic concerns. The point of view expressed in each book, however, does not necessarily represent that of the Club. The Sierra Club has some sixty-five chapters coast to coast, in Canada, Hawaii, and Alaska. For information about how you may participate in its programs to preserve wilderness and the quality of life, please address inquiries to Sierra Club, 85 Second Street, San Francisco, CA 94105. http://www.sierra club.org/books

The revised edition of this book was prepared by Roger Rapoport and his staff at RDR Books, Berkeley.

Library of Congress Cataloging-in-Publication Data
Perry, John, 1914-
The Sierra Club guide to the natural areas of New England/John Perry and Jane Greverus Perry.

p. cm.
Includes index.
ISBN 0-87156-940-X
1. Natural areas—New England—Guide-books.
2. Outdoor recreation—New England—Guide-books.
I. Perry, Jane Greverus. II. Sierra Club.
III. Title.
QH104.5.N4P47 1990 796.5'0974—dc20 89-35736 CIP

Production by Janet Vail
Book design by Mark Ong
Maps by Hilda Chen

Printed in the United States of America on acid-free paper containing a minimum of 50% recovered waste paper, of which 10% of the fiber content is post-consumer waste

10 9 8 7 6 5 4 3 2 1

TO THE RANGERS, FORESTERS,
NATURALISTS, WILDLIFE BIOLOGISTS,
AND OTHER MEN AND WOMEN
WHO CARE FOR OUR FORESTS,
PARKS, AND PRESERVES

CONTENTS

INTRODUCTION

This book is a guide to quiet places, away from crowds and city noises, places to enjoy trees and wildflowers, clear brooks, singing birds, and the flash of a deer's white tail. It is a guide for campers and hikers, birders and canoeists, people who fish and those who hunt.

We had known New England well, but for ten years our work had been in the West. So much had changed! From New York to Bar Harbor, spreading urban development surrounds choked highways. Lakes we remembered as pristine have become busy resorts.

Such contrasts between West and East! Montana's population density is less than 6 people per square mile. In Massachusetts it's 767, while in Connecticut almost 80% of residents live in urban areas. Distances seemed so short; one can cross Massachusetts in an hour. Spaces seemed so small—Montana is more than twice as large as all New England! Montana has 27 million acres of federal land open to recreation; all of New England has 1 million. We had written about western sites covering several million acres. New England's natural areas come in smaller packages.

But after a few days of hiking and canoeing, we put aside West-East comparisons. New England has its own unique natural qualities, its special ambiance. Founded on the hemisphere's oldest rock, the landscape has been carved by a "recent" ice sheet. One mourns the destruction of the primeval forest but rejoices in its successor, risen from stony fields, approaching maturity.

New England has bush pilots who fly people and their canoes to otherwise inaccessible lakes. One can canoe-camp for days, running flat water and white water, seldom meeting another party. New England has many miles of scenic mountain trails. With the returning forest has come a rejuvenated wildlife population, with increasing numbers of moose, bear, coyote, fisher, marten. Few regions have such a diversity of bird species, some at the northern or southern limits of their ranges, some seen only offshore, many breeding in the extensive wetlands. And few regions have such a diversity and abundance of seasonal wildflowers.

Don't come to New England with western expectations. This is a different kind of country, with different opportunities for enjoyment of nature.

Quality of Life and Landscape

Maps of the New England states show many little patches of green: the parks and forests. As one drives the highways, however, most of the region looks green. The original forest was cut long ago, but the forest has returned. Four-fifths of the land again supports trees. However, less than one-tenth of the new forest is on publicly owned land. Most of it is at risk.

In our home state, Florida, one can't see the landscape for the billboards. They are wonderfully absent through most of New England. So is roadside litter, except where natives are outnumbered.

Hundreds of small towns have kept their colonial character: white-painted homes, many more than a century old; neat lawns and hedges; broad, tree-lined Main Streets with no flashing neon signs or golden arches. The character of these towns has been maintained not by ordinances but by the popular will.

New Englanders care about their land. Many landowners, unwilling to see their holdings subdivided and developed, bequeath them to the Audubon Society, The Nature Conservancy, the Society for the Protection of New Hampshire Forests, or other groups for permanent protection.

Traditionally, much recreation has been on private land. In the north, this tradition continues. Many timber companies invite, welcome, or at least permit recreational use of their extensive holdings.

In the south, voluntary associations such as the Connecticut Forest and Park Association have developed networks of hiking trails, linking State lands, crossing private lands with owners' permission. Connecticut's Blue-Blazed Trails, the Appalachian Trail, Vermont's Long

Trail, and many others have been planned, built, and maintained by citizen organizations, a remarkable achievement and testament to the neighborliness of New England land-owners.

Of late, in some parts of New England, rapid growth has swept neighborliness aside. Developer money has overwhelmed tradition. The newcomers are less hospitable. Some resort areas have become gaudy, but not all. There are still natural areas to enjoy.

State Lands

Out West, about half of the land is federally owned. The only large federal lands in New England are its two National Forests; all federal lands combined are less than 3% of the region.

Therefore, providing open green space in a period of rapid growth is a responsibility that has fallen on the States. They are responding by buying more land. Most New England residents now have a park, forest, or other green space less than 10 miles from home.

For residents, this is splendid, but what do these sites offer visitors? Should we include a small natural area within a metropolis? Would visitors struggle through heavy traffic when they can find attractive sites more easily elsewhere? Should we omit everything within the congested coastal corridor?

The New England coast couldn't be overlooked. A beach that's crowded on the Fourth of July may be deserted after Labor Day. The salt marshes are special. So are the tide pools, dunes, islands, estuaries, rocky promontories. We've included the best of the natural areas on and near the coast, noting that one should choose the right time for a visit.

Solitude Is There—If You Can Find It

State Parks are easy to find. They're shown on highway maps and usually have entrance signs. Finding a State Forest or Wildlife Management Area may be more difficult. Often there are no signs at access or entrance roads. Boundaries may be unmarked or marked in ways few visitors will recognize. Frequently we couldn't tell State from private land.

Chiefly, state recreation areas serve state residents. In State Parks we saw few out-of-state license plates. Not that New England lacks tourists, but most go to popular resorts, Acadia National Park, Cape Cod National Seashore, and such scenic areas as Mount Washington and Franconia Notch.

Some state headquarters can provide site maps; others have none. At headquarters, we asked how people find these sites. While acknowledging the lack of maps and signs, our advisors said this was no great problem because most visitors came from nearby. Local hunters, fishermen and women, picnickers, and hikers knew the areas.

You are not unwelcome, and the lack of publicity means you'll have less company. Except in hunting season, most State Forests and Wildlife Management Areas are quiet, many of them are scenic and delightful. We hiked their trails and seldom met other hikers. Our entries will help you find these quiet places. *When in doubt, ask locally.* Folks who live nearby know where to go.

Maps

Most U.S. roads aren't shown on standard state highway maps. Travelers venturing off main highways need more than these. Map resources differ among the New England states. State prefaces say what's available.

A fine series of state and county maps is available to members of the American Automobile Association (there are AAA offices in cities throughout the New England region: consult local phone directories). Most surfaced roads shown on these maps are suitable for ordinary cars, but map legends for other roads should be heeded, especially "graded dirt," "dirt," and "poor or doubtful." Always inquire locally about the condition of unpaved roads, especially if you are driving an RV or towing a trailer. Also, roads in National Forests and Wildlife Refuges usually aren't shown on these maps, and the small roads leading to them and to some of the small Preserves may also not be shown.

However, we were delighted by the DeLorme atlases for Maine, New Hampshire, and Vermont. Rhode Island is so small its official highway map shows and names most streets. On a scale of about 3.5 miles per inch, Connecticut's official map is easy to read. At 5.8 miles per inch, the Massachusetts map is more difficult, but we could find nothing better.

National Forest maps show Forest roads; the highway maps don't. Entries note if site maps are available.

Camping

Out West, we seldom looked for a campsite until our day's work was done. Often, instead of campgrounds we found pleasant places on public land, perhaps beside a lake or stream. Such informal camping is usually prohibited in New England except in the two National Forests; one must use designated campgrounds. (Members of the American Automobile Association can obtain a copy of the *Northeastern CampBook* which lists both private and public campgrounds. It's free to members.)

Some State Parks and State Forests don't offer campgrounds, and some that do were closed to us because we travel with a dog. Commercial campgrounds are usually available, but on summer weekends it's wise to have reservations. Because of our unpredictable schedule, we didn't make reservations, but we always found something.

Especially in southern New England, almost any campground can serve as a base. From a campground in west central Massachusetts, for example, any natural area in the western half of the state is within an hour's drive. Distances are greater in the north, but campsites are less crowded, and one can always camp in the National Forests.

Many State Forests and Wildlife Management Areas (WMAs) have small parking areas along interior dirt roads. They are used mostly by hunters. We often saw indications that people had camped, and we saw no signs prohibiting camping. At headquarters we were told camping is prohibited, and we asked if the rule were enforced. No one suggested ignoring the rule, but some answers were qualified:

- State agencies can't maintain regular patrols, especially on weekends. But some local managers make a point of patrolling.
- Parking a self-contained recreation vehicle overnight is less objectionable than other forms of camping.
- If asked, some local managers may suggest a place to park.
- Fires are strictly prohibited.

Hiking and Backpacking

New England has several thousand miles of fine trails, short and long. Opportunities for day hikes are unlimited. Backpacking may be a problem, however, even on the Appalachian Trail.

Informal trailside camping is prohibited on almost all State lands except in Vermont. Camping along the Appalachian and other long trails is limited to designated sites—State Park and Forest camp-grounds and a few shelters—except in National Forests. One can use the designated sites to plan a weekend backpack, but more extensive hikes, even on the Appalachian Trail, may require spending some nights off trail. Inn-to-inn hiking is popular in some areas.

The hiking guides and other references noted in each state preface are of great value. They describe the long trails and dozens of short trails to waterfalls, lookouts, ponds, and other places of special beauty or interest you're not likely to find without them. Without their descriptions of blazes, landmarks, side trails, and other highlights, you might lose your way. U.S. Geological Society topographic maps are especially helpful. These are often available on site or by writing to:

US Geological Survey
Maps Dept.
12201 Sunrise Valley Dr.
Reston, VA 22092
(800) 872-6277
(703) 648-6045

Canoe Country

Carry a canoe if you can, possibly with camping gear. The canoeing guides noted in the state prefaces describe many spectacular trips through backcountry you can't get to by land. Many wetlands are best seen by canoe.

The rules prohibiting informal camping are less strictly applied to canoe camping. On a few popular waterways, canoeists are asked to use designated sites. More often you can find a suitable site on shore or on an island. If the site seems to be private property and you can find the owner, it's good form to ask permission.

How To Use This Book

Read the prefaces for each state! New England is not homogeneous—Maine doesn't resemble Rhode Island. The six states have great differences in their natural qualities and in opportunities for outdoor recreation.

The entries listed in each state preface, except Rhode Island's, are marked "North," "South," etc. The most populous areas, with the heaviest traffic, are eastern Rhode Island, Connecticut, Massachusetts, southern New Hampshire, and southeastern Maine. The least populated areas with the most open space are northern Maine, New Hampshire, and Vermont.

What's In the Entries

Entries tell how to get to principal site entrances.

A row of symbols shows at a glance the activities offered by each site. In addition to a general description of terrain and noteworthy features, information about flora and fauna is noted if it's available. Often it's not, but information from a similar site is usually applicable.

Some sites are included because of their interpretive programs. This is especially true of Audubon preserves and wildflower gardens where one can learn much about the ecology of a region and see labeled specimens of living plants.

Headings under ACTIVITIES match the symbols above. The symbol for ski touring (cross-country skiing) simply means it's permitted. The text doesn't add "If there's enough snow," and there's no promise of groomed trails.

PUBLICATIONS are those available in 1996 at the site or other headquarters. Some sites have bookstores that offer site-specific and general books and pamphlets that will enhance your visit. Most government publications are free and may be sent on request from state agencies, especially if you send a self-addressed envelope. Site headquarters seldom have resources to respond to mail requests.

Some publications aren't free, especially those of private groups. We noted prices if asked to do so, but caution that prices often change.

Some regional references are listed in several state prefaces, to provide the best service to readers.

HEADQUARTERS is the place to make inquiries. We asked each state headquarters to tell us whether to use site addresses, regional offices, or state headquarters and acted on their advice. Some sites have local managers but no offices. Some have only part-time or visiting managers.

What's Not In the Entries

Entries don't provide information about the following:

- *Entrance and camping fees.* Many State Parks and some forest recreation areas charge entrance fees. Almost all campgrounds do. Fees vary from place to place and year to year.
- *Campground facilities.* Standard campground directories and State-published leaflets provide the data.
- *Picnicking.* Except in a few private preserves where it's prohibited, one can picnic almost anywhere.
- *Hunting and fishing rules and regulations.* Each State publishes its own, annually.
- *Swimming,* unless there's a managed beach. It's prohibited in some public water supply reservoirs. For the most part, it's up to you and at your risk. Many beaches in New England are used more for sunbathing than swimming because of cold water.
- *Winter sports.* Entries note downhill skiing if there's a ski area on the site. New England has many more ski areas, described in special directories. Entries mention cross-country ski possibilities when that information was given to us. Ice skating is rarely mentioned by site managers because it's unmanaged; people skate at their own risk. Ice fishing is popular on some lakes, subject to State regulation.
- *Rules about pets,* except where they are firmly prohibited. Leashes are required where pets are permitted. Pets are almost always barred from public buildings and beaches. The rules in New England State Parks change from year to year, and enforcement is uneven. Except in crowded resort areas, few commercial campgrounds exclude pets.

Hazards

Entries note a few special hazards such as sudden weather on Mount Washington. A more general admonition is not to plan mountain hiking trips during the mud season, generally from snowmelt until about the end of May. You won't enjoy hiking, and boots damage wet trails.

Late spring and early summer is usually the black fly season in the northern woods. Outfitters, pharmacies, and markets sell extrastrength repellents to ward off the vicious beasts. It's wise to have some.

References

In addition to standard field guides, we found these books useful to an understanding of the natural history of New England:

AMC Field Guide to Mountain Flowers of New England. Boston: Appalachian Mountain Club, 1982. Now out of print, but the Green Mountain Club (see entry in preface for Vermont) is selling copies.

DeGraaf, Richard M., and Deborah D. Rudis. *New England Wildlife: Habitat, Natural History, and Distribution.* General Technical Report NE-108. Broomwall, PA: U.S. Department of Agriculture, Forest Service, Northeastern Forest Experiment Station, 1986. This quickly became a classic, although it is now out of print. The Forest Service hasn't committed to a reprint, but says that due to its popularity, a fifth printing "would not be surprising."

Jorgensen, Neil. *A Sierra Club Naturalist's Guide to Southern New England.* San Francisco: Sierra Club Books, 1982.

Kulik, Stephen, Pete Salmansohn, Matthew Schmidt, and Heidi Welch. *The Audubon Society Field Guide to the Natural Places of the Northeast: Coastal.* New York: Pantheon Books, 1984.

Kulik, Stephen, Pete Salmansohn, Matthew Schmidt, and Heidi Welch. *The Audubon Society Field Guide to the Natural Places of the Northeast: Inland.* New York: Pantheon Books, 1984. Both of the Audubon guides are presently out of print.

Peterson, Roger T. *A Field Guide to Eastern Birds,* 4th ed. Boston: Houghton Mifflin, 1980.

Peterson, Roger T., and Margaret McKenny. *A Field Guide to Wildflowers of Northeastern and North-Central North America.* Boston: Houghton Mifflin, 1975.

References specific to states appear in state prefaces.

THE SIERRA CLUB GUIDE TO THE NATURAL AREAS OF NEW ENGLAND

MAINE

Large as the rest of New England combined, Maine has less than a tenth of the region's population. Most of its people live in the coastal region from Portsmouth to Bar Harbor. The extreme south has merged with the Boston metropolis.

This is the part of ME most visitors see, and that has been true for some time. Seacoast towns and villages have long attracted "summer people," often in small colonies, who return regularly for a few months each year during ME's idyllic sailing weather. From the southern border to Bar Harbor, the coast is busy in summer with a variety of people from somewhere else. We saw crowds at every sandy beach. Seaside State Parks were jammed, cars parked along the roads outside their gates. Traffic on the main roads was heavy. The number of antique shops made us wonder if producing antiques is a major industry. The many lobster restaurants made it understandable that the lobster population has declined alarmingly.

Some speculators have made fortunes buying land and selling to developers. Lakes are the developers' prime targets as far north and inland as Moosehead Lake. Lakes and ponds that were isolated 20 years ago are surrounded now by condominiums and tourist businesses. Our ME advisors called the change sudden, dramatic, overwhelming. For the most part, it has been uncontrolled, as developers found loopholes in the state's environmental laws, and localities were without protective restrictions.

"These aren't our people buying the land," one native said bitterly. "Maine folks don't have that kind of money." Frugal ME natives are amazed to see costly houses and condominiums built for only two weeks' occupancy a year. And upset, as these displace the rustic "camps" their families have enjoyed in summer for generations.

But it's still a fascinating coast, only 320 mi. long yet with a 3,478-mi. shoreline and 2,000 islands. And one can find quiet places even in summer. Avoid the sandy beaches. Rocky shores attract fewer people, and such places have a greater diversity of flora and fauna. Acadia National Park has some splendid rocky shore. Beyond Acadia there's no crowding.

Maine Is Different

Away from the coast is a vast area unlike anything else in the U.S., 300 mi. N–S, 300 mi. wide. The terrain is generally hilly and not high. Most of the SE half is below 500 ft. elevation. Most of the NW is a plateau between 1,000 and 1,500 ft. Mountains, extensions of the Appalachian chain, rise to peaks from 3,000 to 5,000 ft. in the central and western sectors. At 5,268 ft., Mount Katahdin is ME's highest point.

The landscape was shaped by glaciers. The state has 6,000 lakes and ponds. With its 32,000 mi. of rivers and streams, ME has more canoe routes than any other eastern state. Little known are its 700,000 acres of bogs and wetlands.

Much of the landscape one sees along inland highways is monotonous: mile after mile of second-growth forest on gently rolling land. Highway planners avoid mountains and ravines. Trees hide most of the lakes and rivers.

Maine's 17.6 million acres of forest cover almost 90% of its land area—the largest percent of any state. But 92% of these forests are privately owned, and one-half of the 92% are owned by a dozen large paper companies and land management corporations that purchased vast acreages from the state in the 19th century.

Thus, ME has far less public land in relation to its size than any other woodland state. But it hasn't seemed to matter. For generations, most outdoor recreation—especially hunting, fishing, and canoeing—has been on private land. In 1996 we chatted with a ME native living near Moosehead Lake, who spoke of the state's good fortune in that so much of its interior is "protected" by paper corporations. She said that her particular area hadn't changed very much, and regarded those who were selectively harvesting ME forests as important benefactors for her community, both economically and as a means of holding the line against overdevelopment. Not all ME people share that perspective, however. Shortly after we spoke with this woman, a majority of ME residents across the state voted to approve ballot measures designed to protect the North Maine Woods from clear-cutting and from the possibility of unbridled development in the future. This was in response to the increased development generally within the state, to the increasing efficiency of clear-cutting technology, and to the fact that ME's large paper and timber companies are now as likely to be controlled by those who reside outside of the state, even outside of the country, as not.

The traditional recreation pattern in ME was based on the "camp," typically a lakeshore lodge that was the only habitation on a back-country lake. The camp provided guides, canoes, and equipment. Many people returned year after year to go out with the same guide, who paddled, made camp, cleaned fish, and cooked. People from ME may also refer to the family cottages they own or rent for summer vacations on a lake or pond as a "camp."

Climate

Summer temperatures throughout ME are generally cool, averaging about 70°F. Hot days are unusual. In January average temperatures range from 10°F in the far north to over 20° along the coast. Total annual precipitation averages from 40 to 44 in., with no pronounced wet or dry seasons. Except along the coast, most winter precipitation is snow. January is the snowiest month. The period of snow cover ranges from about 50 days near the coast to 4 months in the NW.

Maps

Besides the excellent American Automobile Association maps (available free to AAA members), Maine is blessed with an array of excellent maps produced by the DeLorme Mapping Company of Freeport.

Maine Atlas and Gazetteer, The. Freeport: DeLorme Mapping Company, 1995.

The *Maine Atlas* has 78 full-page maps with symbols that indicate beaches, nature preserves, wildlife management areas, parks, boat launching sites, canoe trips, trails, and much more. It includes information about a range of subjects from campgrounds to charter fly-in services.

Maps and guides for hiking, canoeing, and fishing are noted under those headings.

Flora and Fauna

There are only a few remnants of ME's primeval forest, predominantly spruce and white pine. The timber industry is now cutting second- and third-growth spruce and pine, as well as poplar, fir, hemlock, and some hardwoods, chiefly maple, beech, and birch.

Although this forest is by far the most extensive plant community, there are many others, from coastal tide pools to subarctic flora on high mountains. Much of the northern region is poorly drained, creating swamps and bogs with their special plant species.

We didn't find a popular guide to ME plants. Entries note what is available for sites such as Baxter State Park, which suggests species one could expect to find in similar habitats. Fox State Forest in New Hampshire is one of several sites that provides good information. Good regional references are:

AMC Field Guide to Mountain Flowers of New England. Boston: Appalachian Mountain Club, 1982. (This is available from the Green Mountain Club, if not elsewhere. See VT Introduction.)

Peterson, Roger T., and Margaret McKenny. *A Field Guide to Wildflowers of Northeastern and North-Central North America.* Boston: Houghton Mifflin, 1975.

We also did not find popular guides to the state's birds and mammals. The Maine Audubon Society has a field checklist of birds. And, of course, there is:

Peterson, Roger T. *A Field Guide to Eastern Birds,* 4th ed. Boston: Houghton Mifflin, 1980.

The state's mammals include three big game species: white-tailed deer, black bear, and moose. Small mammals include bobcat, weasel, squirrel, snowshoe hare, coyote, fox, skunk, fisher, marten, raccoon, beaver, mink, otter, and muskrat. Marine mammals are often seen along the coast and its many islands. Large remote areas with little hunting pressure are valuable reservoirs.

Some of the larger sites, notably Acadia National Park and Baxter State Park, have information about their fauna. The most comprehensive information is provided by:

DeGraaf, Richard M., and Deborah D. Rudis. *New England Wildlife: Habitat, Natural History, and Distribution.* General Technical Report NE-l08. Broomwall, PA: U.S. Department of

Agriculture, Forest Service, Northeastern Forest Experiment Station, 1986. This was not available in the fall of 1996. However, it has been a well-known and much-used publication. Our sources spoke of the likelihood of a fifth printing.

Trails

An estimate of total trail mileage wouldn't mean much in ME. In the vast region of commercial forest land, hikers use logging roads, many of which are busy during timber cutting, then abandoned until the next cutting cycle years later.

The state's four great trail systems are:

- The Appalachian Trail, which begins in Baxter State Park
- Other Baxter trails
- Acadia National Park trails
- White Mountain National Forest trails

Trail information is noted in entries. Also see:

Appalachian Trail Committee. *Appalachian Trail Guide to Maine.* Harpers Ferry, WV: Appalachian Trail Conference, 1993.

Maine Mountain Guide, 7th ed. Boston: Appalachian Mountain Club.

Although these trails attract most of the backpackers, there are also many fine trails for day hikes. Even in midsummer we often hiked for several hours without meeting others. You might try checking the *Maine Atlas* to see what trails are in the region that interests you. Then consult one of the following booklets, which have trail maps in color, and directions:

Hiking, Vol. 1: *Coastal and Eastern Region* (1988). Vol. 2: *Western Region* (1993). Vol. 3: *Northern Region* (1992). Freeport: DeLorme Mapping Company.

Trails in Baxter, the SW region, and the south coast are described, with maps, in:

Gibson, John. *Fifty Hikes in Southern Maine,* 2nd ed. Woodstock, VT: Countryman Press, 1996.

Private Lands

The use of private land for public recreation continues today, with increasing controls. The North Maine Woods (see entry), 2.8 million acres, has entrances where visitors register and select campsites. Some timber companies also have entrance gates and fees. Several didn't respond to our inquiries. One manager telephoned to explain why he wouldn't answer in writing: "We still let people hunt and fish and camp on our land, but we must be free to close gates or areas whenever we need to. We don't want anyone to think he has a right to be on our land."

The general rule seems to be: If a gate or sign tells you to keep out, do so. Otherwise, it's probably OK to enter, but act like a guest. If you're on a canoe trip, riparian camping is permissible unless there's a posted prohibition.

The Public Reserved Lands

Not too long ago it was discovered that the state had not, in fact, sold all that land in the 1800s. In some cases it had sold only the rights to the timber then standing. Having reestablished its title to 450,000 acres, the state began trading and consolidating. Now available to visitors are 29 parcels, from 500 acres to over 43,000 acres. Multiple-purpose management plans call for a minimum of development, preservation of natural qualities, and opportunities for primitive recreation. If you visit one of these units, you're on your own.

We visited most of these sites and pronounce them splendid. The ME Bureau of Parks and Lands has a leaflet, *Outdoors in Maine,* which describes many of the public reserved lands, and offers excellent information generally on recreational opportunities in the state.

State Parks

The ME Bureau of Parks and Lands operates 32 State Parks, large and small, serving a variety of purposes. Size isn't always significant. Some of the smaller Parks adjoin or are within larger areas available for recreation.

Preservation of green space hasn't kept up with development in the south. Areas of private land once freely used for recreation are fast being developed. As the need increases, land prices soar. One town paid over half a million dollars for 1,400 feet of lakefront. The federal funds once available to states for land acquisition have stopped coming. Bond issues have been proposed as an alternative. Developers and their political allies are, of course, opposed to state acquisition of any tract that could be a building site.

Maine has no State Forests. However, the ME Forest Service administers many forest campsites on private lands. (See Camping, below.)

Coastal Islands

The ME Bureau of Parks and Lands manages several hundred small state-owned coastal islands. Hundreds more are state or federal wildlife refuges with restricted access. Most of the islands are rocky and barren, some inundated by high tides. Some are off limits because of seabird colonies. A few, however, are large enough to support some visitation and have interesting features. The Bureau's leaflet, *Your Islands on the Coast,* describes 40 of these and includes warnings that should be heeded. Also available is:

Illustrated Map of the Maine Coast, The. Freeport: DeLorme Mapping Company, 1987.

Monegain, Bernie. *Coastal Islands, A Guide to Exploring Maine's Isles.* Freeport: DeLorme Mapping Company, 1988.

Wildlife Management Areas

We have listed about 13 Wildlife Management Areas, out of a total of more than 40 operated by the ME Dept. of Inland Fisheries and Wildlife. Maine, with its many wetlands, is an important waterfowl production area, and several of the Wildlife Management Areas are wetlands (see entries).

There isn't much printed information available about these sites, but the Dept.'s Information Center (see State Agencies) was very helpful answering our questions.

Camping

Of the State Parks, 13 have campgrounds. Most are open May 15–Oct. 15. Reservations can be made by telephone: (800) 332-1501 within ME; (207) 289-3824 outside using VISA or MasterCard, but we suggest asking for the system information first, by telephone or writing to the Bureau of Parks and Lands.

Pets are not allowed at Sebago Lake State Park or on beaches in other Parks.

Camping is only permitted in campgrounds in State Parks and Acadia National Park. Campsites are assigned at entrance gates of the North Maine Woods. Informal camping is permitted in the Public Reserved Lands and in the White Mountain National Forest.

Forest campsites are available at many locations on private lands in northern ME. The ME Forest Service no longer publishes a list of these sites, but information is available at Forest Service regional offices in Augusta, Ashland, Greenville, and Old Town. Contact the office nearest the area where you wish to camp.

Maine has many commercial campgrounds, but the vocabulary often confuses strangers. A "camp" may offer cabins, guides, fishing, boating, and more—but not campsites for tents or RVs. Consult a campground directory (such as AAA's *Northeastern Campbook*) or consult the Maine Campground Owners Association, 655 Main St., Lewiston, ME 04240; (207) 782-5874. They will send free of charge their *Maine Camping Guide*. For a broader picture, the promotional brochure, *Exploring Maine,* has much useful information. It's available from:

Maine Publicity Bureau
P.O. Box 2300
97 Winthrop St.
Hallowell, ME 04347
(207) 623-0363; (800) 533-9595

The brochure includes a list of Chambers of Commerce, several of which we found remarkably well informed about local trails and other outdoor features.

Canoeing

Maine is canoe country, none finer. We saw 10 canoes on passing cars for every motorcraft towed or carried. The most famous canoe trips are the Allagash Wilderness Waterway and the St. John River. We have entries for them and a number of others. Many trips are described and mapped in various publications, including those we list. The North Woods has countless backcountry water routes known only to professional guides, who know the best places to fish and camp.

AMC River Guide: Maine, 2nd ed. Boston: Appalachian Mountain Club, 1991.

Kellogg, Zip. *Canoeing*, Vol. I: *Coastal and Eastern Rivers* (1993). Vol. 2: *Western Rivers* (1985). Vol. 3: *Northern Rivers* (1986). Freeport: DeLorme Mapping Company.

Ski Touring

A Guide to Cross-Country Skiing on Maine's State Parks and Public Lands is a useful leaflet available from the ME Bureau of Parks and Lands. It gives location, acreage, trails, parking information, map availability, and regulations for the 16 winter recreation areas listed.

Fishing, Boating

Three volumes of fishing maps have descriptions of the waters and tell what species inhabit them. The maps show public launching sites. The Bureau of Parks and Lands leaflet, *Outdoors in Maine*, has a long list of boat-launching sites.

Vanderweide, Harry, and David DeLorme. *Maine Fishing Maps*, Vol. 1: *Lakes and Ponds* (1993). Vol. 2: *Rivers and Streams* (1991). Freeport: DeLorme Mapping Company.

State Agencies

Maine Bureau of Parks and Lands
22 State House Station
Augusta, ME 04333-0022
(207) 287-3821

For U.S. Geological Survey maps of ME, ask for the Bureau's Natural Resources and Mapping Center at this address.

Maine Department of Inland Fisheries and Wildlife
41 State House Station
August, ME 04333-0041
(207) 287-8000

Maine Forest Service (for Forest campsites)
Ashland (207) 435-7964
Augusta (207) 287-2275
Greenville (207) 695-3721
Old Town (207) 827-6191

Private Organizations

Maine Audubon Society
Gilsland Farm
118 US 1
P.O. Box 6009
Falmouth, ME 04105
(207) 781-2330

The society owns 16 sanctuaries in ME. We have entries for several.

Maine Chapter, The Nature Conservancy
Fort Andross
14 Maine St., Suite 401
Brunswick, ME 04011
(207) 729-5181

The Nature Conservancy's mission is to identify and preserve unusual natural areas. In ME, the Conservancy has acquired or received numerous parcels of land subsequently transferred to federal or state agencies. It currently owns and manages 82 preserves totaling about 22,000 acres. We have entries for several.

Maine Forever, 2nd ed., 1989, is the ME Chapter's preserve directory: $5 plus $2 handling. A 24-page booklet, *Protected Lands,* is available free of charge.

Appalachian Trail Conference
P.O. Box 807
Harpers Ferry, WV 25425-0807
(304) 535-6331

The nonprofit ATC, formed in 1925, has day-to-day responsibility for managing the lands through which the Appalachian Trail is routed. It is also the central clearinghouse for information on the trail and publishes guides, maps, and other relevant materials. Contact them to check if they have such materials for a site you plan to visit.

Maine Appalachian Trail Club
P.O. Box 283
Augusta, ME 04330

This is the trail organization in the region. It works cooperatively with the ATC.

North Maine Woods
P.O. Box 421
Ashland, ME 04732
(207) 435-6213

North Maine Woods is a private organization responsible for the management of recreational use areas of commercial forest land in NW ME.

MAINE

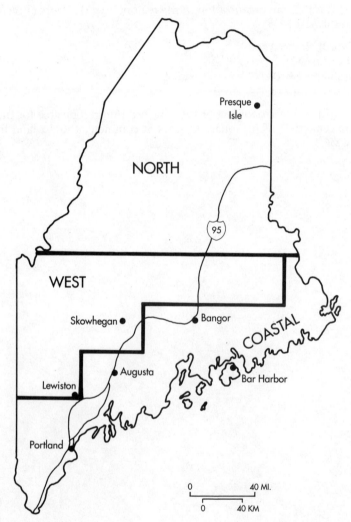

Presque
Isle

NORTH

95

WEST

Skowhegan

Bangor

COASTAL

Augusta

Bar Harbor

Lewiston

Portland

0 — 40 MI.

0 — 40 KM

Natural Areas in Maine

An Alphabetical Listing

Acadia National Park
Coastal

Allagash Wilderness Waterway
North

Appalachian Trail
West

Baxter State Park
North

Bigelow Preserve
West

Bradbury Mountain State Park
Coastal

**Brownfield Bog Wildlife
Management Area**
Coastal

Camden Hills State Park
Coastal

**Chamberlain Lake Management
Unit**
North

**Chesterville Wildlife
Management Unit**
West

Cobscook Bay State Park
Coastal

Deboullie Management Unit
North

Donnell Pond
Coastal

Duck Lake Management Unit
West

Eagle Lake Management Unit
North

East Point Sanctuary
Coastal

Fernald's Neck Preserve
Coastal

Field's Pond Nature Center
Coastal

Four Ponds Management Unit
West

**Francis D. Dunn Wildlife
Management Area (Sawtelle
Deadwater)**
North

**Frye Mountain Wildlife
Management Area**
Coastal

**Gardner-Deboullie Management
Unit**
North

**Georgia-Pacific Corporation
Lands**
West/North

Gero Island Management Unit
North

Gilsland Farm
Coastal

Grafton Notch State Park
West

Great Heath, The
Coastal

Great Wass Island Preserve
Coastal

Gulf Hagas Area
North

Holeb Management Unit
North

Howard L. Mendall Wildlife Management Area
Coastal

Indian Point/Blagden Preserve
Coastal

Josephine Newman Sanctuary
Coastal

Kennebunk Plains Wildlife Management Area/Kennebunk Plains Preserve
Coastal

La Verna and Rachel Carson Salt Pond Preserves
Coastal

Leavitt Wildlife Management Area
West

Lt. Gordon Manuel Wildlife Management Area
North

Lily Bay State Park
North

Little Squaw Management Unit
North

Machias Seal Island
Coastal

Mahoosuc Mountains Management Unit
West

Mast Landing Sanctuary
Coastal

Mattawamkeag Wilderness Park
North

Moosehead Lake
North

Moosehorn National Wildlife Refuge
Coastal

Morse Mountain Preserve
Coastal

Mount Blue State Park
West

Mullen Woods Preserve
Coastal

Nahmakanita Management Unit
North

North Maine Woods
North

Old Pond Farm Wildlife Management Area
West

Peaks-Kenny State Park
West

Petit Manan National Wildlife Refuge
Coastal

Popham Beach State Park
Coastal

Quoddy Head State Park
Coastal

Rachel Carson National Wildlife Refuge
Coastal

Rangeley Lake State Park
West

Reid State Park
Coastal

Richardson Management Unit
West

Rocky Lake Management Unit
Coastal

Round Pond Management Unit
North

Ruffingham Wildlife Management Area
Coastal

R. Waldo Tyler Wildlife Management Area (Weskeag Marsh)
Coastal

St. John River
North

Scarborough Marsh Nature Center
Coastal

Scraggly Lake Management Unit
North

Sebago Lake State Park
Coastal

Seboeis Lake Management Unit
North

Seboeis River
North

Squa Pan Lake
North

Steep Falls Wildlife Management Area
Coastal

Steve Powell Wildlife Management Area
Coastal

Sugar Island Management Unit
North

Sunkhaze Meadows National Wildlife Refuge
Coastal

Telos Lake Management Unit/ Chamberlain Lake Management Unit
North

Vaughan Woods
Coastal

Vernon S. Walker Wildlife Management Area
Coastal

Wells National Estuarine Research Reserve
Coastal

White Mountain National Forest
West

Natural Areas in Maine

by Zone

NORTH ZONE

Allagash Wilderness Waterway

Baxter State Park

Chamberlain Lake Management Unit

Deboullie Management Unit

Eagle Lake Management Unit

Francis D. Dunn Wildlife Management Area (Sawtelle Deadwater)

Gardner-Deboullie Management Unit

Georgia-Pacific Corporation Lands

Gero Island Management Unit

Gulf Hagas Area

Holeb Management Unit

Lt. Gordon Manuel Wildlife Management Area

Lily Bay State Park

Little Squaw Management Unit

Mattawamkeag Wilderness Park

Moosehead Lake

Nahmakanta Management Unit

North Maine Woods

Round Pond Management Unit

St. John River

Scraggly Lake Management Unit

Seboeis Lake Management Unit

Seboeis River

Squa Pan Lake

Sugar Island Management Unit

Telos Lake Management Unit/ Chamberlain Lake Management Unit

COASTAL ZONE

Acadia National Park

Bradbury Mountain State Park

Brownfield Bog Wildlife Management Area

Camden Hills State Park

Cobscook Bay State Park

Donnell Pond

East Point Sanctuary

Fernald's Neck Preserve

Field's Pond Nature Center

Frye Mountain Wildlife Management Area

Gilsland Farm

Great Heath, The

Great Wass Island Preserve

Howard L. Mendall Wildlife Management Area

Indian Point/Blagden Preserve

Josephine Newman Sanctuary

Kennebunk Plains Wildlife Management Area/Kennebunk Plains Preserve

La Verna and Rachel Carson Salt Pond Preserves

Machias Seal Island

Mast Landing Sanctuary

Moosehorn National Wildlife Refuge

Morse Mountain Preserve

Mullen Woods Preserve

Petit Manan National Wildlife Refuge

Popham Beach State Park

Quoddy Head State Park

Rachel Carson National Wildlife Refuge

Reid State Park

Rocky Lake Management Unit

Ruffingham Wildlife Management Area

R. Waldo Tyler Wildlife Management Area (Weskeag Marsh Nature Center)

Scarborough Marsh Nature Center

Sebago Lake State Park

Steep Falls Wildlife Management Area

Steve Powell Wildlife Management Area

Sunkhaze Meadows National Wildlife Refuge

Vaughan Woods

Vernon S. Walker Wildlife Management Area

Wells National Estuarine Research Reserve

WEST ZONE

Appalachian Trail

Bigelow Preserve

Chesterville Wildlife Management Unit

Duck Lake Management Unit

Four Ponds Management Unit

Georgia-Pacific Corporation Lands

Grafton Notch State Park

Leavitt Wildlife Management Area

Mahoosuc Mountains Management Unit

Mount Blue State Park

Old Pond Farm Wildlife Management Area

Peaks-Kenny State Park

Rangeley Lake State Park

Richardson Management Unit

White Mountain National Forest

Acadia National Park

U.S. National Park Service   Coastal
40,000 acres

On Mt. Desert Island. From US 1 at Ellsworth, S on Hwy 3 to visitor center.

Open all year. Some roads, including the Park Loop Rd., may be closed by snow in winter and early spring. Stretches of the Coast Rd. usually remain open. State and town roads are plowed.

This is the only National Park in New England, on the largest rock island off the Atlantic coast. It includes parts of several smaller islands and a mainland peninsula. It is second only to Great Smoky Mountains National Park in number of visitors per year.

Uplift, subsidence, glaciation, and erosion have produced a rugged, rocky shoreline. Mountains up to 1,530 ft. rise abruptly from the sea. At low tide, countless pools are exposed, lively with marine creatures. The island is cut by many deep sounds, harbors, and coves. Somes Sound, a fjord, almost bisects the island. A number of freshwater lakes are on the island. Uplands are heavily forested, but mountain summits are often open and rocky, providing great vistas.

Most National Parks were carved from the public domain. Acadia was created by conservation-minded citizens who contributed most of the land and persuaded Congress to establish, in 1919, the first National Park E of the Mississippi.

The Park doesn't occupy all of Mount Desert Island. The town of Bar Harbor is at the gateway. A map makes the Park look like an unfinished jigsaw puzzle, several large masses and a number of smaller ones, with gaps between, the accumulation of land gifts. Indeed, the boundaries were not fixed by law until 1986.

Thanks to good signs and good Park planning, the jigsaw pattern isn't too confusing on the ground. The island has 200 mi. of paved state and town roads, the Park only 25 mi., including the Loop Rd., the principal tour route. Many portions of the Park are roadless, linked by state and town roads.

For the summer visitor, the first question is where to stay. The Park has two campgrounds, one on the DESTINET reservation system. The other is first come, first served, but it is often full in summer. Nearby are 13 private campgrounds, plus motels and other accommodations, where reservations are necessary in the busy season. Check ahead with Mt. Desert Island Chamber of Commerce. The Park Service will provide a list of private campgrounds.

Stop at the visitor center first. Here one quickly realizes that Acadia can't be fully seen in a day or a week. A year's schedule of naturalist programs may include over 100 activities weekly, including mountain hikes, boat cruises, beaver watches, and amphitheater slide presentations. On your own you can travel the 25 mi. of paved roads, 120 mi. of hiking trails, and 44 mi. of carriage paths used by hikers, cyclists, horse riders, and—in winter—skiers.

If you have only one day, see the sights along the 27-mi. Loop Rd.: spectacular mountains, beaches, and cliffs. There's enough time to walk up Cadillac Mountain, visit the Shore Path, stop at the Jordan Pond Nature Trail, and end the day at one of the amphitheater programs. We spent much of our first day exploring tide pools.

Summer temperatures vary from 45° to 85°F, spring and fall from 30° to 70°. Annual snowfall is about 60 in. Annual precipitation is about 49 in. Rain and fog may occur at any time. Mosquitoes and black flies are most common in June.

Plants: 95% of the Park is forested, an intermingling of northern coniferous and temperate deciduous types. 35% of the area is predominantly coniferous, 40% mixed forest, 20% deciduous. The most common tree species are eastern white and pitch pines, red and white spruce, eastern hemlock, quaking aspen, American beech, pin, red, striped, and sugar maples, northern red oak, balsam fir, northern white-cedar, paper birch.

About 1,500 plant species occur in the Acadia Park area. A checklist of common flowering plants is available, grouped by habitat: coniferous woods, mountains and dry rocky sites, deciduous woods, marsh and pond, bog, roadside and meadow. The luscious wild Maine blueberry grows in the Park, preferring rocky places and poor soil. You may pick and eat what you find, about mid-Aug.

Birds: Checklist available. The birding is exceptional. The checklist shows seasonal abundance, habitats, and confirmed breeding. About 334 species have been reported, an extraordinarily high number that reflects both the diverse nature of the site and the quality of observation. The list includes 70 species reported less than 5 times, such as the magnificent frigatebird, greater white-fronted goose, sandhill crane, South Polar skua, ivory gull, sooty tern, and yellow-headed blackbird, all well out of their normal ranges. There are occasional sightings of the rare peregrine falcon, which has successfully bred in the Park recently.

Mammals, reptiles, amphibians: The Park's checklist shows common species, rare species, and those that have been extirpated, such as the timber wolf, lynx, and cougar. Common species include red fox, raccoon, white-tailed deer, weasels, mink, otter, striped skunk, porcupine, woodchuck, beaver, eastern chipmunk, red and gray squirrels, northern flying squirrel, snowshoe hare, deer mouse, moles, shrews, voles, and two bats. Sea mammals include harbor seal, harbor porpoise, and humpback, finback, and minke whales.

Many common salamanders, snakes, turtles; some less common frogs, toads, and turtles.

Features

The largest mass of the Park is on the E side of the island, beyond the visitor center. Near the middle of the E side are two of the largest water bodies: *Eagle Lake,* about 1¾ mi. long, and *Jordan Pond,* about 1¼ mi. long. The Loop Rd. circles the area E of these lakes, enclosing the Park's highest mountain. Along the route are *Sieur de Monts Spring,* with a nature center and wildflower garden; *Sand Beach,* one of ME's few sandy beaches, popular with sunbathers; *Thunder Hole, Otter Cliffs, Jordan Pond,* and *Bubble Pond.* On the W side of this portion of the Park is Sargent Dr., overlooking *Somes Sound* A spur road goes to the top of 1,530-ft. *Cadillac Mountain,* where the island and coastal views are breathtaking on a clear day. Visibility is best during fall and winter months.

In the early days of the Park, *carriage paths,* a unique way of providing access to automobile-free areas, were financed and planned by John D. Rockefeller, Jr. The graded hard-packed paths, interconnected by 17 stone bridges, extend from near the visitor center to the S coast, chiefly to the W of the Loop Rd.

The smaller mass, W of Somes Sound, has fewer roads and fewer visitors. At the far S is *Seawall Campground.* Bicycles can be rented at *Southwest Harbor.* A nature trail is at *Ship Harbor.* Swimming at *Echo Lake.*

Features Outside Mt. Desert Island

Isle au Haut is about 18 mi. to the SW by water, more than 70 by road and the mail boat from Stonington. There is no car ferry. This remote, densely forested island, a bit over 6 mi. long, has long had a small fishing community and summer colony. In 1943 the S half of the island was given to the Park. It's an island for hikers, with numerous trails to explore the rocky shoreline, marshes, bogs, a narrow lake, and spruce-forested hills. A Park Service campground near the Duck Harbor landing has 5 lean-tos, each accommodating 6 people, available by reservation only. Speak with Park HQ for more information. No other accommodations are available. (The Duck Harbor landing is used only July–Aug. The town landing is 5 mi. from the campground.)

The number of visitors on the island is limited, and on rare occasions day-trippers may be excluded.

Schoodic Peninsula lies E of Bar Harbor. The Acadia National Park area is reached from US 1 at West Gouldsboro, S on Hwy 186. Few Park visitors go here. It's a small piece of the peninsula, about 1½ by 3 mi., with a one-way scenic drive. It preserves a fine section of the coast, and the peninsula as a whole has the flavor of rural, small-town ME, unlike the bustle of Bar Harbor. There is no campground.

The *Islesford Historical Cruise* Lands at Little Cranberry Island for a visit to the *Islesford Museum,* which documents Mt. Desert Island's seafaring heritage.

Interpretation

Visitor center, about 3 mi. N of Bar Harbor on Hwy 3 at Hulls Cove, offers a short orientation film, publications, information about walks, hikes, cruises, evening programs, and more.*Tape tours,* on cassette, are available for purchase or rental. Closed Nov.–April; then Park HQ on Hwy 233, 3 mi. W of Bar Harbor.

Nature center, Acadia Wild Gardens (an orientation to flora on the Island), and *Abbe Museum* (housing artifacts of regional native American cultures) are all at Sieur de Monts Spring, just off the Park Loop Rd. Garden paths open 24 hrs. daily all year. Museum closed Nov. to mid-May; nature center closed Oct.–May.

Nature trails at Jordan Pond (1 mi.) and Ship Harbor (1.3 mi.).

Junior Ranger programs.

Activities

Camping: 2 campgrounds, 522 sites. Blackwoods is open all year, with limited facilities mid-Sept. to mid-May. Reservations through DESTINET, (800) 365-2267, are required at Blackwoods June 15–Sept. 15. No reservations accepted at Seawall, which is open late May through late Sept. 5 group campsites are set aside in the Park to serve formally organized or educational groups only. (Reserve these through Park HQ, not DES-TINET.) Additional Park camping on Isle au Haut.

Hiking: 120 mi. of trails at all levels of difficulty, throughout the Park. Watch for poison ivy, and check for ticks at the end of the day. Expect changeable weather. No trailside camping.

Fishing: Fresh- and saltwater, the former requiring a state license. Freshwater species include trout, salmon, bass. Ice fishing on lakes and ponds Jan.–March.

Swimming: Lifeguards at Echo Lake and Sand Beach.

Boating: Courtesy moorings at Schoodic Peninsula (Winter Harbor), Baker Island, Isle au Haut (Duck Harbor), and near the entrance to Somes Sound. Launching on lakes and ponds. Marinas, powerboat and day-sailer rentals, and other commercial facilities at Bar Harbor and other coast towns.

Cruises: Include several Park ranger-led cruises and trips to Park-owned islands. Check at visitor center.

Canoeing, sea-kayaking: On most of the lakes and ponds on Mt. Desert Island. Most have easy access. Canoe rentals available at the N end of Long Pond on Rt. 102, also in Bar Harbor. Sea-kayaking in the waters around the Island. Guided tours available locally. Ask at the HQ.

Horse riding: Bring your own horse. Wildwood Stables on the Park Loop Rd. near Seal Harbor no longer offers horseback riding. They do rent stall space and campsites to visiting equestrians. The carriage paths are the most popular trails for riding.

Bicycling: Rentals at Bar Harbor and Southwest Harbor. All carriage paths are suitable for mountain bikes, 16 mi. for thin tires. Park Loop Rd. is another favorite route. Bikes may be taken on the ferries for Swans Island and the Cranberry Islands. Bikes prohibited on hiking trails in the Park.

Ski touring: On Park Loop Rd., mostly unplowed in winter, and on carriage paths.

Pets must be kept on leash.

Publications

Leaflet with map.

Beaver Log newspaper. Checklists of birds, plants, mammals, reptiles, amphibians.

Welcome to Acadia National Park.

Written on the Rocks.

Mimeo information sheets: boat cruise and ferry list, hikes with descriptions and difficulty ratings, private campground list and map, wheelchair access guide.

....

Allagash Wilderness Waterway

Maine Bureau of Parks and Lands   North
92 mi. waterway; 200,000 acres, including 30,000 acres of water.

In the North Maine Woods (see entry). All access is by float plane or private road; landowners permit public use but control access. Upstream access at Telos Lake or Chamberlain Lake (see entries). Other access point, from Ashland, Allagash Village.

This fabulous waterway through the forests of northern ME was established by state legislation in 1966 and included in the National Wild and Scenic Rivers System in 1970. It is a protected corridor, not a vast pristine region. Private roads cross or parallel it at several places. Development or other habitat disturbance is prohibited within 500 ft. of the Waterway. Only state-approved timber harvesting is permitted in areas visible from the river within 1 mi. of the shore.

Most of the surrounding land is owned by timber companies. This was once the domain of giant white pines. Now spruce, fir, and other softwood species supply the pulp and paper industries.

However, since the Waterway was established, ME's Bureau of Parks and Lands has acquired nearly 30,000 acres at Telos and Chamberlain Lakes and Round Pond (see entries). Here the mandate is multiple-use management, giving full weight to wildlife and recreation values along with timber production.

For those who travel the Waterway, it is a wilderness experience. Only canoes are permitted N of Chamberlain Lake, although canoes may have motors up to 10 hp. (Inflatable craft are not permitted.) Canoeing the entire route takes 7 to 10 days. The linear trip is only one of many possibilities. The complex includes a variety of lakes, ponds, and streams on either side of the main route. One can make a camping trip of a day, a week, or more, returning to the put-in point.

Allagash Lake, for example, is about 6 mi. W of the main route, linked to Chamberlain Lake by Allagash Stream. This is the only part of the Waterway where all motors are prohibited. Campsites are distributed around the lake. "Ice caves" are on the NE side.

Water conditions vary from year to year, but they are usually favorable from late May into Oct. Ice sometimes persists into late May. In side streams, flow may become inadequate late in the season. High flow rates require extra skill at Chase Rapids. Water level on the Allagash is regulated by a series of dams located on the large feeder lakes in the headwaters.

Drinking water can usually be obtained from a spring or lake. Normal purification methods are recommended. Food, fuel, and other supplies aren't available along the way. You should have both the Waterway schematic map and topos.

Features

From the put-in on Telos Lake, it's 5 mi. to the foot of Chamberlain Lake, then 10 mi. to Lock Dam and a short portage. Then comes 12 mi. on Eagle Lake, and 7 more mi. to Churchill Dam. Below Churchill is the 9-mi. run through Chase Rapids to Umsaskis Lake. Portage service is available in season for those who wish to avoid the rapids. Rapids are rated to class II.

From this point on to Allagash Falls, there are no large lakes. The falls, a 40-ft. drop, are one of the scenic features of the route. The portage around the falls is ⅛ mi. Then it's 13 mi. to Allagash Village, where most trips end. Return transportation can be arranged privately at. Allagash Village or at towns on the St. John River.

Guide service is available. Outfitters offer trips, supplying all but personal gear. Contact the ME Professional Guides Association, P.O. Box 591, Ellsworth, ME 04605; (207) 667-8807.

Activities

Camping: Only authorized campsites may be used. They are scattered along the Waterway, signed, and marked on maps. Sites cannot be reserved, and sharing sites is a wilderness courtesy. Most sites have tables, fireplaces, and pit toilets.

Hiking: There are a few trails to fire towers, providing fine viewpoints.

Hunting: Firearms may not be carried or used within the Waterway boundaries May 1–Oct. 1. Otherwise state game laws apply.

Fishing: Brook trout, togue, lake whitefish.

Canoeing: Each party must register at the Telos-Chamberlain entrance, or at the Churchill Dam, Umsaskis Lake, or Michaud Farm checkpoints.

In winter: Snowmobiles may use unplowed roads (most of which are outside Waterway boundaries) or frozen lakes. Stream channel ice is likely to be thin; some channels remain open. Area is used for ice fishing.

Strict rules govern use of the Waterway. HQ will supply copies of the regulations.

The black fly season is June, extending into July in wet years. Bring an effective repellent.

Publications
Waterway folder with map.

Regulations.

Headquarters
Northern Region, ME Bureau of Parks and Lands, 106 Hogan Rd., Bangor, ME 04401; (207) 941-4014, May–Oct.; (207) 723-8518, Nov.–April.

....

Appalachian Trail
Mixed ownership
281 mi. in ME.
From Mount Katahdin in Baxter State Park to the NH border.

We walked one section of the famous 2,155 mi. trail along the main street of Monson. Two hikers with destinations more distant than ours were replenishing their food stocks. Most of the trail is in backcountry, following the ridges, crossing the state's highest peaks, often far from any road or shop.

Some day the entire trail, from Maine to Georgia, may be on public land or protected by easements. Today ME has more unprotected trail miles than any other state. Until recently there has been no pressing need. Much of the trail is on land owned by timber companies that permit recreation on their holdings.

Getting permission to maintain the trail across private land isn't the only issue. The National Park Service hopes to make the trail a scenic corridor, which has inevitably led to conflict with commercial enterprises such as downhill ski areas. The Park Service would like to acquire enough land to protect the trail's views and to maintain its backwoods character.

Our entries note if the trail crosses or passes nearby. Many other trails, most of them blue-blazed, intersect the Appalachian, linking it with various parks, preserves, and trailheads.

Activities

Backpacking: More than three dozen campsites and shelters are maintained along the trail. Other camping possibilities are on side trails.

Fishing: Many streams, ponds, and lakes are along the route.

Publications

Appalachian Trail Conference. *Walking the Appalachian Trail Step by Step.* Booklet, free.

National Park Service. *Appalachian Trail/Maine to Georgia.* Leaflet and map, free.

......

Baxter State Park

Maine Bureau of Parks and Lands
202,064 acres.

From Millinocket, 18 mi. NW to Togue Pond gatehouse (via unnamed road, ask the way at Park HQ and visitor center in Millinocket). From Greenville, N via Lily Bay/Ripogenus Dam Rd., 70 mi. to Togue Pond gatehouse. From Patten, Hwy 159 W to Matagamon gatehouse, 24 mi.

May 14–Oct. 15, gates open 6 A.M. to 10 P.M. Dec. 1–April 1, contact HQ for hours of access, and for day-use access all year.

We've never been here, though we've been close half a dozen times. Baxter's roads are so narrow that most trailers and motor homes are barred. So are motorcycles, all-terrain vehicles, and pets. We travel in a motor home with a black Labrador, both disqualifying us. This is not a complaint; we hope it's kept that way. Our entry is based on information from the Bureau of Parks and Lands, maps, and talks with people who know the Park well.

Few state governors have left such a legacy. Former ME Governor Percival P. Baxter gave his state the first portion of the Park, including Mount Katahdin, in 1931. His final gift of 7,764 acres in 1962 brought the Park to its present size, one of the largest State Parks in the U.S.

The terms of Baxter's bequest stipulate that the Park be maintained in its wild, natural state. This Park is operated independently of the other ME State Parks for that reason. The Appalachian Trail Conference notes in its literature concerning the Park that "Park personnel exercise a high degree of control over the number of persons entering the Park and their activities."

The Park is surrounded by a vast area of timber company land extending to the Canadian border, crossed by private roads open to public use subject to owners' regulations. (See entry, North Maine Woods.) Like the surrounding lands, portions of the Park were cut over in the past, but the exceptional ruggedness of the terrain protected much of it from ax and saw.

Mount Katahdin, 5,267 ft. high, in the SW quadrant, is the highest point in ME. Almost the entire Park is mountainous, except for the valleys of Trout Brook, and Nesowadnehunk, Wassataquoik, and Katahdin Streams. Of the 46 peaks and ridges, 18 are higher than 3,000 ft. The Park's lowest elevation is 550 ft.

From the Togue Pond gatehouse, the S entrance, a dead-end road goes to Roaring Brook, trailhead for the Mount Katahdin and Chimney Pond Trails. Mount Katahdin is the northern terminus of the Appalachian Trail. It is fitting that such a magnificent achievement should end at the highest point, but one can continue to hike N, all the way to a trailhead at the South Branch Pond.

Also from the Togue Pond gatehouse, a road follows the stream valleys northward near the W boundary, turning NE along Trout Brook. Just at the turn, a road to the W exit is a route to the Allagash Wilderness Waterway (see entry). The Trout Brook road ends at the Matagamon gatehouse on Matagamon Lake, the boundary, meeting the road to Shin Pond. But most of the Park is roadless wilderness, accessible only on foot.

Not by canoe. Although there are streams everywhere—the map suggests there are over 200 mi. of streams, perhaps much more—most aren't canoeable. There is a short canoe run from Nesowadnehunk Lake to the campground, but that seems to be the only one of note.

Lakes and ponds are numerous, but the largest within the Park isn't much over a mile long.

There are 175 mi. of trails within the Park, offering opportunities for short day hikes from the perimeter road or extended backpacking in the interior.

Early arrival is recommended for day use. Access is on a first-come, first-served basis; when parking lots fill up, that area is closed.

Water in the Park is untreated and generally unprotected. All water for drinking or cooking should be treated. Park literature details various means of treating water.

Plants: Over 90% of the Park is forested, chiefly northern spruce/fir. Principal tree species include red, black, and white spruce, balsam fir, eastern white, red, and jack pines, hemlock, sugar and red maples, beech, birches, aspen. The forest is far from uniform. On the South Branch Nature Trail, one can see the traces of a fire that burned over 80,000 acres in 1903. Here and there are the stumps of great white pines cut long ago. The upper slopes have stands of old-growth timber.

A list of 112 wildflowers doesn't note abundance or blooming season. Listed are pink moccasin-flower, white rein orchid, several violets, Dutchman's-breeches, cardinal flower, nightshade, iris, painted trillium, fireweed, evening primrose, fringed gentian, purple clematis, Indian pipe, round-leaved sundew, pitcher plant, trailing arbutus, columbine, yellow avens, spring beauty.

Birds: A checklist of 177 bird species does not give abundance or seasonality, and thus may include species seldom seen. Listed are common loon, pied-billed grebe, green heron, least and American bitterns, Canada and snow geese, green-winged and blue-winged teal, wood duck, common and hooded mergansers, 7 hawks, bald eagle, osprey, peregrine falcon, merlin, kestrel, 9 owls, spruce and ruffed grouse, Virginia and sora rails, American woodcock, yellow-billed and black-billed cuckoos, 7 woodpeckers, 5 swallows, Bohemian and cedar waxwings, loggerhead and northern shrikes, 5 vireos, 23 warblers, and 9 sparrows.

Mammals: The available list isn't a complete inventory of mammals, but it names those the visitor may likely see, with information on when and where. Moose, black bear, and deer are the common big game mammals. Other common species include beaver, muskrat, otter, raccoon, bobcat, lynx, red fox, fisher, marten, snowshoe hare, porcupine, red squirrel, chipmunk, mink, coyote.

Features

Mt. Katahdin, just under a mile high, is the prime attraction. Tell someone you've visited Baxter, and the first question is "Did you climb Katahdin?" Then the next question: "Did you cross the Knife Edge?" One need not, although alternative routes aren't easy. The Cathedral Trail gains 2,300 ft. in 1¾ mi. At Knife Edge, two cirques meet, forming a narrow ridge, in places less than a yard wide with precipices on each side, one of them almost 2,000 ft. down. It's jagged, bare rock, far from level, and often swept by strong winds. Our daughter crossed it sitting down and said she was terrified. No one should try it in bad weather.

Blueberry Knoll is one of numerous day hikes that offers splendid scenery with moderate rather than strenuous effort. From Roaring Brook Campground, it's 3.2 mi., with an elevation gain of 1,600 ft.

Great Basin is the largest of the 7 cirques forming Mt. Katahdin. Several trails cross this great U-shaped valley. Two tarns (steep-banked mountain ponds) are within the basin.

Katahdin Stream Falls is on the Hunt Trail about 1½ mi. from the perimeter road. Four vertical drops totaling about 80 ft. are in a mossy gorge.

Green Falls is more remote, near the center of the Park on Wassataquoik Stream near Wassataquoik Lake. It's a two-stage drop in a handsome setting. Trail access.

Little Niagara and *Big Niagara Falls* are on Nesowadnehunk Stream in the SW corner of the Park. They were named in jest—"Big" Niagara drops less than 20 ft.—but it's a delightful area with many ponds and streams, surrounding the Daicey Pond Campground.

Interpretation

Visitor center is at Millinocket on Hwy 11/157 (right next to McDonald's, the Park literature says!). Displays, slide show, literature. It's a good idea to stop here for information before proceeding to the Park. There's an on-site *visitor center* at Togue Pond entrance.

Daicey Pond Nature Trail circles Daicey Pond in the SW corner of the Park, just off the Appalachian Trail. Many wildflowers in season.

Roaring Brook Nature Trail is near the Roaring Brook Campground. Habitats include forest, bog, stream, pond.

South Branch Nature Trail begins at the South Branch Pond Campground parking lot. This was the area of the 1903 burn. Many wildflowers, birds.

Activities

Camping: 10 campgrounds, 8 accessible by road, including cabins only at Daicey Pond and Kidney Pond. Facilities vary and include lean-tos, tent spaces, bunkhouses, fireplaces, tables. Essentially primitive. *Reservations are essential and must be made either by mail or in person.* ME residents have priority. Contact reservation clerk at HQ. All campgrounds are open May 15–Oct. 15, close for 6 weeks, then open again for winter use Dec. 1–April 1. *Winter use is subject to special regulations.* Permits are required for winter activities within the Park, including camping, and are issued only to parties deemed qualified and properly equipped. Contact HQ well in advance when considering any winter use of Baxter.

Hiking, backpacking: 178 mi. of trails, including the first 10.4 mi. of the Appalachian Trail. All hikers must register at the nearest campground. Backpackers must use authorized sites. This includes 2 backcountry campgrounds in addition to the 8 accessible by road. Hikers should have topos. Other maps may be obtained at campgrounds, Millinocket HQ, or the visitor center at Togue Pond gatehouse. *No children under age 6 are permitted above timberline.*

Bicycles: Allowed on maintained roads only.

Hunting: In designated sections only; inquire. Firearms are prohibited elsewhere.

Fishing: Excellent. Streams and ponds. Chiefly brook trout.

Boating: No trailer-access ramps. Motors are permitted on Matagamon and Webster Lakes.

Canoeing, boating: Boats with motors can be used on Webster and Magamon Lakes, and on Nesowadnehunk Lake, outside the boundary. Canoes can be rented at South Branch Pond, Russell Pond, Trout Brook Farm, Daicey Pond, and Kidney Pond; all have campgrounds.

Ski touring: Season is Dec. 1–April 1; allowed only below timberline. *Snowmobiles* are permitted on the perimeter road only.

All persons entering or leaving the Park must top and register at the gatehouse or HQ.

Special rules govern activities in the Park. Obtain a copy from HQ before making the trip. Vehicles more than 7 ft. wide, 9 ft. high, or 22 ft. long are prohibited.

Gasoline is not available.

Pets are prohibited.

Publications

General information page with trail information and map.

Checklists of birds, wildflowers, mammals.

Mimeo information pages: rules and regulations, guidelines for winter use, nature trail guides for Daicey Pond, Roaring Brook, South Branch.

Headquarters

Baxter State Park, 64 Balsam Dr., Millinocket, ME 04462; (207) 723-5140.

Bigelow Preserve

Maine Parks and Bureau of Lands   West
35,000 acres.

Access over gravel roads off Hwy 27 in Carrabassett; for lake access, Long Falls Dam Rd. runs N from New Portland on Hwy 16 to the E end of the lake.

The principal features of the Preserve are about 20 mi. of the S shore of Flagstaff Lake and the Bigelow Mountain Range. The Preserve occupies much of the land between Hwy 16/27 and the lake, with additional state acreage on islands and a peninsula on the N shore. The 10-mi. W–E range offers some of ME's finest alpine scenery. The Appalachian Trail crosses the high country.

Elevation at the lake is 1,146 ft. Avery and West Mountains are both over 4,000 ft., two others above 3,500. Timberline here is about 3,800 ft. Avery and West Mountains have extensive subalpine heaths. Several glacial tarns are near timberline.

The S slope drops from the ridge irregularly in a series of terraces and cliffs to the Stratton Brook and Huston Brook valleys. Hikers and campers generally enter the Preserve on the Stratton Brook Rd. to trailheads where the Appalachian Trail crosses or at the outlet of Stratton Brook Pond; both have limited parking.

The N slope is a more continuous grade down to the lake and adjoining swamp. Flagstaff Lake is sometimes labeled Dead River Flowage. North and South branches of the Dead River join at Stratton. The dam is at the E end. The lake covers 20,000 acres, up to 3 mi.

wide, with numerous bays, coves, and islands. Much of the shoreline is marshy. The lake is shallow.

Plants: Northern hardwood forests predominate at lower elevations, beech/birch/maple intermixed with spruce/fir. From 2,000 to 2,700 ft. this gives way to a boreal forest of red spruce/balsam fir/European white birch. Still higher the trees become smaller, until in the sub-alpine zone they are low, matted, and shrublike, the pattern called *krummholz*. The highest peaks are treeless, containing patches of low shrubs, herbs, grasses, and sedges broken by rock outcrops.

Other habitats in the Preserve include:

- *Cedar swamp:* northern white-cedar with red spruce, balsam fir, yellow birch, and eastern hemlock. The shrub understory includes blueberry. Growing on the sphagnum mat are three-seeded sedge, sensitive fern, cinnamon fern, ostrich fern, goldthread, and starflower.
- *Black spruce bog:* with black spruce, red maple, northern white-cedar, and larch.
- *Heath and open bog:* shrubs including leatherleaf, sheep laurel, labrador tea, bog laurel, blueberry, cranberry.
- *Wet meadow:* with sedges, grasses, cattail, iris.

Birds: A preliminary list records only species seen or heard during the site inventory. They include common loon, black duck, red-tailed and Cooper's hawks, ruffed and spruce grouse, spotted sandpiper, American woodcock, common snipe, 5 woodpeckers, 2 flycatchers, 2 swallows, gray and blue jays, raven, crow, red-winged blackbird, scarlet tanager, pine and evening grosbeaks, black-capped and boreal chickadees, white-breasted and red-breasted nuthatches, winter wren, 4 thrushes, veery, golden-crowned and ruby-crowned kinglets, solitary and red-eyed vireos, 13 warblers, purple finch, pine siskin, dark-eyed junco, 3 sparrows.

Mammals: The site inventory listed mammals likely to occur, then noted those whose presence was confirmed: shrew, voles, mice, snowshoe hare, chipmunk, woodchuck, gray and red squirrels, beaver, muskrat, porcupine, raccoon, marten, fisher, mink, striped skunk, bobcat, red fox, coyote, white-tailed deer, moose, black bear.

Activities

Camping: Campsites at Stratton Brook Pond, Huston Pond, and along the shore of Flagstaff Lake. Camp in any suitable place, but permit is required for fires except at designated campsites.

Hiking, backpacking: The Bigelow Mountain Trails, from Stratton E along the ridge, are joined by the Appalachian Trail, Firewarden's Trail, and others. Two lean-tos are on the ridge.

Fishing: Warmwater species, chiefly pickerel and yellow perch, in Flagstaff Lake. The North Branch of the Dead River is good for brook trout, the South Branch somewhat less so.

Boating: Ramps near Stratton and at Bog Brook, on the E end. Drawdowns, especially in the fall, may impede launching.

Canoeing: Whitewater runs on both the North and the South Branches and on the lower Dead River below the dam. Rapids to class IV.

Ski touring, snowmobiling: Extensive trails and unplowed roads. Adventurous cross-country skiers enjoy mountain vistas and views of the lake. A lodge is open weekends. Call (207) 778-4111 for map and information.

Publication
Information page with map.

Headquarters
ME Bureau of Parks and Lands, 25 Main St., P.O. Box 327, Farmington, ME 04938; (207) 778-4111.

Blagden Preserve
See Indian Point/Blagden Preserve.

Bradbury Mountain State Park
Maine Bureau of Parks and Lands   Coastal
320 acres.

From US 95 take Freeport-Durham Exit 5 mi. to Pownal.

Open all year.

This small Park offers 41 sites for camping and a choice of short hikes up through open forest to the summit of Bradbury Mountain (460 ft.), with a view over Casco Bay and the surrounding countryside. Trails vary in difficulty, range from ½ to 2 mi. in length. Guided walks available, year-round. 3 mi. of cross-country ski trails, as well as access to local snowmobile trails. Maps available at the Park.

Headquarters

Bradbury Mountain State Park, Pownal, ME 04069; (207) 688-4712.

....

Brownfield Bog Wildlife Management Area

Maine Department of Inland Fisheries and Wildlife   Coastal
5,454 acres.

SE of Fryeburg. Just off Hwy 160 about 1½ mi. NE of East Brownfield Village.

The Saco River Valley is a picturesque and popular waterfowl hunting area. The Saco River flows into and through Brownfield Bog, to and beyond Lovewell Pond. The WMA, its terrain relatively flat, is at about 360 ft. above sea level. It includes 1,100 acres of floodplain, 970 acres of marshland, 3,384 acres of upland. An access road from Hwy 160 passes Bald Bog, skirts the river channel, and ends at Great Bog.

No lists of fauna are available, but the diversity of habitats indicates a good variety of species.

Birds: Nesting waterfowl include black, ring-necked, and wood ducks. Introduced Canada geese have nested.

Activities

Camping: Nearby, the Appalachian Mountain Club has a site at Walker's Falls, chiefly for canoeists on the Saco River.

Hunting: Deer, waterfowl, grouse, woodcock.

Fishing: Brown trout and smallmouth bass in the river and pond, pickerel and bullhead in bogs.

Boating: Ramp near point where the river enters the pond. Pond is about 2½ mi. long.

Canoeing: A popular 33-mi. canoe route on the Saco River passes the bog. Put-in off Hwy 160 or at Lovewell Pond.

Headquarters

ME Dept. of Inland Fisheries and Wildlife, 41 State House Station, Augusta, ME; (207) 287-8000.

....

Camden Hills State Park

Maine Bureau of Parks and Lands   Coastal
5,474 acres.

On US 1, 2 mi. N of Camden.

Park accessible all year, *campground open May 15–Oct. 15.*

Maine's largest coastal park has over a quarter-million visitors a year. The campground is usually full from mid-July to Labor Day, often by noon. Most campers are transients, and 85% of all visitors are from other states.

Almost all of the visitors come through the main entrance. The great majority drive the scenic 1 mi. road to the top of Mt. Battie. Tens of thousands per year hike to the top. It's not to be missed, even if you're there on a crowded day, but there's much more to the Park, large areas most visitors don't see.

The Park extends about 5 mi. on an axis parallel to US 1, although it has less than half a mile of highway frontage. Its boundaries are very irregular, touching or crossing other roads at several places. The trail system extends throughout the Park. A small block opposite the main entrance extends to the sea. The shore is a steep, rocky bluff offering no access to the water, though salt- and freshwater beaches are nearby. The land rises to Megunticook Mountain, which overlooks Lake Megunticook.

About 85% of the Park is forested, a mixed forest with northern red oak, American beech, red maple, white ash, European white birch, red spruce, white pine, balsam fir, eastern hemlock, northern white-cedar.

Features

Mount Battie attracted visitors long before there was a park. The view from the top, 1,380 ft. above the sea, is magnificent, encompassing sea islands, the lake, and distant mountains. The stone tower was built in 1921 at the site of a former hotel. The auto road to the summit is open May 1–Nov. 1.

Maiden Cliff is a sheer drop of 800 ft. down to Hwy 52 on the shore of Lake Megunticook. Ridge Trail leads to the cliff top.

Activities

Camping: 112 sites. Campers will be referred to private campgrounds when sites are full.

Hiking: 30 mi. of trails with access from 5 major trailheads.

Hunting: In undeveloped areas. Inquire.

Ski touring, snowmobiling: Popular in winter. A local snowmobile club maintains several trails as snow permits.

Nearby

Warren Island State Park is on a 70-acre spruce-covered island off Lincolnville in Penobscot Bay. It has docking and mooring facilities, 10 campsites, 2 shelters, water. The Park is designed for the boating public. Contact Camden Hills HQ for information.

Publications

Park leaflet.

Trail map.

Snowmobile trails map.

Headquarters

Camden Hills State Park, Camden, ME 04843; (207) 236-3109 May 1–Oct. 15; (207) 236-0849 Oct. 16–April 30.

Chamberlain Lake Management Unit

See Telos Lake Management Unit. North

Chesterville Wildlife Management Area

Maine Department of Inland Fisheries and Wildlife West
468 acres.

From Farmington, SE on US 2 to Farmington Falls, then S on Pope Rd. and Valley Rd. to Chesterville. Dam is on Little Norridgewock Stream in Chesterville.

The WMA is long and narrow, following the stream for 3 mi. A canoe is the preferred craft, especially at low water. Access is limited to the dam site, where a few cars can be parked and small boats launched. (With two cars, leave one at the dam; put in at Parker Pond in Jay, and canoe downstream.)

From a canoe, wildlife viewing is likely to be good. The waterway is quiet, no roads nearby.

Birds: Wood and black ducks are common. Also hooded merganser, great blue heron, osprey, warblers, flycatchers, red-winged blackbird, ring-necked duck, and blue-winged teal, all of which nest here. In uplands, ruffed grouse, occasional woodcock.

Mammals: Canoeists often see deer, beaver, muskrat, moose. Present but less often seen: mink, otter, bobcat, raccoon, red fox, weasel, snowshoe hare.

Activities

Hunting: Most hunting is for deer.

Fishing: Pickerel, largemouth and smallmouth bass.

Canoeing: May require hauling across old or new beaver dams.

Headquarters

ME Dept. of Inland Fisheries and Wildlife, 41 State House Station, Augusta, ME 04333-0041; (207) 287-8000.

Cobscook Bay State Park

Maine Bureau of Parks and Lands   Coastal
888 acres.

On US 1 4 mi. S of Dennysville.

"This is the unappreciated part of Maine," said one advisor. "This part of the coast, from Bar Harbor to Canada, hasn't had the surge of development you see in the south." Traffic on US 1 is moderate, even on weekends, and the roadside isn't lined with antique shops and lobster restaurants. Cobscook is a coastal park, but on a fine July weekend there were a few vacant campsites.

The Park is on Whiting Bay, an arm of Cobscook Bay, where the tide fluctuation is 24 to 28 ft. The coast is steep and rocky, the upland hilly, with fine views from hilltops, although none rise much over 400 ft. From the campground, we found a trail down to a stony beach, where our presence seemed to interest a loon.

Adjoining the Park is the 6,600-acre Edmunds Unit of the Moosehorn National Wildlife Refuge (see entry). Park employees can provide maps and information. The Refuge offers extensive hiking opportunities.

Plants: About 75% of the Park is forested, spruce and balsam fir predominating. The Park has a list of 50 flowering plant species: wild cherry, pear, and apple blossom in late May–early June, daisy, buttercup, paintbrush, and others June–Aug.

Birds, other mammals: See the species lists for Moosehorn NWR. Coastal and many of the upland species are seen in this Park.

Activities

Camping: 100 sites. May 15–Oct. 15. Many sites at water's edge, secluded among spruce and fir trees.

Hiking: Trails in the Park, up to a locked fire tower, and in the NWR, including its wilderness area.

Fishing: Stream and ocean.

Boating: Launching ramp on Whiting Bay. Boaters should bear in mind the rapid tide changes, swift currents, and eddies.

Ski touring, snowmobiling: On groomed trails.

Nearby

Moosehorn National Wildlife Refuge and Quoddy Head State Park. See entries.

Publication

Leaflet with map.

Headquarters

Cobscook Bay State Park, R.F.D., Dennysville, ME 04628; (207) 726-4412.

Deboullie Management Unit

Maine Bureau of Parks and Lands   North
21,871 acres.

Access by private gravel roads off Hwy 161 in the town of St. Francis on
the north central ME border.

This area of rugged mountains, forests, and crystal lakes is within the
North Maine Woods (see entry). It was managed as commercial forest
before the state acquired it, and extensively logged in the 1950s and
1960s, but new growth is vigorous and the landscape shows few scars.

A management plan published in 1987 divides the site into 6
zones, categories that provide special protection for rare and endangered species, a backcountry closed to motor vehicles, preferred
wildlife habitats, recreation sites, scenic areas, and—finally—timber
production zones.

Only one interior road is maintained, with temporary logging
roads permitted as needed. State managers have been concerned that
too much road improvement and increased access would attract too
many people, with consequent damage to the fragile environment,
especially around the four principal ponds.

Fishing here is very good, camping and hiking delightful. The principal mountains, ponds, and other scenic features are in the SE third
of the site. So are established campsites. The interior road cuts across
the corner of this portion. A strip along the road is zoned for recreation sites, as is the N shore of Togue Pond. Remoteness and snow
conditions make winter use less than popular, though snowmobilers
pass through the unit.

Red River Camps is a traditional sportsman's camp, predating state
ownership, now commercially operated under lease. It provides rustic
accommodations, meals, canoe rentals, and guide services. Lease
terms require that it be kept simple and that some services, such as
canoe rentals, be available to all visitors. The operator also maintains
some short trails to ponds.

Plants: Logging began here in the late 1800s and continued into the
1960s. Cutting, governed by market demand, was mostly for softwoods and high-quality hardwoods. This history has produced a forest that is 42% mixed woods, 33% softwoods, 25% hardwoods. Most

softwood species here are in the 30- to 80-year age classes, while about a third of the hardwoods are over 100 years old. Softwoods are chiefly fir and spruce, with some cedar. Hardwoods include sugar maple, yellow birch, beech, red maple, European white birch, and poplar.

Wildlife: Little information is available on the birds and mammals of the area, other than game species.

Features

Deboullie Mountain, 1,981 ft., is the site's highest point, with a fire tower on top that offers fine views. *Gardner Mountain* isn't quite as high: 1,817 ft. The word *deboullie* is French for "rock slide"—the mountains have steep sides with cliffs and talus slopes.

Elevations of the ponds range from 1,107 to 1,189 ft. Gardner, Togue, and Deboullie Ponds are the three largest, from 1¼ to 1¾ mi. long, each a bit under 300 acres. A dozen other ponds are large enough to appear on the site map.

Cliffs on the S shore of Togue Pond are included in the Scenic Zone. The N shore of Deboullie Pond has "ice caves," small openings in rock crevices that remain frosty into the summer.

Five tracts of old-growth spruce/fir have been designated as Critical Areas, worthy of preservation. All are in the SE portion of the site.

The acreage to the N and W is said to have no features of interest to visitors other than hunters. This portion of the site is managed for timber production, with due regard for environmental quality.

Activities

Camping: Primitive campsites. The North Maine Woods (see entry) manages recreation use throughout the private lands that surround Deboullie and collects fees at their gatehouses. Although fees are not charged at other Bureau of Parks and Lands sites, that is not policy here, and North Maine Woods collects a fee. There are no reservations. One can camp at large, without open fires. Sites are too small for motor homes and large trailer combinations.

Hiking: The principal hiking trails were developed by and for fishermen, linking the several ponds. One trail ascends to the fire tower on Deboullie Mountain. The Bureau continues to improve the trail network.

Hunting: Deer, moose, snowshoe hare, and grouse are present. The limited diversity of habitat conditions makes this a relatively poor area for game production. Most hunters go elsewhere.

Fishing: The principal attraction here, and it is one of the Bureau's chief concerns. Overfishing has already drastically reduced fish populations in one pond. The Dept. of Inland Fisheries and Wildlife is monitoring the ponds, with differing management goals. "Catch and release" is a possible option in one or more ponds.

Boating, canoeing: Canoe is the preferred craft. Hand-carried boats can be launched on the larger lakes.

Headquarters
ME Bureau of Parks and Lands, 22 State House Station, Augusta, ME 04333-0022; (207) 287-3821.

Donnell Pond

Maine Bureau of Parks and Lands   Coastal
14,162 acres.

12 mi. E of Ellsworth off Hwy 182 or 183.

This site encompasses miles of undeveloped shore (including several sand beaches) on Donnell Pond, Tunk and Spring River Lakes, and most of Schoodic, Black, and Caribou Mountains. The three mountaintops provide fine views of Acadia National Park, the ocean, and other mountains nearby.

Boating, hiking, and swimming are popular activities. There are campsites accessible by foot or water on the lake shores. Tunk Lake is a popular fishing spot.

Headquarters
ME Bureau of Parks and Lands, 22 State House Station, Augusta, ME 04333-0022; (207) 287-3821.

Duck Lake Management Unit

Maine Bureau of Parks and Lands West
25,220 acres.

From Burlington, E on an extension of Hwy 188 around the N end of
Nicatous Lake on rough private roads to site.

The region NE of Bangor, bounded by US 2, Hwy 6, US 1, and Hwy 9,
has many lakes, extensive wetlands, and few roads. The thousand-
square-mile region is heavily forested, flat to rolling. Its lakes are generally at between 300 and 500 ft. elevation. Most of the upland is
between 400 and 600 ft., with a few widely scattered mountains.

The management unit is at the center of this region, as remote as
any part of it. It is accessible by road, according to one description
"easily, albeit patiently." Patience here is well rewarded: the road
passes through country as interesting as the destination. Along the
route are several campsites, the put-in for the 23-mi. Narraguagus
River canoe trip, and side roads to large and small lakes, wetlands,
campsites, and hiking trails.

The road traverses the site, passing the E tip of Duck Lake. The
management unit is somewhat higher and hillier than most of the
region, with several hills at about 1,000 ft. Duck Mountain rises to
1,169 ft. Duck Lake has several unusual qualities. At 519 ft., it is one of
the highest lakes of the region. It is a deep, cold-water fishery (salmon
and trout), whereas most nearby lakes are shallower, offering bass,
pickerel, and white perch. It has extensive sand beaches. The lake is
about 1¾ mi. long, 1 mi. wide.

Gassabias Lake, in the S portion of the site, is almost as large. Two
small lakes, Upper and Lower Unknown, are near the NE corner.

Activities

Camping: One vehicle-access primitive site is on Duck Lake. Three
boat-access sites (no latrines, no fires permitted) are on the lake. Two
sites are on Gassabias. One is between the Unknown Lakes. Visitors
may also camp anywhere, with no open fires.

Hiking: The site map shows a few short trails. Some seem to be related
to fishing. There is no trail maintenance.

Hunting: Deer, ruffed grouse; but wildlife populations are relatively low in this region.

Fishing: Duck Lake isn't as well publicized as some of the larger lakes in this semiwilderness region. Fishing pressure is light to moderate. Gassabias and Unknown Lakes have excellent warmwater fishing.

Publication

Information page with contour map.

Headquarters

ME Bureau of Parks and Lands, 22 State House Station, Augusta, ME 04333-0022; (207) 287-3821.

....

Eagle Lake Management Unit

Maine Bureau of Parks and Lands   North
23,882 acres

The town of Eagle Lake is on Hwy 11 about 18 mi. S of Canada. Access to the management unit, across the lake, is via Sly Brook Rd., which connects with Hwy 11 at Soldier Pond (Wallagrass), or by boat from the launch in the town of Eagle Lake.

Not to be confused with Eagle Lake on the Allagash, this one is narrow, L-shaped, about 15 mi. long, linked to the St. John River by Fish River. A minor part of the site is on the S side of the lake, near the town, but the main part, including the campsites, is across.

The site has a few hills; its highest point is about 400 ft. above the lake. Blake Lake is a pond in the site's NW corner, 200 ft. above Eagle Lake, with a hike-in campsite. Alec Brook drops from Blake Lake to Eagle Lake. There are wetlands in the NE corner and between Eagle and Square Lakes. The two lakes are linked by a canoeable water passage, another channel linking Square and Cross Lakes; campsites are on both of these lakes.

Fishing: For salmon and lake trout.

Headquarters

ME Bureau of Parks and Lands, 22 State House Station, Augusta, ME 04333-0022; (207) 287-3821.

East Point Sanctuary

Maine Audubon Society   Coastal
30 acres.

From Biddeford, take Hwy 9/208 (Pool Rd.) S for 5 mi. Left on Hwy 208 toward Biddeford Pool. After 0.6 mi. turn left at the T intersection, bear right through 2 forks to Lester B. Orcutt Blvd., follow it to the point. Gate entrance on left. Park along the street.

Open dawn to dusk.

This is one of the best birding spots in southern ME during migrations. The rocky coastal headland is rimmed with steeply sloping shingle beaches grading up to open meadow and shrub thicket. The 2-mi. loop trail beside the shore allows the hiker to scan near and distant waters for gannets, red-throated loon, auks, terns, and other marine birds. Harbor seals are often seen fishing the channel between East Point and adjacent Wood and Stage Islands, both of which support large colonies of birds. The islands also belong to Maine Audubon. Visitors by boat should stay below high-tide line during summer nesting season, and should beware of the abundant poison ivy on Wood Island.

Headquarters

ME Audubon Society, Gilsland Farm, 118 US 1, P.O. Box 6009, Falmouth, ME 04105; (207) 781-2330.

Fernald's Neck Preserve

Maine Chapter, The Nature Conservancy   Coastal
318 acres.

Off Hwy 52 in Lincolnville.

Open dawn to dusk.

The Preserve is on a peninsula that almost bisects Lake Megunticook. Roads surround the lake, and developers have been active. Local residents bought the site to preserve it. The tip of the peninsula is a town park accessible only by water.

The Preserve has more than 3 mi. of frontage on Lake Megunticook. Its 18,000 ft. of shoreline is irregular, bordered by many plants such as pipewort, arrowhead, bur reed, pondweeds, and bulrushes. Many visitors arrive by boat, and there are several suitable places to beach a canoe or other small craft. Back of the shore is forest, mostly white and red pines and hemlock in the N and W, mixed hardwoods and conifers in the S. A large wetland in the center has pitcher plant, rose pogonia, iris, and various grasses, sedges, and rushes.

There's a well-marked trail system and a brochure in the registration box.

Pets are prohibited.

Nearby
Camden Hills State Park (see entry).

Headquarters
ME Chapter, The Nature Conservancy, Fort Andross, 14 Maine St., Suite 401, Brunswick, ME 04011; (207) 729-5181.

Field's Pond Nature Center

Maine Audubon Society   Coastal
170 acres.

Take US 1A SE from Bangor, cross the Penobscot River to Brewer. Continue (on Wilson St.) to Green Point Rd. (at the McDonald's), turn right, go 1.1 mi. to end. Left on Wiswell Rd. for 1.6 mi., right on Field's Pond Rd. Nature Center is on the left.

Open dawn to dusk.

As we prepared our revision, the Maine Audubon Society informed us that it had acquired a new property, in Holden and Orrington. Because the site is relatively large as Audubon holdings go, we decided to include it sight unseen. The society describes the new acreage as follows: "This beautiful 170-acre property has many attractive features including woods and fields, a lakeshore and brook, an island, and wetlands, as well as an impressive variety of plant and animal life that we are still identifying. Local chapter officers and staff of Maine Audubon have started to plan for the nature education center that will eventually be built on the property. Chapter volunteers have already begun offering regular field trips and nature walks, and we welcome visitors."

Headquarters
ME Audubon Society, Gilsland Farm, 118 US 1, P.O. Box 6009, Falmouth, ME 04105; (207) 781-2330.

....

Four Ponds Management Unit
Bureau of Parks and Lands   West
6,015 acres.

This site lies just E of Mooselookmeguntic Lake. Foot access only; no vehicles. S of Rangeley Lake. Appalachian Trail crosses the site, between Hwys 17 and 4. Foot access from Hwy 17 by Appalachian Trail or Hwy 4 in Sandy River.

The Bureau plans to keep this site quiet, closed to vehicles. From Hwy 17 it's about a 1½ mi. walk. The N boundary is less than a mile from Hwy 4, but across a lake. Hikers and fishermen are the principal visitors.

"Four Ponds"? We counted 7. The 3 on the W side of the site are relatively high, over 2,300 ft. The Appalachian Trail ascends to 2,970 ft. near the site's midpoint. To the E, the terrain slopes downward. Long Pond, to the NE, is at 1,729 ft., a drop of some 600 ft. in 3½ mi. (According to our maps, the water body on the W side is also named "Long Pond." The former has an alias: "Beaver Mountain Lake." Beaver Mountain, 3,160 ft., is to the N.

The management plan permits timber harvesting, but not around the ponds or near the trails. The Appalachian Trail passes beside attractive ponds, ascends gradually through heavily shaded corridors, and emerges at viewpoints.

Activities
Camping: An Appalachian Trail lean-to is at Sabbathday Pond and there is a campsite at Little Swift River Pond. Trailside camping is permitted anywhere. No open fires.
Fishing: Native and stocked brook trout.

Snowmobiling: The unit is crossed by a trail extending from Rangeley to Weld.

Headquarters

ME Bureau of Parks and Lands, 22 State House Station, Augusta, ME 04333-0022; (207) 287-3821.

Francis D. Dunn Wildlife Management Area (Sawtelle Deadwater)

Maine Department of Inland Fisheries and Wildlife   North
300 acres.

From I-95 N of Millinocket, W and N on Hwy 159 to town of Shin Pond, then NW on Huber Rd., about 12 mi.

This is also known as the Sawtelle Deadwater area. Our first draft didn't include it. Then we had a note: "They should include Sawtelle—a great place to see moose, deer, and waterfowl from canoe!" With the note came some history. The deadwater was formed by a dam that powered a sawmill. When the mill was moved in 1955, wildlife biologist Francis D. Dunn urged his department to buy or lease the site to manage it for waterfowl. Thirty years passed before the department agreed to buy and the owner agreed to sell. The site was dedicated to Dunn in 1985.

Since then the dam has been maintained, wild rice planted, Canada geese released, and nest boxes installed for wood ducks and hooded mergansers.

The best time to see moose is in July. Reports of 10 to 15 feeding at the same time are not uncommon.

Activities

Fishing: For brook trout and yellow perch.

Canoeing: Best way to see the wildlife. There's little upland on the site.

Headquarters

ME Dept. of Inland Fisheries and Wildlife, 41 State House Station, Augusta, ME 04333-0041; (207) 287-8000.

Frye Mountain Wildlife Management Area

Maine Department of Inland Fisheries and Wildlife   Coastal
5,176 acres.

From Belfast, W on Hwy 3 beyond North Searsmont to Hwy 220. N on
Hwy 220 about 7 mi. Site is on right. A gravel road crosses the site to
Hwy 137.

The forested site is managed to promote wildlife production. Patches
of timber are cut to create openings and new growth. Strips have been
cut in reverting fields, followed by plantings of grasses and legumes.
Beneficiaries of this treatment include deer, pheasant, grouse, snowshoe hare, woodcock, and squirrel.

The entrance road climbs the shoulder of the mountain, through a
young hardwood forest. We saw one grove of white pine and scattered
hemlock, spruce, and fir. The understory was heavy, with many ferns.
Along the roadside were summer flowers, notably black-eyed Susan
and asters.

The site is moderately popular in all seasons. 12 mi. of gravel roads
provide good access to most of the site and include a spur to the top
of Frye Mountain, 1,140 ft., the site's highest point, which has a fire
tower.

Activities

Hiking: Best time is late spring and summer.

Fishing: For brook trout.

Hunting: Deer and small game.

Ski touring, snowmobiling: Unplowed roads are used. The Bureau also
grooms snowmobile trails.

Headquarters

ME Dept. of Inland Fisheries and Wildlife, 41 State House Station,
Augusta, ME 04333-0041; (207) 287-8000.

Gardner-Deboullie Management Unit

See Deboullie Management Unit.   North

Georgia-Pacific Corporation Lands

450,000 acres, plus 350,000 acres in New Brunswick.   West/North

Numerous large and small landholdings on both sides of the U.S.—Canada border, from the vicinity of Calais to the vicinity of North Amity on US 1 S of Houlton. Access from US 1, Hwy 6, and other routes.

The company's Woodland Division operates these lands on a multiple-use plan, making them available to the public for outdoor recreation. This watershed of the St. Croix River is a region of thick forests, many lakes and streams, including Grand Lake, Big Lake, and others.

To use these lands, write to HQ for the Sportsmen's map, then relate this to the corresponding maps in the DeLorme *Atlas*. Most other lands in this vast area are owned by other timber companies that generally permit public use. Keep in mind that these are private lands whose owners can restrict or prohibit use at will, and who can eject persons who misbehave.

For more information about these lands, including campsites, stop at the nearest local office of the Maine Forest Service.

Activities

Camping: Permitted at designated sites only. Open fires require a permit from ME Forest Service.

Fishing: East Grand Lake, also called Grand Lake, is one of several fine fishing areas. It covers over 16,000 acres, with a maximum depth of 128 ft. Salmon, brook trout, lake trout, smallmouth bass, white and yellow perch, pickerel, hornpout, smelt, whitefish.

Boating: Ramps on East Grand Lake and others.

Canoeing: Grand Lake Stream is part of a complex of waterways, including lakes and streams.

Visitors are excluded from areas being logged. Private roads must be driven with caution. Trucks have the right of way—and their drivers expect it.

Publication

Sportsmen's Map of Washington County and Western New Brunswick.

Headquarters

Georgia-Pacific Corp., Woodland, ME 04694; (207) 427-3311.

Gero Island Management Unit

Maine Bureau of Public Lands   North
3,845 acres.

Water access only. At the head of Chesuncook Lake, NW of Millinocket. A popular camping stop for canoeists on the West Branch of the Penobscot River. Launching at the S end of the lake is accessible by private road from Millinocket. Also launching at the N end, W side, at campsite near Umbazooksus Stream.

Chesuncook Lake, ME's third largest lake, is one element in a complex of interconnected lakes and rivers in a region where travel is chiefly by water. Elevation at the lake is 942 ft. The lake is long, narrow, with several arms and bays. At the N end, the roughly circular Gero Island rises to a high point of 1,080 ft. A grove of old-growth white pine is on the N end of the island.

The management unit includes a strip of land that faces the island on the W shore of the lake, the site of what was Chesuncook village. The village now has four year-round residents. It is dominated by a century-old hotel, still operating, reached only by water.

Activities

Camping: 4 primitive campsites are on this side of the island. 3 private campsites are on the mainland. Many informal sites are available to canoe campers.

Fishing: Fine fishing for salmon, brook and lake trout, white and yellow perch.

Boating: The lake is about 24 mi. long, with little shoreline development. It can be very rough, which calls for sound boats with reliable motors.

Headquarters

ME Bureau of Parks and Lands, 22 State House Station, Augusta, ME 04333-0022; (207) 287-3821.

Gilsland Farm

Maine Audubon Society   Coastal
60 acres.

From Portland, N on I-295 to Exit 9, Falmouth Foreside. N on US 1 for
1.9 mi., bear left at small Maine Audubon sign before junction with Hwy
88. Left at Gilsland Farm sign, to parking area.

Open dawn to dusk.

This is the headquarters of the Maine Audubon Society, with 2 mi. of
self-guiding trails through diverse habitats beside the Presumpscot
River: salt marsh, secondary hardwoods, red oak woodland, oak/hem-
lock woodland, shrubland, large open meadows, orchards, and a pond.

HQ has list of bird species recorded. The meadows support nesting
bobolinks and meadowlarks, winter forage for Canada geese, and hunting grounds for migrating birds of prey. Woodland and shrub edges
draw migrating warblers, thrushes, and finches, while adjacent tidal
flats offer opportunities to observe large numbers of feeding shorebirds.

Resident mammals include many different rodents, woodchuck,
weasel, and red fox.

Interpretation

Bird and mammal exhibits, nature library, energy education center at HQ.

Guided nature walks are scheduled throughout the year.

Bookstore offers guides and other items related to appreciating the out-
of-doors.

Headquarters

ME Audubon Society, Gilsland Farm, 118 US 1, P.O. Box 6009, Falmouth, ME 04105; (207) 781-2330.

Grafton Notch State Park

Maine Bureau of Parks and Recreation   West
3,192 acres.

25 mi. NW of Bethel on Hwy 26, between Upton and Newry.

Hwy 26 is one of ME's most scenic routes, and Grafton Notch is its principal feature. The notch is in the Mahoosuc Mountains Management Unit (see entry). Hwy 26 crosses the Park. Indeed, the Park has no entrance. Along the road are parking areas for such features as Screw Auger Falls, Mother Walker Falls, and Moose Cave Gorge. Each is a short walk from the parking area, and each has an exhibit panel.

Farther on are trailheads. The Appalachian Trail crosses Hwy 26 here. Within the Park are trails to Old Speck Mountain and Table Rock. The highway crosses the Park at 1,100 ft. elevation. The high country is on either side in the Mahoosuc Mountain Management Unit.

There is no camping here, no campground nearer than a commercial one at Newry.

A major snowmobile trail traverses the Park.

Nearby

Step Falls Preserve of the Maine Chapter, *The Nature Conservancy* is on the N side of Hwy 26 just S of the Park. A trail through a dense stand of balsam fir and hardwood forest climbs about ½ mi. for a fine view of the falls, which cascade down 200 ft. in less than ⅛ of a mi.

Headquarters

ME Bureau of Parks and Lands, 22 State House Station, Augusta, ME 04333-0022; (207) 824-2912; off season, (207) 624-6080.

....

Great Heath, The

See The Great Heath.

....

Great Wass Island Preserve

Maine Chapter, The Nature Conservancy   South
1,579 acres.

From Jonesport on Hwy 187, S over bridge to Beals Island. Continue through Beals to Great Wass Island and by dirt road to Black Duck Cove and parking.

Open dawn to dusk.

Here one can enjoy a wild oceanic island without benefit of boat. The open exposure to the ocean makes this habitat unusual, with a shoreline more typical of the subarctic than of the temperate zone. The interior has one of the state's largest stands of jack pine, near the southern limit of its range. The coastal raised peat bogs are typical of Canada's Maritime Provinces. The intertidal zone has unusual algal species and several invertebrates usually found below the tidal zone.

The Cape Cove Trail traverses moss-floored spruce/fir forest, open jack pine woods, a point from which to observe a large bog, a swamp with pitcher plants and sundews, and ends at the eastern shore. The Mud Hole Trail traverses European white birch woods and ends on the NE shore. Those who don't mind slippery rocks and frequent fogs can hike the shore between the two trails and to points south.

The wildlife includes species typical of northern bogs and boreal forests, as well as coasts. Harbor seals are often numerous on the ledges off the E coast.

Trail information is available at the registration box.

Headquarters
ME Chapter, The Nature Conservancy, Fort Andross, 14 Maine St., Suite 401, Brunswick, ME 04011; (207) 729-5181.

....

Gulf Hagas Area

Mixed ownership   North

From Brownville Junction, N 5.5 mi. on Hwy 11, then left on gravel road 6.8 mi. to Katahdin Iron Works. Pay the gate fee and ask about road conditions. Get map and directions. It's another 14 mi., with several turns.

Gulf Hagas has been called "the Grand Canyon of Maine" and even "the Grand Canyon of the East." It's well worth the trip, but there's much more than the canyon to see and do in this region. Some day, perhaps, the roads will be paved and the roadsides commercialized. Today the region still has the beauty and flavor of backwoods ME.

The Katahdin Iron Works is now restored as a State Historic Site. The rail siding that once served it is gone. This is the put-in for a run on the West Branch of the Pleasant River, continuous steep rapids that can be run only at medium high water. Nearby Silver Lake has land-locked salmon.

Gulf Hagas is a rocky gorge in which the river drops 400 ft. in 4 mi. in a series of 5 waterfalls. The vertical slate walls may be 300 to 400 ft. deep. Several trails lead to viewpoints. It's a National Natural Land-mark.

Just before arriving at the gulf, the road crosses the Appalachian Trail. Not far off the road the trail crosses the Hermitage, a grove of 175-year-old white pines, a preserve of the Maine Chapter of The Nature Conservancy. Nearby is Screw Auger Falls. These are not the falls of the same name at Grafton Notch.

There is no designated campsite beyond Brownville Junction.

Holeb Management Unit

Maine Bureau of Parks and Lands   North
19,651 acres.

From Jackman on US 201 the state highway map shows no roads in to Holeb Pond. The DeLorme *Maine Atlas* shows an unimproved road from US 201 near Dennistown, N of Jackman, to the Turner Brook Inlet campsite on the NE shore, with boat launching nearby. Many people launch at Attean Pond.

Holeb is best known for fishing and canoeing, especially for he Moose River Bow, a canoe-camping circuit. It's well known, so don't expect to be alone on a prime weekend.

W of Jackman are several lakes. Jackman is on Wood Pond, which is linked by streams to Attean Pond on the S and Little Big Wood Pond to the NW. Holeb is about a mile W of Attean. The Canadian Pacific RR runs near the S shore of Holeb and the N shore of Attean on its way to Jackman.

Holeb and Attean Ponds are N of Attean Mountain, a small W–E range rising to a 2,453-ft. peak from the lake elevation of 1,231 ft. Holeb is over 3 mi. long, its widest point about 1 mi.

Most of the shores on Attean and Holeb Ponds and a significant length of the Moose River, including Holeb Falls, lie within the boundaries. The river passes close to Holeb Pond's W shore, with Holeb Stream as a connecting passage.

The canoe trip, a scenic journey through mountainous country, is a circuit, requiring no car shuttle. Most canoeists who make the circuit begin at the NE corner of Attean Pond. The hard work is a portage from Attean to Holeb, which 74 ft. higher. At the W end of Holeb is a short stream connection to the Moose River, which meanders around the S side of Attean Mountain to the SE corner of Attean Pond. The circuit is 34 mi. It can be done in 2 days, but why hurry?

The site includes several small ponds and bogs. Large wetlands are on the N side and along the Moose River to the SE. The area was timber company land and will continue under multiple-use management, timber harvesting harmonized with wildlife and recreation. Upland vegetation is mixed forest near the lakeshore, giving way to spruce/fir on the higher slopes.

Little information on flora and fauna is available, but both are probably similar to that found at the lower elevations of the Bigelow Preserve (see entry).

Activities

Camping: Numerous primitive campsites are available. The Turner Brook campsite at the NW corner of the lake is the only one accessible by car. Although one may camp anywhere, only 2 mi. of access road are within the site boundaries, with few feasible sites. For boat campers, several undeveloped sites are on the N shore. Canoeists have several sites along the Moose River.

Hiking: The site map shows only two short trails, their locations suggesting they were made by fishermen. The *Maine Atlas* map shows a third along the S shore of the lake. We were told that hikers, chiefly fishermen, use the railroad right-of-way. (From Jackman, the Sally Mountain Trail, about 4 mi. long, leads to a fire tower overlooking Attean Pond, an ascent of about 1,000 ft.)

Hunting: Deer, bear, small game.

Fishing: Harry Vanderweide in his *Maine Fishing Maps,* Vol. 1 (see ME introduction, "Fishing, Boating"), says that Holeb and other lakes of the region "have strong fisheries for brook trout and landlocks." Holeb and Attean are said to offer "a true Maine fishing experience for brookies."

Canoeing: The Moose River trip includes some rips and drops to class II and requires portaging around several waterfalls.

Boating: Launching at Turner Brook for "modest-sized craft."

Publication
Information page with map.

Headquarters
ME Bureau of Parks and Lands, 22 State House Station, Augusta, ME
04333-0022; (207) 287-3821.

....

Howard L. Mendall Wildlife Management Area/Sandy Point Wildlife Management Area

Maine Department of Inland Fisheries and Wildlife   Coastal
242 acres. Sandy Point, 540 acres.

Parking and boat launching on US 1A between Frankfort and Prospect.
Sandy Point: Off US 1 N of Sandy Point. After going under a railroad
bridge, take the first left turn, Muskrat Rd., unsigned. In 0.1 mi., WMA
sign and dirt road.

The Mendall Marsh occupies most of a peninsula between the Penobscot River and the South Branch of the Marsh River. The parking and
boat-launching ramp are on the W side of the South Branch. Driving
N, the first sign we saw marked a good dirt road that served as
entrance to a parking area. Beyond, the road continued through a
small grove of birch, maple, and aspen and out to the end of a short
causeway in the river.

A hand-carried boat could be launched here; a ramp is further N.
From US 1A, access to the site is by boat. It was too late in the day for
us to explore the E side, but the map suggests taking Hwy 174 E from
Prospect and looking for an unimproved road on the left.

The department began acquiring the site in 1970 as part of its effort
to save ME's remaining coastal marshes from destruction. It includes
open water, tidal flats, and salt marsh, an estuarine community with a
rich flora and fauna. Typical marsh plants are cordgrass, black rush,
salt grass, bayonet grass, and many others.

In spring, many ducks and geese pause here for resting and feeding
before proceeding N up the Penobscot River valley. They find aquatic
plants, snails, crustaceans, and small fish here while inland marshes
are still frozen. Many shorebirds frequent the mud flats.

Sandy Point Wildlife Management Area

It looked like just another freshwater marsh. A local resident stopped and told us it was once a muskrat farm. The birding is excellent, he said. Waterfowl include black duck, ring-necked duck, blue-winged and green-winged teal, wood duck, hooded merganser, common goldeneye, and mallard. The dirt road penetrates the marsh. A car can drive in to the turnaround, but we suggest caution if it looks muddy. Part of the marsh can be overlooked from the highway.

The wetland complex includes both shallow and deep marsh, 34 acres of open water, over a hundred acres of bog. Three streams flow from the N and NW, crossing Meadow Rd. and joining within the site. Below the wetland, the combined stream cuts through the hill to enter the Penobscot River. Hunting in season.

Headquarters

ME Dept. of Inland Fisheries and Wildlife, 41 State House Station, Augusta, ME 04333-0041; (207) 287-3821.

Indian Point/Blagden Preserve

Maine Chapter, The Nature Conservancy   Coastal
110 acres.

On Mt. Desert Island. After crossing the Hwy 3 bridge to the island, bear right on Hwy 102. In 1.8 mi., turn right on Pretty Marsh Rd. In 1.7 mi., bear right at fork. Entrance is in 200 yds.

Closed after 6 P.M.

Visitors to Acadia National Park may enjoy a brief visit here. In 1947 a great fire burned much of central and eastern Mt. Desert Island. This area escaped and thus provides an interesting comparison of vegetation types. Most of the preserve is forest: tall coastal red spruce, northern white-cedar, and balsam fir. The Preserve has over 1,000 ft. of frontage on Western Bay, rocky, gravel beaches with schist outcrops. Harbor seals can often be seen on nearby small islands. Osprey nest near the shore.

Visitors are asked to register at the caretaker's house and to stay on the marked trails.

Headquarters
ME Chapter, The Nature Conservancy, Fort Andross, 14 Maine St., Suite 401, Brunswick, ME 04011; (207) 729-5181.

....

Josephine Newman Sanctuary

Maine Audubon Society   Coastal
119 acres.

From Woolwich on US 1, S on Hwy 127 9.1 mi. to Georgetown. Turn right at Sanctuary sign to parking area.

Open dawn to dusk.

This small coastal site is located in a transition region between ME's southern and Downeast coasts. It has a remarkable natural diversity of habitats. It also has one of the most outstanding guides we've ever seen, a booklet of some length that interprets every aspect of the site, excellent in concept, text, illustrations, and design. It even includes a week-by-week calendar of natural events at the Sanctuary.

Bounded on two sides by salt marsh, the preserve has 2 mi. of walking trails that wind through mature stands of red oak, white pine, red spruce, and hemlock, past a cattail marsh and former beaver pond, along a cascading brook, and beside the rocky shore and tidal mudflats of Robinhood Cove.

Plants: The booklet contains a map of the many plant communities in considerable detail, making it useful far beyond the Sanctuary's borders. Also included are lists of the common trees, shrubs, wildflowers, grasses, sedges, ferns, mosses, and lichens.

Birds: The booklet lists species known to breed in the Sanctuary and also of visitors or migrants, with notes on seasons and preferred habitats.

Mammals, reptiles, amphibians: Included are lists of mammals, amphibians, and reptiles. Mammals include snowshoe hare, white-tailed deer, coyote, and mink.

Nearby
Reid State Park (see entry).

Publication
Forests, Fields, and Estuaries, $3.50.

Headquarters
ME Audubon Society, Gilsland Farm, 118 US 1, P.O. Box 6009, Falmouth, ME 04105; (207) 781-2330.

Kennebunk Plains Wildlife Management Area/ Kennebunk Plains Preserve

Maine Department of Inland Fisheries and Wildlife/
Maine Chapter, The Nature Conservancy   Coastal

1,041 acres/136 acres.

Off Hwy 99 outside Kennebunk.

The Wildlife Management Area, purchased in 1987, contains 450 acres of sandplain grassland, rare in ME, and 600 acres of surrounding forest. The Nature Conservancy manages the open grassland for the Dept. of Inland Fisheries and Wildlife, focusing its effort on protecting rare and endangered species. The Dept. manages the surrounding forest and streams for deer, gamebirds, and fish. An adjacent 136 acres at the SE end of the Plains is both owned and managed by The Conservancy.

Sandplain grasslands dominated by such grasses as little bluestem and poverty grass and woody bushes like blueberry are increasingly rare throughout the world. They are dependent on nutrient-poor soils and extremely dry conditions. Kennebunk Plains sits on 70 ft. of sand and gravel deposited by glaciers 12,000 years ago.

The Plains supports a number of grassland nesting birds that are unusual in ME, such as upland sandpiper, grasshopper and vesper sparrows, eastern meadowlark, and horned lark. There are more than 1 million northern blazing stars here, by far the largest population of this plant species in the world. Through careful management, these and other plants continue to recover from fatal herbicide applications during the years of commercial blueberry production here. Other unusual species are upright bindweed and toothed white-topped aster. The northern blazing star blooms and turns the Plains purple at the end of summer.

The forests and streams surrounding the grasslands provide important habitat for deer, turkey, grouse, and fish. One inhabitant is the northern black racer, ME's largest snake. Its range has been contracted severely and the snake is known today at only a few locations in S ME.

There are informational signs at the Preserve parking area off Hwy 99. Visitors are asked to observe carefully all posted regulations in either area. From May–Sept. the WMA roads are closed to vehicles. Visitors to the Preserve area are asked to walk on dirt roads only, at any time—grassland birds nest on the ground and may be endangered even by foot traffic. There are no vehicles permitted in any Conservancy Preserves at any time, nor are pets allowed. Blueberry picking is for personal consumption only, and is restricted to designated areas.

Publications

Leaflet for the Wildlife Management Area.

Protected Lands, (brochure), ME Chapter, The Nature Conservancy.

Headquarters

The Nature Conservancy, Midtown Mall, 160 Main St., Sanford, ME 04073; (207) 490-4012. ME Dept. of Inland Fisheries and Wildlife, 328 Shaker Rd., Gray, ME 04039; (207) 657-3258.

La Verna and Rachel Carson Salt Pond Preserves

Maine Chapter, The Nature Conservancy   Coastal
119 acres and 78 acres.

From Newcastle on US 1, S on Hwy 130 to New Harbor. For La Verna, 3 mi. N on Hwy 32. At Tibbitts Rd., park along Hwy 32 and walk ½ mi. to the shore, keeping right at the turnaround. For Rachel Carson, 1 mi. N on Hwy 32; park on the seaward side and use the steps.

Both Preserves front on Muscongus Bay. La Verna has 3,600 ft. of rugged shore on Brown's Cove, with cliffs and steep ledges on the N end, gravel beach on the S. Behind the shore are a dense spruce fir forest, swamp, freshwater mash, and reverting farmland. Birding is good, and the site is excellent habitat for deer and small mammals. As of this revised edition, La Verna is temporarily closed except by water access.

At this ¼-acre "salt pond" that now bears her name, author and naturalist Rachel Carson gathered some of the material for *The Edge of the Sea* (1955). Low tide exposes a variety of seaweeds with barnacles, blue mussels, hermit and green crabs, periwinkles, starfish, and green sea urchins. Preserve also includes upland forest with trails.

Pets are prohibited.

Headquarters
ME Chapter, The Nature Conservancy, Fort Andross, 14 Maine St., Suite 401, Brunswick, ME 04011; (207) 729-5181.

Leavitt Wildlife Management Area
Maine Department of Inland Fisheries and Wildlife · West
6,408 acres.
From Dover-Foxcroft, 8 mi. SE on Hwy 15. The county line is the site's center.

Between Dover-Foxcroft and Bangor, this is a place to hike with little likelihood of meeting other visitors except in hunting season. Primarily upland, it has a mixture of old fields and orchards and mixed forest. The highest terrain is Bull Hill, extending E from Hwy 15; some hawk watchers come here during the migration. Hatch Hill and High Cut are W of Hwy 15.

A small bog is also on the E side. Several streams have beaver dams, attracting waterfowl and aquatic furbearers.

Activities
Hiking: Opportunities include interior roads, including old logging roads. Good berrying in season.

Hunting: Chiefly for deer, bear, and small game.

Headquarters
ME Dept. of Inland Fisheries and Wildlife, 41 State House Station, Augusta, ME 04333-0041; (207) 287-8000.

Lt. Gordon Manuel Wildlife Management Area

Department of Inland Fisheries and Wildlife   North
6,452 acres.

From Houlton, S on US 1, W on local road to Hodgdon. Parking, launching, and picnic area at the dam. Access to land area by Horseback Rd. and Town Line Rd.

Open daily as weather permits. Roads usually inaccessible by cars Dec.–May.

A water power dam on the South Branch of the Meduxnekeag River was built here in the late 1800s, forming a marsh that attracted waterfowl. Abandoned in the 1950s, the dam washed out, the marsh dried, and waterfowl declined. The site was acquired by the department, a new dam was built, and waterfowl returned.

From the dam, the marsh extends S for 2½ mi., with a maximum width of 2,000 ft. Adjacent upland is a mixture of hardwood stands and reverting fields.

The marsh is best seen by boat. Motors are prohibited. 2 primitive boat launches are available.

More recently about 6,000 acres of upland were added to the WMA. This upland is a mixture of old fields, woodlands, swamps, small wetlands, and streams.

Birds: Upland species include grouse, woodcock. Nest boxes have been placed for common goldeneye, wood duck, and hooded merganser. Other waterfowl seen here include blue-winged and green-winged teal, black duck, ring-necked duck, common merganser, grebes, and Canada goose. Many shorebirds and songbirds frequent the area.

Mammals: Reported species include beaver, muskrat, mink, otter, red fox, coyote, fisher, marten, weasel, skunk, raccoon, snowshoe hare, deer, moose, black bear.

Headquarters

ME Dept. of Inland Fisheries and Wildlife, 41 State House Station, Augusta, ME 04333-0041; (207) 287-8000.

Lily Bay State Park

Maine Bureau of Parks and Lands   North
924 acres.

From Greenville, 9 mi. N on the E shore of Moosehead Lake. (On the road to Kokadjo.)

Open May 1–Oct. 15.

This has long been one of our favorite parks. We're not alone; it's often full, but one can usually get a campsite, and all the sites are attractive. Many are on the shore where one can keep a boat and swim.

The chief attraction is Moosehead Lake, ME's largest, 40 mi. long, 20 mi. wide. (See entry.) Although the lake has attracted vacationers and fishermen and women for more than a century, until recently most development has been at the S end. Now development is spreading northward, but most of the shoreline is still wild, with no road access.

The shore is very irregular, with many bays, coves, and peninsulas. The Park itself has 7 mi. of shoreline. Near shore the water is generally shallow with numerous rocks and snags, but it's clear and one can navigate or wade, cautiously.

Many large and small islands are in the lake, some with private summer homes. Some have primitive campsites; others are available for picnics. Sugar Island (see entry) is just offshore from the Park.

Beyond the Park, the road extends NE into a region of almost unbroken forest, with countless lakes and streams, access to the North Maine Woods and Baxter State Park (see entries) and Ripogenus Dam between Chesuncook Lake and the West Branch of the Penobscot River. Several dirt roads to the left approach the lakeshore at places where one can often see moose in the early evening. We've seen moose more closely from a canoe.

W of Greenville is a popular trail to the Big Squaw Mountain fire tower and the less-known Little Squaw Management Unit (see entry).

Activities

Camping: 91 well-spaced sites around 2 loops, many along the shore. Arrive early for choicest sites. Group camping is available.

Hiking: There is a shoreline hiking trail in the Park. There are unlimited opportunities nearby. Gatehouse has information.

Hunting: Prohibited during the Park's open season or when crews are working. Otherwise state regulations apply.

Fishing: Moosehead Lake is famous for its salmon, brook trout, and lake trout.

Swimming: There is a swim area on the lake.

Boating: 2 boat launch sites with boat slips. The lake can be very rough. Rocks and shoals are common near shore.

Canoeing: Rentals available at Greenville.

Ski touring, snowmobiling: On several mi. of unplowed roads. The Park facilities are closed during the winter. Snowmobiling is popular in the area.

Publication

Information page with map of campground.

Headquarters

Lily Bay State Park, Greenville, ME 04441; (207) 695-2700; (207) 941-4014 off-season.

Little Squaw Management Unit

Maine Bureau of Parks and Lands   North
15,047 acres.

From Greenville, NW on Hwys 15/6 to Dyer Rd., gravel surface, which passes through the management unit.

The site is near the S end of Moosehead Lake. Big Squaw Mountain is a popular day hike. Little Squaw Mountain is a minor ridge trending WSW from near the highway, not as high as Big Squaw but offering a good view of the lake. The site is best known to fishermen, those who don't mind a bit of hiking. Little Squaw Pond is about 2 mi. from the road, Big Squaw Pond another half mile. Big Indian Pond, the largest pond, is at far SW corner, accessible by a rough gravel road from Dyer Rd. All the ponds are surrounded by forested hills, spectacular when the fall colors are at their best.

Activities

Camping: Primitive campsites are at each of the principal ponds. Trailside camping is permitted anywhere, with no open fires.

Hiking: Chiefly on old logging roads. A trail from a trailhead on Dyer Rd. leads to Big Squaw Pond, then Little Squaw Pond, then along the ridgeline to a trailhead behind the Greenwood Motel, where parking is available.

Headquarters

ME Bureau of Parks and Lands, 22 State House Station, Augusta, ME 04333-0022; (207) 287-3821.

....

Machias Seal Island

25 acres   Coastal

At the mouth of the Bay of Fundy, between Maine and Nova Scotia. By charter boat from Lubec, Cutler, Jonesport.

Birding season May–mid-Aug.

This tiny island is reached by boat from ports in ME. Each year it attracts many birders because of its seabirds. More than 2,000 pairs of Arctic terns nest here, some 800 pairs of Atlantic puffins, with smaller numbers of many other species such as the common tern, razorbill, Leach's storm-petrel (seldom seen), and various land birds.

From the landing, visitors may use the boardwalk, footpaths to blinds, and a mowed area.

Information

It is not an Audubon Preserve, but the Maine Audubon Society, 118 US 1, P.O. Box 6009, Falmouth, ME 04105; (207) 781-2330, has offered occasional tours. We also obtained information from a charter boat operator: Barna B. Norton, RR #1, Box 990, Jonesport, ME 04649; (207) 497-5933.

Mahoosuc Mountains Management Unit

Maine Bureau of Parks and Lands   West
27,253 acres.

Heading N, take the Sunday River Rd. out of Bethel; traveling S, take the East B Hill Rd. between Andover and Upton. The management unit has 2 portions, W and E of Hwy 26, separated by and adjacent to Grafton Notch State Park. Hikers access from the State Park. A major trailhead is in New Hampshire on Success Pond Rd.

Hwy 26 is one of ME's most scenic highways. Grafton Notch has long been a famous resort because of its spectacular setting. The Mahoosuc Range is wild and rugged, with forested slopes, steep gorges, cataracts and waterfalls, cirques, glacial tarns, subalpine heaths, even a few "ice caves," small caves where ice forms and may last all summer. Several peaks rise to over 3,500 ft. Old Speck, 4,180 ft., is ME's third highest. On the E, Baldpate Mountain has twin peaks, both over 3,500 ft.

Most of the management unit is accessible only on foot. Bull Branch Rd. penetrates the W portion from the SE. East B Hill Rd. crosses the N tip of the E portion. Otherwise there are only a few logging roads, not shown on the site map and in uncertain condition.

It's a glorious place for hiking, particularly along the high elevation country. This is the only state land where one can camp almost anywhere, pitching a tent trailside or near one's car. (Fires require Forest Service permits except at designated campsites.) Most hiking has been on the Appalachian Trail, and trail sections near the highway have had heavy use.

Plants: At the base of the mountains is mixed forest. At about 2,500 ft. this gives way to spruce/fir forest; this dominates the slopes to about 3,300 ft., where it becomes spruce/fir krummholz, trees reduced to the stature of shrubs by severe climate and thin soil. At the highest elevations are subalpine heaths and exposed rock covered with lichens. Here also are alpine bogs with delicate plant species.

Multiple use is the governing policy here. About 17,000 acres, the lower-elevation forest, are managed for commercial timber production. Harvesting is planned to promote growth of yellow and European white birch and sugar maple. The high slopes won't be cut, nor will areas designated for recreation or buffer zones around lakes and streams. Cutting is planned in consultation with wildlife biologists, to maintain or improve habitats.

Birds: Most of ME's upland bird species occur here, as well as species characteristic of more northern habitats, including the spruce grouse, gray jay, and boreal chickadee.

Mammals: Most upland species are probably here but not abundant.

Features

The Cataracts are on a trail off East B Hill Rd. Frye Brook cascades over several falls in the gorge between Baldpate and Surplus Mountains.

Speck Pond, a mountain tarn on Old Speck Mountain, is the highest lake in ME. On the Appalachian Trail, it's not far from the State Park and Hwy 26, but the trail is steep and difficult. A shelter is nearby.

Observation tower atop Old Speck Mountain has splendid views.

Mahoosuc Notch, 1,500 ft. below Mahoosuc Arm, is noted for lush growth of ferns and mosses and a nearby 250-year-old stand of yellow birch.

Alpine bog and heath areas are on Mahoosuc, Goose Eye, and Carlo Mountains. Hikers are asked to keep off, as the plants are highly vulnerable to trampling. Walkways have been placed in a few areas.

Activities

Camping: Car camping is difficult. Grafton Notch State Park has no campground. The nearest commercial campgrounds are about 10 mi. N or S. Roadside camping in the management unit isn't prohibited, but there isn't much road. Little more than 1 mi. of Bull Branch Rd. is inside the boundaries.

Most trailside camping is along the Appalachian Trail, in lean-tos or shelters, with tent platforms at Speck Pond, all maintained by the Appalachian Trail Club.

Hiking, backpacking: The trail system was here before the state acquired the land. The principal trails originate outside the boundaries. The main stem is the Appalachian Trail, entering near Baldpate in the N, crossing the State Park, then following the Mahoosucs past Mt. Carlo to the New Hampshire border. The section at Mahoosuc Notch is said to be the most difficult mile anywhere on the trail. Along the way are side trails suitable for day hikes as well as overnights. Several of these—Speck Pond, Mahoosuc Notch, Goose Eye, and Carlo Col— originate in NH. All are well described in hiking guides.

Hunting: Game species are very limited.

Fishing: Opportunities are limited. The principal fishing streams are along Hwy 26 and Bull Branch Rd.

Ski touring, snowmobiling: The State Park is the principal base for parking.

This is remote country. Hikers should know the degree-of-difficulty rating of any trail before starting and be prepared for contingencies, including weather changes.

Publication
Leaflet with map.

Headquarters
ME Bureau of Parks and Lands, 22 State House Station, Augusta, ME 04333-0022; (207) 287-3821.

Mast Landing Sanctuary

Maine Audubon Society   Coastal
140 acres.

From US 1 in Freeport, across from the L. L. Bean store, take Bow St. 1 mi. to Upper Mast Landing Rd., on left. Up hill, and Sanctuary is on the right.

Open dawn to dusk.

The site is operated as a nature day camp in summer, but hikers are welcome. Wooded ridges, fields, and orchard slope down from 100 ft. above sea level to salt marsh along Mill Stream, which cascades over a historic dam before flowing into tidal waters of the Harraseeket River. Runoff has cut deep ravines, several of which have hemlock stands. Habitats include a red maple/alder swamp. Most of the site is forested. A brochure describes the Sanctuary's natural communities and cultural history.

The site has 3.5 mi. of trails.

Publication
Brochure.

Headquarters
ME Audubon Society, Gilsland Farm, 118 US 1, P. O. Box 6009, Falmouth, ME 04105; (207) 781-2330.

....

Mattawamkeag Wilderness Park

Penobscot County North
1,018 acres.

From US 2 at Mattawamkeag, 8 mi. E on Park Rd. From I-5, Lincoln-Mattawamkeag Exit.

Open May 15–Oct. 15.

The Park is centered on a low hardwood ridge surrounded by softwood forest and wetlands, with 2 mi. of frontage on the river. The surrounding region, while not true wilderness, is large roadless, flat to hilly, forested with extensive wetlands. The central feature is the Mattawamkeag River, a scenic fishing stream with rapids. You're on your own for winter activities.

Activities

Camping: 52 sites; 12 shelters.

Hiking: 15 mi. of trails.

Fishing: Brook trout and salmon. The river has large granite pools.

Canoeing: From Kingman on Hwy 170, a 12-mi. run to the Penobscot River at Mattawamkeag, passing the camp. Rapids to class III. The river can be canoed later in the season than most.

Publications
Information leaflets.

Headquarters
Mattawamkeag Wilderness Park, Box 5, Mattawamkeag, ME 04459; (207) 736-4881.

Moosehead Lake

40 mi. N–S, 20 mi. W–E; 420 mi. of shoreline.   North
Greenville is at the S end.

Maine's largest lake lies between the state's developed and undeveloped areas. To the N are few paved roads and few towns; most of this territory is owned by timber companies, accessible by their private roads.

The lake's elevation is 1,029 ft. Surrounding it are forested hills, generally rising no more than 400 ft. above the shore. Behind them are a few mountains more than 3,000 ft. high.

The lake's shape is very irregular. So is that of a moose's head, but it requires great imagination to see a resemblance. The lake has many arms, bays, coves, and peninsulas, and in the lake are numerous large and small islands. Maximum depth is 246 ft. Many of the bays and coves are shallow, and boaters should beware of rocks near shore and occasionally well out.

Moosehead has been a famous resort for more than a century. Outfitters, inns, lodges, marinas, and other commercial development are centered at Greenville, and this is still the primary point of access. Hwy 6/15 now runs halfway up the W side to Rockwood, which has similar but fewer services. Lily Bay State Park (see entry) is on the E side. Most of the shore beyond these points is roadless.

Primitive campsites are scattered around the lake and on several of its islands. We saw many quiet coves, far from any road, where one could camp from a boat or canoe. Sugar Island (see entry), off Lily Bay, is state land. By canoeing near dusk, we often paddled close to a moose.

Moosehead is one of the state's best fisheries for salmon, brook trout, lake trout, hornpout, smelt, lake whitefish, round whitefish, others.

Boaters venturing far from base should watch the weather. Storms can develop suddenly, and the lake can be very rough. However, it's almost always possible to find shelter behind an island or in a cove.

Ice-out is usually by mid-May.

Contact the Moosehead Lake Region Chamber of Commerce for a listing of campgrounds in the area.

Information
Moosehead Lake Region Chamber of Commerce, P.O. Box 581, Greenville, ME 04441; (207) 695-2702/2026.

....

Moosehorn National Wildlife Refuge
U.S. Fish and Wildlife Service   Coastal
Baring Unit, 17,200 acres; Edmunds Unit, 7,200 acres.

Baring Unit: on US 1 a few miles SW of Calais. Edmunds Unit: on US 1 about 2 mi. N of Whiting.

Open weekdays 7:30 A.M.–4:00 P.M.

This part of the ME coast is irregular, with countless bays, coves, and inlets, and many offshore islands. Tidal fluctuations are extreme, about 24 ft. in the Cobscook Bay area (Edmunds Unit).

Except for the coastline, it's not a dramatically scenic area, but it has natural diversity and rich wildlife. The land is highly glaciated, with low rolling hills, elevations from 50 to 480 ft. The two units, about 25 mi. apart, have about 100 water/marsh areas. Lakes and ponds range from 20 to 400 acres, with many smaller ponds and flowages. About a tenth of the Refuge area is wetlands.

Plants: The forest is easily accessible, so it's been cut more than once, and planned harvesting continues within the refuge. Some scattered stands of old-growth white pine remain. Most of the cover is relatively young aspen, beech, birch, maple, spruce, fir, and pine. We saw one area that had been burned and was now green with weeds and dotted with wildflowers.

Birds: This is the only federal refuge where the American woodcock is intensively studied and managed. The average summer woodcock population here is 1,800; more than 3,000 are here in spring and fall migrations. Their spectacular mating ritual can be seen in clearings in early spring.

The best birding season generally is May 10–30. A checklist of over 200 bird species is available. Seasonally abundant or common species include common loon, pied-billed grebe, great and double-crested cormorants, American bittern, great blue heron, Canada goose, wood duck, green-winged and blue-winged teal, American black duck, ring-necked duck, common goldeneye, bufflehead, common and hooded mergansers, belted kingfisher.

Also osprey, northern harrier, broad-winged hawk, kestrel, ruffed grouse, many shorebirds and gulls. Bald eagle frequents both units.

Also great horned and barred owls, common nighthawk, whip-poor-will, blue jay, chimney swift, ruby-throated hummingbird, 5 wood-peckers, 6 flycatchers, 4 swallows, crow, raven, black-capped chick-adee, red-breasted nuthatch, brown creeper, winter and sedge wrens, golden-crowned and ruby-crowned kinglets, veery, 3 thrushes, snow bunting, evening grosbeak, bobolink, gray catbird, cedar waxwing, many warblers, sparrows.

Mammals: Annotated list available. Abundant or fairly abundant species include shrews, mice, voles, moles, little brown myotis (bat), snowshoe hare, woodchuck, chipmunk, red squirrel, northern flying squirrel, beaver, muskrat, mink, river otter, raccoon, jumping mice, porcupine, red fox, coyote, white-tailed deer, black bear.

Baring Unit

This is the larger of the 2 units. The entrance is off US 1, ½ mi. S of its junction with Hwy 191. Refuge HQ is about 3 mi. from this turn. At HQ are a bulletin board and an exhibit with information and map. A nature trail is on the road leading in to HQ. One can hike on interior roads that are closed to vehicles. There is no tour route.

Baring has 4,680 acres designated as wilderness. HQ is near the edge of the wilderness, and several trails lead from here to points of interest in the wilderness, including Bearce Lake, largest in the refuge. The refuge also has several miles of frontage on Hwy 191, with several trailheads.

Edmunds Unit

We thought this unit was less interesting than Baring, except that it adjoins Cobscook Bay State Park (see entry) and provides good hiking opportunities for campers. The Park gatehouse can supply a map and information. N of the Park entrance, on the other side of US 1, is North Trail, the beginning of a 5½ mi. auto loop, a pleasant but unex-citing drive through the woods. On the E, the unit borders on Cob-scook Bay between the Dennys and Whiting Rivers. The unit boasts several miles of rocky shoreline where up to 24-ft. tidal fluctuations occur twice a day.

Edmunds has 2,780 acres of wilderness. The loop route passes along the wilderness boundary. Old roads provide hiking routes. The portion of the area we saw has an understory too dense for bushwhacking.

Activities

Hiking: 60 mi. of trails in the two wilderness areas.

Hunting: For deer, with special regulations. Inquire at HQ.

Fishing: Smallmouth bass, yellow perch, pickerel, brook trout. Fishing areas are designated on the bulletin board at HQ.

Canoeing: On Bearce Lake and Vose Pond. No Motors. Bearce Lake access from Hwy 191.

Ski touring, snowmobiling: On roads and trails.

Publications

Leaflet with map.

Unit maps.

Checklists of birds, mammals.

Headquarters

Moosehorn National Wildlife Refuge, RR 1, Box 202, Suite 1, Baring, ME 04694-9703; (207) 454-7161.

....

Morse Mountain/Morse Mountain Preserve

Private Corporation/Maine Chapter, The Nature Conservancy   Coastal
600 acres/37 acres.

From US 1 at Bath, S on Hwy 209. Where it turns left, continue straight on Hwy 216 for about 1 mi. Entrance is on left.

We noticed this site in the *Maine Atlas*. When Popham Beach and Reid State Parks (see entries) are overcrowded, we thought this might be a quiet seaside. The map shows 1½ mi. of private dirt road crossing a salt marsh and wooded hill from the entrance to the mile of sandy beach.

The smaller Nature Conservancy acreage is tied to a 600-acre conservation easement under other ownership. We saw no sign, just a gap in a stone wall, but people knew about the place. The small parking area inside the wall was full, and many cars were parked along the road outside. This, too, seems to be a site worth exploring before or after the warm months.

Mount Blue State Park

Maine Bureau of Parks and Lands   West
5,021 acres.

From Dixfield on US 2, N on Hwy 142. For lakeside, turn left on West Rd. from Berry Mills; for mountain trails, continue to Weld, then on Maxwell Rd. Alternatively, from Wilton 14 mi. NW on Hwy 156 to Weld.
Open May 15–Oct. 1.

The Park is in two pieces, the smaller one on the shore of Webb Lake, the larger in mountainous terrain. The smaller attracts the campers, picnickers, fishers, and swimmers; the larger attracts hikers and backpackers.

Webb Lake, elevation 678 ft., is about 4 mi. long. The Park has about ¾ mi. of shoreline. Although there is some development around the lake, the surrounding country is largely roadless, most of it owned by timber companies.

The larger portion of the Park is mountainous, about 5½ mi. W–E. From Maxwell Rd. one can drive to the base of Mt. Blue via Center Hill Rd. and Mt. Blue Rd. It is then a ¾ mi. hike to the summit at 3,187 ft., a gain of 1,800 ft.

The Park, like the surrounding region, is almost entirely forested, spruce/fir with some hardwoods. Wildflowers, chiefly in openings and along roadsides, include trailing arbutus, lady's slipper, violets, dogwood, wild rose, goldenrod, iris, jack-in-the-pulpit, daisies, buttercups. Several streams flow to the lake.

Activities

Camping: 136 sites. Adirondack shelters available for large groups.

Hiking, backpacking: Trails and logging roads in the surrounding area offer opportunities for extensive hiking and backpacking, to such destinations as Tumbledown Mountain, Little Jackson Mountain, Rangeley Lake, and the Appalachian Trail.

Hunting: In designated sections. Deer, bear, raccoon, rabbit, coyote, partridge, woodcock, waterfowl.

Fishing: Lake and stream. Salmon, brown trout, bass, perch, pickerel. Ice fishing.

Swimming: Sand beach with bath house; may be supervised.

Boating, sailing: Ramp. Rentals available.

Canoeing: Rentals.

Horse riding, bicycling: Extensive multiple-use trail is open to all-terrain vehicles, horses, and bicycles.

Ski touring, snowmobiling: Extensive ski trail system through forest and fields. Snowmobile trail to Rangeley Lake, about 30 mi. Many opportunities on unplowed roads.

Headquarters
Mount Blue State Park, Center Hill, Weld, ME 04285; (207) 585-2347; (207) 585-2261 off-season.

Mullen Woods Preserve

Maine Chapter, The Nature Conservancy   Coastal
117 acres.

From Newport, E on US 2. Where it bends right, just before East Newport, continue straight on Bangor Rd., then left on Stetson Rd. and left on Durham Bridge Rd. Just over the bridge, right on Rutland Rd. After a sharp left, go 1 mi. Park on Rutland Rd. and walk in. Entrance is a grassy track between fences on the right.

Great white pines once were common in ME forests. Although the original stand here was cleared in the 18th century, many of those now growing are over 150 years old, some taller than 100 ft. The forested area of the tract includes mixed conifers and hardwoods, a stand of younger white pine, and some mature hemlock. A small stream bounded by cedar thickets meanders through the N section. An old field is being used for silvicultural test plots.

Stay on the paths. Pets are prohibited.

Headquarters
ME Chapter, The Nature Conservancy, Fort Andross, 14 Maine St., Suite 401, Brunswick, ME 04011; (207) 729-5181.

Nahmakanta Management Unit

Maine Bureau of Parks and Lands **North**

42,818 acres; crossed by 1,820-acre Appalachian Trail corridor.

Access is from the towns of Kokajo or Brownville over gravel roads.

This vast forested landscape is the largest unit in ME's public reserved lands system. It is embroidered with magnificent lakes, streams, and wetlands, and includes thousands of acres of roadless wilderness. Over 50 mi. of undeveloped shoreline encircle the many lakes and ponds.

The Appalachian Trail crosses the unit following the shore of Nahmakanta Lake. The large Debsconeag Lakes backcountry area offers experienced hikers the opportunity to explore a seemingly boundless complex of low mountains and ponds. At the same time, vehicle-accessible campsites offer convenient access to scenic ponds and trailheads for day use. A popular snowmobile trail crosses the unit, linking the towns of Greenville and Millinocket.

People planning to visit this enormous area need to contact the ME Bureau of Parks and Lands for specific information.

Headquarters

ME Bureau of Parks and Lands, 22 State House Station, Augusta, ME 04333-0022; (207) 287-3821.

North Maine Woods

North Maine Woods **North**

2,800,000 acres.

Northern ME, roughly from Baxter State Park to Canada. The private road system is controlled at checkpoints. The one most used by recreationists is 6 Mile Checkpoint, W of Ashland on American Realty Tote Rd.

Summer season: May opening to Sept. 10. Fall: Aug. 20–Nov. 30; summer season permits not valid.

This huge forested region is privately owned. The owners, individuals and corporations, chiefly timber companies, have formed the North Maine Woods organization to provide for multiple-use management, including recreation. It is open to public use, subject to rules and restrictions adopted by the owners.

Much of this land was sold at about the time ME was separated from Massachusetts in 1820. It was usually sold in blocks of 36 sq. mi., called townships, at the time often roadless and inaccessible. Even today many of these townships have names like T 12 R 15. Often several individuals joined in purchasing a township. Paper companies began large-scale acquisitions early in the 20th century. Sales, transfers, and bequests have produced some complex partnerships, such as a paper company and a number of individuals.

Don't come here unless you understand the nature of the area and have obtained the basic information and regulations publication. Motorists sometimes plan to drive the American Realty Rd. (as labeled on state highway maps) from Ashland W to Quebec, only to discover that it can't be used as a through route; travelers must leave by the checkpoint through which they entered.

The region is commercial forest, not wilderness. Not shown on highway maps are more than 2,000 mi. of permanently maintained roads and additional miles of temporary roads built for forest operations. Large areas have been cut over twice, and third growth is being harvested. Some sections are tree farms, supporting even-aged single-species stands. Earlier cutting in other large areas has been followed by natural succession, and a mixed forest is maturing.

Sculptured by the ice sheet, the terrain is hilly and irregular, most of it between 1,000 and 1,400 ft. elevation, cut by countless large and small stream valleys, with many rivers, lakes, and wetlands.

The N ME woods have long been known to hunters and fishermen from throughout the U.S. and elsewhere. Before most of the present roads were built, parties were conducted by professional guides who paddled the canoes, made camp, cleaned fish, and cooked meals. In the 1920s John's great-uncle came here each summer, wearing his Norfolk jacket, knickers, and laced boots, carrying his cased salmon rods, meeting his favorite guide.

Huge areas are still roadless, and only those familiar with the area know the water trails and portages to the many quiet, isolated lakes and ponds. Registered guides still conduct parties.

With more roads came a rapid increase in the number of visitors. The ensuing problems compelled owners to control access. With the complex ownerships, the only feasible solution was a consortium to manage public use. Differences of viewpoint persist. Some owners would prefer to exclude visitors altogether, but all within the boundaries entrust the North Maine Woods consortium with publishing and administering public use regulations.

Despite the roads, the region is still huge, wild, and primitive. Fewer people live here than in the past. There are no motels, gas stations, shops, restaurants, or tow trucks. The principal law officers are the state's fish and wildlife wardens and fire control rangers, each of whom has a large territory. Visitors who get in trouble are on their own.

Entrances are controlled. Visitors must register and pay fees. Those who wish to camp must obtain permits to use authorized campsites.

The St. John River, Allagash Wilderness Waterway, and Deboullie Management Unit are within the North Maine Woods; see separate entries.

Flying service by floatplane—of people, canoes, and gear—is available at Shin Pond, Portage Lake, Millinocket, and Greenville. Bush pilots know many out-of-the-way spots.

Activities

Camping: Several hundred primitive campsites are available, most with fireplace, table, and privy. Camping is permitted only at authorized sites. Reservations can be made by calling or writing HQ a minimum of 1 month before arrival, or one can chance what's available on entering. For sites inaccessible by motor vehicle, a fire permit must be obtained from the ME Forest Service before entering.

Hiking, backpacking: Aside from abandoned roads and trails to a few fire towers, hiking routes are limited. Checkpoint attendants, wardens, and rangers can usually suggest something.

Hunting: Subject to state laws and local regulations of landowners. Inquire. Special entry permits may be required.

Fishing: As many perennial visitors know, it's great if you know where to go. The guides do.

Canoeing: Canoeing is the best way to travel off road, the only means of access to large areas. Good maps are essential, and many visitors depend on registered guides.

Ski touring, snowmobiling: Permitted on unplowed roads.

Trail bikes and all-terrain vehicles are prohibited. 4-wheel-drive vehicles must stay on rights-of-way. Mobile homes are prohibited. Travel trailers and vehicles up to 28 ft. are permitted through certain checkpoints only.

Quotas may limit visitor numbers. This usually happens only in hunting season.

End of May through July is black fly season.

All water should be boiled at least 1 minute before drinking.

Publications

Basic information, regulations, free.

North Maine Woods Sportsmans Guide map, $3.

Lists of cooperating flying services, outfitters, guides.

List of campsites.

List of publications and order form.

Headquarters

North Maine Woods, P.O. Box 421, Ashland, ME 04732; (207) 435-6213.

....

Old Pond Farm Wildlife Management Area

Maine Department of Inland Fisheries and Wildlife   West
450 acres.

From I-95 at Howland, Exit E on Hwy 6, the Trans-Maine Hwy. In 1 mi. turn N on Hwy 116. In about 2 mi., fork left on North Howland Rd. In 1 ½ mi., turn N on Seboeis Rd. In about 1½ mi., site is on left at bridge.

This site interested us because of its unusual history. Until the late 1800s, there was a large pond here, the water retained by an esker. Some men blasted through this glacial ridge, releasing a flood that caused downstream damage all the way to Bangor. Then followed ditching and unsuccessful farming, grazing, and mining enterprises, after which the land was allowed to revert, grasses and sedges growing in moist areas, woody plants where there was drier ground.

Title passed from owner to owner until someone in Fish and Game observed that it had been state property all the time. All "great ponds," ponds larger than 10 acres, belong to the state. Draining a pond doesn't change its legal status.

So the department dammed the outlet, flooding the old bottom and creating a new pond and marsh. The WMA is near a waterfowl migration route, and its attraction was increased by developing goose pasture, building nesting islands, and blasting potholes. Nearly all species of ducks found in ME's freshwater wetlands are now seen here. Bald eagles are often sighted, and ospreys nest. Standing near the bridge, we looked out over this restored habitat, which shows few signs of its past abuse.

Just beyond the bridge, a short dirt road leads to a parking area for about three cars and launching for hand-carried boats.

Headquarters
ME Dept. of Inland Fisheries and Wildlife, 41 State House Station, Augusta, ME 04333-0041; (207) 287-8000.

....

Maine Peaks-Kenny State Park

Maine Bureau of Parks and Lands   West
839 acres.

From Dover-Foxcroft, N on Hwy 153 for 6 mi.

Open May 15–Sept. 30.

Most visitors come here for water-based recreation. The Park has a 2-mi. frontage on 6,000-acre Sebec Lake, which is over 10 mi. long. The Park is attractive, with wooded campsites, a sand beach at the foot of an expanse of lawn. Most of the site is covered by young mixed forest: spruce/fir with northern hardwoods.

To the N of Sebec Lake is a vast region of forest and lakes, mostly land owned by timber companies, with extensive opportunities for primitive camping, backpacking, hunting, fishing, and canoeing.

Activities

Camping: 56 well-spaced sites. Likely to be full weekends and holidays.

Hiking: 3 trails are within the Park, ½ to 2 mi. Other opportunities are nearby.

Fishing: Lake and stream. Salmon, trout, togue, pickerel, smallmouth bass, perch.

Swimming: Lake. May be supervised.

Boating: Sailboats and powerboats are allowed on the lake; a ramp is outside the Park at the end of Hwy 153.

Headquarters
Peaks-Kenny State Park; Dover-Foxcroft, ME 04426; (207) 564-2003;
(207) 941-4014 off-season.

Petit Manan National Wildlife Refuge

U.S. Fish and Wildlife Service   Coastal
3,335 acres.

From Ellsworth, about 30 mi. S on US 1. Just beyond Steuben, turn S on
Pigeon Hill Rd. to parking area.

Open during daylight hours.

The refuge occupies a peninsula between Dyer Bay and Pigeon Hill
Bay and several nearby islands. Petit Manan Point is rugged,
windswept, with rocky shoreline, cobble beaches, fresh- and saltwater
marshes, beaver flowages, heath, and mixed forest. Small tide pools
can be found on the E side of the point. The highest land is 144 ft.
above sea level. Bois Bubert Island, on which the refuge has 1,155
acres, is much like the point; it can be reached only by boat. The other
islands are much smaller and visiting is discouraged, especially in
nesting season.

Birds: Checklist available. Almost 300 species have been recorded,
including black duck, eider, black-backed, herring, and laughing gulls,
osprey, bald eagle, peregrine falcon, ruffed and spruce grouse, whimbrel, common, arctic, and roseate terns, black guillemot; in winter,
common and red-throated loons, great cormorant, snowy owl.

Mammals: Include white-tailed deer, beaver, mink, muskrat, raccoon,
weasel, red fox, coyote, striped skunk, snowshoe hare, porcupine.

An information exhibit is at the parking area. Two unimproved
trails begin here: Shore Trail, 1 mi. round-trip of rather strenuous hiking to the shore of Pigeon Hill Bay; Birch Point Trail, 3 mi. loop to
Dyer Bay through woods and blueberry fields.

The manager advises that the best time for a visit is late summer,
when the weather is best and black fly and mosquito numbers have
decreased.

Parts of Petit Manan Point and Bois Bubert Island are private property. Please observe refuge boundary signs.

Publications

Information page.

Map.

Bird checklist.

Headquarters

Petit Manan National Wildlife Refuge, Main St., P.O. Box 279, Milbridge, ME 04658; (207) 546-2124.

....

Popham Beach State Park

Maine Bureau of Parks and Lands   Coastal
529 acres.

From US 1 at Bath, S on Hwy 209 to beach.

Open Apr. 15–Oct. 30, 9 A.M.–dusk.

It is said to be a fine sand beach with tide pools and rock outcrops. We don't know. On a sunny day in August, the parking area was full and dozens of cars were parked along the road outside. Try it in the fall.

Headquarters

Popham Beach State Park, Phippsburg, ME 04562; (207) 389-1335.

....

Quoddy Head State Park

Maine Bureau of Parks and Lands   Coastal
481 acres.

From US 1 at Whiting, NE on Hwy 189 toward Lubec. Entering Lubec, S on South Lubec Rd., then E to Quoddy Head.

Open May 15–Oct. 15, 9 A.M.–dusk.

Quoddy Head is the easternmost point of land in the U.S. It's a scenic area, with rock cliffs rising 80 ft. from the ocean, Gulliver's Hole (a foaming sea pocket), a lighthouse, a dense evergreen forest, and a short trail that includes a boardwalk through a peat bog. It's an easy detour for visitors to Campobello Island. The nearest camping is at Cobscook Bay State Park (see entry).

Headquarters
Quoddy Head State Park, Lubec, ME 04652; (207) 733-0911; (207) 941-4014 off-season.

Rachel Carson National Wildlife Refuge
U.S. Fish and Wildlife Service   Coastal
4,500 acres.
From Wells, N on US 1, then right a short distance on Hwy 9 E.

The refuge is presently a chain of 10 small units, coastal marshes extending from near Kittery Point to the Spurwink River S of South Portland. The acreage represents about ⅔ of the total area planned for acquisition. Most of the units have little or no upland. The only visitor facilities are at the unit N of Wells.

Wells is a busy, congested resort town. Just outside, the refuge is a quiet, delightful woodland overlooking a salt marsh, tidal channels, and estuary. Exhibits at the parking area describe the site and its purpose. A 1 mi. loop trail passes through the white pine forest to overlooks and a boardwalk.

An extensive bird list is available, identifying over 250 species seen at the refuge. At midday in August we saw more butterflies than birds. We enjoyed the visit.

Publications
Self-guiding interpretive leaflet.

Annotated bird checklist.

Mimeo information pages: spring wildflowers, trail guide, visiting the refuge.

Headquarters
Rachel Carson National Wildlife Refuge, Rt. 2, Box 751, Wells, ME 04090; (207) 646-9226.

....

Rangeley Lake State Park

Maine Bureau of Parks and Lands   West
691 acres.

From Rumford N for about 30 mi. on Hwy 17; from Farmington NW for about 40 mi. on Hwy 4.

This is an attractive camp on the shore of a lake that has been a well-known resort for more than a century. The lake is about 8 mi. long, covering 6,000 acres. Roads encircle it, and there is development. However, much of the surrounding territory is mountainous, forested, and undeveloped, with many isolated streams and ponds.

The Park has 1½ mi. of lakeshore, and most recreation is water-based. No trails are within the Park, but it's a good place to camp for day hiking at Sabbathday Pond, Elephant Mountain, Bald Mountain, and Saddleback Mountain (which is on the Appalachian Trail).

Activities

Camping: 50 well-spaced sites set among spruce and fir trees.

Fishing: Chiefly salmon. Also brook trout.

Swimming: Supervised beach.

Boating: Ramp; dock; rentals.

Ski touring, snowmobiling: Marked snowmobile trail, 30 mi., to Mount Blue State Park.

Headquarters
Rangeley Lake State Park, Rangeley, ME 04970; (207) 864-3858; (207) 624-6080 off-season.

Reid State Park

Maine Bureau of Parks and Lands   Coastal
766 acres.

From Woolwich on US 1, S and E on Hwy 127, then S on Seguinland
Rd., a total of about 14 mi.

The Park has 1½ mi. of sand beaches, a warm saltwater pond for swimming, dunes, marshes, ledges, and other natural attractions, including
spruce trees growing close to the high-tide mark. Birding is said to be
good, in season, with gannet, eider, and scoter offshore, shorebirds in
late summer, many upland species.

What we saw on a warm summer weekend was a roadside lined
with cars that couldn't be parked inside and a beach thronged with
people. One can usually find parking on weekdays, we were told. It
could be quiet and pleasant in spring and fall.

Headquarters
Reid State Park, Georgetown, ME; (207) 371-2303.

Richardson Management Unit

Maine Bureau of Parks and Lands   West
17,757 acres.

From Andover (at the intersection of Hwys 120 and 5), N on S Arm Rd.
to private campground and boat ramp at the S end of Lower
Richardson Lake. Hwy 16 W from Rangeley crosses the N end of the site;
a boat launch site is at the N end of Upper Richardson Lake.

The 4,200-acre upper lake and 2,900-acre lower lake are joined at a
shallow narrows. The upper lake is separated from Mooselookmeguntic Lake by a dam. All 3 are within the Rangeley Lakes complex, in a
hilly, forested region with a few roads. The lakes are noted for excellent salmon and trout fishing. The shore is undeveloped except for a
few private cottages. Upper Richardson has numerous sand beaches.

The public land lies between the Richardson Lakes and Mooselook-meguntic. Land access is from the S. The gate is not closed except possibly at spring breakup.

Elevation at the lakes is 1,448 ft. The public land is heavily forested, relatively flat, with isolated hills up to 2,130 ft. Three small ponds are in the N portion of the site near Hwy 16.

Activities

Camping: Designated lakeshore sites at the South Arm Campground.

Hiking: On woods roads.

Hunting: Deer, moose, bear, grouse, but in relatively low numbers.

Fishing: Lake, brown, and brook trout, salmon, hornpout, bullhead. Best fishing June–Sept. Excellent Sept. fly fishing in Rapid River, outlet of the lower lake. Marked fly fishing areas in upper lake.

Boating, canoeing: Launch at S and N ends. Ice-out about May 5.

Headquarters

ME Bureau of Parks and Lands, 22 State House Station, Augusta, ME 04333-0022; (207) 287-3821.

Rocky Lake Management Unit

Maine Bureau of Parks and Lands   Coastal
10,904 acres.

From East Machias on US 1, N about 8 mi. on Hwy 191, which cuts across the SE corner of the site.

"I like this site," our advisor said. "It's underutilized. Excellent warmwater fishing. Sand beaches. A good canoe trip."

The boundaries are well marked at the highway with blue-and-white signs. About 3 by 6 mi., the site is in a region of lakes and wetlands. The land is flat to gently rolling, the elevation about 200 ft. Rocky Lake, about 4½ mi. long, is in the E half of the unit. The W half is crossed by the East Machias River and Huntley Brook, with associated wetlands. Second Lake, about 1 mi. long, is on the N boundary. A launch site for hand-carried craft and a campsite are at the dam, on the E side of Rocky Lake, about ½ mi. off the access road.

Rocky Lake is indeed rocky. Boats with motors must be operated cautiously. It has miles of undeveloped shoreline and many small coves and islands.

Activities

Camping: 4 vehicle-access campsites on Rocky Lake, 1 on Second lake. The Mud Landing site is marked at the highway. Walk down before trying the road with a trailer. Camp in any suitable place; no open fires.

Hiking: A few short trails are within the boundaries, miles of back roads and trails nearby.

Hunting: Game populations are generally low.

Fishing: Chiefly bass, white perch, pickerel. Called excellent. Atlantic salmon in the East Machias River.

Canoeing: A 50-mi. trip begins at the end of the lake, curves S into Second Lake, then down the East Machias River through Hadley Lake to the ocean. Some moderate whitewater and areas of open water.

Headquarters

ME Bureau of Parks and Lands, 22 State House Station, Augusta, ME 04333-0022; (207) 287-3821.

Round Pond Management Unit

Maine Bureau of Parks and Lands   North
20,349 acres.

Most visitors are traveling the Allagash Wilderness Waterway (see entry). Land access is from Ashland, W on American Realty Rd. through the North Maine Woods (see entry), turning N at Musquacooks Lakes.

Maine is blessed with an abundance of "Round Ponds." We counted 3 on the Allagash Waterway, and there may be more. This one is at Mile 88 from Telos Landing. About 2 mi. long, the pond is a backwater surrounded by forested hills.

It's a pleasant, scenic rest stop for canoeists, with 4 campsites, a 2 ½ mi. trail to an old fire tower, and abundant wildlife, including loons and other waterfowl.

The Waterway itself has a protected corridor of 500 ft. on each side.

Headquarters
ME Bureau of Parks and Lands, 22 State House Station, Augusta, ME 04333-0022; (207) 287-3821.

....

Ruffingham Wildlife Management Area

Maine Department of Inland Fisheries and Wildlife   Coastal
610 acres.

From US 1 at Belfast, about 10 mi. W on Hwy 3. At North Searsmont, site and dam are on the right. Access by canoe or along the shore.

The region has many pond and freshwater marshes but few are state-owned. This site, acquired as a waterfowl nesting area, has a freshwater marsh, open water, and a strip of land as buffer. It offers an attractive opportunity for quiet walking, canoeing, and wildlife viewing.

Bartlett Stream and Thompson Brook flow from the N into the 386 acres of wetland.

Plants: Principal species include grasses, cattail, bulrush, wild rice, pondweed, coontail, spatterdock.

Birds: Nesting species include black duck, ring-necked duck, blue-winged and green-winged teal, wood duck, hooded merganser, common goldeneye, Canada goose. Other species include woodcock, kestrel, owls, various songbirds.

Mammals: Include muskrat, otter, mink, flying squirrel, deer.

Canoeing: Put-in at the dam on Hwy 3.

Headquarters
ME Dept. of Inland Fisheries and Wildlife, 41 State House Station, Augusta, ME 04333-0041; (207) 287-8000.

R. Waldo Tyler Wildlife Management Area (Weskeag Marsh)

Maine Department of Inland Fisheries and Wildlife   Coastal
533 acres.

From US 1 at Thomaston, E about 1 mi., then right (S) on Buttermilk Lane to Weskeag Marsh. Sign is on right on hill overlooking the marsh.

The bridge at South Thomaston crosses the Weskeag River. A dam was built near here around 1850 to hold tidewater to operate a mill. Upstream is an extensive salt marsh. From Buttermilk Lane, we looked out over rolling fields and woodlands to the marsh below. The Weskeag complex covers about 900 acres. State acquisition began with 180 acres. It now includes 360 acres of salt and fresh marsh, 120 acres of forest, about 50 of fields. The marshes provide rich habitat for shellfish, eels, striped bass, and other fauna.

The WMA sign is the only marker. We saw no boundary postings. There's no parking area, but one can pull off onto the shoulder or into a field.

Birds: No list available. Site is a migration and wintering area for teal, black duck, and Canada goose. Also mentioned as common are yellowlegs, herons, songbirds.

Headquarters
ME Dept. of Inland Fisheries and Wildlife, 41 State House Station, Augusta, ME 04333-0041; (207) 287-8000.

St. John River

North Maine Woods   North
134 river miles.

In the North Maine Woods, roughly paralleling the Quebec border. Access by private road or float plane.

The St. John is about 400 mi. long, the last half in Canada. In May–June it offers a unique opportunity for canoeing through an almost roadless forest on a swift-flowing stream with rapids to class III. The longest run begins at Fifth St. John Pond. Here access is by vehicle or flying boat, bringing canoe and gear. Most trips begin at Baker Lake, 20 mi. downstream. Here there is road access, but the spring road conditions and the difficulties of arranging a car shuttle persuade many to fly in.

Most travelers take 7 to 10 days for the journey to the junction with the Allagash River. It's possible to continue farther, even on through New Brunswick.

The lakes and streams are state property, but the land is privately owned, managed by the North Maine Woods consortium (see entry). Once this was a forest of great trees. The river was the only way to transport huge logs to mills. Only traces remain of the small settlements of loggers and supporters. The present-day forest is mostly spruce/fir with aspen, birch, and alder. Through the North Maine Woods organization, the landowners permit public recreation, subject to their rules. The wilderness quality of the waterway is protected by the St. John River Resource Protection Plan, adopted by the Maine Land Use Regulation Commission.

It's a wilderness adventure, not to be taken casually, through seemingly endless forest with abundant wildlife. You're on your own. Although a few private roads cross the waterway, you might wait a long time to see a vehicle pass. The mile-long Big Black Rapids, class III, is 30 mi. from a settlement.

Water conditions can change rapidly, so it's important to get last-minute advice from the North Maine Woods, (207) 435-6213, or ME Forest Service, Ashland District, (207) 435-7964. The season begins after ice-out, usually about May 1. By mid–June there may be too little water in the river for canoeing.

Everyone using the river must register at checkpoints or when meeting a ranger on the river.

Flying services at Greenville, Shin Pond, Portage Lake, Allagash Village, and other places can deliver you and your gear to any of several points on the river. Guides and outfitters also can arrange waterway trips.

Activities

Camping: At designated sites only.

Fishing: Chiefly brook trout. Possibly muskellunge, a new species migrating from Quebec.

The black fly season is May–June; ask locally about repellents.
Be sure to boil water before drinking, or bring your own.

Publications

St. John River Pocket Guide 12-page folder with map, information. On waterproof paper. $3.

North Maine Woods Sportsman's Guide Map. $3.

Mimeo information pages: rules and regulations, fees, flying services, outfitters and guides.

Headquarters

North Maine Woods, P. O. Box 421, Ashland, ME 04732; (207) 435-6213.

Sandy Point Wildlife Management Area

See Howard L. Mendall Wildlife Management Area.

Sawtelle Deadwater Wildlife Management Area

See Francis D. Dunn Wildlife Management Area.

Scarborough Marsh Nature Center

Maine Audubon Society   Coastal
On 3,100 acres of mixed ownership, private and state.

From US 1 in Scarborough, E ¾ mi. on Hwy 9/Pine Point Rd.

Open from dawn to dusk.

From mid-June to Labor Day the Maine Audubon Society operates the Nature Center, which serves as the site's visitor center with many active programs. The center also has canoe rentals and a store. Parking at the center is limited to about 12 cars, but there's ample parking along the highway.

The Nature Center is the ideal starting point for exploring ME's largest salt marsh. The coastal wetlands were being destroyed by dredging, drainage, filling, and polluting, depriving waterfowl of essential resting, nesting, and feeding habitat. Acting on a cooperative plan, the U.S. Fish and Wildlife Service assembled the Rachel Carson National Wildlife Refuge (see entry), while the (Maine) Dept. of Inland Fisheries and Wildlife acquired the Scarborough, and improved nesting habitat with dams and dikes.

The marsh is at the confluence of the Dunstan and Nonesuch Rivers, its soil held in place by cordgrass, cattails, rushes, and sedges. It provides critical habitat, based on salt, brackish, and fresh waters, or a broad array of wildlife, particularly birds.

Birds: A summer bird list is available. It includes (omitting uncommon and rare species), double-crested cormorant, Canada goose, mallard, black duck, wood duck, green-winged and blue-winged teal, common eider, common merganser, Virginia and sora rails, common tern, 4 gulls, 3 herons, black-crowned night-heron, snowy egret, American bittern, many shorebirds, glossy ibis, northern harrier, sharp-shinned and red-tailed hawks, osprey, merlin, kestrel, black-bellied and semi-palmated plovers, killdeer, belted kingfisher, common nighthawk, common flicker, eastern kingbird, great crested flycatcher, eastern phoebe, 3 swallows, blue jay, crow, black-capped chickadee, 8 warblers, 4 sparrows, eastern meadowlark, red-winged blackbird, northern oriole, common grackle, northern cardinal, rose-breasted grosbeak.

Mammals: No checklist. Mentioned: vole, muskrat, mink, occasional river otter, woodchuck, raccoon, fox, deer, moose.

Interpretation

Nature Center has exhibits, slides, talks, literature.

Weekly programs include "Wildflowers and Wild Edibles," "Family Marsh Adventure," "Dusk and Dawn Birding," canoe tours.

Nature trail into the marsh.

Activities

Hiking: The site map shows one foot trail 2 mi. long crossing the marsh. We found other trails or little-used roads to explore the marsh, some of them outside the site boundaries.

Hunting: Waterfowl.

Canoeing: Rentals at the Nature Center, or bring your own canoe.

Publications

Nature Center folder.

Site map.

Summer bird list.

Nature trail guide.

Canoeing guide.

Headquarters

ME Audubon Society, 118 US 1, P. O. Box 6009, Falmouth, ME 04105:
(207) 781-2330. Nature Center (seasonal): (207) 883-5100.

....

Scraggly Lake Management Unit

Maine Bureau of Parks and Lands   North
9,057 acres.

From I-95 N of Millinocket, W and N on Hwy 159 to town of Shin Pond,
then NW on Huber Rd. about 15 mi. Lake-access road is on the right
(Huber Rd. in the DeLorme *Atlas,* also called American Thread Rd., or
Grand Lake Rd.)

The SW corner of this unit touches the NE corner of Baxter State Park
(see entry).

N central ME is a region of lakes and forests, with few roads or settlements. Scraggly Lake, only 3 mi. long, is not among the larger
waters, nor is it famous for fishing, although the fishing is good. It is a
quiet place, attractive to campers, hikers, and people who like to fish.

The lake is irregularly shaped, with many small islands and coves.
At the E end are bluffs over 100 ft. high. Several small ponds are
within the management unit. To the N and S are hills rising to about
400 ft. above the lake level. Land just to the W is flat to gently rolling.
The surrounding land is heavily forested.

Activities

Camping: 10 primitive sites with road access are in a campground on
the E shore. Visitors may camp anywhere, with no open fires. 3 single
water-access sites.

Hiking: The map shows several short trails with no apparent destinations, other than one to Ireland Pond near the N boundary of the unit. A trail loop is on Owl's Head, on the E end, water access. The region has many unmaintained logging roads, some of which can be hiked.

Fishing: Smallmouth bass, white perch, pickerel.

Boating: Ramp, trailer access, on the E shore.

Nearby
Francis D. Dunn Wildlife Management Area (see entry). You pass it on the way. Don't miss it!

Publication
Information page with map.

Headquarters
ME Bureau of Parks and Lands, 22 State House Station, Augusta, ME 04333-0022; (207) 287-3821.

Sebago Lake State Park

Maine Bureau of Parks and Lands   Coastal
1,300 acres.

From Portland, about 30 mi. NW on US 302. Park is on the N shore, between Naples and South Casco.

This lake is New England's third largest. ME's record landlocked salmon was caught here in 1907, and the fishing is still good. But because of its proximity to Portland and other population centers, it's the most heavily used large lake in ME, with increasing shoreline development.

Interpretation
Nature programs.
Ranger-led hikes.

Activities
Camping: 250 sites, usually full July–Aug. Season is May 1–Oct. 1.

Hiking: 4.5 mi. of trail, with views of Sebago Lake and Songo River.

Fishing: For salmon and togue.

Boating: Ramp.

Pets are prohibited.

Headquarters
ME Bureau of Parks and Lands, 22 State House Station, Augusta, ME 04333-0022; (207) 693-6613; (207) 693-6231 off-season.

Seboeis Lake Management Unit
Maine Bureau of Parks and Lands   North
12,902 acres.

From Millinocket SW about 12 mi. on Hwy 11. Look for sign on left. Then S about 2½ mi. on gravel road.

The management unit contains a considerable amount of shoreline on 2 large lakes. The road leads to the N end of Seboeis Lake, a water body about 6 mi. long that is almost entirely within the unit's boundaries. The lake is about 1¼ mi. across at its widest point. As the road approaches the lake, the right fork leads to a launching place for hand-carried boats and passes near primitive campsites. The left fork continues S somewhat E of the lake, turning E to a primitive campsite on the S end of Endless Lake, where the unit has frontage on the SW shore.

Camping and fishing are the principal activities here, with hunting in season. Maps show no hiking trails, but E side road has little traffic unless loggers are active. Terrain is gently rolling rather than mountainous; elevation at the lake is 438 ft., at the hilltops only 745. However, there are impressive views of mountains nearby, including Mt. Katahdin. Plant cover is chiefly forest in various stages of growth. The land near Endless Lake was heavily cut over shortly before the state acquired it. The woods around Seboeis are in better condition.

Seboeis is usually a quiet place. It is only one of many lakes near Millinocket. Several others are larger, better known, with more dramatic scenery and with visitor facilities. Furthermore, Seboeis is subject to drawdowns in dry summers. In the lake are 250-acre Leyford

Island and several others, including little Dollar Island, just big enough for one campsite.

Activities

Camping: The campsites near the head of the lake are small, primitive, only accessible by foot but not far from the road. The island site is accessible by boat. Camp anywhere, but with no open fire.

Huntring: Deer, bear, ruffed grouse, snowshoe hare.

Fishing: Both lakes offer good bass and salmon fishing.

Boating: Launching for hand-carried boats only. Some attractive campsites can be reached by boat.

Swimming: Sandy beaches at the N end of the lake.

Snowmobiling: Popular as part of the route from Milo to Medway.

Publication

Information page with map.

Headquarters

ME Bureau of Parks and Lands, 22 State House Station, Augusta, ME 04333-0022; (207) 287-3821.

Seboeis River

Mixed ownership   North
About 32 river miles.

From the town of Shin Pond on Hwy 159, W on Baxter Park Road (Grand Lake Road) about 6 mi. to the river.

The crossing of road and river is the center of the 714-acre Seboeis River Gorge Preserve of the Maine Chapter, The Nature Conservancy. Upstream is a deep V-shaped gorge, unusual in ME, with steep banks over 165 ft. high. In this section, Godfrey Pitch and Tiger Rips could be called either falls or rapids. Some whitewater experts might try the run, but it's not recommended. The TNC Preserve extends downstream, for a total of 8 mi.

Next to the bridge is a ME Forest Service campground. This is the put-in for a 24-mi. canoe run in scenic mountain country ending just above Whetstone Falls, W of Stacyville, where there is another camp-ground. This is a relatively easy 2-day run, with some class II rapids and a short portage near the beginning.

This is wild, unspoiled country, black ash and white spruce trees beside the river, alders, sedges, and ferns where there is seasonal flood-ing, dense growths of mixed hardwoods and conifers on the hills and ridges. In some stretches, maples overarch the stream. Wildlife is abundant.

Activities

Camping: Primitive campsites at each end of the run and along the river.

Hiking: Unimproved roads parallel part of the river, and there are a few informal fishermen's trails. Otherwise bushwhacking.

Fishing: Good fishing for brook trout.

Canoeing: 4 days recommended for the run.

Headquarters

Maine Chapter, The Nature Conservancy, Fort Andross, 14 Maine St., Suite 401, Brunswick, ME 04011; (207) 729-5181. ME Forest Service, Ashland District; (207) 435-7964.

Squa Pan Lake

Maine Bureau of Parks and Lands — North
17,985 acres.

From Presque Isle, W on Hwy 163 to Mapleton. There, ask directions.

The lake is relatively shallow. The fishing might be acceptable else-where, but not in northern ME, which has such outstanding fishing waters. Nor is the area especially scenic. The terrain is flat to gently rolling except for Squa Pan Mountain, a N–S ridge rising to 1,460 ft.

However, the site does offer quiet camping and hiking. The E shore is undeveloped. One can camp anywhere, without fire. The forest is sufficiently open to invite bushwhacking up to the ridge.

Activities

Camping: Camping at large, but no wood fires.

Boating: The Squa Pan Outing Club charges a fee for road access to the ramp on the NW shore.

Ski touring, snowmobiling: Trails through the woods.

Headquarters

ME Bureau of Parks and Lands, 22 State House Station, Augusta, ME 04333-0022; (207) 287-3821.

Steep Falls Wildlife Management Area

Maine Department of Inland Fisheries and Wildlife   Coastal
2,537 acres.

About 20 mi. NW of Portland via Hwys 25 and 113 to Steep Falls. Just beyond the town, turn right on Turkey Farm Rd., an unimproved road to Adams Pond.

Near Sebago Lake, the site is a mix of forest, wooded swamp, and wetland, with enough open water to attract waterfowl. In addition to Turkey Farm Rd. (reported to us as graveled) there are about 5 mi. of logging roads in various conditions. Tucker and Davis Brooks cross the site.

Some hiking rails have been marked by the operator of a commercial campground on Adams Pond.

Birds: Game species include ruffed grouse, woodcock, ducks.

Mammals: Important deer habitat, especially for wintering. Species reported include snowshoe hare, fisher, red fox, coyote, raccoon, beaver, otter. Bobcat and bear sightings. Moose may visit.

Nearby

Steep Falls, on the Saco River, is on the SW side of the town. The Saco is canoeable, the falls about a 6-ft. drop.

Headquarters

ME Dept. of Inland Fisheries and Wildlife, 41 State House Station, Augusta, ME 04333-0041; (207) 287-8000.

Steve Powell Wildlife Management Area

Maine Department of Inland Fisheries and Wildlife   Coastal
1,755 acres.

From I-95, Exit 26, then E on Hwy 197 to Richmond. The ferry landing is on the Kennebec River where Hwy 197 meets Hwy 24.

Daily 9A.M.–sunset, May 1–Labor Day, by reservation; Labor Day–Sept. 30, open by reservation as staff time and work schedules permit.

This unique WMA in on Swan Island, accessible by the Inland Fisheries and Wildlife ferry (passengers only, no cars). It is the only WMA that is a wildlife sanctuary, and the only one where camping is allowed. It is also the only WMA with a descriptive brochure, self-guiding tour, and guided tours of a restricted area.

Reservations are required. Reservations include a scheduled ferry trip. Only 60 visitors are permitted at one time. Camping is in 6-person Adirondack shelters.

The island was once the headquarters of native American chiefs. Settlement by whites began in colonial times. Houses, ruins, wells, and other structures remain from the years of farming, fishing, lumbering, shipbuilding, and ice cutting. State purchase began in the 1940s. Until 1952 the island was a game research experiment station. Since then management emphasis has been on providing forage crops for the thousands of Canada geese that arrive each spring.

The island (not to be confused with Swan's Island near Acadia National Park) is 4 mi. long, ¼–¾ mi. wide. The ferry landing is at the N end. The WMA includes Little Swan Island and over 500 acres of tidal flats.

Plants: The island has 840 acres of upland forest, 230 acres of improved pasture, with surrounding wetlands and fertile mud flats. Most of the forest is on the W side, the higher and steeper ground. Tree species include white oak, butternut, mulberry, black birch. On the uplands are deep freshwater marshes and areas of open water, with stands of wild rice, cattail, softstem bulrush, and other aquatic plants. Coastal marshes support pickerelweed, spatterdock, wild rice, duck potato, and bulrush. Goose pastures are on the E side.

The island flora has been greatly affected by logging, land clearing, and introduction of new species, and by the overpopulation of deer.

Hunting was first prohibited in the 1890s, when deer populations were low, and the prohibition continued here after mainland hunting resumed. Trapping and relocating deer didn't reduce the overpopulation. A proposal to reduce the herd by hunting was bitterly opposed and abandoned. So damage to the habitat continues, and some deer die during severe winters. The island deer population ranges from 25 to 200.

Birds: As many as 5,000 Canada geese may be present in the spring migration, as well as a variety of ducks. A bald eagle nest on the island has been used for 2 decades. ME's eagle population declined sharply, largely because of pesticides in fish, but recovery is steadily occurring. Wood ducks reproduce in nest boxes at artificial ponds. Waterfowl include black duck, common goldeneye, bufflehead, mallard, blue-winged and green-winged teal, hooded merganser. Also common are many shorebirds, ruffed grouse, songbirds.

Mammals: Include red and gray squirrels, woodchuck, beaver, red fox, raccoon, deer.

Interpretation

The *self-guiding hiking tour* follows the gravel road that runs the length of the island. No private vehicles use the road. The *18-page tour guide* describes the island's history and natural features.

Activities

Camping: From the ferry landing, campers and their gear are carried by Dept. vehicle to the campground. 10 open shelters accommodate 6 persons each. Tent camping is not permitted. Water and firewood are provided. Stays are limited to 2 nights. Visitors must carry out all trash. Reservations are made by written application with fee, submitted at least 7 days before the requested date.

Hiking: Visitors may hike anywhere on the N end of the island. The S end is restricted; visitors must be accompanied by the custodian or obtain permission.

Hunting: On tidal flats below the high-water mark, except in Maxwell Cove.

Boating: Visitors may bring boats by prior arrangement. Because of tides up to 10 ft., small boats aren't recommended.

Swimming and fishing have been inadvisable because of river pollution. Efforts are being made to improve water quality. Inquire.

Pets are prohibited.
No intoxicating beverages permitted.

Publications

Information folder with application form.

Tour guide.

Headquarters

ME Dept. of Inland Fisheries and Wildlife, 41 State House Station, Augusta, ME 04333-0041; (207) 287-8000.

....

Sugar Island Management Unit

Maine Bureau of Parks and Public Lands   North
4,208 acres.

In Moosehead Lake. Nearest boat ramp is at Lily Bay State Park (see entry).

The island is 4½ mi. long, up to 2 mi. wide. It is hilly, rising to about 400 ft. above the lake surface, and heavily forested. The shoreline is rocky, and many rocks lurk below the water; we lost a shear pin on one of them.

A number of private summer residences are along the shore, some of them quite impressive, with private docks. The rest of the land is state owned. There is no public dock, but we had no difficulty getting ashore. Moosehead Lake can be stormy, and overnight campers should be careful about their moorings.

Campers at Lily Bay State Park often come here for picnics. There seem to be no trails, but much of the forest is parklike.

Camping: 3 primitive sites.

Headquarters

ME Bureau of Parks and Lands, 22 State House Station, Augusta, ME 04333-0022; (207) 287-3821.

Sunkhaze Meadows National Wildlife Refuge

U.S. Fish and Wildlife Service   Coastal
9,337 acres.

From Bangor, I-95 N to Exit 51 at Orono. US 2/Hwy 178 to Milford.
Refuge is located on the Sunkhaze Stream in the town of Milford.

Open weekdays 7:30 A.M.–4 P.M.

The refuge surrounds nearly 5 mi. of Sunkhaze Stream and another 12
mi. of tributary streams. The word Sunkhaze is derived from the
Abnaki, meaning "concealing outlet," which refers to the stream's
well-disguised confluence with the Penobscot River.

Major habitats include forest uplands, alder/willow riparian zones,
and cedar swamps, including the second largest peat bog in ME. The
area was designated a national wildlife refuge in the 1980s, when the
peat mining industry began planning to extract peat for commercial
purposes.

The vast expanse of wetlands in the bog and riparian zones attracts
a host of waterfowl and other waterfowl. Prime birdwatching time
here is late spring during the migrations. Beavers are permanent
mammal residents on the refuge and their lodges and dams are frequently encountered during a trip down any of the waterways. Beaver
empoundments help attract the birds and other wildlife. "Their
actions are all that is necessary for habitat management in the bog,"
says the refuge leaflet.

While development of limited visitor facilities is planned for the
future, Sunkhaze Meadows is now a "wild" place. For those contented
to experience the refuge on its own terms, a canoe trip down Sunkhaze Stream or a walk along an old logging trail will be memorable.
Hunting and fishing are allowed in accordance with state regulations
and with specific refuge regulations. (Contact the refuge manager.)
There are cross-country ski opportunities here in the winter, again,
without amenities.

Three satellite areas are administered by the staff of this refuge: the
Carlton Pond Waterfowl Production Area in Troy and the Benton and
Unity Units, located in those respective towns. The Carlton Pond unit
provides valuable nesting habitat for a variety of waterfowl and the
black tern, a species currently on ME's watch list. The sedge wren, an

endangered species in ME, prompted the establishment of the Benton unit. Woodcock are common residents of the Unity unit.

Birds: No checklist available. Over 200 species documented, including woodcock, ruffed grouse, black tern, black and wood ducks, hooded merganser, mallard, blue-winged teal, great blue heron, American bittern, double-crested cormorant, Virginia and sora rails, shorebirds. A great variety of warbler species and other songbirds are also found in this area. Raptors include northern harrier, broad-winged hawk, red-tailed hawk, kestrels. Owls, including great horned and barred, are common at various times of the year.

Mammals: Include beaver, muskrat, porcupine, snow-shoe hare, red squirrel, several species of mice and vole, moose, black bear, white-tailed deer, coyote, river otter, fisher.

Publication
Leaflet with map.

Headquarters
Sunkhaze Meadows National Wildlife Refuge, 1033 S. Main St., Old Town, ME 04468-2023; (207) 827-6138.

Telos Lake Management Unit/Chamberlain Lake Management Unit

Maine Bureau of Parks and Lands   North
22,806 acres.

From Millinocket, NW on Golden Rd. to Ripogenus Dam, then N on Telos Rd.

At the very edge of the North Maine Woods (see entry), Telos Lake is the gateway to the Allagash Wilderness Waterway (see entry). The management unit includes Chamberlain Bridge, a major put-in for the Waterway trip, and the Arm of Chamberlain.

Telos Lake itself is about 5 mi. long, linked to Chamberlain Lake by mile-long Round Pond. On Telos are put-ins for both the Allagash Waterway and for a lesser-known canoe trip eastward through Webster Lake and Webster Brook into Baxter State Park (see entry).

Normal pool elevation of Telos Lake is 945 ft. The surrounding land is forested, hilly to mountainous, from gradually sloping to steep at the shoreline. Highest nearby point is 1,329-ft. Telos Mountain.

The Chamberlain Lake unit is NW of Telos Lake. It includes tracts in Chamberlain, Eagle, and Allagash Lakes. Access is by Telos Rd. or by water.

Activities

Camping: Primitive campsites at Telos Landing can be reached by gravel road. Numerous other sites are accessible by boat. Visitors may camp anywhere, without facilities and with no open fires.

Fishing: Chiefly lake and brook trout. The bureau says a campsite on Coffelos Pond is popular with anglers.

Boating: Launching at Chamberlain Bridge.

Canoeing: Many canoeists are heading for the Allagash. But those who want a circuit rather than a one-way trip can spend days exploring this area, of which the management units are only a part.

Headquarters

ME Bureau of Parks and Lands, 22 State House Station, Augusta, ME 04333-0022; (207) 287-3821.

The Great Heath

Maine Bureau of Public Lands   Coastal
6,067 acres.

From US 1 at Harrington, about 5 mi. N. Access off unmarked gravel roads N of Cherry Field.

Maine has an estimated 5,000 bogs covering more than 700,000 acres. The Great Heath is the largest, one of the largest anywhere. Until recent years, bogs were considered to be wastelands, good for duck hunting or filling. The oil crisis changed that. One acre of bog may contain 1,600 tons of peat, the energy equivalent of 3,800 barrels of oil.

The prospect of extensive peat mining called attention to the natural values of bog ecosytems. The Land and Water Resources Council was directed to identify peatlands that should be preserved because of their rare flora and fauna. The Great Heath has been so identified, to be devoted exclusively to primitive recreation, scientific study, and education.

The bog is crossed by the Pleasant River, which provides canoe access. Canoeists enjoy some flat water paddling along the meanders of the channel. The river has a natural population of Atlantic salmon. Pineo Ridge, a noteworthy glacial feature, abuts the SW boundary.

No interpretive program has been developed.

Headquarters
ME Bureau of Parks and Lands, 22 State House Station, Augusta, ME 04333-0022; (207) 287-3821.

Vaughan Woods Memorial State Park
Maine Bureau of Parks and Lands   Coastal
250 acres.

From South Berwick S ½ mi. on Hwy 236. Turn right on to Vine St. for 1 mi. to intersection with Old Fields Rd. Turn right, watch for entrance to Park.

On Brattle St. one passes "the oldest water power site in America," where an old mill still stands. Vaughan Woods is on the shore of the Piscataqua River, here the boundary between ME and NH. The land was given to the state in 1949 with the proviso that it remain wild, "a sanctuary for the wild beasts and birds."

The handsome old-growth forest of pine and hemlock has moderately steep slopes. Several trails lead down to the river, including a 2-mi. loop trail. The riverside trail is said to be an authentic native American route. When we visited, part of the trail was being improved, using a design to check erosion as well as provide better footing. A spacious parking lot and nearby tables suggest this is a popular picnic site for local residents. About 3 mi. of trails are used by cross-country skiers.

Publication
Leaflet.

Headquarters
ME Bureau of Parks and Lands, 22 State House Station, Augusta, ME
04333-0022; (207) 384-5160; (207) 624-6080 off-season.

....

Vernon S. Walker Wildlife Management Area

Maine Department of Inland Fisheries and Wildlife   Coastal
4,937 acres.

Southern ME. From Sanford, N on Hwy 11 to North Shapleigh, then
right on Mann Rd. Approximate boundaries are Hwy 11 on the W and
N, Mann Rd. on the S.

This is one of the largest WMAs and one we had inadequate time to
explore. Access is somewhat limited. The management plan mentions
2 trails entering from Mann Rd. The map shows others entering from
the N. In our brief visit, we identified only one of these. The management plan mentions "limited vehicle access"; we saw no entering
road. According to Inland Fisheries and Wildlife, the site has 3 management area and 3 information signs.

It's worth exploring because of its size and diversity, a quiet area in
the state's S portion, most of which is being developed rapidly. Both
the Little Ossipee River and Branch Brook are canoeable. There's a
put-in for the Little Ossipee on Hwy 11. The DeLorme *Atlas* mentions
an 11½-mi. canoe trip from here to Ossipee Mills (E of Newfield) with
unrunnable rapids in Newfield.

The site is hilly. Much of the forest burned in 1947, so the woodland is chiefly young second growth. Within the site are 3 ponds and
part of a fourth.

Data on flora and fauna are scanty but promising. There's enough
wetland to attract some waterfowl. Mammals include snowshoe hare,
beaver, otter, mink, raccoon, deer, and occasional moose and bear.
Fishing is chiefly for brook and brown trout.

Headquarters
ME Dept. of Inland Fisheries and Wildlife, 41 State House Station,
Augusta, ME 04333-0041; (207) 287-8000.

Wells National Estuarine Research Reserve

Mixed ownership and administration, local, state, federal.   Coastal
1,600 acres.

I-95, Exit 2 at Wells. Turn left, proceed to traffic light, turn left onto US 1
for 1.5 mi. Turn right at second blinking light onto Laudholm Farm Rd.,
turn left at fork and right into reserve entrance.

Open 8 A.M.–5 P.M.

Estuaries are places where rivers meet the sea. They have distinctive
character, functions, and difficulties in the natural world. The reserve
at Wells was established about 10 years ago as part of the National
Estuarine Research System. The Research System protects estuarine
waters, marshes, shorelands, and adjacent uplands, at the same time
it fulfills research and educational objectives.

Within the reserve are Laudholm Farm, a historic saltwater farm
with original buildings, Rachel Carson National Wildlife Refuge (see
entry) lands, and land belonging to the state of Maine and town of
Wells. This is a real cooperative venture, supervised by ME's Reserve
Management Authority and supported by the nonprofit Laudholm
Trust (a local grassroots organization), both maintaining close ties
with the U.S. Fish and Wildlife Service. Over 250 volunteers offer time
to the program.

At Wells, the Little, Merriland, and Webhannet Rivers meet the
ocean tides, creating a rich habitat for wildlife. 7 mi. of nature trails
allow visitors to observe salt marshes, dunes and barrier beaches, wetlands, forests, and fields. The farm buildings house a visitor center,
exhibit areas, classroom, laboratories, and a residence for researchers.

The 4-mi. coastal sanctuary supports a wide variety of resident and
transient wildlife: harbor seal, river otter, mink, rabbits and hares,
muskrat, white-tailed deer, red fox, raccoon, as well as a variety of
ducks, geese, herons, and egrets. Tom cod, pollock, alewive, flounder,
striped bass, bluefish, sea-run brown trout, and Atlantic salmon swim
in the unpolluted streams and estuary waters. Threatened and endangered species in the reserve include bald eagle, least tern, peregrine
falcon, piping plover, slender blue flag iris, arethusa orchids.

Because the tick that causes Lyme disease is present at the reserve,
as in other parts of southern ME, staff recommend long pants with

socks pulled over, long sleeves, and insect repellent. *Most important, stay on trails.*

Interpretation

The *visitor center* is open daily May–Oct., then weekdays only. Brochures, checklists, and trail maps are available.

Guided tours are offered throughout summer and fall.

Educational programs of many kinds continue all year.

Publications

Leaflet with map.

Tour of the Reserves, A (summarizes the National Estuarine Reserve program and lists the national reserves).

Calendar of events.

Guide to educational programs.

Watermark (newspaper).

Headquarters

Wells National Estuarine Research Reserve, RR 2, P.O. Box 806, Wells, ME 04090; (207) 646-1555.

Weskeag Marsh Wildlife Management Area

See R. Waldo Tyler Wildlife Management Area.

White Mountain National Forest

U.S. Forest Service   West
49,346

On the NH border S and W of Bethel.

See entry in NH, where most of the Forest is located. The ME portion extends S along the border from the Androscoggin River. Hwy 113 crosses the W side through Evans Notch. The principal trailheads are on this route.

The area is mountainous and forested. High point is Speckled Mountain, 2,907 ft. Numerous streams and ponds. S of Bethel is a scenic drive along Patte Brook, with the Crocker Pond campground nearby.

Caribou/Speckled Mountain Wilderness: 12,000 acres was designated in 1990. The area surrounds 2,828-ft. Caribou Mountain and Speckled Mountain. Terrain ranges from valley bottoms to mountain peaks, gentle slopes to rocky cliffs. Many streams flow from the area to the watersheds of the Androscoggin and Saco rivers, with many waterfalls. Vegetation is chiefly northern hardwoods with white pine at mid and lower elevations, spruce/fir on higher slopes, mountain blueberry, cranberry, other shrubs, and wildflowers on exposed mountain tops. "More than 50 mi. of some of the loveliest trails in the East," according to Forest Service supervisor.

Visitor use is light, mostly June–Sept.

Activities

Camping: 2 campgrounds, at Hastings and Crocker Pond, 31 sites. Informal camping in almost any suitable place.

Hiking: Several attractive day hikes go E from Hwy 113. At least 5 trails ascend Speckled Mountain, including the Spruce Hill Trail from Evans Notch. Trailheads are on Hwy 113 and US 2. Ask the visitor center for their informational pages on hiking opportunities in the area.

Ski touring, snowmobiling, snowshoeing: Vary with snowfall.

Publication:

Hiking and backpacking guide.

The Forest Service suggests that visitors consider purchasing: Appalachian Mountain Club. *White Mountain Guide,* 25th ed. Boston: Author, 1992.

Headquarters

White Mountains National Forest, Evans Notch Visitor Center, 18 Mayville Rd., Bethel, ME 04217-4400; (207) 824-2134.

VERMONT

On a map, Vermont and New Hampshire look much alike: about the same size, the Connecticut River a shared boundary, each with a National Forest (the only two in New England), each mountainous, each with many lakes and ponds. But VT has little more than half NH's population, and the difference is widening. In NH more than half of the population lives in urban areas; in VT about one-third. Southern NH has been annexed by the Boston metropolis. VT is a safe distance away. And while both states are roughly triangular, NH's base is in the S; most of VT's area is in the less developed N. Unlike NH, VT has an income tax, small but helpful to state functions.

The Green Mountains divide the state, N–S. At 4,393 ft., Mount Mansfield is the highest peak, but many others in the range exceed 3,000 ft. In the southwest, the Green Mountains merge with the N end of the Taconic Range, while in the NW the mountains drop down on the W to the Champlain Valley. The E and W boundaries are mostly water, Lake Champlain on the W, the Connecticut River on the E. Elevations below 500 ft. are found chiefly on the lowlands bordering Champlain and in the central and southern Connecticut River Valley.

Many rivers flow down the slopes of the Green Mountains. In addition to several hundred miles of rivers, VT has more than 400 lakes and ponds. Lake Champlain, 100 mi. long, is by far the largest. Largest of those wholly within the state is 2,360-acre Lake Bomoseen.

Like other New England forests, those of Vermont were heavily logged in the 19th century. A hundred years ago 80% of the forest had been cleared. As farming and grazing declined, forests regenerated, and today 80% of the land is again forested. Pristine conditions, of course, are not returning except in a few wilderness areas. Most forest areas are managed for timber production.

Like the climate of other New England areas, VT's is highly variable: daily, seasonally, annually, and from place to place. Summer temperatures are generally comfortable. Jan. averages are below freezing statewide, with the lowest readings in the NE. Precipitation is well distributed seasonally and by region, annual averages ranging from 38–45 in. Snowfall varies from 55 in. in valleys to over 120 in. on high elevations.

By far the largest area available for recreation is the Green Mountain National Forest, 5% of the state's land, occupying much of the central and southern portions of the mountain range. Although less than half of the area within the authorized boundaries is government-owned, this is mostly the upper slopes, the rugged terrain of greatest interest to outdoorspeople. VT has no National Park, only one National Wildlife Refuge.

State Lands

When we asked for definitions of State Park and State Forest, the reply was, "Don't worry about it." In fact, the Public Recreation Areas chart on the official state map lists 51 areas as "State Forest or Park," then gives location, facilities, and phone numbers for each, without further identification of the sites. Don't worry about which is which!

By our calculations, VT State Parks total about 26,000 acres, State Forests about 150,000 acres. We have entries for units that have significant natural areas. They're well distributed around the state.

VT has more than 60 Wildlife Management Areas with a total nearing 100,000 acres. Five of the WMAs have more than 5,000 acres each.

Maps and Pathfinding

The official state map and *Vermont Travelers Guidebook* are available from

VT Dept. of Travel and Tourism
134 State St.
Montpelier, VT 05602
(802) 828-3236 or (800) VERMONT

The *Guidebook* includes many useful sources of information about VT, including publications. In the fall, the *Vermont Winter Guide* is available from the same agency.

The following atlas is of great value:

Vermont Atlas and Gazetteer, The. Freeport, ME: DeLorme Mapping Company, 1995.

In addition to its maps, the *Atlas* has information on campgrounds, canoe trips, fishing, hiking, parks and recreation areas, and much more.

However, the best source of all general map information, as well as specific area topos, is:

The Green Mountain Club
RR 1, Box 650, Rt. 100
Waterbury Center, VT 05677
(802) 244-7037

The club will send a free publications list on request, and people there are very pleasant and helpful.

The American Automobile Association also provides excellent maps free of charge to members.

Pathfinding in VT is uniquely difficult because of an admirable law that bans billboards, making the landscape wonderfully uncluttered. Current rules say an establishment may have two signs, each of a small, standard size, on the approaching state roads. In an even-handed way, the rule has been applied to the state's own properties, including Parks and Forests. Thus a large State Forest with miles of highway frontage and multiple entrances can post only the two small signs allowed a restaurant or antique shop!

The Dept. of Forests, Parks & Recreation uses the allowed signs to mark campgrounds and other recreation sites, where most visitors go. Elsewhere it may be difficult to distinguish state from private land or to find trailheads without trail maps.

The DeLorme *Atlas* is of considerable help in finding Parks and Forests.

The Fish and Wildlife Dept. acknowledges that it's difficult for a visitor to find many WMAs. The Dept. has no maps to hand out. Its *Vermont Guide to Hunting* shows site outlines but on a small scale. Local hunters and fishers know where to go. We usually found some-one to ask.

We commented that even off state highways, where the signing rule doesn't apply, we rarely saw WMA signs. Many have been stolen, we were told. We often looked in vain for boundary markings or posted rules.

At headquarters, we were given information about some WMAs and told management plans were being developed for others. We were warned that even a large WMA may not be a good entry for us:

The state may not own timber rights and thus may have no control over logging. We visited a number of WMAs and enjoyed good hiking and birding, but we may have missed a few good ones.

Flora and Fauna

Our bibliographic search turned up few references describing VT's flora and fauna, most technical or out of print. Several regional references are useful:

AMC Field Guide to Mountain Flowers of New England. Boston: Appalachian Mountain Club, 1982.

DeGraaf, Richard M., and Deborah D. Rudis. *New England Wildlife: Habitat, Natural History, and Distribution.* General Technical Report NE-108. Broomwall, PA: U.S. Department of Agriculture, Forest Service, Northeastern Forest Experiment Station, 1986. (Currently out of print. In 1996 a 5th printing seemed a possibility.)

If not available elsewhere, this may be ordered from:

The Green Mountain Club
RR 1, Box 650, Rt. 100
Waterbury Center, VT 05677
(802) 244-7037

There is also a Peterson wildflower guide for the New England area in general:

Peterson, Roger T., and Margaret McKenny, *A Field Guide to Wildflowers of Northeastern and North-Central North America.* Boston: Houghton Mifflin, 1975.

And this bird guide is available:

Birds of Vermont. Available for $5 plus shipping and handling from:

Green Mountain Audubon Society
255 Sherman Hollow Rd.
Huntington, VT 05462
(802) 434-3068

Or there is the Peterson guide, available generally:

> Peterson, Roger T. *A Field Guide to Eastern Birds,* 4th ed. Boston: Houghton Mifflin, 1980.

The Fish and Wildlife Dept. has had a number of useful free information bulletins, including:

> *Wild Mammals of Vermont.*
>
> *Amphibians of Vermont.*

See State Agencies (below) for address.

Hiking Trails

The 265-mi. Long Trail (see entry), extending N to S along the Green Mountains, is the centerpiece of VT's trail system. Before it turns eastward, the Appalachian Trail coincides for more than 100 mi. with the southern portion of the Long Trail.

The state has over 700 mi. of trails, more than two-thirds on federal and state land, the rest on private land. VT's hiking trails, whether on public or private land, are largely maintained by private volunteer groups. The Green Mountain Club, established in 1910, was acclaimed by the state legislature as "founder, sponsor, defender, and protector of the Long Trail system," which now includes a network of subsidiary trails. The club has subsequently become a model for many recreation groups across the country.

There are interesting day hikes elsewhere in VT, especially in State Forests and State Parks. Hiking in Wildlife Management Areas is largely on either currently used or overgrown back roads and on informal trails. Popular multiuse recreation paths may now be found along the shores of Lake Champlain in Burlington and next to Mountain Rd. in Stowe. There are others in Colchester, Essex, Shelburne, South Burlington, and Barre. Additional recreation paths are either under construction or in the planning stage throughout the state.

Backpacking is possible both on the Long Trail and the Appalachian. The Green Mountain Club maintains many shelters, and trailside camping is permissible in the National Forest and in all or portions of most State Forests. The rules are in a leaflet, *Guide to Primitive Camping on State Lands,* available from the Dept. of Forests, Parks & Recreation. The dept.'s *Hiking and Walking in Vermont* lists sources of trail guides and businesses offering conducted hiking tours and inn-to-inn hiking. Also available from the dept. is *Day Hiker's Vermont Sampler.*

Hikers are asked to stay off trails in the "mud season," usually from snow melt in April to Memorial Day.

These are basic references:

Appalachian Trail Committee. *Appalachian Trail Guide to New Hampshire/Vermont.* Harpers Ferry, WV: Appalachian Trail Conference, 1995.

Green Mountain Club. *Day Hiker's Guide to Vermont,* 3rd ed. Waterbury Center, VT: Author, 1995.

—. *Fifty Hikes in Vermont,* 4th ed. Woodstock, VT: Countryman Press, 1994.

—. *Long Trail Guide,* 24th ed. Waterbury Center, VT: Author, 1996.

Camping

For information on camping in the Green Mountain National Forest, see entry.

The Dept. of Forests, Parks & Recreation operates 35 developed campgrounds with more than 2,200 sites in State Parks and Forests. Most open mid-May. Some close after Labor Day, others after the Columbus Day weekend. Most campgrounds have several lean-tos.

Campsites can be reserved by mail with fee, starting the first Tuesday in Jan. Ask for the current *Vermont Campground Guide* and reservation form.

Pets are allowed, on leash, in the campgrounds of most State Parks, but not in day use areas. They are permitted-on leash-on trails.

Canoeing, Boating

Canoeists have a wide range of choices in VT, from challenging white water to canoe-camping trips of several days to quiet exploration of wildlife areas. Two basic references are

Appalachian Mountain Club. *AMC River Guide: New Hampshire, Vermont,* 2nd ed. Boston: Author, 1989.

Schweiker, Roioli. *Canoe Camping Vermont and New Hampshire Rivers,* 2nd ed. Woodstock, VT: Countryman Press, 1994.

Entries describe other opportunities.

The primary boating water is Lake Champlain (see entry). The leaflets *Guide to Fishing* and *Lake Champlain Fishing Guide* (see below) lists many lakes and rivers and boating access, as well as fishing information. Public boat launch sites are marked on the official highway map.

Fishing, Hunting

A *Vermont Guide to Fishing* and a *Vermont Guide to Hunting* (leaflets) are both available from the Fish and Wildlife Dept. The latter has information on hunting areas, rules, and species. The *Lake Champlain Fishing Guide* includes fishing charts and much useful information about fishing in VT (available free from the Dept.).

Many people hunt for the table in VT. Thus, hunting, with proper license and in season, is allowed on just about all of the sites listed and in all the Wildlife Management areas. If this is of concern to you, inquire at the site.

State Agencies

VT Dept. of Forests, Parks & Recreation
103 S. Main St.
Waterbury, VT 05671-0601
(802) 241-3650

VT Fish and Wildlife Dept.
103 S. Main St.
Waterbury, VT 05671-0501
(802) 241-3700

The Green Mountain Club

The Green Mountain Club has, since 1910, been the principal force in preservation of VT forests and in the construction and maintenance of a statewide network of hiking trails (see entry, Long Trail). Its publications include:

Day Hiker's Guide to Vermont, 3rd ed. 1990.

Fifty Hikes in Vermont, 4th ed., 1994.

Long Trail Guide, 24th ed.

Trail Maps: *Camel's Hump* Mt. Mansfield, Tundra Trail (Mt. Mansfield).

Staff will gladly answer mail or telephone inquiries about trails, trail conditions, and shelters.

The Green Mountain Club
RR 1, Box 650, Rt. 100
Waterbury Center, VT 05677
(802) 244-7037

Other Private Agencies

For information on Audubon properties in VT, contact:

Green Mountain Audubon Society
255 Sherman Hollow Rd.
Huntington, VT 05462
(802) 434-3068

The Vermont Chapter of The Nature Conservancy now manages 33 preserves in the state. They will send their free *Vermont Project Directory* on request.

Vermont Chapter, The Nature Conservancy
27 State St.
Montpelier, VT 05602
(802) 229-4425

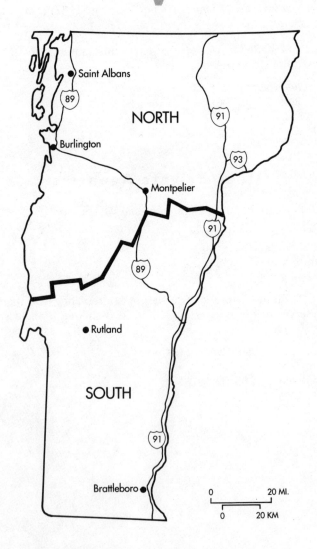

Natural Areas in Vermont

An Alphabetical Listing

Ascutney State Park
South

Atherton Meadow Wildlife Management Area
South

Bill Sladyk Wildlife Management Area
North

Bomoseen State Park/Half Moon State Park
South

Branbury State Park
South

Burton Island State Park
North

Button Bay State Park
North

C. C. Putnam State Forest
North

Camel's Hump Forest Reserve
North

Champlain, Lake
North

Connecticut River
North/South

Coolidge State Forest
South

Cornwall Swamp Wildlife Management Area
South

Dead Creek Waterfowl Refuge
South

Elmore State Park
North

Emerald Lake State Park
South

Gifford Woods State Park
South

Green Mountain National Forest
South

Groton State Forest
North

Jay Peak Area
North

Lewis Creek Wildlife Management Area
North

Little Otter Creek Wildlife Management Area
North

Little River State Park
North

Long Trail
North/South

Lower Otter Creek Wildlife Management Area
North

Maidstone State Park
North

Missisquoi National Wildlife Refuge
North

Mount Mansfield State Forest
North

Mud Creek Wildlife Management Area
North

Pine Mountain Wildlife Management Area
North

Plymsbury Wildlife Management Area
South

Quechee Gorge State Park
South

South Bay Wildlife Management Area
North

Townshend State Park
South

Victory Basin Wildlife Management Area
North

Wenlock Wildlife Management Area
North

Willoughby State Forest
North

Woodford State Park
South

Natural Areas in Vermont

by Zone

NORTH ZONE

Bill Sladyk Wildlife Management Area

Burton Island State Park

Button Bay State Park

C. C. Putnam State Forest

Camel's Hump Forest Reserve

Champlain, Lake

Connecticut River

Elmore State Park

Groton State Forest

Jay Peak Area

Lewis Creek Wildlife Management Area

Little Otter Creek Wildlife Management Area

Little River State Park

Long Trail

Lower Otter Creek Wildlife Management Area

Maidstone State Park

Missisquoi National Wildlife Refuge

Mount Mansfield State Forest

Mud Creek Wildlife Management Area

Pine Mountain Wildlife Management Area

South Bay Wildlife Management Area

Victory Basin Wildlife Management Area

Wenlock Wildlife Management Area

Willoughby State Forest

SOUTH ZONE

Ascutney State Park

Atherton Meadow Wildlife Management Area

Bomoseen State Park/Half Moon State Park

Branbury State Park

Connecticut River

Coolidge State Forest

Cornwall Swamp Wildlife Management Area

Dead Creek Waterfowl Refuge

Emerald Lake State Park

Gifford Woods State Park

Green Mountain National Forest

Long Trail

Plymsbury Wildlife Management Area

Quechee Gorge State Park

Townshend State Park

Woodford State Park

Ascutney State Park

Vermont Department of Forests, Parks & Recreation   South
984 acres.

From I-91, Exit 8, N 2 mi. on US 5, then 1 mi. NW on Hwy 44A.

This is said to be the first U.S. mountain with a developed hiking trail and thus is the ancestor of the Long Trail and Appalachian Trail. Mount Ascutney is not part of a chain, and is visible for miles around. Its peak is 3,144 ft., almost half a mile above its base. Its slopes are generally moderate, steep in places. At one point water trickles over a steep ledge, forming an impressive ice sheet in winter.

The mountain forest is not pristine. It was severely burned in a summer-long forest fire in 1883, then much of it was flattened by a great hurricane in 1938. Its crest is decorated with television, radio, and microwave towers. A motor road goes almost to the top, a trail the rest of the way. It's a splendid view from there. The area has good hiking trails.

Features

Gerry's Falls, seen from a spur off the Windsor Trail.

Crystal Cascade, on the Weathersfield Trail, is where Ascutney Brook plunges 84 ft.

West Peak, near the end of the motor road, is a launch site for hang gliders.

Activities

Camping: 49 sites, including 10 lean-tos, May 17–Oct. 8. Reservations available.

Hiking, backpacking: Trailside camping is permitted. Trail guide available at entrance. Three trails go to the summit. Two can be combined in a 7-mi. circle hike. Snow may remain at high elevations until the end of May.

Hunting: Deer, wild turkey, grouse.

Ski touring, snowmobiling: On scenic road when unplowed.

Publications

Site map.

Guide to the Trails of Ascutney Mountain, available at entrance. $2.

Headquarters

Ascutney State Park, HCR 71, Box 186, Windsor, VT 05089; (802) 674-2060. Reservations and off-season, (802) 886-2434.

....

Atherton Meadow Wildlife Management Area

Fish and Wildlife Department   South
1,042 acres.

Near the MA border, W of Whitingham on Hwy 100, S of the Harriman Reservoir. ("Whitingham Reservoir" on older maps.) Look for sign and parking area about 6½ mi. W of Jacksonville.

The WMA has no frontage on the reservoir, but there is public access at the N end and the fishing is good. The reservoir covers 2,157 acres and is about 8 mi. long.

The WMA's terrain is moderately steep to steep, elevations from 1,500 to 2,078 ft. The site is largely forested with a mix of northern hardwoods and softwoods. Also fields and a large beaver meadow.

One source reports about 4 mi. of trails. Mostly these are routes used by hunters, and there are less or more depending on what you consider a trail. You can get around.

Birds: Include eastern bluebird, black-capped chickadee, brown creeper, goldfinch, purple finch, ruffed grouse, flycatchers, kinglets, vireos, cedar waxwing, American woodcock, woodpeckers, various wood warblers.

Mammals: Include deer, snowshoe hare, red and gray squirrels, chipmunk, red and gray foxes, coyote, bobcat, black bear, raccoon, otter, mink, weasel, fisher, beaver.

Headquarters

VT Fish and Wildlife Dept., Springfield District, RFD Box 33, North Springfield, VT 05150-9726; (802) 886-2215.

Bill Sladyk Wildlife Management Area

(formerly Hurricane Brook Wildlife Management Area)   North
Vermont Fish and Wildlife Department
9,510 acres.

From Island Pond, N 8½ mi. on Hwy 114. Just S of Norton Pond, turn W
on access road and continue to entrance sign.

The turn is onto an unmarked well-maintained gravel road. On the
way in, we passed a marsh with some open water, one of a series of
marshes along the Pherrins River, which parallels the road from Island
Pond. The road penetrates the WMA much farther than the map indicates. We parked and hiked on old logging roads. A broad swath was
cleared on both sides of the road, creating a fine habitat for wildflowers, which were bright and abundant. Prominent were goldenrod,
black-eyed Susan, aster, pussytoes, lobelia, milkweed. The terrain is
rolling, covered with young forest: northern hardwoods along the
ridges, spruce/fir along stream bottoms and in swampy areas. Elevations range from about 1,450 ft. to just over 1,900 ft.

From the entrance, it's about 5½ mi. to the N boundary, which is
the Canadian border. The northern two-thirds of the WMA is roadless. Holland Pond, Beaver Pond, Round Pond, and Halfway Pond are
within the site and can be reached by trail.

On a fine day in Aug., we had the place to ourselves.

Activities

Camping: Permitted in designated areas. No facilities.

Hiking: Miles of trails and woods roads.

Hunting: Deer, bear, grouse, woodcock, snowshoe hare.

Fishing: Ponds, some stream. Brook, brown, and rainbow trout; chain
pickerel.

Ski touring, snowmobiling: Users are warned to stay on established trails
and avoid areas used by wintering deer—places "well-laced with deer
tracks."

Headquarters

VT Fish and Wildlife Dept., St. Johnsbury District, 184 Portland St., St.
Johnsbury, VT 05819; (802) 748-8787.

Bomoseen State Park/Half Moon State Park

Vermont Department of Forests, Parks & Recreation   South
2,379 acres/50 acres.

Take Exit 4 from US 4. Then W on Hwy 4A to Hydeville and N 4 mi. on West Shore Rd. From Hubbardton (on Hwy 30 between towns of Sudbury and Bomoseen), 2 mi. N on Hwy 30, 2 mi. W on Town Rd., then 1½ mi. S on Town Rd.

Lake Bomoseen, about 7 mi. long, covers 2,360 acres. Roads encircle much of the lakeshore, with much lakeside development. The Bomoseen State Park is on an arm of the lake, between it and 191-acre Glen Lake. A separate block to the N, Half Moon State Park surrounds 23-acre Half Moon Pond, with campground and trails.

The Parks are popular, most visitors coming for water-based recreation and camping, although there are hiking trails. Bomoseen has an interesting nature trail. A park naturalist there offers programs from mid-June to Labor Day.

Plants: The terrain is level to rolling, land that was once cleared for pasture and crops. Now it's a mixture of forest, reverting fields, and marsh. The forest is mostly hardwoods: beech, sugar maple, birches; red oak and hickory in the drier sites. Also hemlock, white pine. Many wildflowers appear in spring and summer, notably hepatica, bloodroot, wild rose, violets, jack-in-the-pulpit, goldenrod, asters. Woodland plants include goldthread, partridgeberry, wintergreen, royal fern, mosses. Yellow water lilies in pond shallows. Bulrush and cattail in marshes.

Birds: No checklist. Species include black duck, mallard, blue-winged teal, yellow-bellied sapsucker, wild turkey, eastern kingbird, red-winged blackbird, wood and hermit thrushes, veery, junco, towhee.

Activities

Camping: 66 sites at Bomoseen, 69 at Half Moon; each includes 10 lean-tos. May 17–Sept. 3. Reservations are available.

Hiking: About 10 mi. of trails, including nature trails.

Fishing: Brook and brown trout, yellow perch, northern pike, chain pickerel, largemouth and smallmouth bass, bullhead.

Boating, canoeing: Rentals available at both sites.

Headquarters

Bomoseen State Park, RFD 1, Box 2620, Fair Haven, VT 05743; (802) 265-4242. Reservations and off-season (802) 483-2001. Half Moon State Park, RFD 1, Box 2730, Fair Haven, VT 05743; (802) 273-2848; (802) 483-2001 off-season.

....

Branbury State Park

Vermont Department of Forests, Parks & Recreation   North
96 acres.

From Brandon, E 3 mi. on Hwy 73, then 6 mi. N on Hwy 53.

This small Park on 985-acre Lake Dunmore is a convenient base for hiking in the Green Mountain National Forest (see entry). It's not far from the Long Trail (see entry) and several high peaks. It has a park naturalist in summer and a nature trail. There is also a scenic, rather steep hiking trail to a viewpoint in the National Forest.

Activities

Camping: 44 sites, including 5 lean-tos. May 17–Oct. 8.

Fishing: Rainbow trout, landlocked salmon, lake trout, smelt, yellow perch, northern pike, largemouth and smallmouth bass, bullhead. Boat rental.

Swimming: In Lake Dunmore.

Headquarters

Branbury State Park, RFD 2, Box 2421, Brandon, VT 05733; (802) 247-5925. Reservations and off-season: (802) 483-2001.

Burton Island State Park

Vermont Department of Forests, Parks & Recreation
253 acres.   North

From St. Albans Bay 3½ mi. SW on Hwy 36 and Point Rd. to Kamp Kill
Kare State Park. Passenger ferry to Burton Island runs 8:30 A.M.–6:30 P.M.
at 2-hr. intervals.

This island in Lake Champlain has a 100-slip marina with power
hookups and other facilities, making it a popular stop for cruisers.
Landlubbers can take the Park ferry. The island was once used for
dairy and sheep farming. Now the fields are reverting, and forest has
reappeared on the higher ground.

The island has an abundant bird population as well as deer and
small mammals. A nature trail explains the island's history and
describes its present flora and fauna. A naturalist in residence mid-
June–Labor Day offers walks and talks.

Camping: 42 sites, including 26 lean-tos. May 17–Sept. 3. Reservations available.

Headquarters

Burton Island State Park, Box 123, St. Albans Bay, VT 05481; (802) 524-
6353. Reservations and off-season: (802) 879-5674.

Button Bay State Park

Department of Forests, Parks & Recreation   North
236 acres.

From Vergennes, ½ mi. S on Hwy 22A, then 6½ mi. NW on local roads.

Button Bay is on Lake Champlain (see entry). No doubt most visitors
come for water-based recreation, but the site is noteworthy for its geological features-fossils of coral and sea plants from the period when
this area was covered by a tropical sea. It is also a convenient base for

visits to the Lower Otter Creek and Dead Creek Wildlife Management Areas (see entries).

The site is largely wooded with mixed hardwoods and conifers, including mature hemlock, maple, and beech.

Interpretation

Nature trail and *nature museum* display fossils, remnants of coral reef, signs of later glaciation, present-day flora and fauna.

Naturalist, here in summer, offers guided walks, evening talks, other programs.

Activities

Camping: 72 sites, including 13 lean-tos. May 7–Oct. 8. Reservations available.

Boating: Ramp. Rentals.

Swimming: Both lake and pool.

Headquarters

Button Bay State Park, RFD 3, Box 4570, Vergennes, VT 05491; (802) 475-2377. Reservations and off-season: (802) 483-2001.

C. C. Putnam State Forest

Vermont Department of Forests, Parks & Recreation   North
12,585 acres.

From Waterbury Center on Hwy 100, turn E at post office sign. Local roads E and N about 3½ mi. to Mt. Hunger trailhead.

The Forest has several separate blocks. The one of chief interest has the trail to Mount Hunger, a 3,620-ft. peak in the Worcester Range. The trail extends S to White Rock Mountain and N along the crest of the range.

Nearly 4,000 acres and 3 trails have been added here since our last edition. These serve to connect the Mt. Hunger Trail with other areas, most notably Worcester Mountain to the N. Leaflets about the trail system are available on request.

Camping is permitted here, but there are no facilities. Nearby is the Little River State Park campground in Mount Mansfield State Forest (see entries).

Headquarters

VT Dept. of Forests, Parks & Recreation, Barre District, 324 N. Main St., Barre, VT 05641; (802) 479-3241.

Calvin Coolidge State Forest

See Coolidge State Forest.

Camel's Hump Forest Reserve

Vermont Department of Forests, Parks & Recreation   North
14,789 acres.

From the McCullough Hwy (Hwy 17), about 6 mi. W of Irasville, N to the Winooski River. S access on Hwy 17. Major N trailheads are E from Huntington Center and S from North Duxbury by local roads. (The area S of Hwy 17 us Camel's Hump State Forest. The area N of Hwy 17 is Camel's Hump Park. "Monroe State Park," still shown on some maps, has been incorporated into Camel's Hump State Park.)

This is a preserve for hikers. It is made up of a portion of the State Park and a portion of the State Forest. The Long Trail (see entry) crosses it N to S. Hwy 17 W from Irasville is access to several ski areas, nordic and downhill. The highway climbs to Appalachian Gap, elevation 2,365 ft., just N of the Green Mountain National Forest (see entry). At the top is a parking area and an overlook; the view is attractive but not sweeping. The Long Trail crosses here; going N, the first bit is a rock scramble.

The reserve was established by the legislature in 1969. The proponents' aims included preserving areas of near-wilderness but also recommended multiple-use management, providing for timber, water, wildlife, and recreation. The lack of roads N of Hwy 17 is in part because of legislation but also because of the mountainous terrain. Camel's Hump itself is 4,083 ft. high, third highest in VT, and the skyline is rugged from N to S.

The Hump receives an astonishing 100 in. of annual precipitation. Moisture falling on the peaks and ridges supplies high bogs and marshes, feeding numerous mountain streams that cascade down to rivers in the valleys below.

Plants: Steep terrain didn't dissuade the loggers who clear-cut many of the slopes in the 1800s, while more acres were denuded by fire. Now protected are three Natural Areas: a pristine stand of northern hardwoods on the W slope; a boreal forest of old-growth balsam fir; and the alpine tundra at the summit. Several thousand acres are now pine and spruce plantations, while others are in stages of natural succession with birch, beech, and maple, colorful in the fall.

Wildlife: The information for fauna in the Green Mountain National Forest (see entry) is applicable here; the preserve has comparable habitats. Birds include species favoring wetlands and forest and those that soar along the ridges. Mammals include black bear, porcupine, beaver, raccoon, red fox, bobcat, gray squirrel, chipmunk, mink, otter, occasional coyote. Deer are present but not in great numbers because of the heavy tree cover.

Activities

Hiking, backpacking: The trails up Camel's Hump are among the most popular in VT for day hikes. Each of the 2 principal trails offers about a 7-mi. round-trip, with a vertical rise of over 2,600 ft. The Long Trail is favored by backpackers. Shelters are spaced along the route from Hwy 17 to the N boundary. At-large camping is permitted except in the Research Area adjacent to Burrows Trail and in the Gleason Brook Drainage Area.

Hunting: Bear, deer, small game.

Fishing: Some brook trout fishing in mountain streams, but most of the action is in the Winooski and other valley rivers.

Canoeing: The Winooski River is canoeable for most of its length from Montpelier to Lake Champlain, with a few dams that require portages. Where the river cuts through the Green Mountains between rock cliffs, the current is strong, and there is one ¾-mi. portage.

Ski touring: Ski trail in the NW sector.

Publications

Trail map, showing trailheads.

A Promise Was Made.

Headquarters

VT Dept. of Forests, Parks & Recreation, Essex District, 111 West St., Essex Jct., VT 05452; (802) 878-1564.

Champlain, Lake

100 mi. long; 278,400 acres. North

NY–VT boundary.

For most of its length, the lake's deep-water channel is VT's W boundary. In the S, the lake is as broad as a respectable river. It widens in the N, the boundary swinging toward the W shore, so that the Alburg peninsula, Isle La Motte, Grand Isle, and the Hero Islands are in Vt. On Isle La Motte, on private land, are outcrops of what is said to be the world's oldest coral reef.

VT State Parks on the lake include North Hero, Knight Point, Burton Island, Grand Isle, Sand Bar, Kingsland Bay, Button Bay, and D.A.R. We have entries for Burton Island and Button Bay. The others, while not chosen as natural areas, provide lake access.

The lake's drainage basin is about 8,000 sq. mi. On the VT side are numerous rivers, often with extensive associated wetlands. We have entries for several wetland Wildlife Management Areas. A number of the rivers, such as the Missisquoi, Lamoille, Winooski, Lewis Creek, Otter Creek, Poultney, Mettawee, and tributaries are canoeable. These are usually mentioned in entries for sites such as Dead Creek WMA, which provide access.

Few sections of the shoreline are roadless.

Activities

Camping: At most of the State Parks.

Hunting: Chiefly waterfowl in bordering wetlands.

Fishing: Lake trout, steelhead, landlocked salmon, smelt, sauger, walleye, largemouth and smallmouth bass, northern pike, pickerel, muskellunge, yellow perch, channel catfish. A highly productive ice fishery.

Boating: Many access points, marinas, rental.

Connecticut River

235 river miles.   North/South

The VT–NH border.

The Connecticut River is no wilderness stream. In colonial times, rivers were the avenues of exploration, travel, commerce, and settlement. Dams provided power for mills. Towns and cities grew around the mills. Roads parallel the Connecticut for much of its course. Even so, the canoeist can enjoy quiet stretches, where the banks are greener than when 19th-century logging had stripped them of trees.

Along the VT–NH portion of the river are 13 dams, most operated by power companies. A few rapids are dangerous during the high water of spring runoff, but after mid-June most of it is easy going. The power dams usually retain water at night, releasing it by day. Canoeists should be aware of these fluctuations, lest a canoe beached at night float away when the water rises.

Activities

Camping: With some planning, it is possible to canoe-camp the entire 235 mi. Camping areas include commercial campgrounds, municipal campgrounds, several dam sites, and one State Park. Many owners of riparian land will permit camping, if asked. Superintendents at the dams are your best local information sources.

Towns are frequent enough for provisioning and refilling water jugs.

Fishing: The state fishing guide says the river has brook, rainbow, and brown trout, yellow perch, walleye, northern pike, chain pickerel, largemouth and small-mouth bass, bullhead, and panfish. There is also some shad fishing below the Vernon and Bellows Falls dams.

Boating: Chiefly in dam impoundments. Check locally.

Canoeing: Most of the river offers easy canoeing but consult the publications for dam locations and rough water sections.

Publications

AMC River Guide: New Hampshire, Vermont, 2nd ed. Boston: Appalachian Mountain Club, 1989.

Barton, Mark, et al. (eds.). *The Complete Boating Guide to the Connecticut River,* 2nd ed. Available from the Connecticut River Watershed Council, 1 Ferry St., Easthampton, MA 01027; (413) 529-9500.

Canoeing on the Connecticut River. Available from the VT Dept. of Forests, Parks & Recreation, 103 S. Main St., Waterbury, VT 05671-0601.

Wilson, Alex. *AMC Quiet Water Canoe Guide: New Hampshire/Vermont.* Boston: Appalachian Mountain Club, 1989.

Coolidge State Forest

Vermont Department of Forests, Parks & Recreation   South
14,709 acres.

From Hwy 100 at Plymouth, SW of Rutland, N 2 mi. on Hwy 100A.

The routing is the Forest recreation area, not far from the birthplace of former President Calvin Coolidge. The Forest is made up of several blocks, irregular in shape. Its primary management goal is to maintain and enhance black bear habitat.

Base elevation of the recreation area is about 1,500 ft. Nearby, 2,174-ft. Slack Hill is crossed by a loop trail from the camping area. The area has a small pond for swimming.

In general, all the blocks are forested with a mix of red spruce, hemlock, balsam fir, yellow and European white birches, beech, and sugar maple, with some Norway spruce and pine plantations.

Features

Shrewsbury Peak Natural Area, and *Mendon Peak Natural Area:* about 200 acres within the Forest, at 3,720 ft. and 3,300 ft. This area consists mostly of high elevation spruce/fir forest. The areas have been recognized for years as a nesting habitat for a variety of songbirds dependent upon boreal conditions. Both peaks are located NW of Plymouth. A good trail leads to the summit of Shrewsbury Peak. A connecting trail meets the Appalachian and Long trails, which overlap at this point.

Tinker Brook Natural Area: 45 acres. About 2 mi. SW of Shrewsbury Peak, reached by Hwy 100 and local roads. Its pristine habitat features an old-growth stand of large red spruce and hemlock and the steep, rocky Tinker Brook ravine.

Killington Peak, 4,235 ft., is the highest in the Forest and second only to Mount Mansfield in VT. Driving NW on US 4 from Rutland, pass through Mendon, turn right on Wheelerville Rd., and continue 4 mi. to the trailhead. The round-trip is about 7 mi. The gondola and ski lift operate after the snow leaves, for those who don't wish to hike. The view from the top is superb, despite the towers, gondola terminal, and restaurant. The Appalachian and Long trails cross the mountain; they divide a short distance to the N.

Activities

Camping: One may camp anywhere outside of Natural Areas, though not near traveled roads or beside streams.

Hiking: Principal trails are the combined Appalachian and Long trails, the Shrewsbury and Killington peaks trails, and numerous side trails. Trail connections into other state lands, chiefly Wildlife Management Areas. A "word of caution," says the recreation map, "for most areas are not signed."

Hunting: Deer, bear, snowshoe hare, rabbit, turkey, grouse.

Fishing: Sections of a number of streams are stocked with trout.

Swimming: In small pond.

Bicycling: On trails where permitted (Appalachian and Long trails don't allow bikes) and on Forest roads.

Ski touring, skiing, snowmobiling: Ski area on Killington. Cross-country skiing and snowmobiling on trails and unplowed roads. Map available.

Nearby
The forest adjoins Plymsburg Wildlife Management Area (see entry).

Publications
Recreation leaflet with map.

Primitive camping fact sheet.

Headquarters
VT Dept. of Forests, Parks & Recreation, Pittsford Regional Office, RR 2, Box 2161, Pittsford, VT 05763; (802) 483-2314/2172.

Cornwall Swamp Wildlife Management Area

Vermont Fish and Wildlife Department   South
1,384 acres.

From US 7 about 7 mi. S of Middlebury, E through West Salisbury and Salisbury to covered bridge.

The covered bridge, built in 1865, has a 136-ft. span. A sign posted inside invites you to join the society dedicated to preservation of such bridges. Otter Creek here is about 35 ft. wide and deep enough for canoeing, although a mat of litter had accumulated at the bridge. There's a parking area and the remains of a ramp, suitable now only for a hand-carried boat.

Most of the WMA is N of here, including wetlands on the W side of the creek.

Activities

Hiking: There are supposed to be 5 mi. of trails, and a posted sign asks that visitors stay on the trails. We only saw a track at the edge of an open field, parallel to the creek but separated from it by a fringe of trees.

Hunting: Deer, grouse, woodcock, waterfowl.

Fishing: Brook, rainbow, brown trout, landlocked salmon.

Canoeing: On Otter Creek, from coast S of Burlington to Manchester area.

Headquarters
VT Fish and Wildlife Dept., Pittsford District, RR 2, Box 2161, Pittsford Academy, Pittsford, VT 05763; (802) 483-2172.

Dead Creek Waterfowl Refuge

Vermont Fish and Wildlife Department   South
2,858 acres.

N access: From Vergennes, about 2 mi. S on Hwy 22A, then W about 2 mi. to dead end. S access: Continue S on 22A to Addison, then W on Hwy 17 to creek.

Dead Creek (a branching, slow-moving stream) flows N for about 10 mi., joining Otter Creek W of Vergennes, about 3 mi. from Lake Champlain. (See entry, Lower Otter Creek.) The site occupies the southern 6½ mi., including marsh and a narrow strip of upland on each side.

The N access road ends at a parking area. On the E, the site borders a fenced field, with a jeep track, unused but mowed, going S. On the W side is a fringe of trees. A hand-carried boat could be launched here, although the water is shallow. Walking S, we saw two duck blinds.

The S access leads to a more interesting area. The creek is broader here, with more branches. One can launch a hand-carried boat. There are also greater opportunities to explore the area on foot. The S access road passes the manager's house.

Birds: This is a nesting area for Canada geese and other waterfowl. In season, shorebirds and marshland species are common.

Mammals: Reported species include deer, muskrat, cottontail, gray squirrel, woodchuck, otter, mink, weasel, red and gray foxes, coyote.

Activities

Camping: Permitted at designated sites (no facilities) and at Button Bay State Park (see entry).

Hunting: Goose hunting requires permit and assigned blind. Black duck, mallard, wood duck, teal, pintail.

Fishing: It's not great. Bullhead, pout, northern pike.

Canoeing: The *Vermont Guide to Fishing* (available from the Fish and Wildlife Dept.) marks the entire creek as canoeable, but there's a dam at the N end; when we visited, the water below the dam was too shallow for any craft. We were advised that some areas are posted.

Headquarters

Dead Creek Waterfowl Refuge, Addison, VT 05491; (802) 759-2398.

Elmore State Park

Vermont Department of Forests, Parks & Recreation   North
709 acres.

On Hwy 12, 5 mi. S of Morrisville.

The Park has frontage on the N end of 224-acre Lake Elmore. Most of
the shoreline is privately owned, with increasing development. Most
visitors come for camping and water-based recreation. Much of the
surrounding area is hilly to mountainous forest, privately owned but
available for hiking and cross-country skiing in season. Base elevation
at the park is about 1,000 ft. A 1½ mi. trail ascends 2,608-ft. Elmore
Mountain.

We found the drive N from Montpelier pleasant, traffic light, the
road closely following the Winooski River—a good fishing stream—
and its North Branch.

Activities

Camping: 60 sites, including 15 lean-tos. May 17–Oct. 8. Reservations
available.

Boating: Ramp. Rentals.

Headquarters

Elmore State Park, Box 93, Lake Elmore, VT 05657; (802) 888-2982.
Reservations and off-season: (802) 479-4280.

Emerald Lake State Park

Vermont Department of Forests, Parks & Recreation   South
430 acres.

From Manchester, Rutland, 22 mi. N on US 7 to North Dorset.

The Park is bisected by US 7. The lake covers only 28 acres. It's a pleasant area, however, with many local attractions. US 7 runs in the long, picturesque Valley of Vermont with Batten Kill, a well-known trout stream, and Otter Creek. The Emerald Lake Natural Bridge spans a deep ravine. US 7 is on or near the W boundary of Green Mountain National Forest (see entry). To the N and S of the park are trails connecting with the Long Trail (see entry). The 80-ft.-deep lake has a sand beach.

Elevation at the valley is about 1,000 ft. The nearby Dorset area trails lead to 3,770-ft. Dorset Peak and 3,230-ft. Mount Aeolus. There is also a nature trail that explains, among other things, why the older rock of the Taconic Mountains is on top of younger rock.

Activities

Camping: 105 sites, including 36 lean-tos. May 7–Oct. 8. Reservations available.

Boating, canoeing: Rentals available.

Headquarters

Emerald Lake State Park, P.O. Box 485, East Dorset, VT 05253; (802) 362-1655. Reservations and off-season: (802) 483-2001.

Gifford Woods State Park

Vermont Department of Forests, Parks & Recreation   South
114 acres.

From the junction of US 4 and Hwy 100, N ½ mi. on Hwy 100.

The Park itself isn't much more than an attractive wooded campsite, but it's a good base. Close by is Sherburne Pass, where the Long Trail and Appalachian Trail part company. Also nearby are the Pico and Killington ski areas, and trout and bass fishing in Kent Pond.

Camping: 48 sites, including 21 lean-tos. May 7–Oct. 8. Reservations available.

Publication

Local trail map.

Headquarters
Gifford Woods State Park, Killington, VT 05751; (802) 775-5354.
Reservations and off-season (802) 886-2434.

Green Mountain National Forest

U.S. Forest Service   South
360,000 acres of Forest land; 629,019 acres within boundaries. (Now
also administers the Finger Lakes National Forest in New York.)

Extends N from the MA border about half the length of VT. Two
sections, N and S of Rutland. Numerous access routes from US 7 on the
W, Hwy 100 on the E.

The Green Mountains are VT's spine, N to S. The Long Trail (see
entry), following the ridge, is the U.S.'s oldest long-distance hiking
route. It was conceived by the Green Mountain Club in 1910, built by
its members, and completed, from MA to Canada, in 1930. The club
still maintains the trail, many side trails, and numerous shelters.

The Green Mountain National Forest was established in 1932, 20
years after the VT sections of the Long Trail came into use. It began
with an acquisition of 1,842 acres. The authorized boundaries have
since been expanded. Tracts have been acquired when owners were
willing to sell and when purchase money was available. 25,089 acres
of wooded wildlife habitat have been purchased by The Nature Conservancy and transferred to the Forest. These projects have served to
protect sections of the Appalachian and Long trails, as well as many
square miles of remote forest in the Green Mountains. Although
other such tracts may be added, no large increase in Forest acreage is
contemplated. In general, the Forest has high, rocky, sloping woodlands. Other lands within the boundaries include farms, a few towns,
ski areas, resorts, and private woodlands. The Forest's 360,000 acres is
half of all the publicly owned land in VT.

Thanks to the pioneering work of the Green Mountain Club, the
patchwork of public and private land doesn't inhibit enjoyment of
these scenic mountains. From Canada to MA, private owners have

approved public use of the Long Trail and side trails crossing their lands.

Mount Ellen, at the upper end of the N half is the Forest's highest point: 4,083 ft. (VT's highest is 4,393-ft. Mount Mansfield.) Although this doesn't rival Colorado's towering Fourteeners, the Green Mountains are steep and rugged enough to challenge any hiker, with views from high points well worth the ascent. Rugged and diverse, with lakes, ponds, streams, and waterfalls, cliffs and rocky peaks, all in deep green forest.

The pattern of vegetation is far from uniform, for the Forest is made up of tracts with a variety of histories of past uses and abuses. The long-range Forest Plan identifies 15 types of management areas. Included are 59,598 acres of wilderness, 12,100 acres of roadless primitive areas, and 77,600 acres of semiprimitive areas with few roads. Semiprimitive areas may be managed for timber production; the objective is large sawtimber, trees allowed to grow for years longer than most private woodland owners can afford. An additional 48,000 acres of roaded natural areas will be managed for high-quality sawtimber and wildlife habitats.

Plants: 90% of the area is forested. Hardwoods predominate—maples, birches, beech, and oaks—with hemlock and white pine interspersed at lower elevations, spruce and fir on higher slopes. Much of the understory is dense, with witch hazel, hop hornbeam, striped and mountain maples, shadbush, hobblebush, blueberry, and viburnum. Common wildflowers include Canada mayflower, red and painted trilliums, sessile bellwort, asters, goldenrods, bunchberry, clintonia, Indian cucumber-root, foamflower, goldthread, orange and yellow hawkweeds, jewelweed, jack-in-the-pulpit.

Birds: Checklist available. Recorded species include woodcock, black-billed cuckoo, ruby-throated hummingbird, wild turkey, ruffed grouse, great blue heron, 5 hawks, peregrine falcon, 4 owls, 5 woodpeckers, whip-poor-will, great crested flycatcher, eastern kingbird, eastern wood-pewee, crow, black-capped chickadee, robin, white-breasted and red-breasted nuthatches, 3 thrushes, veery, 2 vireos, 13 warblers, other songbirds.

Mammals: Reported species include deer, moose, black bear, raccoon, porcupine, red and gray squirrels, red and gray foxes, skunk, beaver, otter. Bobcat, fisher, and coyote are present but seldom seen.

Features

Six *Wildnerness Areas* encompass 59,598 acres.

In the N half, *Bread Loaf Wilderness:* 21,480 acres. Straddles the ridge and includes about 11 mi. of the Long Trail. Bread Loaf Mountain, 3,823 ft., is its highest point. Mt. Grant, Mt. Cleveland, Mt. Roosevelt, and Mt. Wilson are over 3,500 ft. Bristol Cliffs, 3,738 acres, is near the town of Bristol, just S of the scenic New Haven River Gorge. Steep slopes, cliffs, remote ponds, vistas.

In the S half, *Big Branch Wilderness* and *Peru Peak Wilderness:* 6,720 and 6,920 acres. These parallel, separated by a narrow corridor, both crossed by the Long Trail.

Lye Brook Wilderness: 15,680 acres. On the W slope of the mountains, the Long Trail skirting its NE boundary. It has ponds, streams, meadows, including the attractive Trestle Cascade on a branch of Lye Brook.

George D. Aiken Wilderness: 5,060 acres. S of Woodford State Park, on a plateau between two ski areas.

White Rocks National Recreation Area: 22,760 acres. In S half, just N of the Big Branch and Peru Peak wildernesses. Several Forest roads provide access. Limited timber management is practiced here with the objectives of improved wildlife habitat, recreation opportunities, and scenic values. The Long Trail is near its W boundary.

Interpretation

Robert Frost Wayside and Trail, on Hwy 125 E of Ripton. The trail has exhibits with excerpts from the poet's works. His farmhouse is nearby.

Nature trail at the Hapgood Pond campground in the S sector.

The National Forest has no visitor center or nature center. Wildlife biologists and other specialists are available at the Rutland HQ to answer questions. Nature centers are nearby at Branbury and Emerald Lake State Parks (see entries) and Merck State Forest.

Activities

Camping: 5 campgrounds, 106 sites. May to mid-Oct. Also campground in nearby State Parks. Dispersed camping is allowed throughout the Forest. Popular hike-in sites are at Silver Lake, Grout Pond, Little Rock Pond, Stratton Pond, Bourn Pond, and Little Pond. Reservations accepted.

Hiking, backpacking: Of the Long Trail's 265 mi., 130 are within the Forest. Together with many side trails, this is part of a statewide network of 440 mi. Trailside camping is permitted in almost any suitable place, and there are also shelters maintained by the Green Mountain Club at intervals. Trampling has caused damage around some of the popular ponds, and hikers are asked to walk softly and observe rules.

Hunting: Deer, bear, rabbit, snowshoe hare, grouse, wild turkey, woodcock.

Fishing: 440 mi. of streams and 2,800 acres of ponds offer some good fishing for native brook, brown, and rainbow trout. Angler access is good where Forest lands abut waterways. A fisheries management program with professional staff was initiated in 1987. The Forest is making major efforts to restore the Atlantic salmon. The headwaters of the White and West Rivers are important spawning and rearing habitat.

Canoeing: Limited opportunities on ponds and streams; some white water in spring runoff.

Ski touring, skiing: 7 ski touring centers are within the Forest boundaries. Downhill ski areas are nearby. Cross-country skiing is permitted on all public lands in VT.

Publications

Forest map and general information.

Mimeo information pages: directory of campgrounds; trails, day hikes.

Pamphlets: *Grout Pond Recreation Area, Hapgood Pond Recreation Area, White River Travelway.*

Headquarters

Forest Supervisor, Green Mountains National Forest, 231 N. Main St., Rutland, VT 05701; (802) 747-6700. Reservations (802) 824-6456 May 1–Oct. 1; (802) 241-3499 Jan. 1–April 30.

Ranger Districts

Manchester R.D., Rts. 11 and 30, Box 1940, Manchester Center, VT 05255; (802) 362-2307. Middlebury R.D., RR #4, Box 1260, Middlebury, VT 05753; (802) 388-4362. Rochester R.D., RR #2, Box 35, Rochester, VT 05767; (802) 767-4261.

Groton State Forest

Vermont Department of Forests, Parks & Recreation   North
25,625 acres.

From I-91, Exit 17. Then NW 9 mi. on US 302, N on Hwy 232. In about
2 mi., this road enters the Forest. Major entrance on right in 5 mi.

This is VT's largest state recreation area. The terrain is rolling to steep.
Signal Mountain's elevation is 3,348 ft. Several mountains are over
2,500 ft. There are many glacial boulders, ledges, rock outcrops. The
area is almost entirely forested.

The Forest sprawls, with irregular boundaries, but this hardly matters as most of the surrounding area is undeveloped forest. Indeed, the
Forest's trail map doesn't show boundaries, and a number of trails cross
neighboring land. Lake Groton, the largest water body, is about 3 mi.
long. There are several large and small ponds as well as swamps, bogs,
and streams.

About half of the visitors come from nearby, to swim and fish in
summer, hunt in the fall, snowmobile and ski tour in winter. Hiking is
popular. Trailside camping is permitted, but few hikers camp.

Most campers are from out of state, often stopping here for a day or
two en route to other destinations. The main season is from Labor Day
to the end of Sept. Recreation areas are popular but seldom crowded;
only rarely are all campsites occupied. Winter campsites are available.

Plants: Like many forests of this region, Groton reflects a history of
abuse. It was heavily logged before 1900. Then great fires destroyed
much of the soil's fertility. Recovery is slow. What is seen from the
road is young mixed hardwood forest—maple, beech, birch—with an
understory of shrubs and saplings and a carpet of herbaceous plants,
ferns, mosses, lichens, and grasses. The forest on higher ground is
mostly spruce/fir with considerably less understory.

The available plant list includes trees, shrubs, ferns, club mosses,
and horsetails. The extensive list of herbaceous flowering plants is
coded for season and habitat.

Birds: Over 100 species have been reported. The bird list is annotated for season, abundance, and habitat. Nesting species include red-tailed and broad-winged hawks, barred owl, grouse, woodcock, 5 woodpecker species, kingfisher, ruby-throated hummingbird, 5 flycatchers, wood and hermit thrushes, veery, many wood warblers, northern oriole, rose-breasted grosbeak, scarlet tanager, various finches and sparrows. Loons visit occasionally.

Mammals: Reported species include black bear, deer, red fox, porcupine beaver, red squirrel, flying squirrel, chipmunk. A few moose frequent the Forest.

Interpretation

The *Groton Nature Center,* near Big Deer Campground, is a large building with exhibits and films. An amphitheater is just outside.

Field trips and other special programs are conducted by naturalists.

A ½-mi. *nature trail* starts at the Nature Center.

Activities

Camping: 250 sites, including over 50 lean-tos. Open Memorial Day weekend through Columbus Day weekend. 5 winter camping areas. Reservations are available.

Hiking, backpacking: 40 mi. of developed trails lead to various mountains, ponds, bogs. An abandoned railroad bed has recently become part of a multiuse trail that extends from Wells River to Montpelier. Trailside camping is permitted except in certain prohibited areas.

Horse riding, bicycling: On multiuse trail.

Hunting: Regulated by Fish and Wildlife Dept. No hunting near developed areas.

Fishing: Trout in streams, warmwater species in lakes and ponds.

Swimming: Lake Groton and Ricker Pond.

Boating: Lake Groton and Ricker Pond. Ramps, rentals.

Canoeing: Access also at Kettle, Levi, and Osmore Ponds.

Ski touring, snowmobiling: 12 mi. of marked roads and trails.

Publications

Fact sheet.

Trail map.

Nature trail guide.

Plants of the Groton State Forest.
Birds of the Groton State Forest.

Headquarters
Groton State Forest, Marshfield, VT 05658; (802) 584-3820/3823.

Half Moon State Park
See Bomoseen State Park/Half Moon State Park.

Hurricane Brook Wildlife Management Area
See Bill Sladyk Wildlife Management Area.

Jay Peak Area
Mixed ownership   North
Near the Canadian border, W of Hwys 100 and 101.

The Long Trail (see entry) follows a chain of peaks northward to its terminus. Jay Peak, 3,861 ft., highest in this area, is within a small State Forest best known for its ski resort. Trail hikers enjoy a sweeping view from the top. Several other peaks along the route exceed or approach 3,000 ft. Most of the area is privately owned forest land, available to visitors for hiking. The Green Mountain Club maintains shelters along the Long Trail.

From the S slope of the mountain, Jay Brook flows SW through terrain favored by cross-country skiers. Good trout fishing. On the E side, Jay Branch flows E to the Missisquoi River. Near North Troy, it passes through Jay Branch Gorge, rough and rocky, with a 15-ft. waterfall.

The Missisquoi is one of VT's longest rivers, flowing N past North Troy into Canada, turning W and SW back into VT, then W to Lake Champlain. (See entry, Missisquoi National Wildlife Refuge.) S of North Troy it drops over Big Falls, one of VT's largest and most spectacular. The 68 mi. from North Troy to Champlain are canoeable, with some rapids and portages.

Lewis Creek Wildlife Management Area

Vermont Fish and Wildlife Department   North
1,796 acres.

From Starksboro, S about 2½ mi. on Hwy 116, then E on Ireland Rd. to
parking areas.

The site is on the W slopes of the Green Mountains. Terrain is gentle
to moderately steep, rising from 1,000 ft. at Lewis Creek to 2,560 ft.
atop Hillsboro Mountain. In the past the area was logged, farmed,
grazed, and abandoned. Now it is 95% forested, chiefly with sugar
maple, beech, and yellow birch, with one tract of hemlock and yellow
birch. Logging is now managed for wildlife habitat improvement.

Except in hunting season, few visitors come here. The site offers an
opportunity for quiet day hiking on about 6 mi. of old logging roads.
There has been some off-road vehicle activity that the dept. hopes to
control.

Lewis Creek is canoeable below Prindle Corners, not here.

The site has 3 beaver colonies. Other wildlife include red fox,
snowshoe hare, coyote, ruffed grouse, occasional black bear. It's a deer
wintering area.

Headquarters

VT Fish and Wildlife Dept., Essex District, 111 West St., Essex Junction,
VT 05452; (802) 878-1564.

Little Otter Creek Wildlife Management Area

Vermont Fish and Wildlife Department   North
1,048 acres.

From US 7 at Ferrisburg, W about 1 mi. Turn right on first paved road
and go N 2 mi. Parking area is across the creek.

The creek is broad, attractive, fringed by marsh and trees, with many
water lilies. From the road, which carries little traffic, one can over-

look open water and marsh. We saw two outboard craft motoring toward Lake Champlain, about a mile downstream. Upstream is a quiet wetland area with good birding.

Activities

Camping: Permitted at designated areas for hunters during waterfowl season. No facilities.

Hunting: Waterfowl.

Fishing: Northern pike, largemouth bass.

Boating, canoeing: A good launching ramp is at the parking area.

Headquarters

VT Fish and Wildlife Dept., Essex District, 111 West St., Essex, VT 05452; (802) 878-1564.

Little River State Park

Vermont Department of Forests, Parks & Recreation   North
12,000 acres.

From Waterbury, 1½ mi. W on US 2, then right under the overpass and 3½ mi. N on Little River Rd.

The developed area of the Park is near the dam of Waterbury Reservoir, an impoundment about 6 mi. long between steep-sided forested hills. It is part of the Mount Mansfield State Forest (see entry). Indeed, in the state's informal if somewhat confusing way, the Park is also called the Little River Block of the Forest (a part of which is also called the Woodward Hill Block).

Whatever the name, it's delightful. Many of the campsites are across a cove from the busier day-use beach and ramp. The sites are well spaced on the forested hillside. We swam from the rocky shore just below our camp. Elevation at the shore is about 550 ft.

Some private development has occurred, chiefly on the E side of the lake. However, while canoeing for several hours, we were passed by less than a dozen motor craft. The water was clear, the swimming fine.

Interpretation

Natural trail along Stevenson Brook, self-guiding.

The *"History Hike"* is fascinating if the printed guide is available. The center spread is a historical map of the Little River area, where the first European settler arrived in 1790.

Activities

Camping: 101 sites, including 20 lean-tos. May 17–Oct. 8. Reservations accepted.

Hiking, backpacking: Several trails from the campground offer opportunities for day or overnight hikes. Trails extend through the Mount Mansfield State Forest, to the Long Trail, and to Camel's Hump Forest Reserve (see entries). Maps carry the State Forest name but are available at the Park office.

Hunting: In the State Forest.

Fishing: For brown, lake, and rainbow trout, yellow perch, smallmouth bass, smelt.

Boating, canoeing: Ramp. Rentals.

Publications

Trail maps.

Nature and history trail guides.

Headquarters

Little River State Park, RFD 1, Box 1150, Waterbury, VT 05676; (802) 244-7103. Reservations and off-season: (802) 479-4280.

....

Long Trail

Green Mountain Club   North/South
265 miles.

From Canada to MA.

What a magnificent achievement! In 1910 a small group with a large vision founded the Green Mountain Club. By 1917 GMC volunteers had surveyed, cleared, and marked a trail from Killington to MA and published the first guidebook. (Our 1996 copy is the 24th edition.) By 1930 the trail had been completed from border to border, 265 miles. It is the oldest long-distance hiking trail in the U.S.

Of its distance, about 10% crosses privately owned land. It was more before the Green Mountain National Forest was assembled and acquisitions by government and the Green Mountain Club were added to the publicly owned sections. The GMC had to persuade landowners to grant easements for routes acceptable to them. GMC volunteers maintain the trail and its shelters, and relocate trail sections when necessary.

In addition to the trail itself, the system includes almost 100 side trails, totaling 175 mi. Volunteers have built and now maintain 62 rustic cabins and lean-tos which provide overnight shelter.

The southern portion of the trail is also the Appalachian Trail, which turns E at Sherburne Pass.

It is not the aim of the GMC to make this route a smooth path for Sunday walks. We've hiked sections that were wet, muddy, steep, and rocky, sometimes encountering deadfalls and windfalls not yet cleared. As trail use has increased, more work has been required to control erosion and to prevent detours through fragile plant communities.

For much of the trail, the hiking season begins at the end of May. The spring mud season is no time be on it, and better winter routes are available for ski touring and snowshoeing. GMC's Waterbury Center office will respond to letters or telephone calls asking about trail conditions and can suggest sections suitable for winter and spring hikes.

For anything more than a short day hike, the guidebook is essential. Having it adds much to the enjoyment of any outing. The GMC invites all hikers to membership, even those who can't volunteer to help.

Publications

Day Hiker's Guide to Vermont, 3rd. ed., 1990.

End-to-End (set of 21 topo maps covering the Long Trail).

Long Trail Guide, 24th ed., 1996.

The following items are free: *Day Hiker's Vermont Sampler, The Long Trail: A Footpath in the Wilderness, Winter Trail Use in the Green Mountains*, Publications list.

Headquarters

Green Mountain Club, Inc., RR #1, Box 650, Waterbury Center, VT 05677; (802) 244-7037.

Lower Otter Creek Wildlife Management Area

Vermont Fish and Wildlife Department   North
452 acres.

From Vergennes, W and N on local roads toward Fort Cassin.

Canoeing is by far the best way to see this site. Topography is flat. Most of the area is flooded in spring and in a wet fall. The creek is canoeable from the public landing at Vergennes to Lake Champlain. A take-out is at Fort Cassin. The WMA is in several parcels, but boundaries aren't apparent.

The biologist who prepared the management plan said the site has "tremendous" fish and wildlife resources, high praise for a relatively small area. The Vermont Natural Heritage Program has also taken note of the wildlife, especially the least bittern, common moorhen, and black tern.

Plants: About 43% of the site is forested. Plants include silver and red maples, American elm, black ash, swamp white oak, one area of eastern hemlock. Also buttonbush, dogwood, cattail, water lily, bulrush.

Birds: Numerous nesting species, including Canada goose, black duck, mallard, green-winged teal, grouse, wild turkey.

Mammals: Include beaver, muskrat, cottontail, mink, raccoon, gray squirrel, deer.

Activities

Camping: At Button Bay State Park (see entry).

Hunting: Waterfowl, upland game.

Fishing: Bass, bullhead, carp. Northern pike and chain pickerel spawn here.

Canoeing: Otter Creek offers the longest canoe trip in VT, 100 mi. from Dorset at high water.

Headquarters

VT Fish and Wildlife Dept., Essex District, 111 West St., Essex Junction, VT 05452; (802) 878-1564.

Maidstone State Park

Department of Forests, Parks & Recreation   North
469 acres.

From Bloomfield, 5 mi. S on Hwy 102, then 5 mi. SW on State Forest Hwy.

Maidstone Lake covers 796 acres, a rough oval about 2½ mi. long. Both shores have roads and seasonal residences. The Park, at the S end, isn't large, but the country for miles around is wild, and scattered hills up to about 2,100 ft. elevation. Away from the lake, there's ample solitude.

The forest has mixed northern hardwoods. Bird life includes warblers, finches, woodpeckers, loon. Mammals include moose, black bear, deer, raccoon, bobcat, snowshoe hare, porcupine, fisher.

Activities

Camping: 83 sites including 37 lean-tos. May 17–Sept. 3. Reservations available.

Fishing: Rainbow and lake trout, yellow perch.

Boating: Ramp. Rentals.

Headquarters

Maidstone State Park, RD 1, Box 455, Guildhall, VT 05905; (802) 676-3930. Reservations and off-season: (802) 479-4280.

Missisquoi National Wildlife Refuge

U.S. Fish and Wildlife Service   North
6,338 acres.

Near the Canadian border on the E shore of Lake Champlain. HQ is on Hwy 78, 2 mi. NW of Swanton.

Open in daylight hours.

The refuge includes most of the delta of the Missisquoi River, on both sides of the channel. The delta is low-lying, marshy, cut by numerous winding creeks, with open water and wooded swamp. Narrow strips of cropland are on ridges. It was established to maintain and enhance feeding and resting areas for migrating waterfowl.

From HQ, the Black Creek and Maquam Creek interpretive trails pass through 1½ mi. of wooded lowland. These may be flooded in spring and early summer. The first portion is just a pleasant walk in the woods. After that it's close to the creeks, but thickets can block the view. There are 2 active beaver houses along Maquam Creek. Ask at HQ what other parts of the refuge can be visited on foot. At the boat ramp, we saw a jeep track behind a gate marked "Area Closed." In most federal refuges, this means "Keep Out," but at HQ we were told only vehicles are prohibited.

Much more can be seen from a canoe. But at HQ we were told there's no nearby place to rent canoes.

The refuge doesn't have a great number of visitors. Of those, many stop by in summer, as we did, when waterfowl numbers are low. It's a pleasant stop, but we don't recommend making a long detour.

Birds: A checklist of 200 species is available. The largest concentrations of waterfowl occur in April, Sept., and Oct. The most numerous nesting species are black duck, mallard, wood duck, and common goldeneye, with a few blue-winged teal and hooded merganser. Other nesting species include great blue heron. American bittern, common moorhen, many songbirds. Nearly 200 nest boxes are located throughout the refuge. Waterfowl and shorebirds are seasonally abundant.

Mammals: Checklist of 35 species available. White-tailed deer are common, as are otter, red fox, beaver, red and gray squirrels, cottontail, muskrat. During high water in April–May, deer may be forced onto higher ground, as many as 30 in a group.

Activities

Hunting: Special regulations. Waterfowl, deer, upland game. "Frog-picking," July 15–Sept. 30.

Fishing: River and lake.

Boating, canoeing: Ramp on Hwy 78, 2 mi. below junction with Dead Creek. There is a second ramp at Mac's Bend Rd., open during hunting season. The Missisquoi is canoeable for almost 70 mi., from North Troy to Lake Champlain, an upper section passing through Canada. Some rapids, dams, unrunnable drops.

Ski touring: On refuge nature trails.

Publications

Leaflet with map.

Checklists of birds, mammals.

Black Creek and Maquam Creek Trail.

Fishing.

Headquarters

Missisquoi National Wildlife Refuge, P.O. Box 163, Swanton, VT 05488; (802) 868-4781.

Mount Ascutney State Park

See Ascutney State Park.

Mount Mansfield State Forest

Vermont Department of Forests, Parks & Recreation North
30,500 acres.

Two principal areas: From Stowe on Hwy 100, NW on Hwy 108; from Waterbury, 1½ mi. W on US 2, then right under overpass and 3½ mi. to Little River State Park.

The Forest has two principal blocks, the northern featuring Mt. Mansfield, the southern the Waterbury Reservoir. It includes 3 State Parks: Little River (see entry), Smugglers Notch, and Underhill. The entire area is in the Green Mountains. Mt. Mansfield, 4,393 ft., is the state's highest.

This is VT's best-known ski country. The famous mountain has been nastily scarred by the clear-cut slopes, more conspicuous in summer than winter. People look up from the valley to see the profile of a reclining giant's face, its features labeled on maps: Adam's Apple, The Chin, The Nose, The Forehead. In the warm months, many hike or drive to the top for the splendid views. Some features can be seen only by walking: Smugglers Cave, Lake of the Clouds, Bear Pond, Cave of the Winds.

It's great hiking country. More than 40,000 visitors per year walk around the Mt. Mansfield summit, a considerable threat to its delicate plant life. No such crowds are on the Long Trail as it follows the peaks southward through the N sector of the Forest. It then veers to the W, passing the Bolton Valley Ski Area. Side trails link it to the trail complex in the Little River sector. Portions of the trail are steep, rough, difficult.

Plants: As one ascends the mountain, a northern hardwood forest is gradually replaced by spruce/fir. Mt. Mansfield rises several hundred feet above timberline, and the summit has a complex of fragile alpine plant communities: sedge tundra, peat bogs supporting leatherleaf, bog laurel, and black crowberry; heath, with alpine brilberry and mountain cranberry; and rare species usually found miles to the N.

Birds: No species record has been kept. Species noted at lower elevations include yellow-bellied sapsucker, veery, 2 thrushes, solitary vireo, 2 warblers, red-breasted nuthatch, golden-crowned kinglet, scarlet tanager, ruffed grouse, American woodcock. Near timberline: gray-cheeked thrush, blackpoll warbler, dark-eyed junco, white-throated sparrow, raven. Hawks aloft in migration.

Mammals: Hunting is prohibited on the E side of the northern sector. Species reported include snowshoe hare, porcupine, gray fox, squirrel, cottontail, bobcat, deer, black bear.

Features

The *summit ridge* is owned by the University of Vermont and state protected as a Natural Area. Green Mountain Club ranger-naturalists are stationed on the summit to provide information and protect the rare flora.

The *Beaver Meadow* block: 3,000 acres. In the Morrisville-Morristown area, has been added to the Forest since our first edition. A trail system is being constructed on an old road system.

Smugglers Notch between Mt. Mansfield and Sterling Peak, has spectacular cliffs, ledges, boulders, arctic flora.

Sterling Pond is on the Long Trail not far from *Elephant's Head*. A GMC shelter is at the pond, with a resident caretaker in hiking season.

Waterbury Reservoir; Little River sector. See entry for Little River State Park. Ricker Mountain, 3,401 ft., is the highest peak in this sector, which is generally mountainous, with two principal streams, Cotton Brook and Stevenson Brook, flowing to the reservoir. The sector has many trails.

Activities

Camping: Smugglers Notch State Park, on the road from Stowe, has 38 sites, 14 lean-tos. (We were informed that these facilities may be relocated at some future time.) Underhill State Park, reached from Essex Junction (I mi. E on Hwy 15, 8 mi. E on local roads too steep for trailers, including 4 mi. of gravel) has 25 sites, 15 lean-tos. Little River State Park (see entry) has 101 sites, 20 lean-tos. Season: May 17–Oct. 8.

Hiking, backpacking: One of the most attractive segments of the Long Trail. Many trails for day hikes. Trailside camping is permitted except in the Smugglers Notch Ski Area and Moscow Tree Seed Orchard.

Fishing: Chiefly in Waterbury Reservoir, recently drained and refilled.

Boating: Reservoir.

Ski touring: *Many trails, some maintained, in Mt. Mansfield sector.*

Skiing: *Chiefly Mt. Mansfield ski area in Stowe.*

Publication
Trail maps.

Headquarters
VT Dept. of Forests, Parks & Recreation, Barre Regional Office, 324 N. Main St., Barre, VT 05641; (802) 479-3241.

....

Mud Creek Wildlife Management Area

Vermont Fish and Wildlife Department   North
1,019 acres.

On Hwy 78 0.7 mi. NE of its intersection with US 2.

If you've just visited the Missisquoi National Wildlife Refuge (see entry) and are traveling W on Hwy 78, this site is worth a stop. Look for a small parking area on the right where the road crosses Mud Creek. A not-too-visible sign says this is a Fishing Access site. Across a small bridge are jeep trails, easy hiking. It seemed possible to launch a canoe and paddle up Mud Creek, how far we don't know. The wetlands along the creek attract waterfowl.

Camping: permitted for hunters during waterfowl season at designated areas.

Headquarters
VT Fish and Wildlife Dept., Essex District, 111 West St., Essex Junction,
VT 05452; (802) 878-1564.

....

Pine Mountain Wildlife Management Area

Vermont Fish and Wildlife Department   North
2,274 acres.

S of US 302, about 4 mi. E of West Groton. Most acreage is in the NE
corner of the town of Topsham. Site's NE corner is in SE Groton and SW
Ryegate, on the Wells River. Includes Melvin Hill in Newbury. Access by
old railroad bed.

Pine Mountain, 1,492 ft., is at the WMA's center. Highest point is
1,632-ft. Burnham Mountain, near the S boundary. Lowest elevation
is 900 ft. on Keenan Brook. Terrain is moderately rolling with some
steep slopes, several streams flowing to the Wells River, a portion of
Scotts Brook Swamp in the SW.

The site is almost entirely forested with a mixture of mature northern hardwoods and softwood species. Timber harvesting is planned
largely for wildlife habitat management.

Wells River is a scenic stream with numerous ledges, falls, cascades,
and pools. For some miles it flows close to US 302. A few short
stretches are canoeable if one doesn't mind frequent portages.

The site map shows no trails, but bushwhacking is feasible, and the
1½ mi. walk from the highway to the top of Pine Mountain is a quiet,
pleasant day hike.

Wildlife: Includes bear, deer, bobcat, fisher, snowshoe hare, occasional moose, 1 active beaver colony, grouse, wood duck, woodcock.

Headquarters
VT Fish and Wildlife Dept., Barre District, 324 N. Main St., Barre, VT
05641; (802) 479-3241.

Plymsbury Wildlife Management Area

Vermont Department of Fish and Wildlife   South
1,860 acres.

About 1 mi. NE of North Shrewsbury. Town Hwy 20 crosses the S
portion. Access to N sector by Northam Rd. and Grouse Hill Rd.

The WMA adjoins a block of Coolidge State Forest (see entry) on the N.
The area is between the two portions of the Green Mountain and Finger Lakes National Forests, on the W slope of the mountains. Terrain is
hilly, gentle to moderate slopes, with several crests near 2,400 ft. The
WMA has two principal watercourses. Great Roaring Brook crosses the
S third, Tinker Brook the NE corner. Neither is canoeable, nor is either
rated high as a fishery, although there are trout in Great Roaring Brook.

The site is almost entirely forested with trees of pole to sawlog size.
About 1,000 acres are northern hardwoods, primarily beech, birch, and
maple. Softwoods predominate in about 450 acres, chiefly spruce/fir. A
40-acre wooded swamp is in the N central sector.

Because of easy access, the WMA and adjacent Forest have considerable recreational use, chiefly by local residents: primitive camping,
hiking, hunting, fishing, birding. Annual snowfall is about 120 in.,
snow cover lasting about 100 days, and this attracts cross-country
skiers and snowmobilers.

Wildlife: Includes bear, deer, fisher, red fox, coyote, bobcat, raccoon.
Beaver impoundments are along Great Roaring Brook. Moose have
been seen. Small numbers of waterfowl visit the area: black duck,
wood duck, mallard, common and hooded mergansers.

Nearby
Coolidge State Forest adjoins the WMA.

Headquarters
VT Fish and Wildlife Dept., Pittsford District, RR #2, Box 2161, Pittsford Academy, Pittsford, VT 05763; (802) 483-2172.

Putnam State Forest

See C. C. Putnam State Forest.

Quechee Gorge State Park

Vermont Department of Forests, Parks & Recreation   South
612 acres.
On US 4. 3 mi. W of I-89 junction with (Exit 1).

When we first saw it in 1978, the Park had only 76 acres. From an
overlook near the highway bridge, one looks down into the 155-ft.-
deep rocky gorge of the Ottauquechee River. One could also hike a
short trail. Since then the state has become the manager of land on
both sides of the highway, on both sides of the gorge. On the S it
extends for about a mile. On the N it includes Deweys Mills Ponds.

The walls of the gorge, steep to almost vertical, have plants from
grasses to stunted trees clinging to ledges and crevices. Surrounding
the gorge is northern hardwood forest with intermixed conifers: hemlock, beech, sugar, and red maples, red spruce, white and red pines,
yellow birch. In the understory are mountain maple, hobblebush,
beaked willow, bush honeysuckle, witch hazel. Seasonal wildflowers
include columbine, bishop's cap, harebell, flowering raspberry, little
cinquefoil, fringed loosestrife, sandwort, purple nightshade, violets,
asters.

Activities

Camping: 54 sites, including 6 lean-tos. May 7–Oct. 8. Reservations
available.

Hiking: A 1-mi. loop trail provides fine views of the gorge from above
and below, passing through forest, crossing streams.

Publication

Geology brochure.

Headquarters
Quechee Gorge State Park, 190 Dewey Mills Rd., White River Junction, VT 05001; (802) 295-2990. Reservations and off-season: (802) 886-2434.

South Bay Wildlife Management Area

Vermont Fish and Wildlife Department   North
1,559 acres.

S end of Lake Memphremagog. From Coventry on US 5, E 4 mi. on local road.

Lake Memphremagog, partly in Canada, is the second largest VT lake and one of its best fishing waters. Newport, at the S end of the main lake, is a popular resort. South Bay extends for about 2 mi. S of Newport. Beyond is the WMA, largely marshland on the Barton River, with some frontage on the bay.

Birds: The WMA is primarily for waterfowl. Seasonally common species include Canada and snow geese, black tern, black duck, wood duck, blue-winged teal, lesser scaup, common merganser, American bittern, Virginia rail, killdeer, common snipe, osprey, shorebirds.

   Boating: Ramp on South Bay.

Headquarters
VT Fish and Wildlife Dept., St. Johnsbury District, 184 Portland St., St. Johnsbury, VT 05819; (802) 748-8787.

Townshend State Park

Vermont Department of Forests, Parks & Recreation   South
856 acres.

3 mi. N on Town Rd. from its junction with Hwy 30.

The U.S. Army Corps of Engineers has dammed the West River, backing up a long, narrow pool. The State Park is below the dam. The Corps' Recreation Area offers swimming, boating, and fishing; the Park has camping and hiking.

Elevation at the reservoir is about 478 ft. From the campground, the land rises to the S, to a high point of 1,680 ft. on Bald Mountain. On a contour map it looks like an easy ascent, but the trail to the top, at times steep and rocky, gains over 1,100 ft. in less than 1 mi. The trail passes an alder swamp, pine grove, an ancient European white birch. Much of the forest has young beech, with maples and hemlock.

Activities

Camping: 34 sites including 4 lean-tos. May 7–Oct. 8. Reservations available.

Hiking, backpacking: Although the site isn't large, trailside camping is permitted. We saw no trail extensions into adjoining areas.

Fishing: Rainbow and brown trout.

Swimming: Beach at Corps' Recreation Area.

Boating: Ramp at Corps' Recreation Area.

Canoeing: West River.

Headquarters

Townshend State Park, Rt. 1, Box 2650, Townshend, VT 05353; (802) 365-7500. Reservations and off-season: (802) 886-2434.

....

Victory Basin Wildlife Management Area

Vermont Fish and Wildlife Department   North
4,970 acres.

From St. Johnsbury, E on US 2 to North Concord, then NE on local road. Beyond Victory the road crosses the WMA. There are 3 parking areas.

The WMA is part of one of the largest wetland/wilderness areas in the Northeast Kingdom (the local name of the Northeast Highlands). The land is generally flat and wet, with occasional ridges and hills. Elevations range from 1,100 to 1,400 ft.

The Moose River parallels the road through the site, which includes 1,800 acres of wetlands, from cedar swamp to cattail marshes. Also within the site are over 1,000 acres of northern hardwood forest and almost 2,000 acres of spruce/fir, interspersed with old fields and other openings. Flora include rhodora azalea, Labrador tea, leatherleaf, pitcher plant.

Birds: Waterfowl populations are generally low. Nesting species include mallard, black duck, wood duck, hooded merganser. Upland species include several rather uncommon in VT, such as gray jay, olive-sided flycatcher, black-backed pileated, and three-toed woodpeckers, rusty blackbird, spotted sandpiper, common snipe.

Mammals: Many beaver ponds. An important deer wintering area. Moose are resident. Other species include black bear, coyote, red fox, bobcat, snowshoe hare.

Activities

Camping: Permitted at designated areas. No facilities.

Hiking: Unmaintained logging road and bushwhacking.

Hunting: Deer, snowshoe hare, grouse, woodcock.

Fishing: Brook trout. Moderate fishing pressure.

Canoeing: Canoe access. A management document says Moose River is canoeable only at high water to Damon's Crossing, below that all year, with white water below Mitchell's Landing.

Headquarters

VT Fish and Wildlife Dept., St. Johnsbury District, 184 Portland St., St. Johnsbury, VT 05819; (802) 748-8787.

Wenlock Wildlife Management Area

Vermont Fish and Wildlife Department   North
1,994 acres.

NE VT. Generally S of Hwy 105 between Island Pond and Bloomfield. From Island Pond, just under 8 mi. E on Hwy 105, then right on dirt road toward South America Pond.

Boundaries don't matter much here, in this least populous part of VT. Essex County, in the NE corner, is mostly between Hwy 114 and the Connecticut River, the NH boundary. The Nulhegan River, paralleled by Hwy 105, crosses its middle, W–E. This is the Northeast Highlands (also locally called the Northeast Kingdom). Most of the land is owned by timber companies that permit recreational use of their lands. The map shows few roads, but there's a network of old logging roads that may not be suitable for a car but serve as hiking trails.

Elevations along the Nulhegan River are about 1,000 ft. Most of the county is hilly to mountainous, several peaks rising above 3,000 ft. The WMA occupies lowlands along the river and its tributaries, including bogs and beaver ponds, with a few knolls and ridges about 1,400 ft. elevation. Much of the site is spruce/fir forest, with a few hardwood knolls. Annual snowfall is 80–100 in., winter snow depth usually about 2 ft.

Moose Bog, a fascinating natural feature, is W of the dirt access road, reached by a track to the right about 0.2 mi. from the highway; in about half a mile look left for a trail. Sphagnum moss has formed a floating mat thick and strong enough to support shrubs, chiefly heath species such as leatherleaf, Labrador tea, bog rosemary, bog laurel, and cranberry. Pitcher plant and sundew are also seen.

Birds: This is a birding hot spot, frequented by local birding societies, chiefly in spring and early summer. A Christmas bird count takes place here. Some boreal forest species are seen here that are uncommon to rare elsewhere in VT. Nesting and migratory waterfowl include mallard, black duck, goldeneye, ring-necked duck. Breeding species include spruce grouse, three-toed and black-backed woodpeckers, gray jay, Cape May warbler. Other notable species include boreal chickadee, rusty blackbird, yellow-bellied flycatcher, Swainson's thrush, Tennessee and blackpoll warblers, Lincoln's sparrow, white-winged crossbill.

Mammals: Deer population is high, especially in winter. Moose are present most of the year. Black bear are often here. Snowshoe hare are abundant. Other species include beaver, fisher, red fox, coyote, bobcat.

Activities

Camping: At nearby Brighton State Park: 84 sites. Season is mid-May–Columbus Day weekend. Reservations available: Island Pond, VT 05846; (802) 723-4360. *No pets.*

Hunting: Chiefly for upland game.

Fishing: Low to moderate trout populations in the river and beaver ponds.

Canoeing: The river is canoeable from Nulhegan Pond to its end, but the portion just below the pond is narrow, and one class IV section is often portaged.

Ski touring, snowshoeing: Good opportunities.

Headquarters
VT Fish and Wildlife Dept., St. Johnsbury District, 184 Portland St., St. Johnsbury, VT 05819; (802) 748-8787.

Willoughby State Forest

Vermont Department of Forests, Parks & Recreation   North
7,422 acres.

On both sides of the S end of Lake Willoughby, extending almost to US 5. From I-91, exit at Barton, then S on US 5.

If you plan to hike here, get a trail map first. Trailheads aren't easy to find, though the trails are blazed. The forester we spoke with in 1996 said that trail improvements are being made at this time. He also suggested obtaining a U.S.G.S. topo map for the area.

The Forest has two parts. The smaller, on the E side of the lake, includes 2,751-ft. Mt. Pisgah. Route 5A follows the lakeshore. From here the mountain's flank rises steeply to vertical rock cliffs. We saw two attractive cascades beside the road. The Mt. Pisgah Trail begins at an inconspicuous trailhead on the highway, where there's no parking, and ends S of the lake. It's an energetic hike, rewarded with some fine vistas.

The larger part of the Forest is W of the lake. Until 1969 this was a patchwork, much of it open farmland on which the CCC (Civilian Conservation Corps) planted trees in the 1930s. Then the state acquired 5,000 acres to unify the tract, giving it control of the forest around Mt. Pisgah and its twin peak across the lake, Mt. Hor. Two other prominent peaks in this portion are Bartlett Mountain, SE of Mt. Hor, and Wheeler Mountain at the N tip of the site. Facing the cliffs of Mt. Pisgah are the cliffs below Mt. Hor. Arctic flora are said to grow on these cliffs.

Elsewhere the slopes are generally moderate to steep. This portion has a network of trails, including loops around a cluster of ponds: Marl, Duck, Blake, Vail, and Bean.

Plants: Generally young forest, mixed hardwoods at lower elevations, red spruce and balsam fir on upper slopes. Blueberry and blackberry are common. Many wildflowers and ferns.

Birds: Species observed include boreal chickadee, American goldfinch, red crossbill, great crested flycatcher, ruffed grouse, cedar waxwing, various raptors, warblers.

Mammals: Bear, deer, porcupine, fisher, bobcat, beaver, snowshoe hare, cottontail, red and gray squirrels, chipmunk.

Activities

Hiking, backpacking: Trailside camping is permitted except in the cliff area and on the W shore of the lake. A good trail system, plus old roads in various conditions.

Fishing: Salmon, rainbow and lake trout, yellow perch in the lake; some trout fishing in ponds.

Boating: State ramp on Lake Willoughby.

Ski touring, snowmobiling: Said to have some of the best snowmobiling on state land.

Publications

Public use map (trails).

Snowmobile trail map.

Headquarters

VT Dept. of Forests, Parks & Recreation, St. Johnsbury District, St. Johnsbury, VT 05819; (802) 748-8787.

Woodford State Park

Vermont Department of Forests, Parks & Recreation   South
400 acres.

From Bennington, 10 mi. E on Hwy 9.

This Park on Adams Reservoir is within the Green Mountain National Forest (see entry), at an elevation of 2,400 ft. Although we saw no trails leading from the site, it is surrounded by a network of National Forest trails, with trailheads on Hwy 9 both E and W of the site. The Long Trail crosses the highway between Bennington and the Park. The Prospect Mountain ski area is nearby.

Camping: 102 sites, including 20 lean-tos. May 7–Oct. 8. Reservations available.

Headquarters
Woodford State Park, HCR 65, Box 928, Bennington, VT 05201; (802) 447-7169. Reservations and off-season: (802) 483-2001.

NEW HAMPSHIRE

New Hampshire is magnificent, a state of high mountains and green forests, 1,300 lakes and ponds, with waterfalls and cascades, fine rivers, scenic highways, and long trails.

From the Canadian border to the MA line is almost 200 mi. The northern tip is less than 20 mi. wide, the base almost 100 mi. The Connecticut River is most of the western boundary; on the E is ME and an 18-mi. seacoast with 131 mi. of shoreline.

Terrain is dominated by the White Mountains. Elevations below 500 ft. are found only near the coast and in central and southern river valleys. Elsewhere the base elevation is 500 to 1,500 ft., except in the extreme N, where elevations reach 2,500 ft. Rising above the base are numerous hills and mountains. Many White Mountain peaks exceed 4,000 ft. Eight peaks in the Presidential Range exceed 5,000 ft. The highest is 6,288-ft. Mount Washington.

Logging the NH forests began in the 1600s, much earlier than in states to the S and W. By 1865 half of the land area had been cleared, and some farmers were abandoning their land. Much of it came back in white pine; browsing cattle kept down competitive deciduous species. Today 85% of the land is again forested.

Southern NH is experiencing severe environmental problems. Although the state had little more than a million residents in the last U.S. Census, its growth rate is double that of the next highest New England state. Almost all the explosive growth is in the S.

The numerous lakes and ponds have become almost a liability. By law, any water body of 10 acres or more is a Great Pond and state property, but the early lawmakers failed to assure public access. Today the state has legal access to only a third of its Great Ponds. On the state's largest lake, Winnepesaukee, a famous resort for 200 years, the state owns only one 600-ft. bit of shore.

In the past, one could always find a lakeside campsite or launch a boat. Today more and more lakes in the S are ringed by houses, condominiums, motels, marinas, and fishing camps.

For years the character of NH communities and the pristine quality of the lakes were maintained by consensus, the popular will. NH citizens scorned zoning and other government regulation of land use. When the wave of development rolled outward from Boston, money overwhelmed consensus. Developers swarmed, buying whatever acreage they could, especially around lakes. Once they had titles, few rules limited what they could do.

Citizen hostility to government is written into the tax structure; no income tax, no sales tax. Per capita taxes are the nation's lowest. Agencies such as the Division of Parks and Recreation have very small budgets. In seasons past, funds have sometimes been so limited that park officials couldn't say when parks would open for the season.

One reason for past legislative indifference to parks is the great mass of the White Mountains National Forest, 11.5% of the state's area, far above the eastern average for public land. Also, most private forest land was open to recreation. In the forested northern two-thirds of NH, it still is.

The state and citizen organizations are seeking more green space in the fast-growing S. Parks and Recreation now oversees 42 State Parks totaling in the neighborhood of 30,000 acres, most of them in the southern half of the state. The largest state landholding, 13,000-acre Pisgah State Park, is in the S. So are most of the woodlands of the Society for the Protection of New Hampshire Forests.

New Hampshire State Parks, an informational booklet, as well as other information on parks and recreation can be obtained from:

New Hampshire Division of Parks and Recreation
P.O. Box 1856
Concord, NH 03302-1856
(603) 271-3556

The New Hampshire Office of Travel and Tourism Development, at the same postal address as the Div. of Parks and Recreation, puts out the *Official New Hampshire Guidebook,* annually. Although it has a tourist orientation, this publication contains useful information for the camper and hiker, including a list and description of state recreation areas by region and a list of state agencies and other information sources within the state. (800) 386-4664 or (603) 271-2343.

Climate

New Hampshire's weather is influenced by elevations, prevailing west-
erlies, and the sea. It's highly changeable, with wide daily and annual
temperature swings, great differences between the same seasons in different years. The N is cooler than the S. Some of the nation's wildest
weather is recorded atop Mount Washington. Summer temperatures
throughout the state are called "delightfully comfortable" by the
National Climatic Center. Snowfall is heavier in the N, but snow cover
is continuous throughout the winter except, at times, near the coast
and the MA border.

Maps and Pathfinding

This atlas is very useful to travelers and trip planners:

> *New Hampshire Atlas and Gazetteer, The.* Freeport, ME: DeLorme
> Mapping Company, 1995.

In addition to its large maps, the *Atlas* has information on the campgrounds, canoe trips, fishing, hiking, ski touring, and much more. It
shows the boundaries of State Parks but not those of State Forests or
Wildlife Management Areas. Finding route numbers and town names
isn't easy with other maps. The *Atlas* shows the names of many rural
roads; few of these roads have street signs at intersections.

The official state highway map shows State Forest boundaries but
not those of WMAs. The Fish and Game Dept.'s publications *Hunting
Digest* and *Fishing: Recommended Waters* seem to provide as much
printed information as is available. Call the Dept. for further help in
locating sites.

We often had difficulty finding a State Forest or Wildlife Management Area. Many aren't identified by signs or boundary markers.

Flora and Fauna

With habitats ranging from ocean beaches to New England's highest
peak, summaries would have little meaning. Where information was
available, we've included it in entries. For example, the entry for Fox
Forest relates bird species to habitats. Such data are generally applicable to similar sites.

These regional references have much information relevant to New Hampshire:

AMC Field Guide to Mountain Flowers of New England. Boston: Appalachian Mountain Club, 1982. (Obtainable from the Green Mountain Club in Vermont if not elsewhere.)

DeGraaf, Richard M., and Deborah D. Rudis. *New England Wildlife: Habitat, Natural History, and Distribution.* General Technical Report NE-108. Broomwall, PA: U.S. Department of Agriculture, Forest Service, Northeastern Forest Experiment Station, 1986. (This has been unavailable in 1996, but another printing is likely.)

Kulik, Stephen, Pete Salmansohn, Matthew Schmidt, and Heidi Welch. *The Audubon Society Field Guide to the Natural Places of the Northeast: Inland.* New York: Pantheon Books, 1984.

Peterson, Roger T. *A Field Guide to Eastern Birds,* 4th ed. Boston: Houghton Mifflin, 1980.

Peterson, Roger T., and Margaret McKenny. *A Field Guide to Wildflowers of Northeastern and North-Central North America.* Boston: Houghton Mifflin, 1975.

Trails

Most backpacking and much day hiking is on the 250 trails in the White Mountain National Forest (see entry), a 1,200-mi. network. Most of the Appalachian Trail mileage in NH is within the Forest. Information sources include the following:

AMC White Mountain Guide, 25th ed. Boston: Appalachian Mountain Club, 1992.

Appalachian Trail Committee. *Appalachian Trail Guide to New Hampshire/Vermont,* Harpers Ferry, WV: Appalachian Trail Conference, 1995.

Doan, Daniel. *Fifty Hikes in the White Mountains,* 4th ed. Woodstock, VT: Countryman Press, 1990.

___. *Fifty More Hikes in New Hampshire,* 3rd ed. Woodstock, VT: Countryman Press, in press.

Trail Map and Guide to the White Mountain National Forest. Freeport, ME: DeLorme Mapping Company, 1987.

The *AMC White Mountain Guide* and *Fifty More Hikes* also describe hikes in the southern region. One of the most popular hiking areas here is Mount Monadnock (see entry), northern terminus of the Metacomet-Monadnock Trail, which begins in CT, and the E end of the Monadnock-Sunapee Greenway.

Trailside camping is permitted in the National Forest. It is prohibited on state lands except at designated sites. (To our surprise, we learned that the Society for Protection of New Hampshire Forests permits trailside camping at some of its sites, with permission only.)

Most of the northern third of NH is timber company land. We asked a few timber companies about their public use policies and got no official answers. As we understand it, visitors won't be challenged unless they ignore postings, interfere with timber operations, or misbehave by building fires or littering. Landowners have the right to close any road or area to visitors. Most hiking in these forests is on used and unused woods roads rather than trails.

Camping

The White Mountain National Forest has 21 campgrounds. Informal camping is permitted anywhere except in restricted areas. The season is generally mid-May to mid-Oct. 7 campgrounds are open all year, but without services or road plowing.

The state has 17 campgrounds in Parks and recreation areas, offering over 1,000 sites. The season generally opens mid-May, with closing dates either mid-Oct. or mid-Dec. 2 State Parks are open all year.

Reservations are now accepted at 11 of the State Parks, and pets are permitted in 10. Ask the NH Division of Parks and Recreation to send the brochure *Camping New Hampshire State Parks* (1996), which gives particulars on each area as well as reservation and fee information.

The American Automobile Association's *Northeastern CampBook* (free to members) also lists private campgrounds.

Canoeing

New Hampshire has many splendid canoe runs, from easy floating to challenging white water, including canoe-camping trips of several days. The DeLorme *Atlas* gives brief descriptions of many. More detail is provided by:

AMC River Guide: New Hampshire/Vermont, 2nd ed. Boston: Appalachian Mountain Club, 1989.

Schweiker, Roioli. *Canoe Camping Vermont and New Hampshire Rivers,* 2nd ed. Woodstock, VT: Countryman Press, in press.

Boating, Fishing

We found no comprehensive list of public boat-launching sites. However, the volume of fishing maps shows launch sites on 81 lakes, 16 rivers, and Great Bay.

New Hampshire fishing is excellent, from rushing mountain trout streams to saltwater bays, estuaries, and open sea. The fishing maps volume tells what species can be caught, not only in the mapped waters but in several hundred other ponds and streams.

Swasey, Charlton J., and Donald A. Wilson. *New Hampshire Fishing Maps.* Freeport, ME: DeLorme Mapping Company, 1993.

Hunting

New Hampshire mammals include black bear and moose as well as deer and small mammals. Moose, once near the vanishing point, have increased enough for a short hunting season to be allowed. Game bird species include waterfowl, grouse, woodcock, turkey, pheasant. Information can be obtained from

New Hampshire Fish and Game Department
2 Hazen Drive
Concord, NH 03301
(603) 271-3421

Private Organizations

Society for the Protection of New Hampshire Forests
54 Portsmouth St.
Concord, NH 03301
(603) 224-9945

Since 1901 the society has led the effort to restore and preserve forests. The White Mountain National Forest was established through its efforts, as well as several State Parks and State Forests. The society has 96 preserves, some of them model woodlands. Its unique headquarters complex and surrounding preserve are well worth a visit. On a wooded hill overlooking the Merrimack River and the city of Concord, the HQ uses innovative means to minimize energy required for heating or cooling in any season. A cassette tour is offered, and a 2-mi. interpretive hiking trail explores native plants on the 90-acre site. Our contact spoke of great bird-watching opportunities there, including winter birdwatching on cross-country skis. He was also glad to recommend specific society sites for specific outdoor interests—for birding, say, or canoeing, or wildflower observation.

Publications include *Land Map and Guide,* describing many of the Society's preserves. A 1-page listing of complete holdings, with acreage, date of purchase, and location is also available, along with information pages on a number of the areas.

Audubon Society of New Hampshire
3 Silk Farm Road
Concord, NH 03301
(603) 224-9909

As part of its comprehensive program of nature education and preservation, the society maintains 21 preserves, most of them in the southern third of NH. Some, like Paradise Point, have nature centers with many activities. Others, like Deering, are isolated and quiet refuges. Many publications, including *Wildlife Sanctuaries and Programs Centers,* free, with S.A.S.E. Trail maps for individual centers are 50 cents each.

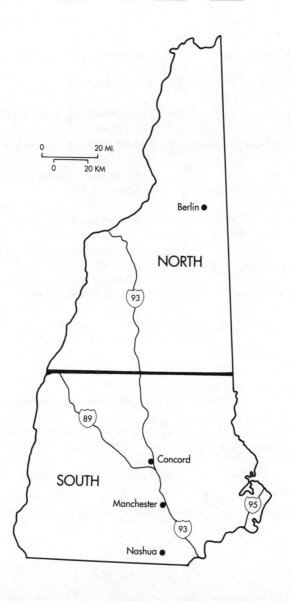

NH

NEW HAMPSHIRE

0 — 20 MI.
0 — 20 KM

Berlin ●

NORTH

93

89

● Concord

SOUTH

Manchester ●

95

93

Nashua ●

Natural Areas in New Hampshire

An Alphabetical Listing

Androscoggin River
North

Annett State Forest
South

Appalachian Trail
North

Bear Brook State Park
South

Cardigan State Park and State Forest
North

Charles L. Peirce Wildlife and Forest Reservation
South

Coleman State Park
North

Connecticut Lakes State Forest
North

Connecticut River
North/South

Crawford Notch State Park
North

Deering Wildlife Preserve
South

Dixville Notch State Park
North

Echo Lake State Park
North

Enfield Wildlife Management Area
South

Fox State Forest
South

Franconia Notch State Park
North

Franklin Falls Reservoir
South

Gap Mountain
South

Gile Memorial State Forest
South

Grafton Pond Reservation
South

Great Bay National Estuarine Research Reserve
South

Hemenway State Forest
North

Hopkinton and Everett Lakes
South

John Hay National Wildlife Refuge/Hay Reservation
South

Jones Brook Wildlife Management Area
South

Kearsarge, Mount
South

Lake Francis State Park
North

Lake Umbagog National Wildlife Refuge
North

Lost River Reservation
North

Merrimack River
South

Miller State Park
South

Monadnock, Mount
South

Monadnock-Sunapee Greenway
South

Moose Brook State Park
North

Mount Sunapee State Park
South

Odiorne Point State Park
South

Ossipee Lake/Heath Pond Bog
North

Pack-Monadnock Mountain
South

Paradise Point Nature Center
South

Pawtuckaway State Park
South

Peabody Forest
North

Pillsbury State Park
South

Pine River State Forest
North

Pisgah State Park
South

Pondicherry Wildlife Refuge
North

Rhododendron Natural Area
South

Squam Lakes Region
North

Taves Reservation
South

Wapack National Wildlife Refuge
South

Washington, Mount
North

White Lake State Park
North

White Mountain National Forest
North

Willard Pond Preserve
South

Natural Areas in New Hampshire

by Zone

NORTH ZONE

Androscoggin River
Appalachian Trail
Coleman State Park
Connecticut Lakes State Forest
Connecticut River
Crawford Notch State Park
Dixville Notch State Park
Echo Lake State Park
Franconia Notch State Park
Hemenway State Forest
Lake Francis State Park
Lake Umbagog National Wildlife Refuge
Lost River Reservation
Moose Brook State Park
Mount Cardigan State Park and State Forest
Ossipee Lake/Heath Pond Bog
Peabody Forest
Pine River State Forest
Pondicherry Wildlife Refuge
Squam Lakes Region
Washington, Mount
White Lake State Park
White Mountain National Forest

SOUTH ZONE

Annett State Forest
Bear Brook State Park
Charles L. Peirce Wildlife and Forest Reservation
Connecticut River
Deering Wildlife Preserve
Enfield Wildlife Management Area
Fox State Forest
Franklin Falls Reservoir
Gap Mountain
Gile Memorial State Forest
Grafton Pond Reservation
Great Bay National Estuarine Research Reserve
Hopkinton and Everett Lakes
John Hay National Wildlife Refuge/Hay Reservation
Jones Brook Wildlife Management Area
Kearsarge, Mount
Merrimack River
Miller State Park
Monadnock, Mount
Monadnock-Sunapee Greenway

Mount Sunapee State Park

Odiorne Point State Park

Pack-Monadnock Mountain

Paradise Point Nature Center

Pawtuckaway State Park

Pillsbury State Park

Pisgah State Park

Rhododendron Natural Area

Taves Reservation

Wapack National Wildlife Refuge

Willard Pond Preserve

Androscoggin River

35 river miles.   North

From Errol to Berlin beside Hwy 16.

With rapids to class II and III and a relatively long season, this is one of NH's most popular canoe runs. The shoreline is relatively undeveloped, but there's little public land along the route.

Annett State Forest

New Hampshire Division of Forests and Lands   South
1,336 acres.

From US 202 at Jaffrey, SE on local roads past Squantum.

The Forest includes more than half of the shoreline of Hubbard Pond, an irregularly shaped water body about 1¼ mi. long. Hubbard Pond Rd. crosses the Forest, which is typical of southern NH: flat to rolling terrain, second-growth northern hardwoods with some pine and hemlock.

Activities

Hiking: On old woods roads.

Hunting: Deer, small game.

Fishing: Smallmouth bass, pickerel, bullhead, yellow perch.

Adjacent

Perry Reservation (Society for the Protection of New Hampshire Forests, 504 acres). From Jaffrey, 4.5 mi. E on Hwy 124. Park at historical marker for Wilder Chair Factor.

The site has 2 mi. of frontage on Hwy 124. The central feature is Tophet Swamp. It can be explored by canoeing on the Gridley River, but with several beaver dam portages.

Headquarters
NH Div. of Forests and Lands, P.O. Box 1856, Concord, NH 03302-1856; (603) 271-3556.

Appalachian Trail
Mixed ownership North

Maine to Vermont.

The trail enters NH from ME in the Mahoosuc Range, N of the White Mountain National Forest. Most of its NH mileage is within the Forest, and most trail hiking is here. Between the Forest and the VT border, the trail is mostly on private land, with some sections on public roads.

Bear Brook State Park
New Hampshire Division of Parks and Recreation South

9,585 acres.

From Manchester, N on US 3, then NE on Hwy 28 to sign on right.

The principal recreation area on Catamount Pond can accommodate 1,500 visitors in the picnic area, more on the beach and in the play areas. It's crowded in good weather. However, the trail system is extensive, and relatively few visitors venture beyond the developed area.

It was originally a National Park site. Facilities were built by the Civilian Conservation Corps. It was leased to the state in 1941 and eventually transferred to state ownership.

Terrain is rolling to steep. Elevation of Bear Hill is 800 ft., about 400 ft. above its base; Hall Mountain, in the S of the Park, rises to 925 ft. The area is heavily wooded. Bear Brook flows N from Hall Mountain marsh. There are 5 ponds in addition to Catamount and a number of small streams.

Interpretation

Bear Brook Nature Center is operated cooperatively with the NH Audubon Society. *Exhibits, nature trails, daily naturalist programs in summer.*

Activities

Camping: 93 tent sites. Mid-May to mid-Oct. The camping area is reserved for campers and has its own beach. Reservations through Labor Day. Pets OK.

Hiking: Over 30 mi. of hiking trails.

Hunting: Deer and small game.

Fishing: Brook trout and panfish; ponds and streams. One pond is reserved for fly fishing.

Swimming: Supervised beach.

Canoeing: Catamount Pond, Beaver Pond. Rentals available.

Ski touring: On marked trails apart from those used by snowmobilers.

Publications

Information for campers.

Headquarters

Bear Brook State Park, RFD 1, Box 507, Allenstown, NH 03275; (603) 485-9869. Reservations: (603) 271-3628.

Cardigan State Park and State Forest

New Hampshire Division of Parks and Recreation/New Hampshire Division of Forests and Lands   North
5,655 acres.

Off US 4 and Hwy 118, about 4½ mi. from Canaan.

Mount Cardigan, 3,121 ft., is popular with hikers. A network of trails surrounds the mountain, offering several routes to the top. More than a century ago, vegetation on the upper slope was destroyed by fire. Consequent erosion stripped the dome to bare rock. A fire tower is at the top, and the sweeping vistas are fine.

Hiking: The shortest and easiest route to the summit is West Ridge Trail, 1.3 mi. High trails lead to nearby peaks including Firescrew, 3,040 ft., and South, 2,290 ft. More than 30 mi. of trails in the network.

Nearby

Cardigan Mountain Reservation: 1,200 acres. Just E of the Park boundary. The Appalachian Mountain Club maintains a lodge here for hikers and backpackers, and many choose to use this as a starting point for hiking the area. There are 50 mi. of trails on the reservation. Some campsites are available. From Bristol, N on Hwy 3A to S end of Newfound Lake, then 9.3 mi. W. Contact: AMC Cardigan Lodge, RFD 1, Box 712, Bristol, NH 03222; (603) 744-8011.

Wellington State Beach. On Newfound Lake, 4 mi. N of Bristol off Hwy 3A.

Paradise Point Nature Center (see entry).

Headquarters

NH Div. of Parks and Recreation, P.O. Box 1856, Concord, NH 03302-1856; (603) 271-3556.

....

Charles L. Peirce Wildlife and Forest Reservation

Society for the Protection of New Hampshire Forests   South
3,576 acres.

From Hwy 9 in Stoddard, 2 mi. W on Hwy 123. Turn right at fire station. Cross bridge, bear right on dirt road about 1 mi. Park on left. Trout-n-Bacon Trailhead at small brook, about 100 ft. back.

This appears to be the society's largest property. The site extends about 4 mi. N from the trailhead. Terrain is hilly. Some areas are intensively managed for timber and wildlife. Others will remain wild. The site is noted for its wildflowers. The 5-mi. Trout-n-Bacon Trail offers outstanding views from Bacon Ledge and leads to scenic Trout Pond. Altogether, over 20 mi. of trails and woods roads ascend ridges, traverse deep forests, pass beaver dams. Many organizations have chosen this site for field trips.

There is camping here by permission only.
No bicycles or motorized vehicles.

Adjacent

Thurston V. William Family Forest, 379 acres, another society property, adjoins on the NW. Features include old-growth forest with large birch, white pine, sugar and red maples, beech, hemlock, and white ash. Access is a bit complicated, so we recommend obtaining the society's *Lands Map and Guide,* which has map and directions. It is recommended that hikers have compasses.

Headquarters

Society for the Protection of NH Forests, 54 Portsmouth St., Concord, NH 03301; (603) 224-9945.

....

Coleman State Park

New Hampshire Division of Parks and Recreation/New Hampshire
Division of Forests and Lands   North
1,685 acres.

From US 3 at Colebrook, 6 mi. E on Hwy 26 to Kidderville, then N on Diamond Pond Rd. about 6 mi.

Northern NH is mountainous, rugged, largely roadless except for logging roads. Coleman is on Little Diamond Pond, in the spruce/fir country, surrounded by near-wilderness. Hwy 26 is a scenic route, crossing the White Mountains at Dixville Notch. The developed Park area is 33 acres, the rest managed as a State Forest.

In this area, the state has developed an extensive network of snowmobile trails on timber company land. The distances between roads or settlements are great, snows usually deep, winters cold. One section of the Androscoggin Trail crosses the Park, a 55-mi. hiking route. Hiking guides mention no trails in this north country, but the woods invite the adventurous.

Activities

Camping: 30 tent sites on the shore of Little Diamond Pond. Mid-May to mid-Dec. (Limited services after mid-Oct.) No reservations. Pet permitted.

Fishing: Trout.

Boating: Boat launch. Small boats only.

Headquarters

Coleman State Park, RFD 1, Box 183, Colebrook, NH 03576; (603) 237-4520.

....

Connecticut Lakes State Forest

New Hampshire Division of Forests and Lands   North
1,548 acres.

Both sides of US 3 for about 10 mi. S of the Quebec boundary.

The Forest is a narrow strip of land beside the highway. It would be called a parkway in more developed country. The country beyond the strip is rugged, wild, and densely forested, roadless except for logging roads. The strip provides access to First, Second, and Third Connecticut Lakes, through which the Connecticut River flows.

The general elevation is 1,200 to 1,400 ft., with nearby ridges over 2,000 ft. Most surrounding land is privately owned. Timber companies generally tolerate visitors on their land, but keep away from areas being logged and don't get in the way of logging trucks. Unused logging roads soon revert to muskeg.

Birds: The NH Audubon Society considers this a prime birding area, especially for Canadian Zone species, but we couldn't find a local list. Reported species include black-backed and northern three-toed woodpeckers, spruce grouse, woodcock, saw-whet owl, raven, Philadelphia vireo, Traill's and yellow-bellied flycatchers, boreal chickadee, red-breasted nuthatch, crossbills, purple finch, goldfinch, evening grosbeak, Swainson's thrush, gray jay, ruby-crowned and golden-crowned kinglets, 7 warblers. On the lakes: common loon, ring-necked duck, goldeneye, mergansers.

Mammals: All species common to the region, including moose, black bear, white-tailed deer, bobcat, fox, otter, raccoon, porcupine.

Features

First Connecticut Lake: 2,807 acres. Lake has a 19-mi. undeveloped shoreline in near-wilderness. Some of the best trout and salmon fishing in NH. Ice-out about May 1. Unpaved ramp near the dam. Some adjoining marshes.

Second Connecticut Lake: 1,286 acres. 11 mi. of wooded shoreline. Also good trout and salmon fishing. Ice-out about mid-May. Launch on Idlewild Rd., off US 3.

Third Connecticut Lake: 278 acres, at the Quebec border, is a natural body, not dammed. Launch site but no ramp. Good fishing.

East Inlet Natural Area: Managed by The Nature Conservancy. The access road is on the right, just N of Second Connecticut Lake. East Inlet Pond is about 2 mi. up this road. About 3 mi. beyond is a trail to a 143-acre tract of virgin red spruce and balsam fir at Norton Pool on East Inlet Stream. This area is open to the public but serviced by a private road.

Activities

Camping: 20 primitive sites at Deer Mountain Campground, 20 mi. N of Pittsburg on Hwy 3. Mid-May to mid-Dec. (Limited services after mid-Oct.) Reservations accepted. Pets OK. Camping also at Lake Francis State Park (see entry), outside of Pittsburg.

Fishing: Trout and salmon.

Headquarters

Connecticut Lakes State Forest, RFD 2, Box 241, Lancaster, NH 03584; (603) 538-6965. Reservations: (603) 271-3628.

....

Connecticut River

Mixed ownership   North/South
260 river miles.

From Pittsburg to Vernon Dam near MA border.

New England's longest river forms most of the VT–NH boundary. From the Canadian border, it flows through the Connecticut Lakes (see entry). The first canoe trip begins at the upper end of First Connecticut Lake.

The river valley was settled early in the colonial period. The primeval forest was felled and huge logs were floated down the river. Dams provided power for mills. Roads were built on both sides of the river. Along some sections, however, new forests on the floodplain shut out the sound and sight of road traffic and sometimes farmland lies between river and road.

Most canoeists choose these quiet sections, but it's possible to canoe the entire 260 miles. Although river flow is controlled by dams, all but the segment just below Pittsburg can be floated at any time, and that segment most of the time. The several portages are not difficult. Long segments of flat water and quick water are punctuated by class I and II rapids and some avoidable hazards.

Camping: May be a problem. Only a few public or private campgrounds are along the way, often more than a day's travel apart. However, one can usually find an informal site without attracting unfavorable attention.

Fishing: From the Connecticut Lakes to North Stratford, this is a blue-ribbon trout stream. Farther down, it becomes a warmwater bass fishery.

Publications

AMC River Guide: New Hampshire, Vermont, 2nd ed. Boston: Appalachian Mountain Club, 1989.

Barton, Mark, et al. (eds.). *The Complete Boating Guide to the Connecticut River,* 2nd ed. Available from the Connecticut River Watershed Council, 1 Ferry St., Easthampton, MA 01027; (413) 529-9500.

Wilson, Alex. *AMC Quiet Water Canoe Guide: New Hampshire/Vermont.* Boston: Appalachian Mountain Club, 1989.

....

Crawford Notch State Park

New Hampshire Division of Parks and Recreation   North
5,950 acres.

At Hart's Location on US 302, 12 mi. N of Barlett.

This 6-mi. mountain pass through some of the most rugged terrain of the White Mountains has been a well-traveled route since stagecoach days. The scenic 1½-mi.-wide strip is surrounded by White Mountain

National Forest (see entry). The Notch is at 1,773 ft. Several nearby peaks are well above 3,700 ft., still higher ones not far off. The Appalachian Trail crosses the Park, and other trails lead to points of interest.

When loggers were felling white pines all around, the then owner of the Notch kept his forest intact. In 1911 the Society for the Protection of NH Forests persuaded the state legislature to buy it, before the National Forest was established.

Features

Arethusa Falls, one of NH's highest, is reached by a moderately steep 1 ½-mi. trail.

Silver Cascade can be seen from the road.

Frankenstein Cliff is W of the highway, across from the campground.

A *nature trail* is near the Park office.

Activities

Camping: 30 tent sites at Dry River Campground. Pets OK.

Fishing: Nearby trout streams.

Headquarters

Crawford Notch State Park, P.O. Box 177, Twin Mountain, NH 03595; (603) 374-2272.

....

Deering Wildlife Preserve

Audubon Society of New Hampshire   South
500 acres.

W of Manchester. S on Hwy 149 at Hillsboro. Go 1 mi., turn left onto Clement Hill Rd. After 1½ mi. look for preserve sign marking right turn; parking area is ⅜ mi., on right.

Open dawn to dusk.

For a quiet hike in an out-of-the way forest, this is the place. The society told us in 1996 that many improvements have been made here since our first edition.

From the parking area take the yellow-blazed trails into the woods. The forest now is mostly a mix of northern hardwoods, trees 4-6 in. in diameter, but we saw a few ancient white pines, so gnarled and twisted the loggers had let them be. A few hundred yards into the woods we came to a massive stone wall, once the boundary of a field.

Follow the trail out of the forest into the old orchard, where it's possible to find scarlet tanagers and indigo buntings singing together from the tops of the apple trees. Many wildflowers in spring. At Black Fox Pond there are signs of beaver activity, and a host of green frogs during warm weather. Wood ducks and hooded mergansers frequent the nesting boxes here. At this point either continue via yellow blazes to pine, balsam fir, and hemlock forest and back to Old Clement Rd. or make other trail choices on the property. (The red-blazed Hemlock Woods Trail is evidently a fine place to look for porcupines.) We suggest taking a good look at the guide to the area before beginning your hike.

Winter and spring road conditions can make travel difficult. Call HQ before setting out in those seasons.

Publication
Trail guide, 50 cents.

Headquarters
Audubon Society of NH, 3 Silk Farm Rd., Concord, NH 03301; (603) 224-9909.

DePierrefeu Willard Pond Sanctuary
See Willard Pond Preserve.

Dixville Notch State Park
New Hampshire Division of Parks and Recreation   North
137 acres.

On Hwy 26 between Colebrook and Errol.

Hwy 26 is a fine scenic highway. The Notch is a rocky cleft in the mountains (at 1,600 ft.) through which the highway squeezes. A scenic gorge and waterfalls are on Flume and Cascade Brooks. Hiking trails and woods roads lead to Table Rock and to nearby mountains in the surrounding near-wilderness area. The vistas here are often dramatic.

Headquarters
NH Div. of Parks and Recreation, P.O. Box 1856, Concord, NH 03302-1856; (603) 271-3556. On site: (603) 788-3155.

Echo Lake State Park
New Hampshire Division of Parks and Recreation   North
396 acres.

From North Conway on US 302, 1.5 mi. W on Westside Rd.

Open dawn to dusk daily from Memorial Day, daily late June to Labor Day.

Most visitors come to picnic and swim, but there are attractive hiking trails around Echo Lake and up to Cathedral and White Horse ledges. The Park is a popular rock climbing site. Cathedral Ledge can also be reached by an auto road that offers beautiful views of the White Mountains and of the Saco River Valley, some 700 ft. below.

Headquarters
NH Div. of Parks and Recreation, P.O. Box 1856, Concord, NH 03302-1856; (603) 271-3556. On site: (603) 356-2672; (603) 788-3155 off-season.

Enfield Wildlife Management Area
New Hampshire Fish and Game Department   South
2,600 acres.

From Enfield Center, S on Hwy 4 A. Right on Bog Rd. about 2 mi. Sign and parking on right.

When we visited, a rough washboard on Bog Rd. helped cars churn up clouds of dust. At other times, birders would enjoy walking the road, which offers brook, ponds, marsh, fields, and woods.

The sign and small parking area are the trailhead for Cole Pond. It's a mile-plus hike on a pleasant trail, ascending gradually from swamp forest to a 17-acre pond in a scenic setting. Fly fishing only. The couple we met on the trail had been swimming. "Delightful!" they said.

The forest is mostly mixed northern hardwoods with a few scattered large white pines, the understory generally light enough to permit bushwhacking.

No site map is available, and we saw no boundary signs. Along Bog Rd. are unmarked gates that may indicate state land. The WMA includes frontage on George Pond, at the 4A-Bog Rd. intersection, which attracts many waterfowl in season. The WMA borders 96-acre Smith Pond (which is closed to fishing) and 7-acre Halfmile Pond. Prospect Hill, 2,100 ft., seems to be the highest point. On the upper slopes, the mixed hardwoods merge into spruce/fir.

Activities

Hunting: Deer, upland game.

Fishing: Brook trout in Cole Pond. Brook trout, largemouth bass, pickerel, bullhead, and yellow perch in George Pond.

Swimming: Unsupervised, in Cole Pond, other ponds.

Nearby
Grafton Pond (see entry).

Headquarters
NH Fish and Game Dept., 2 Hazen Dr., Concord, NH 03301; (603) 271-3421.

....

Fox State Forest
New Hampshire Division of Forests and Lands South
1,432 acres.

From US 202 at Hillsborough, NW on Hwy 107.

In 1922 Caroline A. Fox donated the original 348 acres and established a trust fund that has supported a continuing program of research and education. Far more information about flora and fauna is offered here than at other state sites, in publications, exhibits, classes, and nature trails.

The area is hilly, moderately rugged. Much of it was open farmland in the 1930s. The resident research forester undertook comparative studies, letting some sections revert naturally, planting others with larch, Scotch pine, jack pine, spruce, and Douglas-fir. Most of the site is again forested. Some portions of the original forest remain, never logged so far as is known.

The site has over 20 mi. of roads and foot trails.

Plants: Lists of trees, flowering plants, and ferns are available. Native trees include white, red, and pitch pines, red and black spruce, balsam fir, eastern red cedar, tamarack, eastern hemlock; hardwoods include black willow, trembling and large-toothed aspen, butternut, shagbark hickory, black, yellow, paper, and gray birches, speckled alder, red and white oaks, sugar, red, and striped maples. Also identified are the numerous introduced species, American and exotic. The extensive shrub list includes American yew, sweet gale, spice bush, witch hazel, shadbush, wild plum, dogwoods, blueberries, snowberry, withe rod.

Birds: Summer checklist suggests where to look for various species. Species include doves, ruby-throated hummingbird, yellow-bellied sapsucker, 4 woodpeckers, eastern phoebe, eastern wood-pewee, tree and barn swallows, black-capped chickadee, tufted titmouse, 2 nuthatches, eastern bluebird, northern oriole, rose-breasted grosbeak, 5 hawks, kestrel, 4 swallows, indigo bunting, ruffed grouse, 3 owls, many warblers. In marshes: pied-billed grebe, great blue heron, American bittern, black and wood ducks, mallard, hooded merganser, belted kingfisher, red-winged blackbird.

Mammals: Include snowshoe hare, red and gray squirrels, chipmunk, fox, porcupine, raccoon, beaver, skunk, otter, muskrat, mink, white-tailed deer, occasional bobcat.

Interpretation

Forestry museum.

Environmental center used chiefly for classes, groups.

Mud Pond natural area, reached by 1-mi. trail, has a quaking bog with insectivorous plants, beaver lodge.

Hemlock Ravine natural area, along Gerry Brook, has an old-growth stand of beech and hemlock.

Black Gum Swamp natural area is a glacial kettle that has evolved into a forest growing on a deep bed of peat.

Nature trails include Mushroom Trail, Tree Identification Loop Trail.

Publication

Fox Forest Notes (bulletin series).

Trail guide (leaflet with map).

Checklists of plants, birds.

Headquarters

Fox State Forest, School St., Hillsboro, NH 03244; (603) 464-3453.

....

Franconia Notch State Park

New Hampshire Division of Parks and Recreation   North
6,440 acres.

On I-93 about 10 mi. S of Franconia.

The 8-mi.-long pass between the peaks of the Franconia and Kinsman ranges is one of the most spectacular areas in the White Mountains. It is also one of the busiest. A recent Park leaflet says, "Interstate 93 through Franconia Notch has resulted in over $20 million dollars in new visitor facilities . . ." (and considerably more traffic and congestion!). The Notch is surrounded by the White Mountain National Forest, however, and numerous trails offer routes to places of quiet beauty.

Elevations in the Park range from 1,200 to 2,000 ft. Nearby peaks include 5,249-ft. Mt. Lafayette, 4,040-ft. Cannon Mountain. The Pemigewasset River flows through the Notch. Profile Lake and Echo Lake are beside the highway.

Since I-93 is now the only road through the Notch, it's advisable to have the Park leaflet or other detailed map at hand, so as to choose the right exit. To drive from HQ to the campground or the Flume visitor center, one must get back on the Interstate.

Plants: Trees of the valley floor are mostly northern hardwoods, uncut since the late 1800s: yellow birch, beech, sugar maple. Above 2,000 ft. on the hillsides are mature red spruce and balsam fir with some European white birch, the less accessible areas never logged. Flowers of the valley include Dutchman's-breeches, spring beauty, violets, trilliums, Solomon's seal. On slopes up to 4,500 ft. are subalpine flowers, many blooming in May and early June. Above timberline, some arctic species occur.

Birds: Large flocks of Canada and snow geese often migrate through the valley. Other waterfowl are sometimes seen on the lakes. Many hawks come through, as well as golden and bald eagles and raven. About 100 species have been recorded.

Mammals: Severe winters and deep snow limit resident mammal populations. Bear and moose are occasional visitors. Deer are present, not abundant. More common species include red fox, weasel, snowshoe hare, porcupine, mink, fisher, raccoon, bobcat, chipmunk, mole, woodchuck. Most streams are too rapid for beaver.

Features

The *Flume* is a unique geological area with an 800-ft. gorge, walls 70-90 ft. high, width as narrow as 12 ft. Other features include Avalanche Falls, Liberty Gorge and Cascade, water-washed Table Rock, glacier-deposited boulders. The area has a network of trails.

Old Man of the Mountains is a 40-ft. "profile" in granite 1,200 ft. above Profile Lake. The profile is formed of 5 rock ledges jutting from a sheer cliff.

Cannon Mountain, a ski area, has North America's first aerial passenger tram, which transports summer visitors to the top for fine vistas. An observation tower is near the tram station. One can also hike to the top, which is at 4,180 ft. Many species of alpine flowers in season.

The *Basin,* beside the highway, is a 20-ft. granite pothole at the base of a waterfall.

Interpretation

George Gilman visitor center has film introduction to the Park's natural and cultural history.

Interpretive panels are located throughout the Park.

Activities

Camping: 97 sites. Late May to mid.-Oct. Reservations accepted.

Hiking, backpacking: The Appalachian Trail crosses the Park. Several Appalachian Mountain Club huts are within hiking range. Local trails to Artist Bluff, Bald Mountain, Lonesome Lake, Mt. Pemigewasset, other points of interest.

Fishing: Brook rout stocked in Echo and Profile Lakes.

Swimming: In Echo Lake.

Bicycling: Bike path.

Skiing, ski touring: At Cannon Mountain.

Publications

Leaflet with map.

Flume Guide, The.

Roaring River Nature Trail Guide.

Headquarters

Franconia Notch State Park, Franconia, NH 03580; (603) 823-5563. Reservations: (603) 823-9513.

....

Franklin Falls Reservoir

New Hampshire Fish and Game Department/New Hampshire Division of Forests and Lands South 3,704 acres.

Along the Pemigewasset River between Bristol and Franklin. Access from Hwy 3A and 127.

The Franklin Falls Dam near Franklin was built by the U.S. Army Corps of Engineers for flood control. The reservoir, on the long, narrow floodplain, is normally empty, and the Pemigewasset River flows through. In the late 1960s, the river was heavily polluted. Now it's clean enough for fishing and pleasant canoeing. Perhaps for swimming, although we wouldn't try it after a rainstorm. The area is managed by the NH Div. of Forests and Lands, whose first task is forest improvement.

Activities

Hunting: Pheasants have been stocked.

Fishing: Brook and rainbow trout. Sections near the road are heavily fished, remote sections lightly.

Canoeing: The run from Bristol to Franklin, 15 mi., depends in part on water releases from a hydroelectric dam. Rapids to class II, with stretches of flat water.

Headquarters

NH Fish and Game Dept., 2 Hazen Dr., Concord, NH 03301; (603) 271-3421.

Gap Mountain

Society for the Protection of New Hampshire Forests   South
1,142 acres.

From Troy, take Hwy 12 0.4 mi. S. Turn left on Quarry Rd. Go 0.8 mi. and park at a sharp left turn in the road. Hike up hill, look for white blazes on left, which take you to the site.

Many fine natural areas in New England have been saved from development by concerned citizens and landowners. The story of Gap Mountain is more complex than most, acquisitions being made over more than a decade. The *Monadnock Guide,* available from the society, tells how it was done.

SW of the more imposing Mount Monadnock, Gap has three main peaks, the highest 1,862 ft. It's an easier climb. The northern and middle peaks are mostly open. The wooded southern peak is a protected natural area. The land also includes two bogs and a rich variety of flora and fauna. The Metacomet-Monadnock Trail crosses the site. There are superb views, and seasonal blueberries.

No camping. No wheeled or motorized vehicles on this or any society property.

Publications
Monadnock Guide.

Headquarters
Society for the Protection of NH Forests, 54 Portsmouth St., Concord, NH 03301; (603) 224-9945.

Gile Memorial State Forest

New Hampshire Division of Forests and Lands   South
6,681 acres.

Crossed by Hwy 4A, near Springfield.

The DeLorme *Atlas* map shows the boundaries of the Forest but not the private inholdings, of which there are many along Hwy 4A. We saw one Forest sign where the highway leaves the Forest on the SE side; also a parking area and trailhead at Mud Pond. Several old woods roads along the highway looked promising for hiking but not for vehicles without 4-wheel drive.

The terrain is flat to rolling, with a few hills and scattered small wetlands. The land, once cleared, is now heavily forested with mixed northern hardwoods, pine, and hemlock.

Except in hunting season, the site has few visitors.

Headquarters
NH Div. of Forests and Lands, P.O. Box 1856, Concord, NH 03302-1856; (603) 271-3556.

Grafton Pond Reservation
Society for the Protection of New Hampshire Forests   South
940 acres/235-acre lake.

From Enfield, SE on Hwy 4A. Left on Bluejay Rd.

A natural pond was raised by a dam. The society acquired the surrounding land in 1984, assuring that the lake would remain undeveloped. With depths to 66 ft., a rocky shoreline, and many small islands, it's a lightly fished, highly regarded smallmouth bass fishery. The 7-mi. shoreline provides many nesting sites for loons. Many anglers fly-fish from canoes.

Motors are limited to 6 hp.
Camping is prohibited.

Nearby
Enfield Wildlife Management Area (see entry).

Headquarters
Society for the Protection of NH Forests, 54 Portsmouth St., Concord, NH 03301; (603) 224-9945.

Great Bay National Estuarine Research Reserve

New Hampshire Fish and Game Department   South
5,280 acres.

10 mi. inland along the Piscataqua River, which forms the NH–ME border. Access at Adams Point in Durham; water access via Little Bay or the Piscataqua River.

Great Bay is part of the National Estuarine Research Reserve System. It is a large "drowned river valley" estuary, made up of over 4,000 acres of tidal waters and mud flats and roughly 50 mi. of inland shoreline. 800 acres of upland habitat include salt marsh, tidal creeks, mixed woodlands, and fields that have been logged and cleared since colonial times. Research activities are an important part of all the Estuarine Reserves. Here focus is on an eelgrass disease, on the protection of oyster beds and clam flats from pollution, and on the study of bird populations, including the bald eagle. The U of NH and the Friends of Great Bay also help support Great Bay programs.

Interpretation
Sandy Point Interpretive Center. At S end of Great Bay has a *2 mi. self-guided nature trail* through the salt marsh. Also exhibits on the estuary. Special *educational programs* for all ages are scheduled throughout the year. Open all year, call for hours. Center is reached from Depot Rd., off Hwy 101, at Greenland.

Publication
Tour of the Reserves, A.

Headquarters
Great Bay NERR, NH Fish and Game Dept., 225 Main St., Durham, NH 03824; (603) 868-1095. Sandy Point Interpretive Center (603) 778-0015.

Hay Reservation

See John Hay National Wildlife Refuge/Hay Reservation.

Hemenway State Forest

New Hampshire Division of Forests and Lands   North
1,958 acres.

From Conway 9 mi. SW on Hwy 16 to Chocorua; W 2 mi. on Hwy 113,
then NW on Hwy 113A.

The Forest, just S of the White Mountain National Forest, is rolling to
hilly, mostly in conifers, chiefly white pine. The *Big Pines Natural Area,*
125 acres, is a 150-year-old coniferous forest on a wild river. The
largest white pine has a 42-in. diameter.

Hiking: On old woods roads and local trails. Trail to lookout tower.
Nearby, off Hwy 16, are trails to Mt. Chocorua and other destinations.
(Mt. Chocorua has been called the state's most-climbed mountain,
but the most popular hiking routes are from the Kancamagus Hwy on
the N.)

Nearby

Lovejoy Marsh Wildlife Preserve, 6 mi. from Conway, is a beaver marsh
with good birding. A dirt road crosses the marsh. *Chocorua Lake,* 222
acres, at the base of Mount Chocorua, is 3 mi. further. Fishing for
brook trout, smallmouth bass, pickerel, hornpout, best from mid-
April to early June. Hand-carried boats can be launched; no motors.
White Lake State Park (see entry). Camping.

Headquarters

NH Div. of Forests and Lands, P.O. Box 1856, Concord, NH 03302-
1856; (603) 271-3556.

Hopkinton and Everett Lakes

U.S. Army Corps of Engineers/New Hampshire Division of Parks and
Recreation/New Hampshire Fish and Game Department   South
7,342 acres of land; 650 acres of permanent water.

W of Concord. From I-89, Exit 2, then W on Hwy 13 to Dunbarton. Or
Exit 6 from I-89, then 3 mi. W on Hwy 127.

The Hopkinton Dam on the Contoocook River and the Everett Dam on the Piscataquog River, some miles to the S, were built in 1962-63 for flood control. They formed relatively small permanent pools connected by a canal and Drew Lake, with far more extensive storage areas branching along the floodplains of the two rivers and tributary streams. The project required relocation or abandonment of state and local roads, a railroad line, power and telephone lines.

The maps suggest a cluttered area. It isn't. Driving along the secondary roads we saw some private homes, but most of the land above the floodplain is heavily wooded, young northern hardwoods with scattered white pines, spruce and fir intermixed on upper hillsides.

Birds: No checklist or species record is available, but the variety of habitats indicates a diversity of species, including water fowl and shorebirds in season.

Mammals: Fish and Game says all upland species except moose and bear.

Features

The federal land is available for public use. Most of it has been leased to the state agencies for recreation management. The person we spoke with on-site in 1996 said that they are now promoting the lakes as "a natural resources area." The principal feature are shown on the DeLorme *Atlas* maps, but the map available from the Corps is easier to read. Sites of special interest include

Elm Brook Pool Park: near Hopkinton Dam and Information Center. Boat launch, swimming, picnicking, nature trail.

Clough State Park: swimming, picnicking.

Drew Lake and canal: Boat launch.

Stark Pond: 60-acre open water marsh. Fishing.

Stumpfield Marsh: 95-acre open marsh. Boat launch, fishing.

The sites with swimming and picnicking are crowded on warm summer weekends.

Activities

Hiking: Trails, both marked and unmarked; bushwhacking is feasible.

Hunting: Good waterfowl hunting. Pheasant stocked.

Fishing: We saw a few people fishing.

Bicycling: Both mountain bikes and ATVs are popular.

Snowmobiling: A major activity in this area, according to HQ.

Nearby
Smith Pond Bog, 55 acres, a Audubon Society preserve, has a kettlehole pond surrounded by a bog with a red maple swamp. Boardwalk. Great botanical diversity. Access is by Hwy 9, ½ mi. W of Hopkinton Village. Trail is opposite Gage Hill Rd.

Publication
Leaflet with map.

Headquarters
U.S. Army Corps of Engineers, Hopkinton Lake, 2097 Maple St., Contoocook, NH 03229-3370; (603) 746-3601.

....

John Hay National Wildlife Refuge/Hay Reservation

U.S. Fish and Wildlife Service/Society for the Protection of New Hampshire Forests   South
163 acres/673 acres.

From Concord, about 30 mi. NW on Hwy 103 to the S end of Lake Sunapee. Access to the area is from Hwy 103A.

Open dawn to dusk.

The refuge occupies the estate of John Hay, who was personal secretary to President Lincoln, and later secretary of state in the administrations of Presidents McKinley and Theodore Roosevelt. The Hay family's 1987 bequest to the U.S. Fish and Wildlife Service included the 10-acre site of the family home, The Fells, and its landscaped gardens, which are presently administered at the refuge as a State of New Hampshire Historic Site. The concern of the family was for the preservation of migratory bird habitat on the property.

The Society for the Protection of NH Forests holds 673 adjacent acres and also offers a variety of conservation education programs at the NWR. Much of the society's property is managed as a productive woodlot, but natural areas are preserved along Beech Brook.

The person we spoke with at the refuge noted that this is an atypical NWR in that it includes structures and formal gardens and also because it is mostly forested upland. There are impressive stands of hemlock and white pine here that are over 200 years old—unusually pristine for this area—in addition to 1 mi. of undeveloped shoreline on Lake Sunapee. Beach Brook flows through the refuge into the lake. The diverse habitat supports a variety of upland migratory birds, while others, like ruffed grouse and the pileated woodpecker, are residents. Large mammals include white-tailed deer and black bear.

Trails include the *John Hay II Forest Ecology Trail* in the NWR, a 1-mi. self-guided trail that begins at The Fells, passes by the gardens, into the woods, along the lakeshore, and eventually back to the house.

Camping, bicycles, and motorized vehicles are prohibited.

Publications
Information sheet.
John Hay II Forest Ecology Trail.

Headquarters
U.S. Fish and Wildlife Service, c/o Refuge Manager, Great Meadows NWR, Weir Hill Rd., Sudbury, MA 01776-1427; (508) 443-4661. Society for the Protection of NH Forests, P.O. Box 325, Newbury, NH 03255; (603) 763-5958.

....

Jones Brook Wildlife Management Area
New Hampshire Fish and Game Department   South
863 acres

NW of Rochester. From Middleton Corners, N 2½ mi. on Wolfeboro Rd. (Kings Highway on the DeLorme *Atlas* map). The next ¾ mi., on the right, is WMA frontage. Walk-in dirt road in ½ mi.

Varied habitat. Steep, rocky, burned-over terrain in the N. Flat with good softwood cover in the S. A 25-acre, fly-fishing only, trout pond is in the center. All upland game, including moose. A major deer wintering area.

Headquarters
NH Fish and Game Dept., 2 Hazen Dr., Concord, NH 03301; (603) 271-3421.

Kearsarge, Mount

New Hampshire Division of Parks and Recreation/New Hampshire
Division of Forests and Lands   South
4,460 acres.

NW of Concord. S side: From I-89, Exit 8; Hwy 103 to Warner, then N.
N side: I-89 Exit 10; N on local road toward Wilmot Flat.

Not to be confused with Kearsarge North Mountain near North Conway, Mt. Kearsarge is a complex including Rollins and Winslow State
Parks, a State Forest, and Fish and Game lands. At 2,937 ft., it's the
highest point for some miles around and provides fine vistas. The top
is bare rock showing glacial striae. Upper slopes have stunted, wind-
torn spruce. Lower are mixed conifers and northern hardwoods.

On the N side, a scenic drive in Winslow State Park ends in a parking area and viewpoint. From here, it's a steep mile-long trail to the
summit and a fire tower. On the S side, a drive in Rollins State Park
leads to an easy ½-mi. trail.

Lake Francis State Park

New Hampshire Division of Parks and Recreation
38 acres.

7 mi. NE of Pittsburg by US 3. Turn right onto River Rd. Entrance is 2
mi. past the covered bridge.

Open mid-May to mid-Dec.

It's just a small campground but it's on a 2,051-acre lake in gorgeous
country at the gateway to the Connecticut Lakes. The lake is artificial,
supplying water for hydropower. The shore is heavily forested and
undeveloped. The Park attendant knew of no hiking rails nearby. The
DeLorme *Atlas* map shows a few, and we saw many little-used woods
roads.

Activities

Camping: 40 sites, 5 of which are walk-in. Waterfront sites are available.

Fishing: Maximum lake depth is 85 ft. Excellent rainbow trout and salmon fishing. Also, large pickerel.

Boating: Ramp.

Canoeing: A stopping point for those headed for the upper Connecticut Lakes region.

Swimming is prohibited.

Headquarters

Lake Francis State Park, RFD 1, 37B, Pittsburg, NH 03592; (603) 538-6965. Reservations: (603) 271-3628.

....

Lake Umbagog National Wildlife Refuge

U.S. Fish and Wildlife Service   North
8,500-acre lake, over 4,000 acres of surrounding lands.

On the NH–ME border. From Errol on Hwys 16NE and 26SE.

The refuge became official in 1992, thanks to partnerships involving the states of NH and ME, timber companies, conservation organizations, private landowners, and the federal government. Since then, the refuge has grown by more than 4,000 acres. The combination of ownerships and easements in the area now protects nearly all of Lake Umbagog's shoreline in NH, and also significant portions of the shores of the Androscoggin and Magalloway Rivers.

The region is a splendid mix of habitats: river oxbows, heath bog, swamp forests, ponds, marshes. Trees include northern conifer species, notably jack pine, as well as hardwoods such as red oak.

Traditional uses of the area such as hiking, birding, hunting, fishing, canoeing, and boating are expected to continue, says the Fish and Wildlife Service. This is a fine, quiet wilderness for canoeists to explore. Except for 2 put-ins and unmapped logging roads, the shoreline is roadless, and some of the wetlands can't be reached on foot. The lake is shallow but clear, with good fishing. (When we visited in midsummer, however, the water was too warm for good brook trout angling.)

Both the Magalloway and Androscoggin Rivers are canoeable, and a put-in on the Magalloway off Hwy 16 provides good access to rivers and lake.

The lake itself, over 10 mi. long and quite shallow, has more than 50 mi. of shoreline, many islands, and extensive wetlands and marshes along the rivers—it's the largest freshwater marsh complex remaining in the state. This provides ideal habitat for waterfowl to nest and raise their young during the summer. Forested swamplands and upland areas are important habitat for many bird species, including 24 different warblers.

Birds: Only bald eagle nest in NH is here. Also largest number of nesting osprey in NH. Species include peregrine falcon, common loon, wood duck, hooded and common mergansers, mallard, scaup, 3 scoters, black duck, goldeneye, American bittern, great blue heron, northern harrier, gray jay, spruce grouse, black-backed and northern three-toed woodpeckers.

Mammals: Unusually large population of moose, white-tailed deer, black bear, beaver, fisher, coyote, and bobcat.

Activities

Camping: Shoreline sites owned by the state of NH and private landowners offer many camping options. For information, reservations, contact Umbagog Lake Camps, P.O. Box 181, Errol, NH 03579.

Fishing: Maximum depth is 48 ft., for most of the lake it's 10–22 ft. Salmon, brook trout, pickerel, yellow perch, hornpout, smelt.

Boating: Ramp on Hwy 26 E of Errol.

Canoeing: The Magalloway is canoeable from Wilsons Mills, ME, on Hwy 16; the Androscoggin for about 30 mi. below Errol Dam. Before trying either, consult Fish and Wildlife's *Exploring Lake Umbagog* (see Publications).

Publications

Fact sheet.

Map.

Bird checklist.

Exploring the Lake Umbagog National Wildlife Refuge by Canoe.

Headquarters

Lake Umbagog NWR, P.O. Box 280, Errol, NH 03579; (603) 482-3308.

Lost River Reservation

Society for the Protection of New Hampshire Forests   North
152 acres.

From North Woodstock on I-93, W about 8 mi. on Hwy 112 to Kinsman Notch.

Open daily, 9 A.M.–4 P.M.; July–Aug. 9 A.M.–6 P.M.

The reservation, the society's first, was acquired in 1912, the year the society persuaded Congress to establish White Mountain National Forest. In scenic Kinsman Notch, surrounded by the Forest, the reservation includes a dramatic rocky gorge with waterfalls, great tumbled boulders, caves, giant potholes with crystal-clear water, a nature garden with 300 varieties of native wildflowers, a small natural history museum, a nature center, and several trails. An easy, ¾ mi. self-guided tour takes about 1 hour.

The Lost River vanishes beneath the jumble of boulders. Visitors can explore the natural caves and passages underneath these huge rocks.

There is an entrance fee.

Activities

Camping: The Wildwood Campground (26 sites) of the U.S. Forest Service is about 2½ mi. N on Hwy 112.

Hiking: The Dilley Trail is a scenic route up the Kinsman Notch Cliffs to the Appalachian Trail. Some of the spruce trees on the upper cliffs are more than 400 years old. The Kinsman Notch Ecology Trail passes a beaver pond.

Publication
Tour leaflet.

Headquarters
Lost River Reservation, North Woodstock, NH 03262; (603) 745-8031.

Merrimack River

60 river miles. South

From Franklin to the MA border.

The Merrimack River has friends: the Merrimack River Watershed Council. Flowing through the state's most heavily populated region, the river became heavily polluted. Today it's clean enough to support fish populations. Efforts to restore significant numbers of the anadromous Atlantic salmon and shad are ongoing.

The upstream watershed has several flood-control dams. There are dams built for waterpower along the river. However, the council identified a 33-mi. segment of the river, S from the confluence of the Pemmy and the Winnepesaukee, as free flowing and worthy of inclusion in the national Wild and Scenic River system.

The 60 mi. in NH are canoeable, with portages around dams. Stretches of flat water are punctuated with some class I and II rapids. In general, the upstream segments are the most attractive.

On shore, the Society for the Protection of NH Forests' innovative Conservation Center is located on a bluff overlooking the Merrimack. (See NH Introduction.) From here the *Les Clark Nature Trail* leads the visitor on a steep forest walk, down to the floodplain of the river. Cardinals, orioles, and rose-breasted grosbeaks can often be seen along the trail. The preserve is open for hiking year-around during daylight hours.

Information

Merrimack River Watershed Council, 56 Island St., P.O. Box 1377, Lawrence, MA 01842-2577; (508) 681-5777.

Miller State Park

New Hampshire Division of Parks and Recreation South
83 acres.

On Hwy 101, 3 mi. E of Peterborough.

NH's oldest Park sits atop South Pack Monadnock Mountain. A paved road ascends to the 2,288-ft. summit. Most visitors come for the view or to picnic. The vista includes Mount Monadnock (see entry) 12 mi. away.

Hiking: Hiking trails also lead to the summit. The Wapack Trail is a 21-mi. route from Ashburnham, MA, to and across the Pack Monadnocks.

Adjacent
The Wapack National Wildlife Refuge (see entry) can be reached by the Wapack Trail.

Headquarters
Miller State Park, Peterborough, NH 03458; (603) 924-3672.

....

Monadnock, Mount

New Hampshire Division of Parks and Recreation/Society for the
Protection of New Hampshire Forests   South
5,000 acres.
Off Hwy 124, 4 mi. N of Jaffrey.

Is it a natural area? Some say only Mount Fugi attracts more climbers. Here several thousand come on pleasant weekends, 125,000 in a year. Once one could drive a toll road to the summit. That road is now a hikers' route. Halfway House, a resort built in 1861, is gone. Once there were 80 trails to the summit; now there are 40 mi. of maintained trails on the mountain.

The 3,165-ft. peak is by no means the state's highest, and it rises less than 2,000 ft. from its base. But it is a monadnock, an isolated mountain on a plain, and thus conspicuous.

The original forest was much abused. After logging came sheep grazing, and what forest remained was burned, they say, to drive off wolves. By 1820 the upper 300 to 500 ft. were stripped of soil. The top is now bare rock. On the lower slopes, a regenerated forest is a healthy mix of conifers and hardwoods.

The townspeople of Jaffrey led the preservation movement, buying some of the land in 1884. State acquisition began in 1905. In 1913 the Society for Protection of NH Forests began purchases. Most of the

Mountain and lower slopes are now owned by the society and leased to the state. Monadnock State Park now occupies 1,009 acres.

Interpretation

Monadnock visitor center has exhibits, slide programs, publications, nature trails, guided hikes. Several summit trails begin here.

Activities

Camping: 21 sites at the State Park. Open year-round. *No pets.* Many trails start near the campground.

Hiking: 40 mi. of trails. Among the most popular summit trails are the White Dot Trail, the White Cross Trail, and the Pumpelly Trail (the easiest, also the longest). This is the E end of the 51-mi. Monadnock-Sunapee Greenway (see entry). It is also the northern terminus of the Metacomet-Monadnock Trail that extends from CT across MA.

Publications

Leaflet.

Forest Nature Trail Guide.

Monadnock Guide.

Headquarters

Monadnock State Park, Jaffrey, NH 03452: (603) 532-8862.

Monadnock-Sunapee Greenway

Society for the Protection of New Hampshire Forests/Appalachian
Mountain Club   South
51 trail miles.

From Mount Sunapee State Park through Pillsbury State Park to Mount Monadnock (see entries).

In 1976 the Society for the Protection of NH Forests and the Appalachian Mountain Club completed the initial clearing of this remarkable footpath connecting Mounts Monadnock and Sunapee. The route follows highlands wherever possible, dropping down into meadows and streams, on the divide between the Connecticut and Merrimack River watersheds. Although the trail is anchored in state lands, the two sponsoring organizations had to seek easements or permissions from private landowners to cross properties. Obtain information about overnight hiking from the society, AMC, or the NH Div. of Parks and Forests.

Publication
The Monadnock-Sunapee Greenway Trail Guide.

Headquarters
Society for the Protection of NH Forests, 54 Portsmouth St., Concord, NH 03301; (603) 224-9945. Appalachian Mountain Club, 5 Joy St., Boston, MA 02108; (617) 523-0636.

Moose Brook State Park

New Hampshire Division of Parks and Recreation   North
755 acres.
Off US 2, 2 mi. W of Gorham on Jimtown Rd.

This is a good base for sightseeing, hiking, and fishing. The park, at the foot of the Crescent Range, lies between and close to two portions of the White Mountain National Forest. The Presidential Range is to the S. Moose Brook, a trout stream, is tributary to the nearby Androscoggin River.

Camping: 56 sites. Mid-May–mid-Oct. Pets OK.

Headquarters
Moose Brook State Park, RFD 1, Berlin, NH 03570; (603) 466-3860.

Mount Washington

U.S. Forest Service   North
Within the White Mountain National Forest.
From Hwy 16 N of Pinkham Notch.
The toll road is open mid-May to late Oct., weather permitting.

The highest peak in the northeast, 6,288 ft., is one of 11 in the Presidential Range, 6 of the others towering over 5,000 ft. Visitors can drive to the top on a toll road, ride up on the cog railway, or hike on any of several trails. In doing so, they cross the timberline more than 1,000 ft. below the summit and enter into a region of near-arctic conditions.

The mountain is broad and massive, with 3 major ridges, secondary ridges, numerous valleys and ravines. Slopes range from gentle to steep. Many streams rush over falls and cataracts.

Mount Washington has long attracted attention and visitors. The Summit House was built in 1852. The toll road to the summit was completed in 1861; the cog railway in 1869. In 1867 the state sold 2,000 acres, including the summit. Later Dartmouth College bought 60 acres, surrounding the summit. Still later the state repurchased the summit. This is now Mount Washington State Park, but the state's title is subject to easements and leases pertaining to the toll road, cog railway, weather station, and television broadcasting facilities.

The first weather observatory was built in 1870. There is much weather to observe, considered by some to be the world's worst. The highest wind velocity ever known on Earth's surface was recorded at the summit: 231 mph. Combine this with subzero temperatures and the windchill factor rivals anything Antarctica can offer. More than once hikers who set out on fine, sunny days have been caught in sudden, blinding blizzards and perished.

Plants: Vegetation below timberline is typical of the White Mountain National Forest (see entry). At that elevation, the forest becomes krummholz, a low tangle of spruce and fir, stunted and twisted by fierce wind and cold. Above is the largest alpine zone in the eastern U.S., extending to neighboring mountaintops. Here are low-growing sedges and heaths, carpeting mosses, and wildflowers that bloom even as they poke up through melting snow in June.

Features

The summit has the observatory, visitor information, rest rooms, cafeteria, museum, souvenir shop—and shelter from high winds. Open daily.

Great Gulf and *Tuckerman Ravine* are large glacial cirques, dramatic features attractive to hikers and mountain skiers.

Alpine Garden, a natural feature noted for its wildflowers, is on a trail between the auto road and Tuckerman Ravine.

Glen Ellis Falls is one of several impressive falls and cataracts.

Hiking, backpacking: Several trails ascend the mountain. The Appalachian Trail crosses it. Trails link with the trail network of the National Forest. Many people hike the mountain, but all should be warned: It's dangerous at any season.

The climb is steep and strenuous: about 4,000 ft. in 4 mi. 100-mph winds can occur in any season, along with rain, snow, or cold to threaten hypothermia. Weather, including clouds and fog, can blind the hiker, and this is a grave threat above timberline where the trails are marked only by stone cairns. Many hikers, leaving one cairn before they can see the next, have become hopelessly lost.

Even if it's a sunny July day, be prepared. First and foremost that means understanding the hazards and how to meet them. It requires trail maps and knowing how to read them, a compass, proper clothing, and survival gear. Know in advance what to do if bad weather strikes.

Trailside camping is not permitted above timberline between May 1 and Nov. 1. We'd think it inadvisable at other times.

Headquarters

White Mountain National Forest, 719 N. Main St., Laconia, NH 03246; (603) 528-8721. NH Div. of Parks and Recreation, P.O. Box 1856, Concord, NH 03302-1856; (603) 271-3556.

Mount Sunapee State Park

New Hampshire Division of Parks and Recreation   South
2,174 acres.

On Hwy 103, 3 mi. W of Newbury.

Mount Sunapee, 2,743 ft., was fast being stripped of trees when the Society for the Protection of NH Forests bought its first 600 acres in 1911, including a 256-acre remnant of virgin timber, and Lake Solitude, a small glacial lake. Holdings were increased until the state bought the land in 1948.

It's a busy place. In winter it's a ski area. In summer the main chair lift takes visitors to the top, where the lodge offers meals and views. Across the road is Sunapee State Beach, with bathhouse, refreshment stand, picnic area, and launching ramp on 4,085-acre Sunapee Lake.

For those who seek quiet places, there are fine hiking trails, notably the 51-mi. Monadnock-Sunapee Greenway (see entry), which links Mounts Sunapee and Monadnock.

Camping is available at Pillsbury State Park (see entry).

Headquarters
Mount Sunapee State Park, Sunapee, NH 03772; (603) 763-2356; (603) 763-4020 in winter.

Odiorne Point State Park
New Hampshire Division of Parks and Recreation   South
330 acres.
S of Portsmouth on Hwy 1A, at Rye.

This fragment of protected seacoast and tidal marsh is a war relic. After Pearl Harbor, the army commandeered the site and evicted residents to install coastal defenses. It became a Park in 1961. It has both sandy and rocky shores, with stands of Scotch pine and oak, wild rose thickets. It is the last undeveloped stretch of NH coast.

Interpretation
Seacoast Science Center offers interpretive programs and educational exhibits about the coastal environment.

Interpretive panels are placed throughout the Park.

Activities
Hiking: Trails.

Boating: Boat launch.

Bicycling: Paved trail.

Headquarters
Odiorne Point State Park, Route 1A, Rye, NH 03870; (603) 436-7406. Seacoast Science Center: (603) 436-8043.

Ossipee Lake/Heath Pond Bog

New Hampshire Division of Parks and Recreation   North
Lake: 3,092 acres. Bog: 744 acres.

The lake is at Center Ossipee, NE of the intersection of Hwys 16 and 25. The Bog parking area is about 2 mi. E, on the S side of Hwy 25.

The state owns most of the sandy S lakeshore, but there is no developed access. Most of the shore has escaped residential development thus far, although there are clusters. The lake is best known for fishing.

Heath Pond Bog is a National Natural Landmark, a wild area, fragile, left undeveloped and little publicized. A floating mat of peat covered with sphagnum moss supports a unique plant community, including insectivorous plants, orchids, heaths. Trees around the pond are chiefly spruce and tamarack. Visitors are asked to stay on the trail.

Activities

Hiking: Trail around the bog.

Fishing: Salmon, lake and brook trout, pickerel, smallmouth bass, cusk, yellow perch, suckers, hornpout, smelt.

Boating: Fishing map shows a launch site on E shore.

Nearby

Pine River State Forest (see entry).

Headquarters

NH Div. of Parks and Recreation, P.O. Box 1856, Concord, NH 03302-1856; (603) 271-3556.

Pack Monadnock Mountain

See Miller State Park; Wapack National Wildlife Refuge.   South

Paradise Point Nature Center

Audubon Society of New Hampshire   South
43 acres.

I-93 Exit 23 to Hwy 104, W to junction with Hwy 3A, 9 mi. N, then 1
mi. W on North Shore Rd.

Open daily, Memorial Day weekend–Oct. 1.

This small site has much of interest. From the parking lot one walks
up a trail through a fine old forest, chiefly hemlocks, many of them
large. At the top is the Nature Center, which has good wildlife
exhibits, a library and study area, literature, and a room for talks and
film showings. The hill overlooks 3,000 ft. of unspoiled shoreline on
Newfound Lake, a precious asset where almost every other inch has
been developed. Near the shore is a small swamp.

The site has 5 self-guiding nature trails: Loop, Swamp, Ridge, Point,
and Lakeshore.

The rapid development around Newfound Lake has brought a new
constituency to the Nature Center, which now offers evening programs.

Nearby

Hebron Marsh: 36 acres. Also operated by the Audubon Society, in con-
junction with the town of Hebron. It's another mi. W, toward Hebron.
When we visited, there was no sign; we were told to look for the red
cottage with a white picket fence and take the dirt road just to the S.
The site has a marsh and pastures on the river. An observation tower
overlooks the marsh, a good place to look for waterfowl beginning in
Sept.

Quincy Bog is a small private preserve on the N side of the road,
between Hwy 3A and the Nature Center. It's well marked. Ask about it
at the center.

Publications

Leaflet.

Nature trail guides.

Headquarters
Audubon Society of NH, Hebron, NH 03241; (603) 744-3516 or 224-9909.

......

Pawtuckaway State Park
New Hampshire Division of Parks and Recreation/New Hampshire Division of Forests and Lands   South
6,500 acres.

At Raymond, 3½ mi. N of the intersection of Hwys 101 and 156.

Pawtuckaway Lake, 903 acres, is about 3 mi. long, narrow, with many arms, coves, and bays. The Park occupies most of the W shore, plus 2 islands accessible by bridges.

In summer the 900-ft. beach, 25-acre picnic ground, camping areas, and boating facilities attract crowds from nearby population centers. However, almost 5,000 Park acres are undeveloped, and hikers can find quiet trails. To the W are the Pawtuckaway Mountains, 3 low ridges; the highest is 1,011-ft. North Peak. Fine views are seen from the fire tower on South Peak. The forest is mostly oak/hickory. A stream flows through a hemlock ravine.

Burnham's Marshes lie between Fundy Cove and Neal Cove, the northern and southern arms of the lake.

Activities
Camping: 193 sites. Mid-May to mid-Oct. Reservations accepted.

Fishing: A bass tournament is held here each spring. Smallmouth and largemouth bass, pickerel, yellow perch, hornpout.

Boating: Ramps at the Park and at the dam.

Canoeing: Rentals available.

Headquarters
Pawtuckaway State Park, RFD 1, Raymond, NH 03077; (603) 895-3031. Reservations: (603) 271-3628.

Peabody Forest

Society for the Protection of New Hampshire Forests   North
83 acres.

From Gorham, 3½ mi. E on US 2. Left across the river. E 1 mi. on North Rd. to trailhead on left.

The trail passes among large white pines and hemlocks in the S, then northern hardwoods. The Peabody Trail continues beyond the site along Peabody Brook toward Giant Falls and the Mahoosuc Range.

Headquarters

Society for the Protection of NH Forests, 54 Portsmouth St., Concord, NH 03301; (603) 224-9945.

Pillsbury State Park

New Hampshire Division of Parks and Recreation/New Hampshire Division of Forests and Lands   South
5,250 acres.

On Hwy 31, 3½ mi. N of Washington.

Open daily from Memorial Day to late Oct.

The last of several sawmill owners here was one of the founders of the Society for the Protection of NH Forests. In 1920 he deeded 2,400 acres to the state as a forest reservation. In the 1930s the Civilian Conservation Corps restored ponds once choked with sawdust, and rebuilt dams. The site was opened as a State Park in 1952, but only 151 acres have been developed; the rest remains a near-wilderness, the regenerated forest healing past wounds. The Park is a key link in the 51-mi. Monadnock-Sunapee Greenway (see entry).

Base elevation is about 1,200 ft., with hills rising to over 2,000 ft. Seven ponds, the largest over ½ mi. long, are scattered through the site.

Activities

Camping: 38 primitive sites on 150-acre May Pond, including walk-in and canoe-in sites. Pets OK.

Hiking: 20 mi. of trails. The Monadnock-Sunapee Greenway (see entry) crosses the Park.

Fishing: Largemouth bass, pickerel, hornpout, yellow perch.

Canoeing: Hand-carried craft can be used.

Headquarters

Pillsbury State Park, Washington, NH 03280; (603) 863-2860.

Pine River State Forest

New Hampshire Division of Forests and Lands   North
3,084 acres.

Pine River flows N from Pine River Pond, crossing Hwy 16 about 7½ mi. S of Center Ossipee, 2.7 mi. S of Hwy 28. It flows N to Lake Ossipee, crossing Hwy 25 about ½ mi. E of Hwy 16.

The Forest doesn't appear on the DeLorme *Atlas* map. It is noteworthy for a remarkable esker, some exceptionally large white pines, and the river. The esker, a ridge 7 mi. long, 120 ft. high, formed in the last ice age, is reached by an old road off Hwy 16, site of an abandoned hatchery. The pines are here, too.

Pine River is canoeable for 20 mi., usually all year. Class II rapids are in the 5 mi. from Pine River Pond to Granite Rd. From there the river flows gently through unspoiled forest, with stretches of sandy bottom, deep pools. Many wildflowers in season. Some canoeists camp on the way. It's a little-known stream, with good fishing for brook trout.

Nearby

Ossipee Lake/Heath Pond Bog (see entry).

Headquarters

NH Div. of Forests and Lands, P.O. Box 1856, Concord, NH 03302-1856; (603) 271-3556.

Pisgah State Park

New Hampshire Division of Parks and Recreation/New Hampshire
Division of Forests and Lands   South
13,066 acres.
Off Hwy 63, 2 mi. E of Chesterfield.

A 20-square-mile wilderness in fast-growing southern NH may seem
improbable, but a management plan adopted in 1987 by the state's
park, forest, and wildlife agencies would maintain Pisgah as a place
"where visitors can experience a sense of relative solitude and remoteness from 'civilization.'" The site was acquired in 1968. Since then
several studies have defined its natural and cultural resources. The
evolving management plan was influenced by an opinion survey
showing that most respondents want no further development.

Just leaving it alone won't preserve it, however. For almost 20 years
the land was looked after by one part-time custodian who had two
other parks to oversee. The multiple entrances were uncontrolled. If
there were rules, no one gave them much heed. Off-road vehicles
roamed the area, damaging vegetation, soil cover, and foot bridges.

It was called "the Pisgah wilderness" before the state bought it. Terrain is mostly a series of low ridges dividing valleys that have streams,
ponds, and marshes. The highest point is 1,416-ft. Davis Hill. Mt. Pisgah is 1,303 ft. Pisgah Pond, the largest water body, is about 1½ mi.
long, Fullam Pond about half that length.

Plants: 95% forested: mixed hardwoods with white pine and hemlock. Prominent species are beech, yellow birch, red oak. Flowering
plants include azalea, rhodora, mountain laurel, hobblebush.

Birds: No list. Observed: waterfowl, herons, many hawks, owls. Fall
roosting of grackles at Fullam Pond. Many warblers in season.

Mammals: Include beaver, bobcat, fisher, coyote, red fox, porcupine,
raccoon, deer.

Activities

The management plan lists activities judged "generally appropriate":
hiking, nature study, cross-country skiing, picnicking, fishing, hunting, nonmotorized boating, and berry picking. "Only in designated

zones": snowmobiling, ATV use, motorized boating, horseback riding, and sled dog training. "Only under applicable permit": primitive camping, archeology digs, large group outings, trapping, and field dog trials. "Generally inappropriate": camping in vehicles, swimming, sailing, speed boating and water skiing, using off-road vehicles, and target shooting.

These recommendations were made in 1987. In view of the chronic underfunding of NH's resource agencies, full realization may be years away.

Hiking: At least 30 mi. of old logging roads.

Hunting: Probably the chief activity now. Deer, grouse.

Fishing: In several ponds. Trout, bass.

Headquarters

NH Div. of Parks and Recreation, P.O. Box 1856, Concord, NH 03302-1856; (603) 271-3556. On site: (603) 239-8153.

....

Pondicherry Wildlife Refuge

Audubon Society of New Hampshire/New Hampshire Fish and Game
Department   North
310 acres.

From Whitefield on US 3, follow signs E to Whitefield Airport. Drive the old railroad right-of-way as far as possible, then walk. Beyond Big Cherry Pond is a trail, often wet, to Little Cherry Pond.

Open dawn to dusk all year.

The refuge was designated a National Natural Landmark in 1974. Of significance here are the more than 60 acres of open and nearly open sphagnum-heath bog which surround the 2 ponds and present black spruce/tamarack bog forest.

The area is relatively flat, poorly drained, densely forested with northern conifers and a few hardwoods. Both ponds are completely natural and are dammed only by beaver dams. Both have cattails and other emergent plants. Little Cherry Pond has many yellow water lilies.

The two ponds are important as breeding areas for green-winged teal and ring-necked duck, both rare summer residents in NH, as well as for black and wood ducks and occasional hooded mergansers.

Birds: Other summer residents include great blue heron, pied-billed grebe, American bittern, Virginia and sora rail, northern harrier, common snipe, mourning and Wilson's warblers, rusty blackbird, Lincoln's sparrow. Over 40 species of waterbirds, including rare species, have been recorded during migration periods.

Mammals: Include moose, black bear, white-tailed deer, beaver, snowshoe hare, raccoon, skunk, coyote.

Fishing: Pickerel, hornpout, yellow perch. No motorized craft.

Publication
Trail guide, 50 cents.

Headquarters
Audubon Society of NH, 3 Silk Farm Rd., Concord, NH 03301; (606) 224-9909.

Rhododendron Natural Area

New Hampshire Division of Parks and Recreation   South
294 acres.

Off Hwy 12, 2½ mi. N of Fitzwilliam.

The Park, donated to the state by the Appalachian Mountain Club, was named for the exceptional 16-acre colony of rhododendrons, the largest such assemblage in New England, a National Natural Landmark. The rhododendron bloom in early to mid-July. The site has many other wildflowers. From April through Sept. some are always in bloom.

Many species of rhododendron are native to Asia and eastern North America. Exotics have been introduced, and many hybrids have been developed. Common in the North Carolina mountains, rhododendrons are at the northern limit of their range in NH and thus unusual.

Wildlfowers seen along the 1-mi. Wildflower Trail include

- *April–May:* bloodroot, Dutchman's breeches, hepatica, mayflower, bellwort, blue flag, bunchberry, clintonia, columbine, fringed polygala, foamflower, goldthread, jack-in-the-pulpit, painted trillium, shadbush, Solomon's seal, starflower, wake-robin, wild oats.

- *June–July:* checkerberry, dewdrop, heart-leaved aster, mountain laurel, partridgeberry, pink lady's-slipper, pipsissewa, red baneberry, rhododendron, shinleaf, twinflower, white baneberry, wood azalea, wood sorrel.
- *Aug.–Sept.:* Indian pipe, wild lettuce, wood aster, woodland aster.

Hiking: The 160-mi. Metacomet-Monadnock Trail (see entry in MA) crosses the Park.

There are views of Mount Monadnock and other mountains in the region.

Publications

Leaflet with map.

Wildflower Trail guide.

Headquarters

NH Div. of Parks and Recreation, P.O. Box 1856, Concord, NH 03302-1856; (603) 271-3556 or 532-8862.

Squam Lakes Region

Squam Lakes Association and others   North

At Holderness on US 3.

Squam Lake, 6,765 acres, is a natural water body whose level was raised by a dam. It has a 61-mi. rocky, wooded shoreline. Linked to it by a narrow waterway is 408-acre Little Squam Lake. Both are long-established fishing and summer vacation sites with moderate shoreline development. *On Golden Pond* was filmed here.

The Squam Lakes Assoc. was organized in 1905, with the primary mission of protecting the lake's water quality. Its current publication admonishes residents to keep soap, detergent, and human waste out of the lake, to use fertilizer sparingly and not at all within 150 ft. of the water, to have septic tanks pumped every 3 years, and not to use lumber treated with creosote or pentachlorophenol for docks or decks.

It also manages shorefront property for public use, maintains trails on the surrounding mountains, has a 200-acre wildlife sanctuary, and offers programs for children. The association owns Moon Island, available for low-impact recreation. It promotes conservation and good land use practices. Would that other NH lakes had such protectors!

Activities

Camping: The association maintains 9 primitive lakeside campsites, several of which require boat access. Reservations required.

Hiking: More than 40 mi. of trails extend N into the Squam Mountains and beyond to the trails of the White Mountain National Forest.

Fishing: Squam Lake is well known for its salmon and lake trout. Also smallmouth bass, pickerel, white and yellow perch, hornpout, whitefish, cusk, smelt.

Boating: Ramps at Holderness and elsewhere.

Publications

Squam Lakes Trail Guide, $3.25.

Lake charts and range map.

Birds of the Squam Lakes Region, $8.50.

Headquarters

Squam Lakes Assoc., P.O. Box 204, Holderness, NH 03245; (603) 968-7336.

··

Taves Reservation

Society for the Protection of New Hampshire Forests   South
571 acres.

From Keene, E on Hwy 101, then N on road to Otter Dam (Branch Rd.). Turn right at crossroads by Roxbury town hall. In 4 mi., at old Roxbury center, bear left, to parking.

In 1973 the Taves family bought the land to protect a small town from development; 10 years later they gave it to the society, which manages it for forest products and wildlife. The terrain is rough, with steep hillsides and ravines. It includes the watershed of Wheeler Brook. From the entrance a dirt road extends N along Otter Brook, the W boundary. A compass is recommended for off-trail hiking.

The reservation can be seen from Hwy 9, across Otter Brook.

Headquarters
Society for the Protection of NH Forests, 54 Portsmouth St., Concord, NH 03301; (603) 224-9945.

....

Umbagog Lake
See Lake Umbagog National Wildlife Refuge.

....

Wapack National Wildlife Refuge
U.S. Fish and Wildlife Service   South
1,672 acres.

By trail from Miller State Park (off Hwy 101, 3 mi. E of Peterborough) or by Old Mountain Rd. E from Peterborough.

Open dawn to dusk.

We're not sure why this is a federal refuge, but we're glad it's there. The land was acquired by gift, not purchase. On 2,288-ft. North Pack Monadnock Mountain, 1,200 ft. above the valley floor, the site is rugged, unspoiled, forested, with bogs and swamps, ledges, cliffs, open alpine flats, streams. Visitors are few.

Birds: It's a good place to watch the migration of hawks. Also belted kingfisher, green heron, pine siskin, crossbill, pine grosbeak, ruffed grouse, woodcock.

Mammals: Include deer, fisher, mink, squirrel, porcupine, chipmunk, mice, voles, weasel, raccoon, fox, bobcat, snowshoe hare.

   Hiking: The Wapack Trail crosses the site, a 3-mi. segment.
   Camping, hunting, and fires are prohibited.

Headquarters
c/o Great Meadows NWR, Weir Hill Rd., Sudbury, MA 01776; (617) 443-4661.

White Lake State Park

New Hampshire Division of Parks and Recreation   North
624 acres.

From West Ossipee, ½ mi. N on Hwy 16.

The lake is a bit over ½ mi. long with a good natural beach. Parks and Recreation calls it one of NH's most popular camping spots, and it's crowded in the swimming season. However, the site includes some forest, a black spruce bog, and two small bog ponds. It's near Hemenway State Forest (see entry).

Features

White Lake Pitch Pines, a 72-acre National Natural Landmark, is a grove of exceptionally tall and straight old trees.

Tamworth Black Spruce Ponds Preserve: 35 acres. A property of the town of Tamworth, adjoins the Park and is linked by trails.

Activities

Camping: 200 sites. Mid-May–mid-Oct. Reservations accepted. No pets.

Fishing: Trout.

Canoeing: Rentals available.

Publication

White Lake Pitch Pines folder.

Headquarters

White Lake State Park, P.O. Box 273, West Ossipee, NH 03890; (603) 323-7350. Reservations: (603) 271-3628.

White Mountain National Forest

U.S. Forest Service   North
In NH: 724,040 acres within boundaries; 714,336 acres of federal land.
Additional 49,346 acres in ME.

Between Plymouth on the S and Hwy 110 on the N; from the ME
border almost to VT. Crossed by US 2, I-93, US 302, and other routes.

The Forest occupies over 11% of NH's land area, the highest percent-
age of federal land for any eastern state. It wasn't federal land when
the Society for the Protection NH Forests was organized in 1901. Much
of it had been cut over. Only the N slope of the Presidential Range and
a few tracts such as Crawford Notch remained intact. The society
urged Congress to act, but it was 10 years before legislation was passed
and 2 more before the first land was bought for the new National Forest. Acquisition has continued.

The White Mountains dominate northern NH and extend into ME.
Their most striking feature is the Presidential Range, a chain of peaks
named for U.S. presidents; a number of the mountains are more than
a mile high. Mt. Washington, at 6,288 ft., is highest of all. Along the
ridges is an alpine zone about 8 mi. long and 2 mi. wide, treeless and
windswept, with species of shrubs, wildflowers, mosses, and lichens
typical of arctic regions, left here on these lofty islands, many think,
when the last ice sheet receded.

Although the Forest produces timber, about 95% of it is natural in
appearance, showing no conspicuous signs of human alteration. On
the average, 4,000 acres are logged each year, only 750 acres in conspicuous openings. The rest of the 5% includes ski areas, campgrounds, roads, and service areas.

Recreation use of the Forest totals about 7 million visitors per year.
On days when traffic is heavy at Pinkham, Crawford, and Franconia
notches, motorized sightseeing appears to be the chief visitor activity,
but it accounts for only 25% of the visitors. Camping and picnicking
make up 15% of the total, downhill skiing about 15%. Almost half of
the visitor-days are spent in the backcountry: hiking, hunting, fishing, and so on.

Forests that are extensively logged have networks of logging roads. Here the entire road system, including the public highways, totals only 761 mi. Less than half are National Forest roads, and only 180 mi. are open to visitor traffic.

By contrast, there are 1,500 mi. of hiking trails and 125 mi. of cross-country ski trails. About 43% of the Forest is open to winter off-road snowmobile travel on 314 snowmobile trails.

The Forest offers opportunities for extensive backpacking, demanding mountain hikes, or easy day walks in scenic valleys. The hiking season in the mountains is generally from June to mid-Oct., but weather on the mountains can be severe in any season, windier, colder, and wetter than in the valleys. Clouds often shroud the peaks, sometimes reducing visibility to a few feet. Above timberline, where trails are marked by stone cairns, many hikers have lost their way, some their lives. Proper clothing and gear, and knowing what to do in case of trouble, are essential to full enjoyment of these lofty places.

Although most of the Forest is accessible only to those who travel on foot, other travelers can see its most spectacular features. A toll road and a cog railway ascend to the top of Mt. Washington; an aerial tram carries passengers to the top of Cannon Mountain; and other high viewpoints are no less accessible. Scenic highways pass waterfalls, cataracts, and ponds. Along the way are parking areas with short, easy trails to places of interest and beauty.

Great cirques in the mountainsides mark the action of past glaciers. Rivers have cut down through faults, forming steep-sided ravines, here called "notches," of which Franconia Notch and Crawford Notch are best known.

Features

Throughout the Forest are attractive cirques, waterfalls, cascades, pools, ponds, vistas, and other natural attractions, among them:

Presidential Range–Dry River Wilderness: 27,380 acres. Includes 4,930-acre alpine area, treeless, along the ridge tops, with many alpine plants. Wildflowers blooming in the brief summer include alpine azalea, bearberry, bluet, goldenrod, speedwell, black crowberry, bluebell, dwarf cinquefoil, dwarf willow, eyebright, Labrador tea, Lapland rose bay, mountain cranberry, pale laurel.

Great Gulf Wilderness: 5,552 acres. On the N slope of Mt. Washington adjoining the alpine area. Has the largest cirque in the White Mountains, walls rising up to 1,600 ft., with old-growth red spruce and balsam fir. Many trails.

Pemigewasset Wilderness: 45,000 acres. Between Franconia Notch and Crawford Notch. Mountainous, forested, bounded by the Appalachian Trail; also internal trails. Includes *Pemigewasset Extension:* 16,000 acres. Bordering the E side. Steep, heavily forested, no trails.

Sandwich Range Wilderness: 25,000 acres. Lies between the Kancamagus Hwy, Hwy 112, and the S boundary of the Forest. It includes the *Bowl Natural Area,* which has a virgin climax spruce/fir forest and virgin climax northern hardwood forest within a large cirque.

Franconia Notch and *Crawford Notch:* see entries.

Pinkham Notch Scenic Area includes a cluster of features on both sides of Hwy 16, with Mt. Washington on the W, Wildcat Mountain on the E: Tuckerman and Huntington ravines, Alpine Gardens, Crystal Cascades, Glen Ellis Falls.

Snyder Brook Scenic Area, just W of Randolph on US 2: old-growth trees, cascades.

Gibbs Brook Scenic Area, on the slopes of Mt. Pierce, E of US 302. One of the few extensive stands of virgin spruce in New England.

Sawyer Ponds Scenic Area, via Sawyer Ponds Trail from US 2 or the Kancamagus Hwy. Secluded glacial ponds.

Rocky Gorge Scenic Area on the Kancamagus Hwy. A narrow gorge cut by the Swift River bordering tall red spruce.

Nancy Brook Scenic Area, W of US 302, S of Crawford Notch. Cascades and ponds.

Greeley Ponds Scenic Area, S of the Kancamagus Hwy. Trail through Mad River Notch. Isolated Ponds below rugged slopes.

Mount Chocorua Scenic Area, 5,700 acres at the SE corner of the Forest. One of the most-climbed NH mountains. Numerous trails, fine views from the bare summit.

Scenic drives include

- *Kancamagus Hwy,* between Lincoln and Conway. Lower Falls, Greeley Ponds, and Rocky Gorge Scenic Areas, Sabbaday Falls, campgrounds, and trailheads.
- *Jefferson Notch Rd.,* N from Crawford Notch, highest road in NH, narrow and steep.
- *Evans Notch,* from Chatham N on Hwy 113 into ME. The ME portion of the Forest (see entry in ME) is the Evans Notch Ranger District.

Aerial tramways are on Cannon, Black, Wildcat, and Loon Mountains.

Birds: A checklist of 194 species is available. Only 21 of these are generally present in winter. Well over half of those listed are species that breed here but migrate in the fall to more temperate climates. Species common in summer include great blue heron, mallard, black duck, wood duck, black-billed cuckoo, chimney swift, ruby-throated hummingbird, belted kingfisher, eastern kingbird, eastern phoebe, blue jay, raven, crow, 4 woodpeckers, 2 flycatchers, 3 swallows, 2 chickadees, 2 nuthatches, 4 thrushes, 2 kinglets, many warblers, 5 sparrows, eastern meadowlark, red-winged blackbird, common grackle, scarlet tanager, rose-breasted grosbeak.

Mammals: In 1978, moose were gradually moving into NH from ME. Now they are seen more often than deer. Other species include moles, shrews, bats, snowshoe hare, raccoon, woodchuck, chipmunk, red and flying squirrels, red fox, skunk, porcupine, beaver, muskrat, fisher, otter, bobcat, black bear.

Reptiles and amphibians: About 20 species of frogs, toads, turtles, snakes, and salamanders are found in the Forest.

Interpretation

Visitor centers at the Saco ranger station in Conway, at the E end of the Kancamagus Hwy, Hwy 112, and at Androscoggin ranger station on Glen Rd., Hwy 16, in Gorham.

Nature trails at the *Russell Colbath Historic Site* and near the Covered Bridge Campground on the Kancamagus Hwy. Also the *Patte Brook Auto Tour* near Crocker Pond Campground in ME.

Campfire programs at campgrounds throughout the Forest are sponsored by the White Mountain Interpretive Association.

Activities

Camping: 23 campgrounds, 936 sites. Usually open May 15–Oct. 15. Several are open in winter but roads aren't plowed. Most campgrounds are filled during summer and fall peaks. No reservations.

Informal camping elsewhere is permitted except in zones bordering main roads and within Forest protection areas.

Hiking, backpacking: With over a thousand miles of trails to choose among, it's advisable to study one of the hiking guides (see Introduction) before setting forth. The *AMC White Mountain Guide* is the most complete and includes advice on equipment and safety. *Fifty Hikes in the White Mountains* describes a number of short day hikes and a few longer trips. Trailside facilities include 43 shelters, 8 Appalachian

Mountain Club huts, and 8 cabins. The huts, open to the public, are more than their name implies. Madison Hut, for example, can accommodate 50 hikers in three-high bunks. Hut crews provide dinners and breakfasts. Huts are reached only by hiking at least 1½ mi. Some visitors hike hut-to-hut along the mountains; others make a one-night stand.

Hunting: Deer, bear, raccoon, rabbit, ruffed grouse, woodcock, duck.

Fishing: Over 30 species of fish are present in Forest waters. Atlantic salmon are currently being reintroduced into headwaters streams. The best trout fishing is in the Saco and Swift Rivers and their tributaries. The Pemigewasset, once heavily polluted, has good fishing again; it's in the I-93 corridor bordered by Forest land. Fishing is for brown brook and rainbow trout, and perch, pickerel, smallmouth bass.

Canoeing: The Pemigewasset has class I and II rapids below North Woodstock, canoeable except at low water. Its East Branch, draining the Pemigewasset Wilderness, has rapids to class IV April–May and after heavy rains. Another tributary, the Mad River, also has rapids to class IV but for a short season. So does the upper Saco River.

Ski touring: Opportunities are unlimited, with several hundred miles of marked trails for skiing and snowshoeing.

Snowmobiling: Restricted to designated areas and corridors and to times when the minimum snow cover is 6 in. Operators should obtain map and regulations.

Skiing: 4 downhill ski areas are wholly or partly on Forest land. The season may last until mid-June.

Publications

Forest map, $4.

Bird checklist.

Hiking information.

Trout Fishing.

Headquarters
White Mountain National Forest, 719 N. Main St., Laconia, NH 03246; (603) 528-8721.

Ranger Districts
Ammonoosuc R.D., Trudeau Rd., Box 239, Bethlehem, NH 03574; (603) 869-2626. Androscoggin R.D., 300 Glen Rd., Gorham, NH 03581; (603) 466-2713. Evans Notch R.D., 18 Mayville Rd., Bethel, ME 04217; (207) 824-2134. Saco R.D., 33 Kancamagus Hwy, Conway, NH

03818; (603) 447-5448. Pemigewasset R.D., RFD #3, Box 15, Rt. 175, Plymouth, NH 03264; (603) 536-1310.

....

Willard Pond Preserve

(also known as DePierrefeu Willard Pond Sanctuary)
Audubon Society of New Hampshire   South
642 acres.

From Hancock, 3 mi. NW on Hwy 123, then 1½ mi. N on dirt road.

The preserve has about one-third of the shoreline of the 100-acre pond. The rest is largely undeveloped. Much of the site is reverting pasture, but it also has good stands of white pine and hardwoods and a large patch of mountain laurel. The lake is at 1,100-ft. Bald Mountain rises on the W to 2,037 ft. Three hiking trails, a canoe landing, and good birding, here and at nearby marshes.

Headquarters

Audubon Society of NH, 3 Silk Farm Rd., Concord, NH 03301; (603) 224-9909.

MASSACHUSETTS

Every resident of Massachusetts lives within 10 mi. of a public park, forest, or wildlife area. The state has approximately 200 sites open to public recreation. This is remarkable in a state where growth and development often seem out of control.

With only one-eighth of New England's land area, MA has almost half of its population. More than three-fourths of the people live within commuting range of Boston, whose metropolitan area now extends onto Cape Cod and into southern NH.

We had known MA for many years. Returning after a 10-year absence, we were shocked by the changes along the coast and Cape. After 2 days of fighting heavy traffic and seeking almost any overnight parking for our motor home, we considered recommending that readers stay west of I-495.

Still, we couldn't ignore the east's delightful natural areas: the National Seashore, attractive State Parks and State Forests, numerous private preserves. We have entries for them, but those who dislike crowds should plan their visits appropriately. Beaches are best enjoyed out of season. When beaches are crowded, upland areas aren't. Even in winter, don't head toward Cape Cod on a Friday afternoon.

State Forests have fewer visitors than State Parks, Parks without campgrounds fewer than those with camping. Except in hunting season, Wildlife Management Areas have the least visitors.

You can find quiet natural areas in the eastern part of the state, but there's no way to avoid the traffic. It's easier to find quiet places in the western areas, and the forested mountain trails are cool in summer.

We have divided the state into three zones. *East* has the coast and the most congestion. *Central* is hilly, forested, with many streams and rivers. *West* has mountain ranges and river valleys.

Geography and Climate

Excluding Cape Cod, MA measures about 50 mi. N–S, about 150 mi. W–E. The terrain is mountainous along the western border, generally above 1,000-ft. elevation W of the Connecticut River. At 3,491 ft., Mount Greylock is the state's highest. Most of the central region is between 500 and 1,000 ft. The Connecticut River Valley and the coastal region are below 500 ft. The Cape and some coastal areas are flat with many wetlands.

Average Jan. temperatures are in the low 20s in the west, near 30° along the coast. Summers are warm, with less regional variation. Total annual precipitation is 40 to 50 in., with no wet or dry seasons and little regional difference, but the west receives much more snow than the east.

The Connecticut River drains most of the western half of the state, the Merrimack the NE portion. Other rivers are small.

State Lands

Massachusetts has no National Park or National Forest, though the National Seashore is part of the National Park Service system. It has 5 small National Wildlife Refuges and 1 National Estuarine Research Reserve. We've included entries for all these lands. (We cannot quite call them "federal" since the Estuarine Reserve is mostly state property.)

The state has roughly 350,000 acres of public lands, well distributed. The most complete current listing we found for lands managed by the Division of Forests and Parks was in the state's 1996–97 *Getaway Guide,* published by the MA Office of Travel and Tourism. The *Guide* lists 51 State Parks, 30 State Forests, 13 State Reservations, and 1 State Recreation Area. However, this information is considerably at odds with information on the official transportation map we received from the same agency at the same time. (The map, it turned out, was almost 3 years old.) The brochure *Massachusetts Forests and Parks,* revised by the Div. of Forests and Parks in 1995, offers only a partial listing of recreation areas, though it does contain a map that shows them all. The brochure includes directions, facilities, and activities for the sites it lists, and gives numbers to call for further information. None of the literature provides information about when parks and forests are open. However, generally, the season appears to be May–Columbus Day.

The Division of Fisheries and Wildlife (see State Agencies, below, for address) has what appears to be a complete listing of Wildlife Management Areas, with a reasonably current publication date. The WMAs have doubled in number since our first edition—for a total of 102. Fisheries and Wildlife has maps for about half of the areas and will send an interesting publications list of mostly free materials. The list includes the pamphlet *Wildlife Sanctuaries,* with maps and descriptions of the state's 12 sanctuaries, $1.50.

Campgrounds and developed recreation sites in MA usually have entrance signs. So do many WMAs. Often, however, we couldn't tell whether forested land was public or private. Perseverance will be rewarding. Unsigned areas are rarely crowded.

We visited sites that seemed to be candidates for entries. Sites planned for intensive use are omitted unless they include significant natural areas.

Maps

MA has no road atlas comparable to those available in ME, NH, and VT. Nothing, indeed, other than the official transportation map. This map marks parks and forests with names and symbols in their general locations. It doesn't show boundaries and sometimes doesn't show the secondary roads leading to them. Wildlife Management Areas are not marked. The map in the brochure *Massachusetts Forests and Parks* may help you to locate forests and parks a little more precisely; again, WMAs are not included.

The scale of the official transportation map is about 5.8 mi./in. Tourist offices sometimes hand out a smaller version (8.3 mi./in.). Neither served our needs well, but the larger is certainly preferable. American Automobile Association members will find AAA maps more useful, though again, not all sites or roads leading to them will be shown.

The Division of Fisheries and Wildlife will send up to 5 WMA single area maps at a time when an SASE is sent to them at their field headquarters. The Division of Parks and Forests no longer sends out area maps, but they advise travelers to call a specific forest or park that might interest them "to see what they have" in the way of site-specific materials. (We surmise that reduced funding has curtailed the volume of publications by the agency.)

Flora and Fauna

Little published information about plants and animals is available from state agencies, though there are checklists offered for purchase by the Div. of Fisheries and Wildlife. More is available at private preserves, notably those of the Massachusetts Audubon Society. These references were most helpful:

DeGraaf, Richard M., and Deborah D. Rudis. *New England Wildlife: Habitat, Natural History, and Distribution.* General Technical Report NE-108. Broomwall, PA: U.S. Department of Agriculture, Forest Service, Northeastern Forest Experiment Station, 1986. (In 1996 this was out of print but there may be another printing.)

Jorgensen, Neil. *A Sierra Club Naturalist's Guide to Southern New England.* San Francisco: Sierra Club Books, 1982.

Kulik, Stephen, Pete Salmansohn, Matthew Schmidt, and Heidi Welch. *The Audubon Society Field Guide to the Natural Places of the Northeast: Coastal.* New York: Pantheon Books, 1984.

—. *The Audubon Society Field Guide to the Natural Places of the Northeast: Inland.* New York: Pantheon Books, 1984. (Both are presently out of print but you might find copies in used bookshops.)

Peterson, Roger T. *A Field Guide to Eastern Birds,* 4th ed. Boston: Houghton Mifflin, 1980.

Peterson, Roger T., and Margaret McKenny. *A Field Guide to Wildflowers of Northeastern and North-Central North America.* Boston: Houghton Mifflin, 1975.

Sammartino, Claudia F. *The Northfield Mountain Interpreter.* Berlin, CT: Northeast Utilities, 1981, reprinted 1991.

Trails

Massachusetts has several long trails. In the west are 83 mi. of the Appalachian Trail and extensive trails on the Taconic Range. The Metacomet-Monadnock Trail crosses from NH to CT, with sections on both sides of the Connecticut River. In the east are trails linked to RI trails.

Opportunities for overnight hikes are limited, however. Even on the Appalachian Trail, there is no chain of shelters spaced at convenient intervals, and informal trailside camping is forbidden everywhere.

Opportunities for day hiking, on the other hand, are almost unlimited. Thanks largely to the Appalachian Mountain Club and the New England Trail Conference, trails have been established on public and private lands throughout the state. The AMC's comprehensive trail guide includes descriptions of trails as short as 1 mi.:

AMC Massachusetts and Rhode Island Trail Guide, 7th ed. Boston: Appalachian Mountain Club, 1995.

For the Appalachian Trail:

Appalachian Trail Guide to Massachusetts/Connecticut. Harpers Ferry, WV: Appalachian Trail Conference, 1994.

Other guides describe trails to or through places of special interest:

Banfield, Walter (ed.). *Metacomet Monadnock Trail Guide,* 8th ed. Amherst, MA: New England Cartographics, 1995.

Brady, John, and Brian White. *Fifty Hikes in Massachusetts,* 2nd ed. Woodstock, VT: Countryman Press, in press.

Fisher, Alan. *Country Walks Near Boston,* 2nd ed. Boston: Appalachian Mountain Club, 1986.

Griswold, Whit. *Berkshire Trails for Walking and Ski Touring.* Charlotte, NC: East Woods Press, 1983. (Out of print.)

Sadlier, Hugh and Heather. *Short Nature Walks on Cape Cod, Nantucket and the Vineyard,* 5th ed. Old Saybrook, CT: Globe Pequot Press, 1996.

Scheller, William G. *More Country Walks Near Boston.* Boston: Appalachian Mountain Club, 1986. (Out of print.)

With minor exceptions, these guides don't describe trails in WMAs. Most hiking in WMAs is on woods roads and informal trails. We found the WMA site maps adequate.

Camping

Camping has had low priority in the development of MA parks and forests. Only 32 of them have campgrounds. At the extremes are 4 with more than 200 campsites, others with as few as 3. Most of the large campgrounds and more than half of the sites are in the east. They are much in demand in summer.

In the west, we camped several nights in State Parks and State Forests. We were lucky, twice getting the last available site. You might be lucky, too, but don't count on it. The campgrounds are popular. Since our first edition, 11 state campgrounds have begun accepting reservations. We have entries for most of those sites. Contact the Division of Forests and Parks (see State Agencies, below, for address) for their leaflet *Campsite Reservations System,* which lists the sites with their phone numbers, locates them on a map, and explains the reservation procedure. Two brochures, *Camping in Massachusetts State Forests and Parks* and *Access to the Outdoors,* are also available from the Div.

Reservations can also be made at private campgrounds. During the busy season, it's wise to reserve wherever possible. The Office of Travel and tourism's *Getaway Guide* offers a list of private campgrounds by areas within the state. The American Automobile Association's *Northeastern CampBook* (free to members) lists both public and private campgrounds.

Canoeing

Except on the Connecticut River, MA's longest river canoe run is about 10 mi. Most runs are seasonal, and canoeists should inquire about water conditions. There are a few stretches of white water.

AMC River Guide: Massachusetts, Connecticut, Rhode Island, 2nd ed. Boston: Appalachian Mountain Club, 1990.

Borton, Mark C., et al. (eds.). *The Complete Boating Guide to the Connecticut River,* 2nd ed. Available from Connecticut River Watershed Council, 1 Ferry St., Easthampton, MA 01027.

Weber, Ken. *Canoeing Massachusetts, Rhode Island, and Connecticut.* Woodstock, VT: Countryman Press, in press.

Boating

Public access is available at points on a number of rivers and at many ponds, most of the latter small. *Public Access to Waters of Massachusetts* is available at a cost of $3 from the Division of Fisheries and Wildlife (see State Agencies, below, for address).

The state's 1,519-mi. shoreline provides unlimited opportunities for saltwater boating.

Fishing

Freshwater game species include brook, rainbow, and brown trout, landlocked salmon, smallmouth and largemouth bass, chain pickerel, northern pike, tiger muskie, walleye. Trout are stocked in several hundred streams and ponds. Fishing regulations and a list of stocked waters are available from the MA Div. of Fisheries and Wildlife.

For saltwater fishing information, contact

MA Division of Marine Fisheries
100 Cambridge St.
Boston, MA 02202
(617) 727-3151

Hunting

Game species include deer, black bear, small mammals, waterfowl, turnkey, grouse, pheasant, and quail. Seasons, bag limits, and regulations differ in various counties. The *Abstracts of the Fish & Wildlife Laws* is available from Fisheries and Wildlife with an SASE.

State Agencies

All environmental matters in the state are under the jurisdiction of the Department of Environmental Management.

Responsibility for State Parks and State Forests lies with:

Division of Forests and Parks
100 Cambridge St., 19th Fl.
Boston, MA 02202
(617) 727-3180

For information about Wildlife Management Areas, contact:

Division of Fisheries and Wildlife
Field Headquarters
Westboro, MA 01581
(508) 792-7270

The official transportation map and *Massachusetts Getaway Guide*
may be requested from:

Massachusetts Office of Travel and Tourism
100 Cambridge St., 13th Fl.
Boston, MA 02202
(617) 727-3201

Private Organizations

1996 marks the MA Audubon Society's centennial year. As part of its
many activities in nature education and conservation, the society
owns and protects more than 24,000 acres of wildlife habitat in 18
staffed sanctuaries with nature centers across the state.

208 S. Great Rd.
Lincoln, MA 01773
(617) 259-9500

The Trustees of Reservations is a nonprofit organization devoted to
preserving MA properties of exceptional scenic, historic, and ecological value for public use.

290 Argilla Rd., Box 563
Ipswich, MA 01938
(508) 356-4351

Both organizations provided information about their sites. We visited many and have entries for a number. (We usually don't include
sites that limit public access or that are so small and fragile as to be
damaged by too many visitors.)

MASSACHUSETTS

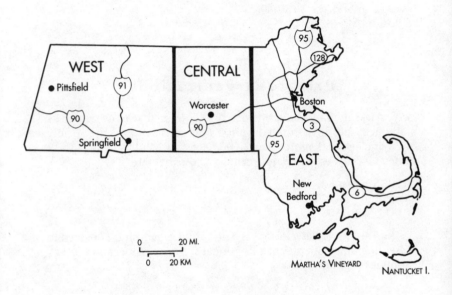

WEST

● Pittsfield

CENTRAL

Worcester

95

128

Boston

3

95

EAST

New
Bedford

6

0   20 MI.

0   20 KM

MARTHA'S VINEYARD

NANTUCKET I.

Natural Areas in Massachusetts

An Alphabetical Listing

Appalachian Trail
West

Arcadia Nature Center and Wildlife Sanctuary
West

Ashumet Holly Reservation and Wildlife Sanctuary
East

Bartholomew's Cobble
West

Beartown State Forest
West

Birch Hill Wildlife Management Area
Central

Blue Hills Reservation
East

Bolton Flats Wildlife Management Area
Central

Borderland State Park
East

Brimfield State Forest
Central

Broadmoor Wildlife Sanctuary
East

Canoe Meadows Wildlife Sanctuary
West

Cape Cod
East

Cape Cod National Seashore
East

Cape Cod Rail Trail
East

Cape Poge Wildlife Refuge. See Martha's Vineyard
East

Catamount State Forest
West

Charles H. Ward Reservation
East

Chester-Blandford State Forest
West

Clarksburg State Park
West

Coatue Wildlife Refuge and The Haulover. See Nantucket National Wildlife Refuge
East

Connecticut River
West

Coskata-Coatue Wildlife Refuge. See Nantucket National Wildlife Refuge
East

Crane Pond Wildlife Management Area
East

Crane Wildlife Management Area
East

D.A.R. State Forest
East

Daniel Webster Wildlife Sanctuary
East

Dorothy F. Rice Sanctuary for
Wildlife
West

Dubuque Memorial State Forest
West

Erving State Forest
West

Eugene D. Moran Wildlife
Management Area. *See* Windsor
State Forest
West

Felix Neck Wildlife Sanctuary.
See Martha's Vineyard
East

Garden in the Woods
Central

Granville State Forest
West

Great Meadows National
Wildlife Refuge
East

H. O. Cook State Forest
East

Harold Parker State Forest
East

High Ridge Wildlife Management
Area
Central

Hinsdale Flats Wildlife
Management Area
West

Hiram H. Fox Wildlife
Management Area
West

Hockomock Swamp Wildlife
Management Area
East

Hopkinton State Park
East

Hubbardston Wildlife
Management Area
Central

Ipswich River Sanctuary
East

Lake Dennison State Park. *See*
Birch Hill Wildlife Management
Area
Central

Laughing Brook Education
Center and Wildlife Sanctuary
Central

Leominster State Forest
Central

Long Point Wildlife Refuge. *See*
Martha's Vineyard
East

Manuel Correllus State Forest.
See Martha's Vineyard
East

Martha's Vineyard
East

Martin Burns Wildlife
Management Area
East

Metacomet-Monadnock Trail
West

Midstate Trail
Central

Millers River Wildlife
Management Area
West

Mohawk Trail State Forest
West

Monomoy National Wildlife
Refuge
East

Monroe State Forest
West

Natural Areas in Massachusetts

by Zone

WEST ZONE

Appalachian Trail

Arcadia Nature Center and Wildlife Sanctuary

Bartholomew's Cobble

Beartown State Forest

Canoe Meadows Wildlife Sanctuary

Catamount State Forest

Chester-Blandford State Forest

Clarksburg State Park

Connecticut River

Dorothy F. Rice Sanctuary for Wildlife

Dubuque Memorial State Forest

Erving State Forest

Eugene D. Moran Wildlife Management Area. See Windsor State Forest

Granville State Forest

Hinsdale Flats Wildlife Management Area

Hiram H. Fox Wildlife Management Area

Metacomet-Monadnock Trail

Millers River Wildlife Management Area

Mohawk Trail State Forest

Monroe State Forest

Mount Grace State Forest/ Northfield State Forest/Warwick State Forest

Mount Greylock State Reservation

Mount Tom Reservation

Mount Washington State Forest

Norcross Wildlife Sanctuary

Northfield Mountain Recreation and Environmental Center

Northfield State Forest. See Mount Grace State Forest

Notchview Reservation. See Windsor State Forest

October Mountain State Forest

Peru Wildlife Management Area

Phillipston Wildlife Management Area

Pittsfield State Forest

Pleasant Valley Wildlife Sanctuary

Quabbin Reservoir

Sandisfield State Forest (York Lake)

Savoy Mountain State Forest

Taconic Skyline Trail

Tolland State Forest

Warwick State Forest. See Mount Grace State Forest

Wendell State Forest

Windsor State Forest

Appalachian Trail

Mixed ownership   West
83 trail mi.

From the VT line and Clarksburg State Park (see entry) to the CT line in
Mount Washington State Forest (see entry).

Western MA is mountainous, the Berkshire Valley framed by the
Taconic Range on the W, the Hoosac Range on the E. The trail here
leads through the Berkshires. Pleasant stretches through wooded hills
and valleys feature such outstanding peaks as Mt. Greylock (see entry)
and Mt. Everett.

Two principles guided trail planning—to keep to the highest
ground, following ridges between peaks, and to stay on public lands
wherever possible. There were and are difficulties, however.

The mountains don't have continuous ridges, and much of the
trail must be on private land. The Appalachian Trail Club and its allies
have had admirable success in obtaining permissions from landowners, but some trail sections had to use public roads. Occasionally a
change of ownership or mind requires rerouting.

MA prohibits trailside camping on its public lands, and most of its
many Parks and Forests don't have campgrounds. AT hikers find a few
shelters, but intervals are too long for hut-to-hut trips. Hikers must
spend some nights off the trail.

We have entries for most of the Parks and Forests along the way.
Trail guides are essential, whether one is planning a long AT hike or
seeking a local access trail for a day trip. There is a regional office
number included in Division of Forests and Parks literature: (413) 442-
8928.

Publications

Appalachian Trail (free National Park Service brochure with map).
Available from Appalachian Trail Conference, P.O. Box 807, Harpers
Ferry, WV 25425-0807; (304) 535-6331.

Official Guides and Maps for the Appalachian Trail (list of publications
available from the ATC).

Walking the Appalachian Trail Step by Step (free booklet from the ATC).

Arcadia Nature Center and Wildlife Sanctuary

Massachusetts Audubon Society   West
650 acres.

From I-91, Exit 18. S 1.3 mi. on US 5 (not easily seen on the state map). Right on East St.; 1.2 mi. to Fort Hill Rd., and turn right (MA Audubon sign). 1 mi. to entrance.

Open 9 A.M.–5 P.M. daily except Mon.

The Sanctuary is on the W side of an oxbow in the Connecticut River. Almost half of the site is floodplain forest, woody swamp, and marsh. Wild rice was planted some years ago. The site is at the crossroads of two bird migration routes. The upland half of the site is forested with mixed hardwoods and conifers planted in the early 1900s. These factors add up to fine birding. Arcadia is also noted for its wildflowers.

A 30-ft.-high blind overlooks the marsh.

Interpretation

Nature center is the base for a lively educational program.

Guided tours and *canoe trips.*

Activities

Hiking: 5 mi. of self-guided trails.

Canoeing: Access to the Oxbow and Connecticut Rivers.

Pets are prohibited. No bicycles on the trails.

Publications

Site map.

Four bird lists, one for each season.

Headquarters

Arcadia Wildlife Sanctuary, 127 Combs Rd., Easthampton, MA 01027; (413) 584-3009.

Ashumet Holly Reservation and Wildlife Sanctuary

Massachusetts Audubon Society   East
45 acres.

On Cape Cod in East Falmouth. From the intersection of Hwys 28 and
151, E on 151 for 4 mi. Left on Currier Rd. to entrance.

Open Tues.–Sun. 9 A.M.–5 P.M.

In this small space one can see 8 species and 65 varieties of holly trees.
On the S side of the Cape, the site's highest point is 18 ft. above sea
level. It includes 27 acres of mixed woodland, 10 agricultural acres,
and an 8-acre pond. Also present is the unusual fall-flowering
Franklinia tree, and a large barn swallow colony, May–Aug.

Two *nature trails* offer tours of the hollies and other site features.
The society maintains an active program including a holly sale at
Christmas, spring open house, Lotus Festival in summer, Franklinia
Festival in the fall, day camp, and seasonal boat tours to Cuttyhunk,
the Elizabeth Islands, and Gay Head.

Pets are prohibited. No bicycles on trails.

Publications

Ashumet Discovery Guide. $1.50.

The Hollies of Ashumet. $1.50.

Headquarters

Ashumet Holly and Wildlife Sanctuary, 286 Ashumet Rd., East Falmouth, MA 02536; (508) 563-6390.

Bartholomew's Cobble

The Trustees of Reservations   West
277 acres.

In Ashley Falls, near CT. 0.5 mi. W on Hwy 7A, then Rannapo Rd. S and
Weatogue Rd.

Open dawn to dusk throughout the year.

A National Natural Landmark, this scenic site is on the Housatonic
River. The Cobble is a natural limestone rock garden, elevations from
600 to 1,050 ft., with an extraordinary diversity of plants: nearly 500
species of wildflowers; 100 of trees, shrubs, and vines; 40 species of
ferns. Best wildflower blooming seasons are April–June and Sept.

Birds: Checklist available. 236 species have been recorded, an extraordinary number for any site, especially one so small.

Interpretation
Small *museum* has displays of wildflowers, birds' nests, Indian artifacts, geology. Open daily April 15–Nov. 1.

Activities
Hiking: 6 mi. of trails.

Publications
Information page.

Map. 50 cents.

Birds at Bartholomew's Cobble. $1.50.

Ledges Interpretive Trail Guide. $3.

Headquarters
Bartholomew's Cobble, P.O. Box 233, Ashley Falls, MA 01222; (413)
298-8600.

Beartown State Forest

Massachusetts Division of Forests and Parks   West
10,897 acres.

From Great Barrington, about 5 mi. E on Hwy 23 to Blue Hill Rd. and
Forest sign. HQ is ½ mi. N, Forest boundary another 1½ mi.

This is handsome country, a high plateau with hilltops of the Hoosac
Range. Mt. Wilcox, at the Forest center, is 2,150 ft.; Beartown Mountain is 1,865. The area has many streams and ponds Lookout points
offer fine views. The site extends N almost to the Housatonic River
and Hwy 102. It is crossed by several roads, woods roads, and trails,
including the Appalachian Trail.

It's surprising that one of the state's largest Forests has a campground with only 12 sites, not surprising that they are usually occupied in season. Even when weekend campers leave on Sunday, others
are waiting to take their places.

Plants: The area is 90% forested with mixed hardwoods, some spruce
plantations. Many wildflowers in season.

Birds: Include wild turkey, grouse, woodcock, hawks, owls, woodpeckers, flycatchers, vireos, finches, crossbills, thrushes, warblers.

Mammals: Include deer, black bear, bobcat, coyote, snowshoe hare,
cottontail, red and gray foxes, red and gray squirrels, porcupine, fisher.

Activities

Camping: 12 sites mid-May–Columbus Day, earlier as conditions permit. All year for self-contained units. Pets OK.

Hiking, backpacking: 5 mi. of the Appalachian Trail, including 2 shelters.

Fishing: Trout stocked in streams. Bass in ponds.

Swimming: 36-acre Benedict Pond.

Ski touring: 11 mi. of marked trails.

Publication

Site map.

Headquarters
Beartown State Forest, Blue Hill Rd., Monterey, MA 01245; (413) 528-0904.

....

Birch Hill Wildlife Management Area/Otter River State Forest/Lake Dennison State Park

Massachusetts Division of Fisheries and Wildlife/Massachusetts
Division of Forests and Parks   Central
20,219 acres.

From US 202 at Baldwinville, left on Old US 202 (Dennison St.). For Lake Dennison, continue NE on US 202 about 6 mi.

This complex includes a large Wildlife Management Area, a large State Forest, and a new State Park, all based in part on land made available by the U.S. Army Corps of Engineers. (Until very recently, Lake Dennison was designated as a State Recreation area.)

The Corps is involved because of Birch Hill Dam, which impounds water only during floods. At other times the lands on the floodplain are available for recreation. Terrain is flat to gently rolling. Millers River, Otter River, and Priest Brook drain most of the site. Brushy fields are interspersed with hardwood and coniferous forests, swampy areas, and wetlands. Forest understory includes dogwood, mountain laurel, viburnum, azalea, blueberry, raspberry.

Paved and dirt roads crisscross the sites, and we saw many trails. We chose one at random that gave us easy hiking through quiet woods, passing a lily pond and marsh. In the past, trail bikes have created a problem for management, but we hope the new State Park will have better control of portions that have been damaged and littered.

Lake Dennison 82 acres, a natural lake, is the activity center of the 4,000-acre State Park.

Birds: Pheasants are stocked in the WMA. Wild turkey, introduced in 1982, are seen occasionally. Common species include woodcock, grouse, waterfowl, flycatchers, woodpeckers, warblers.

Mammals: Stocked with snowshoe hare. Common species include deer, raccoon, cottontail, beaver, mink, muskrat.

Activities

Camping: 151 campsites at Lake Dennison. All year, but after Oct. 15 only self-contained units. 100 sites at Otter River State Forest, seasonal. Lake Dennison campground is usually full on summer weekends; Otter River usually has sites. Reservations accepted for both sites Memorial Day–Labor Day.

Hiking: More than 30 mi. of back roads and trails.

Hunting: Waterfowl, deer, small upland game.

Fishing: Excellent trout fishing in Millers River and Priest Brook. Trout stocked. Warmwater species in the lake.

Canoeing: Streams can be canoed, but watch for rocks and fallen trees. Only boats with electric motors on the lake.

Publication
Birch Hill WMA map shows the entire area.

Headquarters
Birch Hill WMA, Dennison St., Baldwinville, MA 01436; (508) 835-3607. Baldwinville, MA 01436; (508) 939-8962.

....

Blue Hills Reservation

Metropolitan District Commission   East
6,500 acres.

S from Boston on Dorchester Ave. which becomes Randolph Ave./Hwy 28 and bisects the reservation. From E or W, I-95/US 1/Hwy 128 crosses the S portion. See the "Boston and Vicinity" inset of the official highway map.

The Metropolitan District Commission was the nation's first regional park commission. Established in 1893, it acted with remarkable foresight and speed, acquiring within a decade most of the parkland now in the Boston system. Blue Hills was its first large acquisition.

The Blue Hills are monadnocks, massive granite domes thrust up by volcanism, exposed by erosion of glacial till and slate. This part of MA has numerous domes less than 100 ft. high. The Blue Hills rise over 635 ft., affording fine views. Habitats include forest, ledges, rock outcrops, grassy meadows, bog, streams, and ponds. Ponkapog, the largest pond, is bordered by a quaking peat bog.

The developed recreation sites and some trails may be crowded in good weather. The more challenging trails have fewer hikers.

Plants: Wooded areas include scrub pitch pine and red cedar near windswept summits; white pine, sumac, poplar, oaks, hickories, and red maple at mid-elevations; white cedar, red maple, ash, and elm in swamps and bogs. Bog species include pitcher plant and sundew.

Birds and mammals: No checklists available for the Trailside Museum has information.

Interpretation
The Trailside Museum, operated by the MA Audubon Society, is the visitor center for the Reservation. Live native animals, nature walks, talks. Open 10–5. Tues.–Sun.; also Mon. on state holidays.

Activities
Hiking: The 200-mi. trail network is well described in several of the books in the Introduction. Some trails begin at the museum. Principal trails are blazed.

Fishing: Streams, pond.

Swimming: Houghton's Pond.

Canoeing: Ponds.

Ski touring: On trails and unplowed roads.

Headquarters
Blue Hills Reservation, Hillside St., Milton, MA 02186; (617) 698-1802. Blue Hills Trailside Museum: 1904 Canton Ave., Milton, MA 02186; (617) 333-0690.

Bolton Flats Wildlife Management Area
Massachusetts Division of Fisheries and Wildlife   Central
986 acres.

From I-495, Exit 27. NW on Hwy 117. Site is on both sides of Hwy 117 beyond Hwy 110. Parking areas on Hwys 110 and 117.

This river floodplain doesn't get high marks for scenery or hiking opportunities, but it's great for birding. The Still River is close to Hwy 100, the larger Nashua River on the W boundary of the site. Most of the area is open agricultural fields and brushfields, with marshy wetlands, maple swamps, and brushy river banks.

Birds: Said to be one of the best inland spots for egrets, glossy ibis, herons. In migration, the site is said to "teem" with black duck, mallard, pintail, snow goose, blue goose. Also reported: ruff, purple gallinule. American and least bitterns, Virginia and sora rails, hooded merganser, wood duck.

Activities

Hunting: Pheasant stocked in season.

Canoeing: Nashua River.

Publications

Site map.

Birds of Bolton Flats Wildlife Management Area.

Adjacent

Oxbow National Wildlife Refuge (see entry).

Headquarters

Central Wildlife District Office, Temple St., West Boylston, MA 01583; (508) 835-3607.

Borderland State Park

Massachusetts Division of Forests and Parks   East
1,772 acres.

On Massapoag Ave. in North Easton, E of Foxborough.

This was a country estate. Today, both house and surrounding grounds are open to the public as a Historic State Park. The owners were from prominent MA families, and they maintained the property as a game and forest preserve, clearing sections, building dams to form new ponds and fire roads that now serve as trails. Habitats range from low swamp forest in the S to granite hills in the N.

Activities

Hiking: On woods roads and trails, hilly on the N.

Canoeing: Ponds.

Headquarters

Borderland State Park, Massapoag Ave., North Easton, MA 02356; (508) 238-6566.

....

Brimfield State Forest

Massachusetts Division of Forests and Parks   Central
3,250 acres.

S central MA, between Sturbridge and Palmer. From US 20, S on local road W of Hwy 19.

The area is hilly, the highest elevation 1,150 ft. Just N of the State Forest, Steerage Rock on the ridge of Mt. Waddaquadduck was a landmark on the trail from Boston to villages on the Connecticut River. There's a fire tower on the mountain.

The area is forested with mixed northern hardwoods, the understory having azalea, laurel. Many wildflowers in season. Several fast-flowing streams. Dean Pond is the largest of several small ponds. (No boats are permitted on Dean Pond.)

No lists of fauna are available, but the area seems promising for birds.

Activities

Hiking: 24 mi. of forest roads.

*Hunting:*Deer, bobcat, rabbit, raccoon, ruffed grouse, woodcock.

Fishing: Trout in streams.

Headquarters

Brimfield State Forest, Rt. 20, Brimfield, MA 01010; (508) 347-9257.

Broadmoor Wildlife Sanctuary

Massachusetts Audubon Society   East
623 acres.

Between Boston and Framingham. From South Natick, 1.8 mi. W on
Hwy 16.

With frontage on the Charles River, the Sanctuary has woodland,
fields, marsh, and pond. It's a quiet natural island in a heavily settled
region. It's open all year, with activities. April–May and Sept.–Oct. are
the periods with the most visitors. It has a built-in safeguard against
crowding: the capacity of its parking lot. There is no nearby street
parking.

Plants: Checklist available. About half of the site is forested with mixed
hardwoods and softwoods. The list includes white and Norway spruce,
hemlock, Douglas-fir, larch, white, red, and pitch pines, red cedar,
pussy willow, bigtooth aspen, hickories, American hazel, hophornbeam,
birches, American beech, American chestnut, oaks, American elm,
mulberry.

The diverse habitats produce many seasonal wildflowers, including
arrowhead, jack-in-the-pulpit, skunk cabbage, spiderwort, daylily,
Canada lily, clintonia, white trillium, star grass, blue-eyed grass, iris,
lady's-slipper, coralroot orchid, campions, water lily, buttercups,
hepatica, marsh marigold, columbine, pitcher plant, sundew, cinque-
foils, clovers, jewelweed, St. Johnswort, violets, evening primrose, pipsissewa, Indian pipe, loosestrife, speedwell, asters, many more.

Birds: List available. Includes mallard, black duck, blue-winged teal,
wood duck, ring-necked duck, red-tailed and broad-winged hawks,
osprey, kingfisher, kestrel, ruffed grouse, yellow-billed and black-billed
cuckoos, 3 woodpeckers, eastern kingbird, great crested flycatcher,
eastern phoebe, tree and barn swallows, blue jay, black-capped chickadee, tufted titmouse, white-breasted nuthatch, house wren, brown
creeper, brown thrasher, gray catbird, mockingbird, robin, veery, wood
thrush, red-eyed vireo, red-winged blackbird, 6 warblers.

Interpretation

The *visitor center,* in a renovated barn, uses alternative energy systems
to conserve both energy and water. Open 9–5 Tues.–Fri.; 10–5 week-

ends. Information, exhibits, natural history lectures, special events. Announcements in newsletter.

Hiking: 9 mi. of trails feature historic mill sites; a foot bridge over Indian Brook is a fine place to view wildlife.

Pets are prohibited. No bicycles on trails.

Publications
Newsletter.

Trail map. $1.50.

Lists of plants, birds.

Headquarters
Broadmoor Wildlife Sanctuary, 280 Eliot St., South Natick, MA 01760; (508) 655-2296 and (617) 235-3929.

....

Canoe Meadows Wildlife Sanctuary
Massachusetts Audubon Society   West
254 acres.

From Massachusetts Turnpike, Exit 2. Follow US 7 to Holmes Rd., then right 2 mi.

Open daily except Mon., 9 A.M. to dusk.

The site's W boundary is the Housatonic River. From river, floodplain, swamps, brooks, and ponds, the land slopes up to hemlock forest. Fields comprise most of the northern, western, and southeastern portions and contain many seasonal wildflowers.

Visits to these relatively small sanctuaries are rewarding because they have been studied more systematically than most of the larger state landholdings. The resources here include descriptions of each of the eight habitats: fields, coniferous woods, upland deciduous woods, riverbank, lowland deciduous woods, cattail marsh, sedge meadows, and fencerows and planted areas, noting the plant species typical of each.

There is an extensive plant list with common as well as Latin names, and lists of mammals, reptiles, and amphibians, but no bird list. There is a separate leaflet that includes a fascinating discussion of local invertebrates, noting that "few or no preserved areas in the country are being managed to conserve habitat for rare or specialized invertebrates" and that Canoe Meadows is "an ideal area for invertebrate, particularly butterfly, conservation."

Interpretation

Canoe Meadows and the Pleasant Valley Wildlife Sanctuary (see entry) are managed as the Berkshire Sanctuaries. Their seasonal publication includes a calendar of events: nature hikes, canoe tours, nature ski hikes, talks, slide shows, workshops, and more.

Activities

Hiking: 5 mi. of trails. The Wolf Pine Trail passes an unusually large white pine, the Sacred Way Trail, and the reconstruction of an Indian wigwam.

Canoeing: Access to the Housatonic River.

Pets are prohibited.

Publications

Trail map. Checklists of plants, mammals, reptiles, and amphibians.

Invertebrate leaflet.

Self-guiding trail leaflets.

Quarterly newsletter.

Headquarters

Berkshire Sanctuaries, 472 W. Mountain Rd., Lenox, MA 01240; (413) 637-0320.

Cape Cod

Mixed ownership   East

Traversed by US 6, Hwy 28.

Early one New Year's Day we drove the length of the Cape and walked the beach at Race Point, its outer tip. Few people were about that morning, none on the beach, although the day was bright and warm.

Back then, small towns were threaded along US 6. Many unmarked, unpaved roads led to broad, sandy beaches. Small crowds gathered in summer where these roads ended, but those who wanted solitude had only to walk along the shore until they found it. We never knew whether it was forbidden to camp on the beach; no one seemed to care.

We had planned to visit the Cape during our summer fact-finding tour. then we saw the traffic inching along the route from Boston and turned back. Summer wasn't our time.

The Cape today is overwhelmed by growth the part-time town governments couldn't manage. They had loose zoning laws, if any, no comprehensive plans for roads, water, waste disposal, fire protection, or other needs. Developers did what they pleased.

Population on the Cape has grown explosively. From what was once just a summer resort, thousands of all-year residents commute daily to Boston. With land speculators, builders, and a billion-dollar tourist industry demanding more, those who love the Cape struggle to preserve remaining fragments. A great victory came in 1961 when Congress authorized the National Seashore. Towns are now seeking funds to preserve green space.

We have entries for the National Seashore and for:

- Ashumet Holly Reservation
- Cape Cod Rail Trail
- Crane Wildlife Management Area
- Martha's Vineyard (selected natural areas)
- Nantucket National Wildlife Refuge (and 2 contiguous refuges)
- Nickerson State Park
- Waquoit Bay National Estuarine Research Reserve
- Wellfleet Bay Wildlife Sanctuary

Cape Cod National Seashore

U.S. National Park Service   East
25,930 acres; 27,004 acres within boundaries (enclosing 44,596 acres of land and water).

On Cape Cod between Chatham and Provincetown. Access points along US 6.

Thoreau called Cape Cod "the bared and bended arm of Massachusetts." In this image, the National Seashore occupies most of the hand

and forearm. It extends for 40 mi. along the Atlantic Ocean with additional frontage on Cape Cod Bay and Provincetown Harbor.

It was established just in time. Developers coveted the land even then, and heavy lobbying opposed the proposal. Surely Congress would not have approved purchasing at today's land prices, and going higher by tomorrow. But it was possible in 1961, a magnificent acquisition for the people.

The land didn't qualify as a National Park. The National Park Service had to reconcile conflicting interests in deciding what facilities should be developed and where. No campground was provided. Conservationists urged that off-road vehicles be barred, while beach buggy users and vendors wanted no restrictions; the decision allows oversand vehicles to use designated routes in one area. One of the superintendent's many tribulations was deciding what to do about nude sunbathing, traditional on isolated beaches long before 1961.

Historic structures were to be preserved, and the interpretive program would recall the Cape's history. Modest rules would minimize conflicts among fishers, surfers, and sunbathers.

No one knows how many visitors come here. The Seashore records over 5 million *visits*. If you have a week's vacation and go to the beach twice a day, that's 14 visits. You won't find an isolated beach next to your parked car, but walking can provide escape from crowds.

Cape Cod is the product of glaciers. Its beaches, dunes, and cliffs were shaped by wind and wave over centuries. Within the Seashore, banks and cliffs of sand, gravel, and clay rise as much as 175 ft. The diverse habitats include migrating dunes, tidal flats, salt- and freshwater marshes, swamps, kettlehole ponds, and woodlands.

Climate on the Cape is milder than on the mainland because of the moderating influence of the ocean. Spring is cooler, fall warmer. Less snow falls on the Cape, and it remains for shorter periods; occasional winters are snow-free. But the low-lying Cape is exposed to maritime winds and storms. Birds have occasionally been swept here all the way from Yucatán.

Features

Nauset. At the S end of the Seashore, long barrier beaches shelter the extensive Nauset Marsh, a major gathering place for shorebirds and waterfowl. Theme of the Salt Pond *visitor center* is the human and natural history of the Cape. There are 5 *nature trails:* Nauset Marsh, Fort Hill, Buttonbush (designed for the blind), Red Maple Swamp, and Doane Loop (fully wheelchair accessible). *Evening programs* are held at the amphitheater in summer, and sometimes on weekends in spring and fall. There are *guided walks* in summer; weekends only in spring and fall. Activity notices are posted at the visitor center, which is open daily March–Dec., on weekends Jan.–Feb. (508) 255-3421.

Marconi Station. So named because the first U.S. wireless station was here. Wayside interpretive shelters tell the story. Seashore HQ is in this area, as are extensive beaches, the award-winning Atlantic White Cedar Swamp Nature Trail, and the Great Island Trail, which is the Seashore's most difficult trail. The Wellfleet Bay Wildlife Sanctuary (see entry) is adjacent.

Pilgrim Heights. In North Truro. People from the *Mayflower* landed here. The Pilgrim Spring Trail traces a part of their adventure. Nearby are beaches, sand dunes, Small's Swamp Trail, and Cranberry Bog Trail.

Province Lands. At the tip of the Cape. *Visitor center,* the Beech Forest Trail, beaches, dunes, salt marshes. The visitor center has an observation platform, various exhibits; open daily mid-April–Nov. (508) 487-1256.

Beaches. Side roads extend from US 6 to all the principal beaches. Most are on the Atlantic Ocean, but Duck Harbor Beach at Wellfleet and Herring Cove Beach at Provincetown are on Cape Cod Bay. Duck Harbor and several of the ocean beaches are town-owned and managed. Access to some is restricted to cars with stickers available only to town residents and tenants.

Plants: Dune vegetation includes beach plum, cranberry, American beach grass, salt spray rose. Some bay shallows have eelgrass. Back of the dunes are low-lying areas with numerous shallow ponds, freshwater marshes, scrub, and woodland patches. Pond lilies and cattails abound in ponds, cinnamon and wood fern in woodlands. Pitch pine is the predominant tree species, with Atlantic white cedar and red maple in wetter areas. Some fine beech trees, remnants of the original oak/beech forest, remain in the Province Lands area.

Birds: Checklist available. Over 300 species have been recorded. Long, narrow Cape Cod forms a funnel along the Atlantic Flyway. Large numbers of migrating shorebirds, gulls, terns, and ducks pass through, as well as geese, swans, and pelagic birds. Winter residents include Canada goose, brant, black duck, mallard, goldeneye, bufflehead, eider, red-breasted merganser, great black-backed gull, sanderling. Prominent upland species include red-tailed hawk, great crested flycatcher, pine warbler, common yellowthroat, gray catbird, towhee vesper sparrow, horned lark, pheasant.

Mammals: Checklist available. Includes raccoon, cottontail, woodchuck, chipmunk, red, gray, and flying squirrels, muskrat, weasel, red fox, deer. Whales, dolphins, porpoises, and harbor seals are often seen offshore, occasionally beached.

Activities

Camping: The Seashore has no campground. HQ has a list of commercial campgrounds. Reservations are essential in summer. Many of the campgrounds prohibit pets.

Hiking: Nature trails offer opportunities for short walks. The principal hiking route is the ocean beach. Experienced beachcombers know that hiking conditions can change from day to day though low tides generally offer the best footing. According to the Seashore map, the longest distance between access roads is about 8 mi.

Hunting: Upland game and migratory waterfowl may be hunted in designated areas, subject to federal, state, and local rules. Consult HQ.

Fishing: Surf, outside swimming areas. State license is required for fishing in freshwater ponds. Town licenses for shellfishing are required.

Horse riding: On 3 bridle paths only. Stables nearby.

Bicycling: Three rails, 1.6 to 7.3 mi. Rentals available within the towns.

Swimming: Lifeguards are provided at the principal beaches in season. The water is cold.

Pets are prohibited in public buildings and picnic areas and on protected beaches and interpretive trails. They must be kept under restraint in developed areas and wherever visitors concentrate.

Oversand vehicles are restricted to designated routes and must have permits. Driving on the dunes is prohibited.

Publications

National Seashore leaflet with map.

Checklists of birds, mammals, reptiles, amphibians, mollusks.

Self-guiding Nature Trails (leaflet).

Bicycle Trails (leaflet).

Brochures for individual trails (available at visitor centers).

Common Trailside Plants (guidebook for sale at visitor centers).

Headquarters

Cape Cod National Seashore, P.O. Box 250, South Wellfleet, MA 02663; (508) 349-3785.

Cape Cod Rail Trail

Massachusetts Division of Forests and Parks East
25 miles.

On Cape Cod, from Hwy 134 in Dennis to the Cape Cod National Seashore in Eastham. Additional path from Salt Pond visitor center in Eastham to Coast Guard Beach, passing Nauset Marsh.

The route was abandoned by a railroad in 1965. It now provides one of the longest trails in eastern New England, open to hikers, horseriders, and cyclists, closed to motor vehicles. It passes forests, ponds, cranberry bogs, salt marshes, beaches.

Publication

Cape Cod Rail Trail brochure available from the Division of Forests and Parks in Boston.

Headquarters

c/o Nickerson State Park, Route 6A, Brewster, MA 02631; (508) 896-3491.

Cape Pogue Wildlife Refuge

See Martha's Vineyard.

Catamount State Forest

Massachusetts Division of Forests and Parks West
1,125 acres.

From Shelburne Falls, 1 mi. W on Hwy 2, turn on Four-Mile Square Rd.

Here is an opportunity for quiet day hiking in moderately interesting country: rolling to hilly, somewhat rugged, with kettleholes, potholes, marsh, streams, a 47-acre pond, mixed forest. Elevations are from

1,000 to 1,250 ft. Catamounts—mountain lions—no longer den under the ledges, but there may be porcupine.

Hiking: 5 mi. of foot trails; 3 mi. of woods roads.

Headquarters
c/o Mohawk Trail State Forest, P.O. Box 7, Charlemont, MA 01339; (413) 339-5504.

....

Charles W. Ward Reservation

The Trustees of Reservations   East
686 acres.

From I-93, Exit 15. N 5 mi. on Hwy 125; right on Prospect Rd. at Reservation sign.

The site's principal features are a northern bog and 420-ft. Holt Hill, a drumlin, highest point in Essex County. Most of the area is natural woodland, mixed species including some large white pines. The entrance is on a quiet residential street. A site map with contours is on the bulletin board at the parking lot. Elevations appear to range from 180 ft. to the hilltop. On a July weekday, we saw no other visitors.

A self-guiding nature trail through the bog includes a boardwalk, from which we saw a great variety of plant life, including a wild orchid. The nature trail deadends at a small pond fringed with shrubs. There are several miles of hiking and skiing trails.

Publications
(By mail, price includes postage and handling.)

Map. $2.

Bog Nature Trail Guide. $5.

Headquarters
Supt. Bob Murray, 5 Wood Lane, Andover, MA 01845; (508) 682-3580.

Chester-Blandford State Forest

Massachusetts Division of Forests and Parks   West
2,308 acres.

From Springfield, 20 mi. W on US 20.

The highest point is only 1,502 ft., but that's more than 1,000 ft. above the lowest. The forested slopes are steep, with many brooks and streams. The mixed forest is dominated by oaks with many substantial hemlocks.

Sanderson Brook has a 100-ft. cascade. The road to the falls and brookside trail has been closed to vehicles, but it's an attractive quarter-mile walk from the parking area.

Activities

Camping: 15 sites.

Hiking: Trails and forest roads.

Hunting: Deer, bobcat, snowshoe hare, cottontail, raccoon, woodcock, ruffed grouse.

Fishing: Trout in streams.

Headquarters

Chester-Blandford State Forest, Rt. 20, Chester, MA 01050; (413) 354-6347.

Clarksburg State Park

Massachusetts Division of Forests and Parks   West
3,421 acres.

NW corner of MA. From North Adams, about 2 mi. N on M Rd.

A heavily forested site overlooking the Hoosic River. Elevations from about 900 to over 2,200 ft. Rock outcrops and ledges. Trees are mixed hardwoods with white and red pines, spruce. Fine display of fall colors.

Activities

Camping: 47 sites.

Hiking: The Appalachian Trail crosses the Forest. Other trails and woods roads.

Headquarters

Clarksburg State Park, Middle Road, Clarksburg, MA 01247; (413) 663-8469 (Savoy Mountain State Forest).

Coatue Wildlife Refuge and The Haulover

See Nantucket National Wildlife Refuge.

Connecticut River

69 river miles.   West

From VT to CT.

I-91 and US 5 parallel the river from border to border, but they aren't always within sight or earshot of canoeists. Most of the shore is heavily developed in the S, but the N of Northampton much of the course is through farmland. There's almost no riverside state land.

One of the first public access points S of the NH border is where Hwy 2 crosses and the river turns sharply W. At Barton Cove, just E of Turners Falls, the Northeast Utilities Company has a camping, picnicking, and swimming area, with boat ramp.

Several dams impede the river flow. Most canoeing and boating is within their impoundments. The longest unimpeded run is the 36 mi. from Turners Falls to Holyoke. Anyone contemplating a border-to-border cruise should study the route first. Low water can be a problem in some stretches. Portages must be arranged around dams. Some rapids and hazards will be encountered. Even informal campsites are scarce. (See "Canoeing" in Introduction for references.)

Coskata-Coatue Wildlife Refuge

See Nantucket National Wildlife Refuge

Crane Pond Wildlife Management Area

2,123 acres.   East

From I-95, Exit 54. W on Hwy 133 to center of Georgetown. Turn right on North St. 1.8 mi. Left on Thurlow. In about 1.5 mi. look for gated entrances.

This site is W of I-95, lying across the town lines of Georgetown, Groveland, Newbury, and West Newbury. The site map is confusing because the road shown crossing the site appears to change names: Pond St. becomes Star Rd., which becomes Little Rd., the latter two intersecting Seven Star Rd., Bear Hill Rd., and Byfield Rd. Look for steel gates typical of Department of Environmental management (DEM) sites.

We parked at one of the gates and hiked for a while, picking blackberries. Most of the area is abandoned farmland now reverting to brush and forest. About one-fifth is marsh, bog, and open water. We didn't see the Parker River; it's not shown on the site map but the accompanying text says it flows through.

Parking areas aren't shown on the site map, but we saw several along perimeter roads. Motor vehicles, including trail bikes and snowmobiles, aren't allowed inside. The text mentions "a large network of walking trails." Some are overgrown, but we found enough for pleasant hiking. We met no other visitors.

Activities

Hunting: Most native game species are present. Pheasant and snowshoe hare are stocked.

Fishing: Trout are stocked in the Parker River April–May. Bass and pickerel in Crane Pond and Little Crane Pond.

Publications

Site map and description.

Headquarters

Northeast Wildlife District Office, Harris St., Box 2086, Acton, MA 01720; (508) 263-4647.

Crane Wildlife Management Area

Massachusetts Division of Fisheries and Wildlife   East
1,807 acres.

At the W end of Cape Cod, near Falmouth. From Hwy 28, E on Hwy
151 about 3 mi., to entrance and parking.

Terrain is flat to gently rolling, with a few low ridges. Most of it is open
and reverting farmlands, with some scrub forest. The site has a few
small streams and ponds, a small marsh in the SW corner. A separate 53-
acre parcel is managed for quail. A large open area was once an airport.

A network of trails is often used by hikers and horse riders in spring
and summer, and on Sundays in hunting season. Common wildlife
species include pheasant, quail, woodcock, grouse, deer, fox, rabbit,
woodchuck, squirrel.

Publication
Area map.

Headquarters
Southeast Wildlife District Office, 195 Bournedale Rd., Buzzards Bay,
MA 02532; (508) 759-3406.

D.A.R. State Forest

Massachusetts Division of Forests and Parks   West
1,517 acres.

From Goshen on Hwy 9, 1 mi. N on Hwy 112.

This seems to be the most popular State Forest in western MA. In summer the campground begins filling on Thursday evening, and by Friday evening there are no available sites. At times long lines of cars
form early in the morning, waiting for a vacancy.

Visitors come because there's swimming, an attractive campground, an active naturalist program, and pleasant scenery. Terrain is
rolling to hilly, with rock outcrops. Moor's Hill, 1,713 ft., is the highest

point, offering a four-state view from its fire tower. Devil's Den is a craggy cleft on Rogers Brook. Upper and Lower Highland Lakes are each a bit less than a mile long. One side of Lower Highland has private homes.

About two-thirds of the site is undeveloped except for hiking trails. In this portion are streams, ponds, swamps, and a waterfall. The area is forested with northern hardwoods, white pine, and hemlock. The understory includes mountain laurel, azalea, blueberry. Many wildflowers, including lady's-slipper, trillium, swamp pink.

Interpretation
The *nature center* has a naturalist program, including *evening programs, night walks, pond walks,* a 3-mi. *nature trail,* and *special events.*

Activities
Camping: 50 sites, mid-May to mid-Oct. Reservations accepted.

Hiking: 9 mi. of trails and forest roads.

Fishing: Bass, perch, trout.

Canoeing: On both lakes. No boats with motors.

Swimming: In Upper Lake.

Publication
Trail map.

Headquarters
D.A.R. State Forest, Rt. 112, Goshen, MA 01032; (413) 268-7098.

Daniel Webster Wildlife Sanctuary

Massachusetts Audubon Society   East
444 acres.

From Hwy 3 N of Plymouth, Exit 11. Go E about 5 mi. on Hwy 139 to Marshfield Center. Pass 2 stoplights and turn right on Webster St. In 1 mi., turn left on Winslow Cemetery Rd.

Open 9–5, Tues.–Sun.

Once owned by Daniel Webster, the site was acquired by MA Audubon in 1983. On Cape Cod Bay, mostly grassland and riparian land, it drains to Green Harbor Basin, a shallow river controlled by tidal gates.

This site and two other Audubon sanctuaries are managed as the South Shore Sanctuaries.

Birds: About 150 bird species have been recorded. The site attracts migratory waterfowl, shorebirds, and raptors. As many as a thousand ducks may be present at one time.

Mammals: Include red fox, opossum, raccoon, rabbit, field rodents, mink, muskrat, weasel.

Pets are prohibited. No bicycles on trails.

Publications

Leaflet.

South Shore calendar of events: nature hikes, slide shows, etc.

Headquarters

South Shore Sanctuaries, 2000 Main St., Marshfield, MA 02050; (617) 837-9400.

Dorothy F. Rice Sanctuary for Wildlife

New England Forestry Foundation   West
273 acres.

E of Pittsfield. From Hwy 8 in Hinsdale, E on Hwy 143 to South St. in Peru Center (a crossroads). 0.9 mi. S on South St. to Sanctuary sign.

A visitor center is at the parking area about ¼ mi. past the gate. It's open daily May–Aug.; it may be open weekends Sept.–Oct.; closed in winter. A bulletin board provides information when the center is closed. Guided hikes can be arranged when the supervisor is available in summer.

From the parking area, 6 trails lead out through the diverse habitats of the Sanctuary: forest, grassland, reverting fields, swamp, beaver pond. Elevations range from 1,810 to 2,140 ft.

Plants: The site is 90% forested. Tree species include red spruce, eastern hemlock, white ash, sugar maple, European white, gray, and yellow birches, beech, balsam fir, larch, red oak, mountain, red, and striped maples. Wildflowers include lady's slipper, swamp pink, asters, many more.

Birds: Checklist of 68 species available. Includes 16 warblers, hawks, osprey, owls, woodpeckers, grouse, woodcock, ducks. Peak season is spring.

Mammals: Include deer, raccoon, porcupine, beaver, skunk, red fox, red and gray squirrels, weasel, chipmunk, cottontail, bobcat, bear.

Hiking: More than 12 mi. of trails, mostly easy.

Publications

Trail guide.

Checklists of birds, mammals.

Headquarters

New England Forestry Foundation, P.O. Box 1099, Groton, MA 01450; (508) 448-8380.

....

Dubuque Memorial State Forest

Massachusetts Division of Forests and Parks   West
7,822 acres.

NW MA. From Adams, 13 mi. SE on Hwy 116, then N 1 mi. on Hwy 8A.

In the high northern Berkshires, this is part of the large block that includes Mohawk Trail and Savoy Mountain State Forests (see entries). This Forest has a well-developed trail system, with separate trails for hiking, horse riding, and recreation vehicles. It is one of the few where overnight stays are permitted.

The terrain is heavily forested, rugged, elevations from 1,200 to 2,000 ft. The site has several brooks, beaver dams, and 2 ponds, the largest about ½ mi. long.

Plants: The forest is typical of the region: northern hardwoods with some white pine, hemlock, and spruce; azalea and hobblebush in the understory. Seasonal wildflowers include violets, orchids, trillium, touch-me-not, trout lily, spring beauty, gentians.

Birds: Include ruffed grouse, woodcock, hawks, owls, bluebird, scarlet tanager, thrushes, brown thrasher, flycatchers, black-capped chickadee, tufted titmouse, brown creeper, warblers, some waterfowl.

Mammals: Include snowshoe hare, cottontail, red and gray squirrels, red fox, raccoon, skunk, muskrat, beaver, otter, mink, weasel, bobcat, deer. Occasional black bear and coyote.

Interpretation
Nature trail around Hallockville Pond, near HQ on Hwy 8A.

Activities
Camping: 15 wilderness campsites.

Hiking, backpacking: 8 mi. of designated hiking trails; 35 mi. of little-used woods roads.

Fishing: Ponds and streams. Trout, perch, pickerel.

Headquarters
Dubuque Memorial State Forest, Rt. 8A, Hawley, MA 01070; (413) 339-5504 (Mohawk Trail State Forest).

....

Erving State Forest

Massachusetts Division of Forests and Parks   West
4,479 acres.

From Athol, 8 mi. W on Hwy 2A, then N 2 mi. on Wendell Depot Rd.

The camping area is on a steep, forested hillside above a small lake. The opposite shore has private cottages. We were told the campground is often full on weekends.

In the morning we hiked up a steep forest road from the campground. Trees are mostly oak, white pine, and hemlock, with mountain laurel, azalea, blueberry, and honeysuckle in the understory. Seasonal wildflowers include painted trillium, Solomon's seal, bunchberry, clintonia, mayflower.

Birds: Mostly upland forest species: whip-poor-will, flycatchers, wrens, hawks, owls, grouse, woodcock, scarlet tanager, bluebird, thrushes, warblers, chickadee, titmouse. We saw no waterfowl but assume some migrants come through.

Mammals: Include raccoon, snowshoe hare, chipmunk, weasel, cottontail, muskrat, beaver, red fox, red and gray squirrels, bobcat.

Interpretation
Nature trail, 1 mi.

Activities
Camping: 32 sites. May to mid-Oct. Pets OK.

Hiking: 2-mi. trail; 12 mi. of forest roads.

Hunting: Deer, upland small game.

Fishing: Trout in Laurel Lake and streams.

Headquarters
Erving State Forest, Rt. 2A, Erving, MA 01364; (413) 544-3939.

....

Eugene D. Moran Wildlife Management Area
See Windsor State Forest.

....

Felix Neck Wildlife Sanctuary
See Martha's Vineyard.

....

Garden in the Woods
New England Wild Flower Society   Central
45 acres.

From Hwy 128, W 8 mi. on Hwy 20. Left on Raymond Rd. .3 mi. S to Hemenway Rd.

Open April 15–Oct. 31, except Mondays. 9–4.

From early spring through late fall, this remarkable site displays over 1,600 varieties of plants, including many rare and endangered native species. Plants and books on sale.

Pets, picnicking, smoking, and baby strollers are prohibited. Children under 16 must be accompanied by an adult.

Interpretation
Guided walks.

Horticultural and botanical library.

Special events.

Publications
Site leaflet.

Site map.

Plant sales list.

Calendar of special events.

Curtis Trail Guide (self-guiding booklet).

Wildflower Cultivation, Propagation, and Sources.

Headquarters
Garden in the Woods, Hemenway Rd., Framingham, MA 01701; (508) 877-6574.

Granville State Forest

Massachusetts Division of Forests and Parks   West
2,376 acres.

From Hwy 57 just E of Granville town line, S at sign.

The entrance road passes a campground, swimming area, and many scattered picnic sites. On the slopes above the river, the forest is largely mature hemlocks with almost no ground cover. Elsewhere is a fine spring display of mountain laurel. Terrain is steep with many ridges and ravines draining to the Hubbard River. Elevations range from 400 to 1,400 ft. The river, dropping over a waterfall and cascade, descends 450 ft. in 2½ mi.

Activities

Camping: 2 campgrounds, 40 sites. May to mid-Oct.

Hiking: 3 mi. of trails. The AMC guide (see Introduction) describes several trails extending along the river and beyond the Forest.

Hunting: Deer, snowshoe hare, grouse, woodcock.

Fishing: Trout stocked.

Swimming: Stream and small pond.

Ski touring, snowmobiling: 11 mi. of unplowed roads.

Publication
Map.

Headquarters
Granville State Forest, W. Hartland Rd., Granville, MA 01034; (413) 357-6611 or (413) 269-6002 (Tolland State Forest).

Great Meadows National Wildlife Refuge

U.S. Fish and Wildlife Service   East
3,400 acres.

About 20 mi. W of Boston. Two major public use areas: The *Weir Hill visitor center,* Sudbury Unit, is located on Weir Hill Rd. in Sudbury. The *Concord Unit* is located off Monsen Rd. in Concord.

The Refuge is one of the best inland birding sites in MA, whether one travels on foot or by boat. Both of its units are clearly shown on the "Boston and Vicinity" section of the official transportation map. The Sudbury Unit/Weir Hill visitor center is on the Sudbury River. The Concord Unit lies along the Concord River. Together they occupy about 12 mi. of river bottomland and marsh. Walden Pond (see entry) lies between them; Thoreau explored the area and made field notes about its flora and fauna. The state's 411-acre Pantry Brook Wildlife Management Area adjoins the Sudbury Unit on the NW, at the end of Weir Hill Rd.; hunting is permitted there.

Great Meadows Refuge serves as HQ for a complex of 8 National Wildlife Refuges in MA and NH. It was established and is managed for migratory birds, chiefly waterfowl. The floodplain has marshes and impoundments. A fringe of trees grows on the narrow strip of upland, but the range of elevations within the Refuge is only 8 ft. Many waterfowl stop here during the fall migration. The best viewing is from the Dike Trail in the Concord Unit.

Plants: Wetland species include water lilies, American lotus, iris, duckweed, cattail, pickerelweed, arrowhead, loosestrife, wild oats, wild cucumber, buttonbush, sparganium, jack-in-the-pulpit, skunk cabbage, touch-me-not.

Birds: Despite the limited upland habitat, 221 birds species have been recorded in recent years. A checklist is available, prepared in cooperation with the MA Audubon Society.

Seasonally abundant or common water- and shorebirds include great blue heron, black-crowned night-heron, Canada goose, wood duck, black duck, mallard, green-winged and blue-winged teals, American wigeon, ring-necked duck, coot, sora, killdeer, spotted and least sandpipers.

Interpretation

Weir Hill visitor center, in Sudbury Unit, has exhibits, auditorium, information, bookstore. Open daily May–Oct.; closed weekends Nov.–April.

Nature trails include a 1 mi. walking trail that circles the visitor center, passes through upland, along marsh edge, through a red maple swamp and around a small pond. The Concord Unit has 2.7 mi. of trails around an impoundment pool and through woodlands; an *observation tower* and *photography blind* offer further opportunities to view wildlife.

Guided walks are offered spring and fall.

Evening programs and *workshops* are scheduled throughout the year.

Activities

Fishing Both rivers: bass, perch, bullhead.

Canoeing: Both rivers are canoeable to their confluence, traversing both Refuge units. Both are passable at all water levels, with no rapids. Especially at higher water, paddling against a headwind is difficult.

Publications

Refuge leaflet with map.

Bird checklist.

Trail guides for each unit.

The Meadows Messenger (quarterly newsletter).

Headquarters
Great Meadows National Wildlife Refuge, Weir Hill Rd., Sudbury, MA 01776; (508) 443-4661.

H. O. Cook State Forest

Massachusetts Division of Forests and Parks   East
1,620 acres.

On the VT border. From Hwy 2 Charlemont, N 8 mi. on Hwy 8A.

Rugged, forested terrain is sharply dissected by several large streams. Highest elevation is 1,740 ft. Of interest are several hundred acres of Norway spruce and white pine planted in the early 1900s and now reaching maturity. Elsewhere the pattern is familiar: northern hardwoods with red spruce. Azalea and hobblebush are prominent in the understory. Numerous wildflowers in openings.

Hiking: 6 mi. of little-used forest roads.

Headquarters
c/o Mohawk Trail State Forest, P.O. Box 7, Charlemont, MA 01339; (413) 339-5504.

Harold Parker State Forest

Massachusetts Division of Forests and Parks   East
3,500 acres

SE of Andover, between Hwys 125 and 114. Several entrances, well signed.

We were told most visitors come from nearby, chiefly for fishing and camping. Most other campers are transients staying for one night, as we did.

The original forest was cut or burned long ago, followed by farming and pasturing. Now there is again a mature forest cover, some developing through succession, but we also saw extensive plantations. The site includes 10 ponds and a wooded swamp.

Although the site is relatively large, a number of paved and unpaved roads divide it into blocks, none of which seems larger than about 400 acres. The map shows no point more than ½ mi. from a road.

The site is considered poor to fair for birding.

We didn't rate the site highly as an attractive natural area because of road traffic and relatively heavy use. It is an entry because it has one of the few public campgrounds in the region, a base for visits to other sites.

Activities

Camping: 134 sites. Reservations accepted. Pets OK.

Hiking: Trails and woods roads throughout the site.

Hunting: Limited seasonal releases of pheasant and snowshoe hare. Hunting restricted to section E of Jenkins Rd.

Fishing: Berry Pond is stocked with trout but is rated marginal. Fair to good warmwater fishing for bass and pickerel in other ponds.

Publication
Site map showing trails and roads.

Headquarters
Harold Parker State Forest, 1951 Turnpike Rd., North Andover, MA 01845; (508) 686-3391.

....

High Ridge Wildlife Management Area
Massachusetts Division of Fisheries and Wildlife   Central
2,018 acres.

N central MA, near Gardner. From the intersection of Hwys 101 and 140, go SE on 140, left on Smith St., see WMA sign and proceed to parking.

This was once a mental hospital surrounded by productive farm fields. The buildings, across the railroad tracks, are now a minimum security prison. The land is a fairly recent WMA acquisition. Only foot travel is permitted beyond the parking area.

Terrain is rolling, from a base elevation of about 900 ft. to the open ridge at 1,200 ft. that gives the site its name. A mix of agricultural fields, brushy fields, and hardwood forest provides the habitat edges favored by many wildlife species. An arm of Whitman Reservoir penetrates the NE corner. Two small streams with native trout supply several marshy areas.

Wildlife includes deer, waterfowl, grouse, woodcock, rabbit.

The site's attractions are modest, but it's easy hiking and except in hunting season you're not likely to have company. The view from the ridge includes Mounts Wachusett and Monadnock.

Publication
Site map.

Headquarters
Central Wildlife District Office, Temple St., West Boylston, MA 01583; (508) 835-3607.

....

Hinsdale Flats Wildlife Management Area
Massachusetts Division of Fisheries and Wildlife   West
1,454 acres.

E of Pittsfield. From the junction with Hwy 143, go 0.8 mi. S on Hwy 8. Left on Middlefield Rd. (Skyline Trail) 0.7 mi. to WMA sign. Park on roadside.

Middlefield Rd. is at the N end of the WMA, whose N–S length is about 4 times its width. From here, the highest part of the site, one overlooks a large area of rolling fields, dropping down to the forest edge, and seasonally flooded stream bottoms. The East Branch of the Housatonic River is near the W boundary. Bilodeau Brook bisects the area. The site has two small artificial ponds and a beaver pond. Other mammals include otter, mink, muskrat, bear.

Activities
Hunting: Stocked pheasant; also woodcock, grouse, waterfowl, raccoon, gray squirrel, cottontail, deer.

Fishing: Trout in the East Branch and several brooks.

Headquarters
Western Wildlife District Office, 400 Hubbard Ave., Pittsfield, MA
01201; (413) 447-9789.

Hiram H. Fox Wildlife Management Area

Massachusetts Division of Fisheries and Wildlife   West
2,653 acres.

From Hwy 9 near Cummington, drive S on Hwy 112 through Ringville
and angle right on Goss Hill Rd.

We couldn't find a Goss Hill Rd. sign and had to ask. The parking area
is on the right a little over 1 mi. from Hwy 112. From this point, a trail
runs SW.

The site is rolling with some steep ledges and gullies, elevations
from 700 to 1,200 ft., forested with a mixture of hardwoods and
conifers. Meadow Brook crosses the site, as does Little River, close
beside Hwy 112. There are 2 small marshy areas.

Wildlife includes bear, deer, grouse, raccoon, snowshoe hare, gray
squirrel, bobcat, wild turkey, some waterfowl.

Headquarters
Western Wildlife District Office, 400 Hubbard Ave., Pittsfield, MA
01201; (413) 447-9789.

Hockomock Swamp Wildlife Management Area

Massachusetts Division of Fisheries and Wildlife   East
4,430 acres.

From Hwy 24, Exit 15 (just N of I-495). Take Hwy 104 W. Lake
Nippenicket is on the right.

Lake Nippenicket is at the SE corner of the WMA, which extends N to Hwy 106 and W to Bay Rd. in Taunton. State land occupies only about half of this area, in one large but irregular and sprawling block plus numerous detached bits.

Much of the area is wooded, but the chief attractions are the wetlands: maple and cedar swamps, marshlands, open water, and flowing streams. With a map one can find trails and other foot routes, but the best way to explore the area is by canoe.

In the SW corner, Bay Rd. runs between the WMA and Winnecunnet Pond. About 0.6 mi. N, turn right on Toad Island Rd. to a parking area. From here unimproved roads cross and encircle a 450-acre tract on the N side of the Snake River, which is bordered by marshland. This tract was a turkey farm, and the open lands are under cultivation. Pheasants are stocked, and waterfowl frequent the area.

Lake Nippenicket, 368 acres, was formerly owned by a hunting club. About 1½ mi. long, the lake has a boat ramp at the SE corner. There are opportunities to shore fish, bird-watch, or duck hunt along an unimproved road and foot trail on the W side.

Fisheries and Wildlife told us that about all of the wildlife species occurring in SE MA can be found here.

Birds: Of the waterfowl, black duck, mallard, wood duck, and teal are most abundant, but many others stop during migrations. Also pheasant, grouse, woodcock, quail, and many songbirds.

Mammals: Include deer, snowshoe hare, cottontail, squirrels, muskrat, fox, raccoon, mink, weasel, opossum, otter, skunk.

Activities
Fishing: Lake has chain pickerel, largemouth bass, black crappie.

Canoeing, boating: The Town River flows N from the N end of Lake Nippenicket, being joined in about 1 mi. by the S-flowing Hockomock and continuing NE. These two rivers, the Snake, and the lake are canoeable, although the segment of the Town River just beyond the lake is often overgrown.

Publications
Maps of the WMA.

Headquarters
Southeast Wildlife District Office, 195 Bournedale Rd., Buzzards Bay, MA 02532; (508) 759-3406.

Hopkinton State Park

Massachusetts Division of Forests and Parks   East
1,450 acres.

From I-495, Exit 21. E to Hopkinton; N on Hwy 85 to entrance.

Like most State Parks within the I-495 beltway, this one is for day use only. Like most parks with water-based recreation, it is heavily used in warm weather, at least on weekends. We visited about 9 A.M. on a July weekday and saw few visitors.

Hopkinton doesn't fit our definition of "natural area" because it has been developed for intensive use, with recreation field, pavilion, boathouse, bathhouse, 5 launching ramps, and a dozen parking areas. Development is on the N side of mile-long Hopkinton Reservoir. The lake is largely surrounded by hardwood forest.

We include it as an example of sites we generally omit: attractive, popular, but not a quiet place.

Hiking: A trail about 1 mi. long skirts the N boundary of the site. We were told there is undeveloped acreage on the other side of Hwy 85, near Park HQ, but the site map shows only the developed area.

Publication
Site map.

Headquarters
Hopkinton State Park, Rt. 85, Hopkinton, MA 01748; (508) 435-4303.

Hubbardston Wildlife Management Area

Massachusetts Division of Fisheries and Wildlife   Central
600 acres.

From Hubbardston on Hwy 68, E on Westminster Rd. At the fork of Westminster and New Westminster, take your choice; the former crosses the N portion of the site, the latter the S portion.

This area is dotted with many low hills, mostly surrounded by wetlands, most drained by Joslin Brook. Uplands are open fields, brushy fields, and young forest.

Nothing dramatic, but it's a quiet and pleasant area for a day hike with good birding, not in hunting season. Warmwater fish in the ponds.

Publication
Map.

Headquarters
Central Wildlife District Office, Temple St., West Boylston, MA 01583; (508) 835-3607.

....

Ipswich River Sanctuary

Massachusetts Audubon Society   East
2,800 acres.

About 20 mi. N of Boston, in Topsfield. From US 1, E on Hwy 97 at traffic light. Left on Perkins Row. 1 mi. to entrance.

Open Tues.–Sun. 9–5.

The site, a former estate, has many exceptional qualities, not the least of which is the information describing its flora and fauna. Few sites in this region with similar characteristics provide such data.

Its numerous habitats include coniferous and deciduous woods, fields, shrublands, wooded swamp, marsh, bog, and meadow.

Plants: 445 species have been recorded. A list with common and scientific names is available for inspection.

The wooded upland overlooks the Ipswich River. In the early 1900s, the then owner developed an impressive arboretum. At The Rockery, great boulders were arranged in a setting for both endemic and exotic flora. Included are Douglas-fir, Korean, mugho, and Jeffrey pines, dwarf Alberta spruce, sawara cypress, as well as sourwood, mountain laurel, azaleas, and rhododendrons. Exotic species include winged euonymus, Frazier and sweet bay magnolias, mountain and Japanese andromedas, Amur corktree, Oriental photinia, red-veined enkainthus, and many more.

Arboretum Rd., circling Bradstreet Hill, is bordered with azaleas, rhododendrons, and many exotics.

The Wildflower Garden, SE of Bradstreet Hill, was begun in 1951, with the aim of assembling all the spring wildflower species occurring in Essex County.

Birds: 221 species have been recorded. The list is available for inspection. 98 of the species reported nest here. The list includes data on abundance, seasonality, and habitat preference.

An observation tower overlooks the Bunker Meadows Waterfowl Management Area.

Prominent species include black and wood ducks, greater scaup, hooded merganser, Canada goose, bald eagle, osprey, Cooper's, red-tailed, red-shouldered, and broad-winged hawks, kestrel, merlin, northern and loggerhead shrikes, brown thrasher, veery, white-breasted nuthatch, goldfinch, Philadelphia vireo, Henslow's sparrow, 10 warblers.

Mammals: 26 species have been recorded. List is available for inspection and includes deer, raccoon, opossum, red fox, skunk, otter, muskrat, squirrel, weasel.

Reptiles and amphibians: 18 species have been recorded. List is available for inspection and includes many turtles, garter, black, and grass snakes.

Activities

Hiking: 10 mi. of trails.

Canoeing: River ecology float trips on the Ipswich River. Canoe rentals.

Pets are prohibited.

Nearby
Parker River National Wildlife Refuge; Richard T. Crane, Jr., Memorial Reservation; Willowdale State Forest. (See entries.)

Publication
Calendar of events.

Headquarters
Ipswich River Wildlife Sanctuary, 87 Perkins Row, Topsfield, MA 01983; (508) 887-9264.

Kenneth Dubuque Memorial State Forest

See Dubuque Memorial State Forest.

Lake Dennison State Park

See Birch Hill Wildlife Management Area.

Laughing Brook Education Center and Wildlife Sanctuary

Massachusets Audubon Society   Central
340 acres.

From I-91 near Springfield, Exit 4. Take Hwy 83 S to Sumner Ave. E 3.6 mi. on Sumner, then bear right on Allen St. for 4.7 mi. into Hampden. Left 2 mi. on Main St.

With some 250 people enlisted as volunteers, this is one of the Audubon Society's liveliest sanctuaries. The site map shows the way to the Environmental Center, Storyteller's House, goose and deer pen, wildflower garden, nature center, land use ethic exhibit, Smiling Pool, dinosaur tracks, live animal loop, and more. This was the estate of children's author and naturalist Thornton W. Burgess; his house is now the Storyteller's House.

The buildings and other developments occupy 5 acres. Around them are 200 acres of woodland, 37 of swampland, 8 of open fields, Laughing Brook, the Scantic River.

Plants: The wildflower list notes seasonal abundance.

Birds: The bird list is divided into winter and summer residents, with notes on migrants.

Mammals: Although the site is near Springfield and just off a main commuter route, it has deer, porcupine, red and gray foxes, bobcat, as well as opossum, river otter, mink, weasel, beaver, woodchuck, chipmunk, gray, red, and flying squirrels, cottontail, mice.

Interpretation

The Education Center is a 2-story, modern building with library, auditorium, exhibits, program room, solar greenhouse, shop, and offices. Open Tues.–Sun., 10–5; also open holiday Mondays.

Program brochure lists many special events for children and adults, continuing throughout the year. Activities include classes, films, guided hikes, day camps.

Five nature trails, 0.5 to 1.6 mi. Trails visit a glacial esker, red pine forest, boardward near the river, hemlock, grove.

Pets are prohibited.

Publications

Trail map.

Seasonal program brochure.

Sanctuary newsletter, published seasonally.

Introductory guide.

Passport to Nature (brochure for all MA Audubon sanctuaries, includes list of 100 common birds of MA).

Headquarters

Laughing Brook Education Center and Wildlife Sanctuary, 793 Main St., Hampden, MA 01036; (413) 566-8034.

....

Leominster State Forest

Massachusetts Division of Forests and Parks   Central
4,126 acres.

Near Fitchburg and Leominster. From Hwy 2, about 2½ mi. on Hwy 31.

Hwy 31 cuts N–S across the W side of the Forest. Its highest point, 1,234-ft. Crow Hill, and the Mid-State Trail, are in the narrow strip between Hwy 31 and the W boundary. Park HQ is on Hwy 31. Rocky Pond Rd. runs W–E across the middle.

Terrain is rolling to steep, from a base elevation of about 800 ft. Most of it is forested with a mixture of hardwoods, most of them 6- to

8-inch diameter, and white pine. We saw much mountain laurel and were told there are 1,000 acres of it, plus 75 to 100 acres of azalea. Many blueberries and wildflowers.

Activities

Hiking: 28 mi. of trails, some steep. The Mid-State Trail links Leominster with the Wachusett Reservation (see entry). A popular trail ascends Crow Hill, which has a 165-ft. open face and ledge used by rock climbers.

Hunting: Deer and small upland game, in undeveloped areas.

Fishing: Trout stocked in Crow Pond.

Swimming: Pond and stream.

Publication

Site map, showing trails.

Headquarters

Leominster State Forest, Rt. 31, Leominster, MA 01453; (508) 874-2303.

....

Martha's Vineyard

Mixed ownership　　　　　　　　　　　　　　　　　　　　　East
25 mi. W–E, 10 mi. N–S.

Car ferry from Woods Hole. Summer passenger service from Falmouth, Hyannis, and New Bedford. Also air service.

This triangular island lies 7 mi. S of Cape Cod. Vineyard Sound and Elizabeth Island are on the NE, Nantucket Sound on the NW, the Atlantic Ocean along its S base. Of the 3 principal towns, Vineyard Haven and Oak Bluffs are on the N, Edgartown on the SE.

We spent enough time there in the 1940s to enjoy some of its traditions and folkways. Development has changed it. Devoted islanders have helped preserve some significant natural areas, including a State Forest and several private sanctuaries. Magnificent South Beach is still there, but the access routes we used are now marked "No Trespassing." Traffic has come to the dirt roads where we cycled.

It's still attractive. Being an island gives it some insulation. If we do go back, it will be after the summer crowds have gone. Below, we've listed a few natural areas for those seeking quiet places on the island.

Features

Cape Poge Wildlife Refuge: 501 acres; *Mytoi:* 14 acres; and *Wasque Reservation:* 200 acres. All are managed by The Trustees of Reservations and are on Chappaquiddick Island in the SE corner of Martha's Vineyard, a ferry ride from Edgartown. Cape Poge is well known to birders. Located at the N Tip of a barrier beach that encircles Cape Poge Bay, its low sand dunes, cedar thickets, tidal flats, and more than 6 mi. of beach offer habitat and nesting areas for thousands of sea- and shorebirds, including Canada goose, snowy egret, black-crowned nightheron, oyster catcher, least tern. *Headquarters:* The Trustees of Reservations, 290 Argilla Rd., Box 563, Ipswich, MA 01938; (508) 356-4351.

Felix Neck Wildlife Sanctuary: 350 acres. 4 mi. SE of Vineyard Haven on the Edgartown Rd. This outstanding wildlife area is a terminal moraine with a good representation of barrier beaches, salt ponds, marshes, open fields, and pine woods. These fresh- and saltwater habitats along the SE coast of Martha's Vineyard support native waterfowl and nesting osprey. The 4 mi. of self-guided trails are open daily and include a photography blind on Sengekontacket Pond. A visitor center has wildlife exhibits, films, talks, information (open 8–4:30 daily July–Aug., 9–4 Tues.–Sun. the rest of the year). Trail guide and bird checklist available. *Headquarters:* MA Audubon Society, Edgartown Rd., Vineyard Haven, MA 02568; (508) 627-4850.

Long Point Wildlife Refuge: 580 acres. From Edgartown-W. Tisbury Rd., left on Deep Bottom Rd., 1 mi. past airport entrance, then another 3 mi. This is a fine birding area. The glacial outwash plain has pitch pine/oak forest, salt- and freshwater ponds, salt marshes, sandy beaches on the ocean. *Headquarters:* The Trustees of Reservations, 290 Argilla Rd., Box 563, Ipswich, MA 01938: (508) 356-4351.

Manuel Correllus State Forest: 4,343 acres. 4 mi. SE of Vineyard Haven on Edgartown Rd. (across from Felix Neck Wildlife Sanctuary), turn right on Barnes Rd. to park. At the center of the island, this site is, geographically, furthest removed from summer activity. We remember woodlands, bushy fields, windswept hilltops, and fine views. It wasn't a State Forest then. Today the Div. of Forests and Parks' literature mentions hiking, biking, equestrian areas, hunting in season, cross-country skiing. *Headquarters:* Manuel Correllus State Forest, Edgartown, MA 02539; (508) 693-2540.

Martin Burns Wildlife Management Area

Massachusetts Division of Fisheries and Wildlife   East
1,555 acres.

S of Newburyport, between I-95 and US 1. From US 1, SW on Middle
St. Bear right on Orchard St., about 1 mi. to entrance on right.

This is an attractive area for day hiking. On the last day of July we
were the only visitors. The gravel entrance road passes the HQ building. Several parking areas are beyond. A network of trails spans the
site.

The land is gently rolling with many rock outcrops. Primary habitats are brush and young hardwood forest with small clearings, but
there are also large areas of marsh and wooded swamp. We saw many
wildflowers, including large patches of loosestrife.

Wildlife: Most native species are present, including many songbirds.
Hunting: Special rules posted. Mostly for stocked pheasant and
snowshoe hare.

Trail bikes and all-terrain vehicles are prohibited.

Publication
Map with text.

Headquarters
Northeast Wildlife District Office, Harris St., Box 2086, Acton, MA
01720; (508) 263-4347.

Metacomet-Monadnock Trail

Mixed ownership   West
CT–NH.

The trail extends from the Hanging Hills of Meridan, CT to Mount
Monadnock in NH. It enters MA just W of Hwy 187, near Agawam,

and enters NH from the Warwick State Forest (see entry). That the trail even exists is remarkable. It has had far less publicity, official support, and volunteer work than the Appalachian Trail, and the route presented even greater difficulties.

Like the AT, it links a series of State Parks and State Forests, and wherever possible it keeps to high ground. But the mountains framing the Connecticut River Valley aren't as high as those of the Berkshires, and much of the route has had to be over lowlands. Many sections of the trail follow roads, but the planners have been ingenious in piecing together back roads, abandoned rights-of-way, and other lightly traveled routes.

Trailside camping is prohibited in MA, and few of the State Parks and Forests have campgrounds. Those who bike from border to border must spend most nights off the trail. For more information, contact the Appalachian Mountain Club, 5 Joy St., Boston, MA 02108; (617) 523-0636.

Midstate Trail

Midstate Trail Volunteers   Central
92 trail miles.

From Asburnham, near the NH border, to Douglas State Forest on the RI border.

The trail travels the length of Worcester County, linking a chain of State Parks, and Wildlife Management Areas. An earlier footpath from Mount Watatic to Wachusett Mountain fell into disrepair by the 1950s. In 1972 the County commissioners formed an advisory committee to rejuvenate and extend the trail. Planning and clearing the route required permission from landowners in sections between public landholdings. It was dedicated in 1985. The trail, blazed with yellow triangles, is maintained by volunteers. At the N end, the trail connects with the 20-mi. Wapack Trail in NH.

5 Adirondack shelters are available for backpackers. Volunteers lead trail hikes in the summer months.

Publication

Midstate Trail Guide, rev. ed., 46 pages, is available at a cost of $7 ($10 by mail). For more information about the trail, or to order the guide, contact Bob Elms, 143 Nola Dr., Holden, MA 01520; (508) 829-2600. (Recreation outfitters in MA, as well as the Appalachian Mountain Club, may also have the guide for sale.)

Millers River Wildlife Management Area

Massachusetts Division of Fisheries and Wildlife　　　　　　West
2,582 acres.

From Athol, 3–4 miles on Millers River Rd.

Millers River flows W to meet the Connecticut River at Greenfield. The S part of the WMA is a narrow strip along the river, which offers good trout fishing and part of a whitewater canoe run. The larger portion of the WMA extends N, a little E of the Athol-Royalston Rd. Here the terrain is steep and rocky, forested, good habitat for upland wildlife.

Although the road follows the river, access points are limited. People wanting to fish and willing to walk and scramble can find good trout waters where fishing pressure is light.

The Birch Hill Flood Control Dam regulates river flow. Whitewater canoeists are attracted by class III rapids during spring high water.

Publication

Map.

Headquarters

Central District Wildlife Office, Temple St., West Boylston, MA 01583; (508) 835-3607.

Mohawk Trail State Forest

Massachusetts Division of Forests and Parks   West
6,457 acres.

On both sides of Hwy 2 about 18 mi. E of North Adams; 25 mi. W of
the Greenfield/I-91 rotary.

At the N end of the Hoosac Range, the Forest straddles Hwy 2, the
Mohawk Trail. One of the larger State Forests, it has a common
boundary on the W with the 10,500-acre Savoy State Forest (see
entry), making this the largest block of undeveloped land in MA. The
Dubuque Memorial State Forest (see entry) is on the S. The terrain is
hilly to mountainous, with ridges, deep gorges, rock outcrops, and
ledges. Principal streams are the Cold and Deerfield Rivers. Elevations
range from 700 ft. at the rivers to 1,961 ft. at Indian Lookout.

This is a hiker's forest. The adjacent Savoy has a more extensive
trail system, but here there are also woods roads, some used, other
abandoned, and paths worn by hunters and fishermen. Or one can
bushwhack. Except in hunting season, few people are in the backcountry.

Plants: 95% forested, chiefly with beech, birches, and maples; oaks
on S slopes; scattered stands of hemlock, white pine, and spruce.
What we saw of the forest seemed more mature than most others in
MA, with more trees about 100 ft. tall, diameters over 3 ft. Abundant
mountain laurel, azalea, blueberry, raspberry, wild rose. Seasonal wildflowers include bloodroot, Dutchman's-breeches, trout lily, violets,
orchids, trillium, gentians, lily of the valley.

Birds: No checklist. Many grouse, woodcock, hawks, owls, songbirds.

Mammals: Black bear, deer, bobcat, coyote, raccoon, porcupine,
skunk, red and gray squirrels, red and gray foxes, otter, fisher, snowshoe hare, cottontail.

Activities

Camping: 56 sites on the Cold River. Reservations accepted. Pets OK.

Hiking: Trails to Clark Mountain, Todd Mountain, other destinations.

Fishing: Good trout fishing in both rivers.

Swimming: Beach near campground.

Canoeing: White water on some sections of the Deerfield River. Conditions change seasonally and daily, depending on releases from the power dam upstream.

Bicycling: On woods roads.

Headquarters
Mohawk Trail State Forest, P.O. Box 7, Charlemont, MA 01339; (413) 339-5504.

Monomoy National Wildlife Refuge

U.S. Fish and Wildlife Service   East
2,702 acres.

Two islands at the bend of Cape Cod, S of Chatham. Accessible only by private or commercial boat across a mile-wide channel. There is road access to HQ and a 40-acre unit on Morris Island (connected to the mainland by a "neck") in Chatham.

Monomoy, a 10-mile-long barrier beach between Nantucket Sound and the Atlantic Ocean, is a National Wilderness Area, roadless and undeveloped, with no visitor facilities. Most of its visitors are birders. The islands are famous for their spring shorebirds and waterfowl.

The long, narrow Refuge has sand beaches, dunes over 100 ft. high, salt- and freshwater marshes, freshwater ponds and kettleholes, dense thickets of scrub oak, pitch pine, black alder, and willow. The beach often offers good shelling.

Birds: Checklist available. 285 species reported, 75 considered rare. Species nesting here include Canada goose, black duck, piping plover, horned lark, savannah and saltmarsh sharp-tailed sparrows, common, arctic, roseate, and least terns. Migrants include semipalmated and black-bellied plovers, ruddy turnstone, whimbrel, hudsonian godwit, greater and lesser yellowlegs, Wilson's phalarope, red knot, sanderling, pectoral, least, and semipalmated sandpipers, dunlin, harlequin duck, king eider, hooded merganser, bald eagle, osprey, peregrine falcon. Thousands of common eider and white-winged scoter lie just off the beach, along with common loon, goldeneye, bufflehead, red-breasted merganser. Offshore oceanic birds often include shearwater, gannet, jaeger, black-legged kittiwake, razorbill, thick-billed murre, dovekie.

Mammals: Include muskrat, mink, river otter, raccoon, weasel, deer, occasional harbor seal.

Reptiles and amphibians: Include Fowler's toad, diamondback terrapin, Atlantic ridley sea turtle, leatherback sea turtle.

Activities

Hiking: Beach on Monomoy. Short trails on Morris.

Fishing: Striped bass, bluefish, flounder. Best season is May–Oct.

Swimming: Surf, unsupervised.

> *Pets are not permitted on Monomoy.*
> *Permit is required for group visit.*
> *Winds and rip tides often make the crossing to Monomoy dangerous, especially Nov.–March. Safe landings can be made only on the W shore. It is recommended that visitors hire a commercial fishing boat at Chatham.*

Publications

Refuge leaflet with map.

Bird checklist.

Morris Island Trail Guide.

Getting to the Islands (leaflet listing ferry service and guided tours).

Headquarters

Refuge Manager, Great Meadows National Wildlife Refuge Complex, Weir Hill Rd., Sudbury, MA 01776-1427; (508) 443-4661.

....

Monroe State Forest

Massachusetts Division of Forests and Parks   West
4,321 acres.

From North Adams, about 4 mi. E on Hwy 2; 2 mi. E on Tilda Hill Rd.

In the high northern Berkshires, the terrain is mountainous, with steep slopes, rock ledges and outcrops, elevations from 1,700 to 2,730 ft. The SE boundary is a road following the Deerfield River. The Forest has no river frontage but Raycroft Lookout overlooks the scenic river gorge. Dunbar Brook, which runs across the Forest NW–SE, has numerous small falls and rapids.

The area is 95% forested, chiefly with northern hardwoods, red spruce increasing on upper slopes. Wildlife is typical of the area: bear, deer, upland small game, many birds.

Activities

Camping: 3 hike-in sites.

Hiking: 9 mi. of designated foot trails, plus 6 mi. of woods roads.

Hunting: Deer, snowshoe hare, bobcat, raccoon, cottontail, squirrels, grouse, woodcock.

Fishing: Trout streams.

Headquarters

c/o Mohawk Trail State Forest, P.O. Box 7, Charlemont, MA 01339; (413) 339-5504.

Moose Hill Wildlife Sanctuary

Massachusetts Audubon Society   East
1,975 acres.

I-95S Exit 10, left at end of ramp. Right at intersection to Hwy 27N toward Walpole. After 0.5 mi. turn left onto Moose Hill St., go 1.5 mi.

Open 9–5.

The Audubon Society's booklet describing its properties in the state says that Moose Hill is a "haven for wildlife and people in search of quiet solitude." It became the society's first MA sanctuary in 1922.

The terrain is rolling. From a granite bluff at 600-ft. elevation, there's a fine view. Then the land drops down through open deciduous forest to fields and meadows and a red maple swamp traversed by a boardwalk. (The last is a blaze of color in the fall.) 15 mi. of trails lead through the site's several habitats. The Fern Trail has an exceptional number of fern species. Site has a butterfly garden.

Birds: Migrating waterfowl pause at the swamp. Species often seen include Canada goose, hooded merganser, teals. Also goshawk, northern harrier, green heron, bluebird, woodpeckers, grackles, blue jay, tufted titmouse, red-eyed vireo, northern oriole, scarlet tanager, grouse, warblers.

Mammals: Include deer, raccoon, chipmunk, squirrels, skunk, opossum, mice.

Interpretation
Visitor center offers adult classes and school tours.

Pets are prohibited. Bicycles are not allowed on trails.

Publication
Brochure.

Headquarters
Moose Hill Wildlife Sanctuary, 293 Moose Hill St., Sharon, MA 02067; (617) 784-5691.

Mount Grace State Forest/Northfield State Forest/ Warwick State Forest

Massachusetts Division of Forests and Parks   West
11,012 acres

From Athol, W on Hwy 2A, N on Hwy 78. Northfield is W of Hwy 78; Mt. Grace is further N; Warwick is on the road E from Warwick.

These Forests have a common HQ. At 7,100 acres, Warwick is the largest, although the map shows it to be a number of separate blocks. Without maps it would be difficult to know where Forest Land begins and ends, but this is sparsely settled country and boundaries seldom matter.

The pattern is common to N central MA: rolling, forested, elevations generally between 700 and 1,200 ft., a few hills rising higher. Trees are northern hardwoods with some white pine and hemlock; mountain laurel and azalea are prominent in the understory; trillium, lady's slipper, mayflower, Solomon's seal, and clintonia are common wildflowers. Birds and mammals are also typical of the region.

Northfield has several streams and small swamps. It is crossed by several gravel roads. The map shows no trails, but woods roads offer hiking opportunities. Snowmobilers use the area in winter.

Mt. Grace, on the VT border, attracts more hikers, chiefly because the Metacomet-Monadnock Trail (see entry) crosses the 1,617-ft. summit of Mt. Grace. There's a shelter for backpackers on the trail. Several brooks and springs. This area, too, is used by snowmobilers and mountain bikers.

Warwick is also crossed by gravel and woods roads. Sheomet Lake, almost a mile long, has a boat ramp. Numerous brooks. Snowmobiling in winter.

Publications
Maps.

Headquarters
Mt. Grace State Forest, Winchester Rd., Warwick, MA 01264; (508) 544-7474.

Mount Greylock State Reservation

Massachusetts Division of Forests and Parks   West
12,500 acres.
From Pittsfield, about 5 mi. N on Hwy 7, then right following signs.

The state's highest mountain, 3,491 ft., is also one of its most accessible, with auto roads and several trails to the top. At the top a 100-ft. tower gives an even wider sweep to the 360-degree view. You can see 5 states on a clear day. Even when there's a crowd at the top, hiking a mile or two will provide a sense of isolation.

Greylock is an isolated peak on a spur of the Taconic Range, at the S end of VT's Green Mountains. Because of its height and exposure, its climate is cooler and more severe than is usually encountered in MA. Fog, enshrouding clouds, and storms are common. Terrain is generally steep, with rock outcrops and ledges. Roaring Brook is the largest of several streams, "roaring" because of its impressive cascade.

This was MA's first State Park.

Plants: The lower and middle slopes are forested with species typical of the region: northern hardwoods with scattered hemlock and white pine. Ash, spruce, elder, hobblebush, mountain maple, and beech become more common above 3,000-ft. elevation. At the top is a boreal zone with such species as club moss, creeping snowberry, mountain wood fern, large-leafed goldenrod, asters, yellow birch.

Birds: No checklist, but an illustrated folder shows many species and where to look for them. Some species seen here are rare elsewhere in MA. Some more common here than further S are olive-sided fly-catcher, red-breasted nuthatch, brown creeper, winter wren, Swainson's thrush, golden-crowned kinglet. Summer visitors that may breed here include yellow-bellied flycatcher, Tennessee warbler, pine siskin, red and white-winged crossbills.

Mammals: No checklist. Species observed include black bear, deer, coyote, bobcat, red and gray foxes, porcupine, weasel, beaver, snowshoe hare.

Interpretation
Visitor center is open daily, 8–4:30, weekdays, 9–5:30 weekends.

Activities
Camping: 35 sites. Mid-May to mid-Oct. Pets OK.

Hiking, backpacking: This is one of the few sites on the Appalachian Trail with overnight shelters. 35 mi. of hiking trails include 11 mi. of the AT. Most trails to the summit are steep.

Fishing: Trout streams.

Publication
Birds of Mount Greylock.

Headquarters
Mt. Greylock State Reservation, Rockwell Rd., P.O. Box 138, Lanesboro, MA 01237; (413) 499-4262.

Mount Tom State Reservation
Mt. Tom Reservation Trustees   West
1,800 acres.

From I-91N, Exit 17B. N on Hwy 141; see signs.

It's state land, managed by the Trustees, who are the commissioners from Hampden and Hampshire Counties.

The mountain rises to 1,202 ft., offering fine views of the Connecticut River Valley and beyond. The geological record is interesting, providing evidence of ancient crystalline rock, marine deposits, volcanism, stream action, and glaciation. The site has streams and a pond; Lake Bray is about ⅓ mi. long.

It's a popular hiking area. The climb to the top is moderate to fairly difficult, through woods and over ledges to numerous viewpoints.

The Mt. Tom Ski Area is privately owned, not part of the Reservation.

Interpretation

Robert Cole Museum of Natural History, on Reservation Rd., has exhibits on geology, geography, butterflies, insects, birds. Usually open Memorial Day–Labor Day. (413) 527-4805.

Nature trail.

Activities

Hiking: The Metacomet-Monadnock Trail (see entry) crosses the site. Within the site are 20 mi. of trails.

Fishing: Bass and panfish in Lake Bray.

Publications

Brochure with map.

Nature trail pamphlet.

Headquarters

Mt. Tom State Reservation, Reservation Rd., Holyoke, MA 01040; (413) 527-4805.

....

Mount Washington State Forest

Massachusetts Division of Forests and Parks   West
4,169 acres.

SW corner of MA. From South Egremont 5 mi. on Hwy 41, S on Mt. Washington Rd. (Or E from Copake, NY.)

The Southern Taconic Highland straddles the NY–MA border at the S end of the Berkshires. On the MA side are some of the state's highest mountains. Mount Everett, 2,623 ft., is the highest. The area is rugged, scenic, heavily forested, with steep slopes, rock outcrops, and ledges. Some of the nearby mountains are privately owned and inaccessible, but there's plenty of backcountry for hikers.

The principal attraction for visitors here is Bash-Bish Falls, set in a spectacular gorge. The falls are most impressive during the spring runoff but always scenic. The Forest has other falls, too, as well as streams and cascades, mostly away from the road.

Activities

Camping: 15 hike-in sites.

Hiking, Backpacking: The Appalachian Trail crosses Mt. Everett, heading S into CT. On the W is the South Taconic Trail, partially in NY's Taconic State Park. A trailhead for Mt. Everett is at the Berkshire School off Hwy 41. Total of 15 mi. of trails within the Forest.

Headquarters

Mt. Washington State Forest, East St., Mt. Washington, MA 01258; (413) 528-0330.

Myles Standish State Forest

Massachusetts Division of Forests and Parks 14,651 acres.

East

Near Plymouth. From I-495, Exit 2, then 3 mi. N on Hwy 58 to South Carver; then follow signs.

About 40 mi. S of Boston, near major highways, and with the state's largest public campground, this site is heavily used in summer, during hunting season, and when under snow cover. It is also the second largest area of state land.

A glacial moraine and outwash plain, it has sandy flat lowlands broken by a few small, steep-sided knobs. Elevations range from 50 to

240 ft. Of its many kettle ponds, the largest covers 53 acres. The site has a few marshy areas.

Plants: The Forest supports one of the largest assemblages of rare plant species occurring in MA. They are found throughout in 2 rare natural communities: coastal plain pondshore, and pitch pine/scrub oak barrens.

95% of the area is forested, chiefly with dense growth. Ground cover includes blueberry, wildflowers, ferns, mushrooms. Open fields have been planted with seed crops for birds.

Birds: No checklist. Species include hawks, owls, whip-poor-will, nighthawk, chickadee, junco, titmouse, nuthatch, sparrows, scarlet tanager, bluebird, northern oriole, cedar waxwing, woodpeckers, warblers, grosbeaks, marsh birds, waterfowl.

Mammals: No checklist. Species include red and gray foxes, red and gray squirrels, raccoon, cottontail, opossum, muskrat, occasional deer.

Reptiles and amphibians: Garter, black, grass, and hog-nosed snakes, box turtle.

Interpretation
Naturalist programs, June–Aug.

Activities
Camping: 475 sites in several campgrounds. Some open all year.

Hiking: Despite its size, this isn't a hiker's forest. Roads crosshatch the area at intervals of about a half mile, and these roads are used by horse riders, mountain bikers, and motorcyclers. There are many paths, used mostly by hunters and fishermen.

Hunting: Pheasant and quail are stocked. Grouse, rabbit, deer.

Fishing: Bass, perch, pickerel, trout, in the ponds.

Swimming: Two sand-bottom ponds. Supervised in season.

Features
Myles Standish Wildlife Management Area: 2,000 acres. The WMA is managed by the MA Div. of Fisheries and Wildlife and is actually 2 areas within the Forest. The larger lies W of Upper College Pond Rd., S of College Pond. The smaller is a quail area about 1 mi. SE. Both are managed for game birds, with clearings and plantings.

Publications

State Forest map.

Wildlife Management Area map.

Headquarters

Myles Standish State Forest, Long Pond Rd., P.O. Box 66, South Carver, MA 02366; (508) 866-2526.

Nantucket Wildlife Refuges: Coatue Wildlife Refuge and the Haulover/Coskata-Coatue Wildlife Refuge/ Nantucket National Wildlife Refuge

Nantucket Conservation Foundation/The Trustees of Reservations/U.S. Fish and Wildlife Service
476, 792, and 40 acres, respectively.

Ferry from mainland to Nantucket Island. From the town of Nantucket follow Orange St. to Milestone Rd., to Polpis Rd., to Wauwinet Rd. and the Wauwinet gatehouse, about 8 mi.

These Refuges collectively are a barrier beach system that protects more than 21 mi. of ocean, sound, and harbor shoreline on Nantucket Island. They form a long spit that stretches in an L curve to make up the NW shore of the island, moving from its N tip at Great Point SW to Coatue Point, where Nantucket Sound and Harbor meet. The area is mostly glacial debris and soft, shifting sand deposited by wind and water. There are beaches, dunes, salt marshes, and forests of wind-sheared oaks and cedars.

Access is by foot and by 4-wheel-drive vehicle only. Tire pressure must be adjusted to 15 psi prior to entering. Vehicles may travel only on roads and designated crossovers to prevent damage to plants.

The Refuges are cooperatively managed for scientific, educational, conservation, and minimal recreation purposes, and thus portions may be closed at any time to protect wildlife and plants.

From the gatehouse at Wauwinet it is 1.4 mi. to the nearest beach access, 5.4 mi. to Great Point, and 9 mi. to Coatue Point. There are no public buildings, concessions, restrooms, or telephones. These are mainly preserves for picnickers, birdwatchers, students of nature, photographers, day-hikers, surfcasters, and shellfishers (properly licensed). A tire pump is maintained just beyond the gatehouse.

There are no lifeguard-protected beaches, and dangerous current and rip-tide conditions often exist at many locations, especially the E and W beaches at Great Point.

Birds: No checklist. Species include American oystercatcher, common and least terns, herring and great black-backed gulls, and the rare and endangered piping plover. Migratory birds include Canada goose, black duck, eiders, scoters, oldsquaws, scaup.

Mammals: Gray and harbor seals rest here in winter months.

Activities

Fishing: Surf fishing for bluefish and striped bass in Nantucket Sound and ocean.

Shellfishing: Nantucket Harbor and its salt marshes support populations of bay scallops, soft-shell clams, quahogs, and mussels.

Publications
Mimeo information pages, available from Great Meadows National Wildlife Refuge.

Headquarters
Nantucket Conservation Foundation, Inc., 118 Cliff Rd., Nantucket, MA 02554; (508) 228-2884. Nantucket National Wildlife Refuge, c/o Great Meadows National Wildlife Refuge, Weir Hill Rd., Sudbury, MA 01776; (508) 443-4661. The Trustees of Reservations, 290 Argilla Rd., P.O. Box 563, Ipswich, MA 01938; (508) 356-4351.

....

Nickerson State Park
Massachusetts Division of Forests and Parks   East
1,955 acres.

Off Hwy 6A in East Brewster.

Don't expect to find room here in midsummer. At the bend in Cape Cod, the Park is near but not on Cape Cod Bay, near the S end of Cape Cod National Seashore, a few minutes away from ocean beaches. Many use this as a base for visiting the National Seashore, which has no campground.

Cliff Pond, at Park's center, is the largest of 4 ponds within the boundaries that offer swimming, boating, and fishing. The Park has an interpretive program, including an amphitheater.

Activities

Camping: The 420 well-spaced sites are in great demand during the summer season. Reservations accepted. Pets OK.

Hiking: 8 mi. of trails link with the Cape Cod Rail Trail (see entry).

Headquarters

Nickerson State Park, Rt. 6A, Brewster, MA 02631; (508) 896-3491. Reservations: (508) 896-4615.

Norcross Wildlife Sanctuary

Norcross Wildlife Foundation   West
3,000 acres.

From Springfield, E about 15 mi. on US 20; S 15 mi. on Hwy 32; E 1–2 mi. on Monson-Wales Rd.

Open daily except Sun. and holidays; closed also Mon., Jan.–March.

Beyond the reception and museum area, visitors must stay on designated trails. The area of wooded hills, fields, and streams is managed to conserve wildlife, land, and water, with emphasis on research, education, and conservation training. The diverse plant life includes some exotics. Feed crops attract a large bird population.

The museum has natural history exhibits, including rocks, shells, photographs of plants, and bird carvings.

Publications

Leaflet with map.
Bird checklist.

Headquarters
Norcross Wildlife Sanctuary, Peck Rd., Wales, MA 01081;(413) 267-9654.

North Hill Marsh Wildlife Sanctuary

Massachusetts Audubon Society   East
137 acres of land.

N of Plymouth. From Hwy 3A, E 1.3 mi. on Mayflower St. (Duxbury).

Open 9–5 Tues.–Sun.

Freshwater marshes and an oak/pine forest surround a 90-acre pond. Near the coast elevations range from 16 to 140 ft. The site has over 3 mi. of trails.

It's a small natural oasis in a heavily developed area. 122 bird species have been observed here. The South Shore Sanctuaries office has lists of the flora and fauna.

Pets are prohibited. No bicycles on trails.

Headquarters
South Shore Sanctuaries, 2000 Main St., Marshfield, MA 02050; (617) 837-9400.

Northfield Mountain Recreation and Environmental Center

Northeast Utilities   West
2,000 acres.

Close to the VT–NH border. From I-91, Exit 27. E on Hwy 2, across the Connecticut River, then 2 mi. N on Hwy 63.

Center open Wed.–Sun., 9–5 May–Oct. Trails open daily.

Information about the natural history of MA is hard to find. With so little available from government and academic sources, it was astonishing and refreshing to see what a power company has done.

The centerpiece is a splendid 160-page book: *The Northfield Mountain Interpreter.* It has everything you want to know about the region, well written, excellently organized and illustrated. It begins with the origins of Earth, continues through plate tectonics, traces the geologic history of the Connecticut Valley and the beginnings of life. It has a wonderful section on the flora and fauna of the region, not just identifying species but explaining their functions and relationships. For example, one spread shows the diets of animal species, from black bear to turtles, while another lists plants and tells what animals eat them. It recounts the history of the land from native Americans through early settlers to modern times.

The center is at the site of the company's pumped storage hydro-electric station. Recreation facilities include hiking and nature trails, camping and picnic grounds, a pavilion where a variety of performances are scheduled in summer, cross-country ski trails. Activities include riverboat tours, canoe instruction, orienteering instruction, star gazing, and more. It's not all nature-oriented; other activities include jazz cruises, bicycle tours, sing-alongs, and foot races.

Activities

Camping: 27 sites. Reservations needed.

Canoeing, boating: Ramp, rentals. No hp limit. Canoe-camping opportunities.

Ski touring: 25 mi. of maintained trails. Usually mid-Dec.–mid-March.

Publications

Seasonal newsletter with program schedules.

Site map.

Leaflets: *Barton Cove Nature and Camping Area, Hidden Quarry Nature Trail, Northfield Mountain Cross-Country Ski Area.*

Sammartino, Claudia F. *The Northfield Mountain Interpreter.* Berlin, CT: Northeast Utilities, 1981, reprinted 1991. $5.00 in person, $8.50 by mail.

Headquarters

Northfield Mountain Recreation and Environmental Center, RR 2, Box 117, Rt. 63, Northfield, MA 01360; (413) 659-3714.

Northfield State Forest

See Mount Grace State Forest.

October Mountain State Forest

Massachusetts Division of Forests and Parks   West
16,127 acres.

From US 20 at Lenox or Lee, follow signs E to Forest entrance.

One of the largest MA State Forests lies across the Hoosac Range, E of the Berkshire Valley. This portion of the range is a high plateau, elevations generally between 1,800 and 2,000 ft., with a few peaks rising higher. The region is rugged, scenic, heavily forested, with many rock outcrops and ledges. The numerous streams draining the area drop over many falls and cataracts. The largest of several ponds are 212-acre Lake Felton and 200-acre Finerty Pond. From Lake Felton a swift brook rushes through Schermerhorn Gorge, emptying into the Housatonic River.

The Appalachian Trail crosses the Forest. Adjoining the Forest on the W is the 613-acre Housatonic Valley Wildlife Management Area, spread along the oxbows and backwaters of the Housatonic River. Access is from October Mountain Rd.

Plants: 90% of the area is forested with mixed hardwoods, maples, oaks, and birches, with hemlock and spruce. Many flowering shrubs in the understory. Seasonal wildflowers include bloodroot, hepatica, jack-in-the-pulpit, wood and trout lilies, mayapple, lady's slipper, trillium, iris, trailing arbutus.

Birds: No checklist. Abundant populations of woodland species.

Mammals: Include black bear, deer, bobcat, coyote, red fox, red, gray, and flying squirrels, weasel, cottontail, snowshoe hare, muskrat, porcupine, beaver, fisher, raccoon, skunk, otter, mice.

Activities

Camping: 50 sites. All year. Pets OK.

Hiking: 12 mi. of trails, including the Appalachian.

Fishing: Bass, pickerel, bullhead.

Boating: Pond. Ramp.

Headquarters
October Mt. State Forest, Woodlawn Rd. Lee, MA 01238; (413) 243-1778.

Old Town Hill Reservation

The Trustees of Reservations   East
373 acres.

From Hwy 128, Exit 20N, proceed N 16.2 mi. on Hwy 1A. Left on Newman Rd. (200 yds. N of Parker River) to entrance on right.

The trail ascends a hill. At the top one has a sweeping view of Parker River, Plum Island River, Parker River National Wildlife Refuge, and Isles of Shoals. Much of the trail is in forest, but there are also open areas. On the hill are several side trails, and it's easy to make a wrong turn, as we did on the way down, but then one sees more of the site.

Farther on Newman Rd. is another entrance, not as clearly marked, to the floodplain of the river. This open area is less scenic but offers better birding.

Headquarters
The Trustees of Reservations, 290 Argilla Rd., Box 563, Ipswich, MA 01938; (508) 356-4351.

Otter River State Forest

See Birch Hill Wildlife Management Area.

Oxbow National Wildlife Refuge

U.S. Fish and Wildlife Service   Central
711 acres.

From I-495, Exit 29. W on Hwy 2 to Hwy 110; S to Still River. W on Still
River Depot Rd. across railroad tracks to entrance.

Sunrise to sunset. Foot traffic only. Nonhunting dogs on leashes at all times.

The Dept. of Defense transferred this former bombing range to the
Fish and Wildlife Service in 1974. Visitors are warned not to touch
"unusual metallic objects." We saw none. The site is largely open
water, marsh, and swamp, bounded by the Nashua River on the W,
Hwy 2 on the N, railroad right-of-way on the E. It adjoins the Fort
Devens Military Reservation, which is being phased out. (However,
the military presently maintains a right-of-way through the Refuge,
and the sound of gunfire from the training area across the river may
sometimes be heard.) Uplands include a few pine-covered knolls. Several trails cross the Refuge, one beside the river. Elevation ranges from
210 to 250 ft.

Birds: No checklist. The floodplain associated with the Refuge and
with its neighbor Bolton Flats WMA (see entry) is a fine central MA
birding spot during the springtime high-water period. The Refuge is
maintained primarily for migratory birds, notably black and wood
ducks. Other birds include great blue heron, American bittern, snipe,
sandpipers, woodcock, osprey, ring-necked pheasant, ruffed grouse.

Mammals: Species include woodchuck, snowshoe hare, red and gray
squirrels, cottontail, raccoon. There is an active beaver colony. Seen
occasionally: skunk, opossum, river otter, red fox, muskrat, white-
tailed deer.

Reptiles and amphibians: The Blandings turtle, a threatened species,
nests here. Also, spring peeper, wood frog, spotted salamander.

Activities

Hiking: 2 mi. of self-guided trail begins at the parking area.

Hunting: Small game and upland game birds; hunting of waterfowl and deer not permitted. Inquire about special regulations. Only non-toxic shot allowed.

Fishing: Some chain pickerel and bullhead in the river.

Canoeing: Nashua River. Launch adjacent to parking area.

Ski touring.

Adjacent
Bolton Flats Wildlife Management Area (see entry).

Publications
Leaflet with map.

Mimeo information pages.

Headquarters
Refuge Manager, Great Meadows National Wildlife Refuge, Weir Hill, Sudbury, MA 01776; (508) 443-4661.

....

Parker River National Wildlife Refuge
U.S. Fish and Wildlife Service   East
4,662 acres.

On Plum Island. From Newburyport on Hwy 1A, E on Water St. and Plum Island Turnpike, following signs.

Open sunrise to sunset. During summer, capacity is often reached and gates are closed by 9 A.M. Gates usually reopen about 3 P.M.

We'd never seen a Refuge quite like this. It includes over 6 mi. of splendid barrier beach, and crowds of visitors come just to enjoy the beach. When we arrived on a weekday midmorning, cars were queued at the gatehouse. A pleasant woman was handing out maps and leaflets, explaining rules and suggesting which parking area was least crowded. Another hundred cars, she told us, and the gate would be closed. 400,000 people visit the Refuge annually, most of them in summer. There is an admission fee of $5 per vehicle.

The gate is at the N end of the refuge. At the S tip of the island is a small tract called Sandy Point State Park, administered as part of the

Refuge. Parking areas are spaced along the road. Beach access is by boardwalk.

Beach and fore-dunes are barren. Rear dunes, up to 50 ft. high, are heavily vegetated. On the inland side of the road, dikes have created several freshwater marshes and pools. Beyond are 3,200 acres of salt marsh and tidewater. These wetlands can be observed from dikes and a nature trail. Other habitats include glaciated uplands with goose pasture and wooded patches and small glacial drumlins. The beach is closed periodically to protect nesting birds. Call before visiting.

Refuge Events
- *Jan.–Feb.* Snowy owls, rough-legged hawks, northern harriers present and frequently seen flying over marshes or roosting in trees at marsh edges; heavy storms may block Refuge roads for extended periods.
- *March–April.* Marshes thaw; northbound migrations of waterfowl, raptors, and early shorebirds and wading birds; courtship activity of waterfowl around April 1; serviceberry flowers in late April.
- *May–June.* Geese hatch and broods feed in roadside fields; warbler migration peaks in May; beach plums, false heather, and honeysuckle flower; striped bass migration reaches refuge.
- *July–Aug.* Ducks hatch and feed in pools; fox kits play near dens; mosquitoes and greenhead flies in strength; purple loosestrife flowers; concentration of snowy egrets; large flocks of shorebirds and swallows seen in late Aug.
- *Sept.–Oct.* Plum and cranberry picking (check regulations); waterfowl migration under way; hunting permits available September 1; colorful Glasswort in salt marshes; peregrine falcons seen occasionally; monarch butterflies migrate through refuge.
- *Nov.–Dec.* Migrating Canada and snow geese present; American black duck numbers peak; sea ducks rafting in large numbers offshore; snow buntings, horned larks, and Lapland longspurs seen in large flocks; seals sunning on Emerson's Rocks; marshes freeze.

Plants: Species seen along the nature trail include blueberry, greenbrier, grape, chokecherry, blackberry, pin and black cherry, woodbine, raspberry, honeysuckle, bayberry, poison ivy, beach plum, cranberry, spirea, speckled alder, willow, trembling aspen, dune grass, serviceberry, arrowwood, winter berry, cedar, staghorn sumac, wild rose, honeysuckle.

Birds: Checklist records 301 species plus 33 accidentals. The Refuge is along major bird migration routes. Salt marshes are important feeding and resting areas. Peak concentrations of up to 25,000 ducks and 6,000 geese occur in spring and fall. Other habitats attract large flocks of warblers and shorebirds.

Mammals: Species often seen include cottontail, fox, skunk, weasel, muskrat, harbor seal, woodchuck, deer. Woodchucks emerge from hibernation March–April. Red fox kits are sometimes seen on roads at dawn or dusk in June–July.

Interpretation

Visitor contact station at HQ, the old Coast Guard lighthouse at the N tip of Plum Island. (Instead of turning right for Refuge gate, continue on, then left.) Office hours 8–4:30.

Hellcat Swamp Wildlife Trail, begins at parking lot 4 (no beach access). About 2 mi., with spurs and boardwalk, visits dunes, freshwater swamp, freshwater marsh, salt marsh. Observation tower. Trail guide available.

Activities

Hiking: When the crowds have gone, 6 mi. of fine beach. (We repeat, though, this may be closed seasonally. Call before visiting in the off-season.) Back of the beach, 2 mi. of nature trail, 2 mi. of dike. At the S end, trails around the goose browse fields.

Hunting: In designated area. Special regulations. Inquire at HQ.

Fishing: Ocean beach. HQ has fishing leaflet with information and special restrictions.

Swimming: No lifeguards. Relatively cold water, rough surf, strong tides, undertow.

Boating: Launching or landing on the Refuge is prohibited except as specified in waterfowl hunting regulations. Boating in tidewater is governed by state and local regulations.

Pets are prohibited.

Publications

Leaflet with map.

Bird checklist.

Hellcat Swamp Nature Trail guide.

Refuge, hunting, and fishing rules.

Headquarters

Parker River National Wildlife Refuge, Northern Blvd., Plum Island, Newburyport, MA 01950; (508) 465-5753.

Peru Wildlife Management Area

Massachusetts Division of Fisheries and Wildlife West
3,677 acres.

From Hwy 143 E of Peru, turn N on North Rd. The next paved road to the right is East Windsor Rd. In about 1¼ mi. look for an abandoned road on the right. This bisects the site. There is no parking area.

The site lies between Hwy 143 and Pierce Rd., E of North Rd. Trout Brook crosses it NW to SE. From the brook at about 1,500 ft. elevation, hills rise to 2,000 ft. in the SW, 2,050 ft. in the NW. The site is almost totally forested with a mix of northern hardwoods and conifers. The unused woods road crosses N to S. The site now includes Tracey Pond.

Wildlife includes grouse, woodcock, snowshoe hare, raccoon, beaver, black bear, bobcat, deer. The brook has trout.

Headquarters

Western Wildlife District Office, 400 Hubbard Ave., Pittsfield, MA 01201; (413) 447-9789.

Phillipston Wildlife Management Area

Massachusetts Division of Fisheries and Wildlife West
3,384 acres.

From Athol, S on Hwy 32 to Hwy 101, N of Petersham. NE on Popple Camp Rd. WMA is on both sides, before coming to Queens Lake.

The S unit is the larger, extending S about 3 mi. to E Petersham Rd. Bakers Lane, first turn beyond Hwy 101, leads to a parking area. Narrow Lane, turn at Queens Lake, leads to parking near the S end. It runs along a low ridge, from which the land slopes gradually down on both sides to marshes and streams 200 ft. below. Moccasin Brook, on the W side, has a great blue heron rookery. The upland is forested but recently logged; skid roads now serve as trails.

The N unit lies along the East Branch of the Swift River, from which the land rises on both sides. Here the upland has both forest and old fields.

Activities

Hunting: Stocked with snowshoe hare and pheasant. Game species include deer, cottontail, turkey, grouse, woodcock.

Fishing: Trout in several streams.

Publications
Site maps.

Headquarters
Central Wildlife District Office, Temple St., West Boylston, MA 01583; (508) 835-3607.

Pittsfield State Forest

Massachusetts Division of Forests and Parks   West
10,000 acres.

From Pittsfield, W on West St., N on Churchill St., W on Cascade St.

The Forest lies W of Onota Lake, near the NY border, extending from near Hancock almost to US 20 along the ridge of the Taconic Range. Peaks along the range include 2,314-ft. Honwee Mountain, 2,170-ft. Smith Mountain. The slopes are drained by numerous streams with waterfalls and cascades. 9-acre Berry Pond, at 2,150 ft., is the highest in the state. A road leads to the campground there from near Forest HQ.

It's a hiker's forest. The Taconic Skyline Trail (see entry) runs the length of the ridge, passing Berry Pond. More than a dozen trails ascend from the E side, offering opportunities for circuit hikes of 3 mi. or more.

Slopes are moderate to steep, with rock outcrops, ledges, and caves. Most of the area is forested with mixed hardwoods and hemlock. June brings an attractive azalea display. *Wildlife* is typical of the region, including deer and black bear. Hawks follow the ridge in migration. One observer said to look for red-spotted newts along the trail after a spring or summer shower.

Activities

Camping: 31 sites. Mid-May to mid-Oct. Pets OK.

Hiking: 30 mi. of fair trails.

Fishing: Berry Pond is stocked.

Publication

Map prepared by the Appalachian Mountain Club.

Headquarters

Pittsfield State Forest, Cascade St., Pittsfield, MA 01201; (413) 442-8992.

Pleasant Valley Wildlife Sanctuary

Massachusetts Audubon Society West
1,153 acres.

From the intersection of US 7 and US 20 at Lenox, N 3 mi. on US 7; W on W Dugway Rd.; left on W Mountain Rd. to entrance.

Open Tues.–Sun. all year.

Yokun Brook, fed by numerous small streams, flows through a series of many ponds, including beaver ponds, along W Mountain Rd. From here, at an elevation of about 1,250 ft., the land slopes up to a fire tower on Lenox Mountain at 2,124 ft. About 800 acres of the site are forested with northern hardwoods, hemlock, and white pine. 65 acres are open fields, 30 acres alder swamp. Many shrubs and wildflowers.

Birds: Checklist available. More than 60 species nest here. Twice that number have been observed in migrations. Houses and feeding stations attract many for close observation. There is a hummingbird garden.

Mammals: Many beaver ponds and lodges, with muskrats sometimes sharing space. Mink, otter, cottontail, fox, deer.

Interpretation

Year-round *Nature hikes, canoe tours, nature ski hikes, talks, slide shows, workshops,* and more (see Publications, below).

Trailside Museum has wildlife exhibits, observation beehive, nature games. Open in summer.

Nature trails begin at the museum.

Hiking: 7 mi. of trails.

Pets are prohibited. No bicycles on trails.

Publications

Berkshire Sanctuaries quarterly newsletter listing year-round events.

Bird checklist.

Headquarters

Pleasant Valley Wildlife Sanctuary, 472 W. Mountain Rd., Lenox, MA 01240; (413) 637-0320.

Quabbin Reservoir

Metropolitan District Commission   West

55,000 land acres, including 3,500 acres on 60 islands; 25,000 water acres.

From I-90, Exit 8; N 10 mi. on Hwy 32 to Ware; then 6 mi. W on Hwy 9 to three entrances to Quabbin Park area.

It's called the world's largest man-made domestic water supply, providing water to 2.5 million people in 46 towns and cities. The dam on the Swift River was completed by 1939. Submerged were towns, villages, and farms whose beginnings were in the early 1700s. To protect the water supply, 120 sq. mi. of the watershed are maintained in near-wilderness condition. The area is open to passive recreation, with conditions: *no swimming is allowed,* for example, *no horses or dogs, no fires, camping, skiing, hunting, littering.*

The principal public area is Quabbin Park at the S end. Here there are a visitor center, hiking trails, a picnic area, scenic vistas, an observation tower.

The reservoir is surrounded by wooded hills, with wet meadows, marshes, shrubby areas, and reverting fields.

Birds: Checklist available. 250 species have been recorded. Both golden and bald eagles are seen, chiefly in winter. Other raptors include osprey, northern harrier, goshawk, kestrel, red-tailed, red-shouldered, broad-winged, and rough-legged hawks, great horned, barred, saw-whet, and screech owls. Loons and Canada geese have nested. Also red-headed and pileated woodpeckers, black-billed cuckoo, northern shrike, bluebird, blue-gray gnatcatcher, many warblers. Many others in migration.

Mammals: Many beaver, deer, raccoon, porcupine, muskrat, mink. Also chipmunk, red and gray squirrels, red and gray foxes, coyote, snowshoe hare, cottontail. Increasing populations of otter and fisher.

Activities

Hiking: All areas are open to hiking except Prescott Peninsula and the islands.

Fishing: The fishing guide has a map showing areas of lake and shoreline where fishing is permitted. Also regulations. Coldwater species include lake, rainbow, and brown trout, salmon, smelt. Warmwater species include largemouth and smallmouth bass, pickerel, white and yellow perch, bullhead.

Boating: Permitted for fishing purposes only. Three launch areas. 20 hp limit. Rentals.

Publications

Brochure with map.

Trail map.

Watershed map.

Fishing guide.

History and data sheet.

Friends of Quabbin leaflet.

Headquarters

Quabbin Reservoir, P.O. Box 628, Belchertown, MA 01007; (413) 323-7221.

Quaboag Wildlife Management Area

Massachusetts Division of Fisheries and Wildlife   Central
1,445 acres.

From Worcester, W about 20 mi. on Hwy 9 to West Brookfield; S on Davis Rd. to Hill Rd. and parking.

Much of the site is freshwater marsh along the Quaboag River. From here the land slopes up about 250 ft. on the W side of the tract. The site is about ½ mi. downstream from Quaboag Pond, the river's source.

From the pond downstream 9 mi. to Warren, the river is canoeable, usually all year, slow-moving flat water. There is no established put-in or take-out in the WMA, but we saw one or two places where it might be managed. In any case it would be no great task to paddle down from the pond and return, and this would be the best way to see the marsh. Downstream is a 10-mi. stretch of rapids from class II to class IV.

Birds: No checklist. River and wetlands attract heron, egret, American bittern, osprey, marsh wren, sandpipers, many waterfowl in migration.

Activities

Hiking: 3 mi. of roads and trails.

Hunting: Deer, squirrel, cottontail, raccoon, fox, pheasant (stocked), woodcock, waterfowl.

Fishing: Pike, largemouth bass, panfish.

Publication

Map.

Headquarters

Central District Wildlife Office, Temple St., West Boylston, MA 01583; (508) 835-3607.

Richard T. Crane, Jr., Memorial Reservation

The Trustees of Reservations   East
1,339 acres.

From I-95 N of Boston, Exit 45 to Hwy 128 E. Go 6 mi., take Exit 20 to
Hwy 1A N. Then 10 mi. to Hwy 133E, 4 mi. to Argilla Rd. Direction signs
say "Crane's Beach."

Any New England beach open to the public attracts crowds in warm
weather. The Trustees of Reservations have a handsome array of quiet
preserves, but this one is far from quiet in summer. We couldn't pass
through the gate because of our dog but were quite willing to turn
back. The guard told us that as many as 2,000 cars may park before
the gates must be closed. From fall to spring, however, this is well
worth a visit.

It's a fine ocean beach, more than 4 mi. on Ipswich Bay according
to one publication, 6 mi. according to the guard. Back of the beach
are dunes, salt marsh, and steep uplands. The several habitats attract
various bird species. Mammals seen in quiet times include deer, red
fox, striped skunk, otter, muskrat, opossum.

The site includes Great House on Castle Hill, used for cultural
events and occasionally open for tours.

A *nature trail* explores the dunes and red maple swamp.

Pets are prohibited May to mid-Oct., must be under control at other times.

Adjacent

Cornelius and Mine S. Crane Wildlife Refuge: 753 acres. The Trustees of
Reservation also manage this refuge. There's no public transportation
to this cluster of 5 islands and salt marsh in the estuary of the Essex
River. Private boats may land only at a dock on Long Island, Memorial
Day weekend to Columbus Day weekend.

Publication

Pine Hollow trail guide, available at Beach office or from ranger.

Headquarters

Richard T. Crane Memorial Reservation, Argilla Rd., Ipswich, MA
01938; (508) 356-4354/4351.

Sandisfield State Forest (York Lake)

Massachusetts Division of Forests and Parks   West
7,785 acres.

From New Marlborough on Hwy 57, S and bear right on Sandisfield Rd.
Sign points to State Forest. In 3 mi., turn left.

The official description of the Forest says the terrain is hilly, with
brook, streams, and swamps, and a diverse wildlife population.

The entrance leads to 36-acre York Lake, apparently the center of
visitor activity. On a Aug. morning no visitors were there, but an
attendant was prepared to sell tickets. The area includes a bathhouse,
beach, and launching ramp. The lake is fringed with trees.

Beyond the lake the terrain is flat to gently rolling. The surrounding forest is young, interspersed with pine plantations. Nearby a jeep
trail goes a short distance to West Lake, a small pond with no shore
development. A small parking area there seemed to be used mainly by
hunters and anglers.

Hiking: 20 mi. of trails and woods roads.

Headquarters

Sandisfield State Forest, York Lake St., Sandisfield, MA 01255; (413)
258-4774.

Savoy Mountain State Forest

Massachusetts Division of Forests and Parks   West
11,118 acres.

From North Adams, about 5 mi. E on Hwy 2, then 3 mi. S on Central
Shaft Rd. Follow signs.

This is one of the numerous State Forests in northwestern MA. Combined with the adjacent Mohawk Trail State Forest (see entry), it is the largest block of State Forest land. Terrain is rugged to mountainous, elevations from 1,800 ft. to 2,566-ft. Spruce Hill and 2,506-ft. Borden Mountain. A fire tower atop Borden Mountain offers sweeping views. The area has many streams and waterfalls, several ponds, the largest 40 acres. Scenic trails ascend the 2 peaks and lead to such points of interest as North Pond, Balanced Rocks, Crooked Forest, and 80-ft. Tannery Falls.

Plants: About 80% forested with mixed hardwoods, increasing amounts of spruce, fir, and pine at high elevations. Understory of striped maple, mountain laurel, raspberry, blackberry, fireweed. Some reverting fields. Spring wildflower displays. Some boggy areas have typical wetland species. Crooked Forest has trees presumably deformed by an ice storm years back.

Birds: No checklist or reports of observations, other than hawks migrating through in the fall.

Mammals: Bear, deer, snowshoe hare, cottontail, porcupine, fisher, red and gray squirrels, red and gray foxes, woodchuck.

Activities

Camping: 45 sites. May 15–Oct. 15. Reservations accepted. Pets OK.

Hiking: 24 mi. of trails, some rugged. Also woods roads. The Appalachian Trail is several miles W.

Hunting: Bear, deer, rabbit.

Fishing: Trout streams, ponds.

Horse riding: On woods roads.

Swimming: South Pond and North Pond.

Headquarters

Savoy Mountain State Forest, RFD #5, North Adams, MA 01247; (413) 663-8469.

South Cape Beach State Park

See Waquoit Bay National Estuarine Research Reserve.

Stony Brook Nature Center and Wildlife Sanctuary

(Includes Blake State Reservation, 200 acres, managed cooperatively.)
Massachusetts Audubon Society   East
241 acres.

SW of Boston. From Norfolk, S 1 mi. on Hwy 115 to North St. Turn
right.

Trails open daily dawn–dusk.

All the MA Audubon sanctuaries attract birds and birders. One sanctuary specializes in butterflies, another in ferns. At Stony Brook a specialty is the Odonata—dragonflies and damselflies.

About half of the site is forested with mixed hardwoods and white pine. The land slopes down to about 80 acres of wetlands: wet meadow, red maple swamp, Kingfisher Pond, and stream.

Birds: A checklist of 147 species is available, annotated to show seasonal abundance. 23 other species have been recorded once or twice. Spring and fall are the peak seasons.

Interpretation

Nature center has exhibits, including a butterfly garden, gardening for wildlife, nesting boxes and displays on environmental issues. Open Tues.–Sun.

Nature trail, 1.3 mi., passes through the several habitats to the swamp boardwalk.

Guided hikes and *special events* are scheduled all year, as well as *educational programs* for children and adults.

Pets are prohibited.

Publications

Newsletter and program list.

Trail guide and map. $1.

Bird checklist. 50 cents.

Dragonflies. 50 cents.

Headquarters

Stony Brook Wildlife Sanctuary, 108 North St., Norfolk, MA 02056;
(508) 528-3140.

Taconic Skyline Trail

About 23 mi.   West

From US 20 to Mt. Greylock, near the NY border.

Much of this trail is in the Pittsfield State Forest and Mount Greylock
State Reservation (see entries). AMC says it is well blazed but less well
maintained. There are many access trails, chiefly on the E side, especially in Pittsfield State Forest. Campground in Pittsfield State Forest.

Tolland State Forest

Massachusetts Division of Forests and Parks   West
4,893 acres.

From Hwy 8 S of Otis, turn E on Reservoir Rd. Cross the dam and
continue 1.6 mi. to marked campground entrance.

The Forest lies between Hwy 8 and the S end of Otis Reservoir. The
campground, beach, and boat ramp are at the N end of the Forest on a
peninsula that divides Southwest Bay from the main water body.
Between the dam and the campground entrance, a paved road runs S
to the Forest boundary.

We saw no signs identifying Forest land. We inquired at the campground ticket booth, but the attendant didn't know of any area but
the campground. We asked for directions to Forest headquarters.
"This is it," she said, pointing at her booth.

The area covered by the map is rolling to hilly, forested, with a moderate understory. State HQ provided a description that mentions 310-acre Big Pond, evidently beyond the map's scope, and rivers, streams, a waterfall.

Birds: We obtained an interesting bird list, including Cooper's, sharp-shinned, and red-tailed hawks, goshawk, barred, great horned, long-eared, short-eared, screech and saw-whet owls. Also great blue heron, American bittern, common loon, gulls, black skimmer, osprey, belted kingfisher, northern oriole, brown creeper, cedar waxwing, cardinal, purple finch, American goldfinch; evening, pine, and rose-breasted grosbeaks, 3 swallows, woodpeckers, ruby-throated hummingbird, many warblers and sparrows, chimney swift. The list includes no waterfowl, but mallard and Canada goose have been reported.

Mammals: Include red and gray foxes, beaver, bobcat, muskrat, otter, weasel, mink, skunk, snowshoe hare, cottontail, chipmunk, red, gray, and flying squirrels, deer.

Activities

Camping: 90 sites, 35 on the shore, Mid-May to mid-Oct. Reservations accepted. Pets OK.

Hiking: State HQ said "10 mi. of multi-purpose trails bordering reservoir." The map shows some of these trails, but there must also be woods roads.

Hunting: Deer, small game, turkey.

Fishing: Trout stocked in streams. Reservoir: largemouth and smallmouth bass, bluegill, white and yellow perch, pickerel, trout.

Swimming: Beach near camping area.

Boating: Ramp near camping area. No horsepower limit, but a 24-ft. length limit except for pontoon craft.

Publication
Map.

Headquarters
Tolland State Forest, Rt. 8, Otis, MA 01008; (413) 269-6002.

Upton State Forest

Massachusetts Division of Forests and Parks   Central
2,660 acres.

From I-495, Exit 21. NE to Hwy 135 in Hopkinton, then NW on Hwy 135. Just past Whitehall Reservoir, turn left on Spring St., 2 mi. to Westboro Rd.

We saw nothing extraordinary here, but the site offers an opportunity for pleasantly quiet woodland hiking when most sites near Boston are crowded. Off-road vehicles are permitted, but we heard none during our visit.

Hiking: About 6 mi. of trails in 2 loops. Some trail markings.

Headquarters

Upton State Forest, Westboro Rd. Upton, MA 01519; (508) 278-6486 (Blackstone River Heritage State Park).

Wachusett Meadow Wildlife Sanctuary

Massachusetts Audubon Society   Central
1,000 acres.

N of Worcester. From Princeton on Hwy 31, ¾ mi. W on Hwy 62 to Sanctuary sign.

Open Tues.–Sun. dawn to dusk.

One of the society's larger sanctuaries, this adjoins the 2,842-acre Wachusett Mountain State Reservation and is linked to it and other state properties by the Midstate Trail (see entries). On the S slope of the mountain, it was a farm. From Brown Hill, its highest point, 1,312 ft., one looks out over upland meadows, woodland, red maple swamp, ponds, and distant mountains.

Plants: Most of the site is forested with red oak, white pine, hemlock, sugar maple, white ash, and black cherry, beech, birch, and basswood, with an understory including hophornbeam and blueberry. The Crocker maple is one of the largest of its species in North America, over 300 years old. Woodlands include a hemlock ravine, a stand of shagbark hickory, dark groves of hemlock and beech.

As New England's farm acreage has declined, so have populations of bobolink, eastern meadowlark, and other open-meadow species. Here fields are kept open, mowed after the nesting season. Trails pass through or beside both young and old-growth forest, a hayfield, another hayfield allowed to revert, former pastures now growing small trees and shrubs, thick patches of ferns. A boardwalk crosses the red maple swamp that has many cinnamon and royal ferns.

May is the peak season for wildflowers. Prominent are foamflower, painted trillium, three-toothed cinquefoil, dwarf ginseng, wood anemone, marsh marigold.

Birds: No printed checklist, but we saw several records: a tally of 96 species recorded 1964–1973, another of early June sightings. (The best birding season is May to mid-June.) Over the period the top 10 species were rufous-sided towhee, ovenbird, red-eyed vireo, common yellowthroat, blue jay, robin, tree swallow, black-capped chickadee, red-winged blackbird, cliff swallow. By 1996, more than 100 nesting species had been recorded. The farm ponds are home to wood ducks and herons. This is a good place to see the fall migration of hawks, peaking in mid-Sept.

Mammals: A preliminary list included a number of species as "potential" or "possible." Those confirmed as present included shrews, mice, voles, porcupine, woodchuck, chipmunk, red and gray squirrels, snowshoe hare, cottontail, raccoon, weasel, skunk, red and gray foxes, deer, river otter in ponds.

Interpretation

Maps and other orientation material are available at the trailhead, near the parking lot.

Guided hikes are offered on weekends, occasionally on weekdays.

Hiking: 11 mi. of trails. The Midstate Trail, RI to NH, crosses the site. Mountain Trail leads to the State Reservation.

Pets are prohibited.

Publication
Trail map with descriptive text. $2.

Headquarters
Wachusett Meadow Wildlife Sanctuary, 113 Goodnow Rd., Princeton, MA 01541; (508) 464-2712.

....

Wachusett Mountain State Reservation

Massachusetts Division of Forests and Parks   Central
2,842 acres.

From Princeton on Hwy 31, N 3 mi. on Mountain Rd.

At 2,006 ft., Mt. Wachusett is the highest point in central and eastern MA. That's not breathtakingly high, but high enough to have some alpine flora at the summit, giving the mountain exceptional floral diversity. Although there's no camping, the Reservation attracts over 250,000 visitors per year. Many drive the road to the summit, especially in Oct. when fall colors are bright. Some come to ski in winter, many to hike in the warmer months.

The Reservation was created by the Great and General Court of MA in 1899. The mountain's vertical rise is 1,119 ft. From the top on a clear day, one can see Mount Washington, 150 miles away.

Information about the natural history of MA state lands is generally scanty, but here we have a 1978 management plan buttressed by extensive field studies.

Because of its steep slopes, the mountain kept its forest cover after most surrounding forest was cut. By 1900 most of its trees were gone, however, and the slopes were grazed. Forest regeneration began about 1930, so the present cover is rather young. About half the Reservation is now forested. With improved moisture retention, the Reservation now has 4 small ponds, 6 waterholes, and several small streams.

Plants: Dominant species are red oak, shagbark hickory, red, sugar, and mountain maples, witch hazel, hophornbeam, and birches, with aspen and willow at lower elevations, white pine and spruce higher, juniper in dry, exposed locations, some hemlock in damp ravines. Shrubs include azalea, sheep laurel, blueberry, huckleberry. State-protected plants include pink azalea, pink lady's slipper, trailing arbutus, swamp honeysuckle, rhodora, helleborine, rattlesnake plantain, rose pogonia. May brings a display of azalea; June, of mountain laurel. April sees a profusion of bloodroot. Purple trillium appears in May, wood lily in July. Many other wildflowers.

Birds: Checklist of 84 species available. A few pairs of goshawks have nested. Also breeding here: mallard, black duck, ruffed grouse, woodcock, barred owl, whip-poor-will, northern flicker, downy, hairy, and pileated woodpeckers, 16 warbler species, many other songbirds. The annual New England Hawk Watch held here each fall recorded over 10,000 raptors in the report we saw.

Mammals: Deer, an occasional bear, red and gray foxes, raccoon, porcupine, woodchuck, snowshoe hare, red and gray squirrels, cottontail, opossum, weasel, mink, skunk, chipmunk, mice, moles, shrews, bats. As the habitat improves, it is expected that beaver, marten, fisher, bobcat, weasel, and flying squirrel will return.

Reptiles and amphibians: Include snapping, spotted, and painted turtles, water, garter, milk, and smooth green snakes, timber rattlesnake, 5 salamanders, red-spotted newt, 5 frogs.

Features

The summit is the chief attraction. Along the 4-mi. road to the top are several overlooks. At the top are several communications towers and buildings that have to stay, but no major buildings will be added. From the summit, an alpine ski trail goes to the ski area.

Wachusett Meadow Wildlife Sanctuary (see entry) is on the S slope.

Minns Wildlife Sanctuary is a 200-acre preserve on Little Wachusett Mountain. It has some of the best forest cover and a number of rare plant species.

Visitor center near the entrance with information, exhibits, maps.

Activities

Hiking: Trails from the base converge at the summit, about 13½ mi. in all. The Midstate Trail (see entry) crosses the Reservation.

Hunting: Restricted to an area on the W side of the mountain.

Si touring: Designated trails on unplowed roads, beginning at the ski area.

Skiing: Chair lifts and rope tow.

Publications
We were given a sheaf of trail maps, ski trail maps, trail descriptions, etc. Most are currently available.

Headquarters
Wachusett Mountain State Reservation, Mountain Rd., Princeton, MA 01541; (508) 464-2987.

Walden Pond State Reservation

Massachusetts Division of Forests and Parks   East
304 acres.
From Hwy 2 in Concord, 1.5 mi. S on Hwy 126.

To discover where Henry David Thoreau found solitude, go out of season, midweek, on a rainy day. Hiking the trails then, one can imagine what it was like. On fine weekends, parking for a thousand cars isn't sufficient.

Headquarters
Walden Pond State Reservation, Rt. 126, Concord, MA 01742; (508) 369-3254.

Wampanoag Commemorative Canoe Passage

70 river miles.   East
From Scituate on Massachusetts Bay to Dighton Rock State Park on the Taunton River at the head of Narragansett Bay.

The route, a linked series of waterways, is within a few miles of Boston and passes under some of the state's busiest highways. However, if one is seeking quiet places in this bustling metropolis, there's no better way than by canoe. The route was used by the Wampanoag Indians, whose chief greeted the pilgrims.

Paddling the entire route would take 3 to 5 days and require several portages. We found no reliable information about camping. Some canoeists use informal, unsanctioned sites. One can scout the route by land to find accommodations near landings. Most canoeists travel one section at a time.

Publication

Wampanoag Commemorative Canoe Passage, (pamphlet with sketch map and route description) may be available from Plymouth County Development Council, Box 1620, Pembroke, MA 02359; (617) 826-3136.

Waquoit Bay National Estuarine Research Reserve

Massachusetts Department of Environmental Management/Citizens for the Protection of Waquoit Bay
2,250 acres.

On Cape Cod's S shore, between Falmouth and Mashpee. US 6S to Exit 2, then Hwy 130 through Mashpee to Hwy 28. Turn right, go about 5 mi. S to Reserve, on the left.

Habitats represented are salt ponds and marshes, forested areas, barrier beaches, dunes, and open water. No lifeguards. Important species here are such birds as the endangered piping plover and least terns; plants such as sandplain gerardia; fish such as alewifes and winter flounders; and blue crabs.

The Reserve includes *South Cape Beach,* a 400-acre State Park; Washburn Island with 330 acres and 10 campsites (boat access only); and the Swift Estate headquarters. A 450-acre pitch pine/scrub oak uplands tract protects the watershed. These areas are connected by open water, tributaries, salt ponds, and about 15 mi. of shoreline.

Like other reserves in the NERR system, Waquoit Bay serves important research and education functions in relation to estuarine areas. Water-quality monitoring and ecosystem research are ongoing here. There is an education curriculum on watersheds, intern and volunteer programs, evening programs, and interpretive walks for the public.

Nearby

Ashumet Holly Reservation and Wildlife Sanctuary (see entry).

Headquarters
Waquoit Bay National Estuarine Research Reserve, P.O. Box 3092, Waquoit, MA 02536; (508) 457-0495. For South Cape Beach State Park use the Reserve number.

....

Warwick State Forest

See Mount Grace State Forest

....

Wellfleet Bay Wildlife Sanctuary

Massachusetts Audubon Society   East
1,000 acres.

On Cape Cod. On the W side of US 6 just N of the Eastham-Wellfleet town line.

Open: Summer, 8–8. Winter, dawn to dusk; closed Mon.

The society has preserved an unspoiled area on Wellfleet Bay, which opens onto Cape Cod Bay. More than 430 acres are salt marsh. Other wetlands include a diked freshwater pond and brackish marsh and salt marsh tide pools. Uplands are pine woods, large open fields, and a moor overlooking the sea. The Sanctuary is near the Marconi Beach section of Cape Cod National Seashore.

Plants: Woods are chiefly pitch pine. Shrubs include sweet pepperbush, bayberry, beach plum, shadbush, honeysuckle, highbush blueberry, huckleberry, dwarf sumac. Flowering plants include bearberry, sea lavender, butterfly weed, asters, crowberry, heathers.

Birds: Checklist available. The Cape is an exceptional birding area, and the variety of habitats provides excellent opportunities here, especially for shorebirds (late May–early June, and mid-July–mid-Sept.) and sea ducks (winter). About 250 species have been recorded: green heron, mallard, black duck, kingfisher, red-tailed hawk, kestrel, bobwhite, clapper rail, piping plover, woodcock, mourning dove, black-billed cuckoo, great horned owl, chimney swift, ruby-throated hummingbird, northern flicker, eastern kingbird, phoebe, wood-pewee, horned lark, 2 swallows, blue jay, chickadee, mockingbird, catbird, robin, 3 warblers, red-winged blackbird, orchard and northern orioles, boat-tailed grackle, cowbird, cardinal, purple and house finches, American goldfinch, towhee, 6 sparrows.

Mammals: Include red and gray squirrels, red fox, cottontail, muskrat, deer.

Interpretation

A brand new *visitor center* is a model of "green" architecture.

Self-guided *nature trail* with 71 stations.

Guided walks daily in summer.

Guided tours of Nauset Marsh, Pleasant Bay, Monomoy Island.

Canoe trips; pelagic birding trips.

> *Hiking:* 5 mi. of trails.
> Pets are not permitted. No bicycles on trails.

Publications

Site map.

Quarterly newsletter.

Goose Pond Trail guide. $2.

Checklist, *Birds of Cape Cod.* $1.

Headquarters

Wellfleet Bay Wildlife Sanctuary, Off West Rd.–Rt. 6, South Wellfleet, MA 02663; (508) 349-2615.

....

Wendell State Forest

Massachusetts Division of Forests and Parks   West
7,557 acres.

From Greenfield, 12 mi. E on Hwy 2 through Millers Falls, Wendell Rd. over RR bridge to Montague Rd., follow signs.

The Forest lies immediately to the S of Millers River, with Hwy 2 across the stream, but it has little or no river frontage. The Forest map shows an unusual number of roads crisscrossing the area, plus 3 power lines, but this appearance seems to be a mapmaker's artifact. Most are woods roads, carrying little or no traffic, suitable for hiking.

The area is rolling to hilly, less mountainous than are nearby Forests. Forest cover is mostly oak and sugar maple with some hemlock and white pine. Laurel and blueberries are abundant. Ruggles Pond and Wickett Pond are within the Forest, Bowens Pond just outside.

Activities

Hiking: On the Metacomet-Monadnock Trail (see entry), which has an Adirondack shelter. About 30 mi. of trails and woods roads.

Hunting: Deer, rabbit, bobcat, raccoon, woodcock, turkey, grouse.

Fishing: Trout in streams. Bass, perch, pickerel in Wickett Pond.

Swimming: Ruggles Pond.

Canoeing: Millers River is canoeable in season from the NH border to the Connecticut River. The section beside the Forest has rapids to class II.

Horse riding: On woods roads.

Publication
Map.

Headquarters
Wendell State Forest, Montague Rd., Wendell, MA 01349; (413) 659-3797.

....

Willard Brook State Forest

Massachusetts Division of Forests and Parks   Central
2,380 acres.

From Fitchburg, N about 6 mi. on Hwy 31; right on Hwy 119.

The site is hilly with rock ledges, forested with an understory of shrubs, ferns, and wildflowers. We saw large areas of mountain laurel, which blooms in June. Elevation is 350 ft. along Trap Falls Brook, which has a 15-ft. waterfall, 765 ft. on Hwy 119.

Many picnic sites are distributed along the brook. There and in the two camping areas the only auto tags we saw were MA, except for two from NH. Headquarters confirmed the observation: 80% of visitors come from within the state; most others are from NH or transients making an overnight stop.

The campground at Damon Pond is sometimes full, but we were told sites are usually available at Pearl Hill, on New Fitchburg Rd. S of Hwy 119.

Activities

Camping: 21 sites at Damon Pond, 51 at Pearl Hill. Damon Pond season is mid-April through Oct., Pearl Hill a bit shorter. Pets OK.

Hiking: 18 mi. of trails, chiefly in the roadless center of the Park. Also a brookside trail.

Hunting: Small upland game.

Fishing: Trout stocked.

Swimming: Pearl Hill Pond (5 acres) and Damon Pond (2 acres).

Publication

Site map.

Headquarters

Willard Brook State Forest, Rt. 119, Townsend, MA 01469; (508) 597-8802.

Willowdale State Forest

Massachusetts Division of Forests and Parks   East
2,400 acres.

US 1 N to Topsfield, right on Ipswich Rd. Follow signs.

The central feature is Willowdale Swamp. The surrounding higher ground is mixed conifer and deciduous forest with meadows and reverting fields. Several brooks drain to the Ipswich River on the S. Highest point is 194-ft. Bartholomew Hill.

Off-road vehicles are prohibited, which makes for quiet hiking. The diversity of habitats attracts a variety of wildlife. Birding is good.

Hiking: Chiefly on old woods roads, on upland surrounding the swamp. A 3½-mi. circuit hike is described in the AMC trail guide (see Introduction).

Nearby
Ipswich River Wildlife Sanctuary (see entry).

Headquarters
Willowdale State Forest, Linebrook Rd., Ipswich, MA 01938; (508) 887-5931 (Bradley Palmer State Park).

....

Windsor State Forest/Eugene D. Moran Wildlife Management Area/Notchview Reservation

Massachusetts Division of Forests and Parks/Massachusetts Division of Fisheries and Wildlife/The Trustees of Reservations   West
1,743, 1,147, and 3,000 acres, respectively.

From Pittsfield, 11 mi. E on Hwy 9. For the Forest: turn left 2 mi. beyond Windsor at sign. For WMA, turn N at Windsor on Hwy 8A and look for sign. Reservation entrance is on Hwy 9 E of Savoy Hollow Rd.

The 3 contiguous sites are in one of the most scenic areas of the Berkshires. Elevations range from about 1,600 to 2,297 ft. Although several roads cross the area, much of the upland is wild, rocky, heavily wooded. In the Forest, Windsor Jambs is a narrow, picturesque ravine cut by Windsor Jambs Brook.

The WMA surrounds two hills, each about 2,000 ft. high, and occupies the S slope of a third hill that is mostly within the Forest. Whereas the Forest is almost entirely woodland, the WMA has extensive open fields and meadows. It includes Windsor Brook, a shallow marsh, and a beaver pond.

The Reservation includes the area's highest point, 2,297-ft. Judges Hill. Three brooks drain to the Westfield River. A small marsh is at the foot of Judges Hill. The area N of Hwy 9 is mostly spruce and hardwood forest. The open fields and farm buildings S of the road are also part of the Reservation.

Birds: No checklist. The Reservation visitor center can provide information. 175 species have been recorded, 99 of them known to breed here.

Mammals: Include bear, deer, bobcat, porcupine, raccoon, squirrel, woodchuck, fisher, beaver, otter, snowshoe hare, cottontail.

Activities

*Camping:*In the Forest. 24 sites.

Hiking: The Reservation has the best-developed trail system: 25 mi. Trails interconnect with those in the Forest and WMA.

Fishing: Streams and the Westfield River.

Swimming: Pond in the Forest.

Publications

WMA map.

Reservation map.

Headquarters

Windsor State Forest, River Rd., Windsor, MA 01270; (413) 663-8469 (Savoy Mountain State Forest). Western Wildlife District Office, 400 Hubbard Ave., Pittsfield, MA 01201; (413) 447-9789. The Trustees of Reservations, 290 Argilla Rd., Box 563, Ipswich, MA 01938; (508) 356-4351.

....

Wompatuck State Park

Massachusetts Division of Forests and Parks   East
3,500 acres.

About 20 mi. SE of Boston. From Hwy 3, Exit 14, then N on Hwy 228.

It's near Boston, near the coast, and it has one of the state's largest campgrounds. But because the Park has no swimming, the campground is almost never full. Its natural features make it well worth a visit.

The land slopes toward Massachusetts Bay, gently rolling, with some steepsided knobs of rock and glacial debris 50 to 100 ft. high. It has a few streams and small ponds, not large enough for canoeing.

Plants: The site has 3 of the state's oldest forest groves. Forest Sanctuary Climax Grove has large white pine, hemlock, and American beech, some specimens more than 180 years old. Other tree species include pine, elm, white oak, sweet birch. Norway maple, white ash. Understory species include holly, swamp azalea, sheep laurel. Many wildflowers.

Birds: No checklist. Species include pheasant, grouse, goshawk, owls, northern harrier, green heron, quail, many songbirds.

Mammals: Include cottontail, raccoon, skunk, muskrat.

Interpretation
Visitor center at entrance.
Nature trail, self-guiding, 2 mi. through old-growth forest.
Naturalist programs, June–Aug.

Activities
Camping: 400 sites. April 15–Oct. 15. Reservations accepted. Pets OK.
Hiking: 10 mi. of trails.
Hunting: Pheasant, grouse, cottontail.
Ski touring: 10 mi. of trails. Warming room at visitor center.

Publications
Information page.
Trail map.

Headquarters
Wompatuck State Park, Union St., Hingham, MA 02043; (617) 749-7160.

RHODE ISLAND

Smallest of the 50 states. Rhode Island measures less than 50 mi. from N to S, 30 mi. W–E. No place in the state is more than 25 mi. from the sea.

Its population density, 925 people per square mi., is exceeded only by New Jersey's. Almost nine-tenths of the people live in urban areas. The Western half of the state is rural.

Only about 9% of the land is in publicly owned forests, wildlife management areas, and parks. Nevertheless, the landscape is green. Much land once cleared and farmed has reverted to forests, which cover more than half of the state. Well-kept fields, farmyards, and lawns, and the absence of signboards and litter, help make RI pleasing to the eye.

Many citizens want to keep it that way, but the losses today are to developers, not loggers, and are more permanent. The state is buying development rights to preserve some farmland and buying ecologically important sites for parks and wildlife areas.

There's no room for adventurous backpacking. The longest named trail is only 8 mi., although there are connections. The state's highest point is 812 ft., no challenge to mountaineers. We could find no dry-land point as much as a mile from a road. The state has only 6 publicly owned campgrounds, and campsites are in great demand between Memorial Day and Labor Day.

Yet we found quiet places to enjoy. In summer, when crowds gather wherever there's a beach, we hiked forest trails few people use except in hunting season. Coastal wetlands offer splendid birding. Canoeists, too, can enjoy the feeling of isolation. RI has an impressive array of flora and fauna.

The state has an attractive park system, but we don't include sites developed for intensive use. We have included several very small sites, such as those of the RI Audubon Society, because they are protected fragments of natural ecosystems where one can see and learn.

Terrain and Weather

Many outdoors people here look seaward. The state's 420-mi. coastline is a complex of bays, sounds, islands, estuaries, and barrier beaches. Boaters outnumber hikers. Saltwater anglers outnumber people who fish in streams and ponds.

RI has 3 topographic divisions. The narrow coastal plain along the S shore and around Narragansett Bay is below the 100-ft. contour. To the N and E of the bay are gently rolling uplands rising to about 200 ft. The western two-thirds of the state has rolling hills, mostly between 200 and 600 ft., rising to about 800 ft. in the NW corner.

Temperature ranges are relatively wide daily, seasonally, and from year to year, less so on the coastal plain. Annual precipitation ranges from 42–46 in. over most of the state, rather evenly distributed from season to season. Average annual snowfall ranges from 10–35 in. along the coast and 25–60 in. over the western uplands. Around the bay, snow seldom remains for more than a few days. The western interior is usually snow-covered from mid- or late Dec. to mid-March.

Maps

The official highway map shows many street names, including most of those in our directions to sites. It shows all of the public recreation lands and many of the private preserves open to the public.

The Division of Fish and Wildlife issues 8½- × 11-inch maps of the largest and least-developed public areas. We were told some of these are out of date, but we had no difficulty matching them with the official highway map.

Plants

More than 1,800 plant species have been recorded in RI. Oak/hickory is the dominant forest type; oak/pine, pitch pine, eastern red cedar, and white pine make up most of the remainder. Less than one-quarter of the stands have trees of sawtimber size.

We didn't find a convenient plant or wildflower checklist. However, many site managers are good information sources, as are the Ningret National Wildlife Refuge and Audubon Society of RI. Also:

Peterson, Roger T., and Margaret McKenny. *A Field Guide to Wildflowers of Northeastern and North-Central North America.* Boston: Houghton Mifflin, 1975.

Birds

Birders have excellent opportunities here. Observers describe "waves of warblers" seen on Block Island in the fall. Many pelagic birds are seen from ferries. Coastal wetlands are lively during migrations. Wintering waterfowl make birding an all-season activity.

More than 300 species have been recorded in RI. In larger states, we list abundant and common species for typical sites, if we can get the information. Here one such list will serve for the state.

Species that are seasonally abundant or common in suitable habitats include common and red-throated loons, horned and pied-billed grebes, Cory's and greater shearwaters, Wilson's storm-petrel, great and double-crested cormorants, great blue, green, and little blue herons, cattle, great, and snowy egrets, black-crowned night-heron, mute swan, Canada goose, brant, wood duck, green-winged and blue-winged teals, black duck, mallard, pintail, gadwall, American wigeon, canvasback, ring-necked duck, greater and lesser scaups, common eider, old squaw, white-winged, surf, and black scoters, common goldeneye, bufflehead, common and red-breasted mergansers, ruddy duck.

Also turkey vulture. Raptors: sharp-shinned, red-tailed, red-shouldered, broad-winged hawks, northern harrier, osprey, merlin, kestrel. Ruffed grouse, bobwhite, ring-necked pheasant, Virginia rail, coot. Plovers: semipalmated, piping, black-bellied, ruddy turnstone. Greater and lesser yellowlegs. Sandpipers: spotted, solitary, purple, pectoral, white-rumped, least, semipalmated, western. American woodcock, common snipe, whimbrel, willet, red knot, dunlin, short-billed dowitcher, sanderling.

Gulls: great black-backed, herring, ring-billed, laughing, Bonaparte's. Terns: Forster's, common, roseate, least. Mourning dove, yellow- and black-billed cuckoos, screech and great horned owls, whip-poor-will, common nighthawk, chimney swift, ruby-throated hummingbird, belted kingfisher.

Northern flicker, hairy and downy woodpeckers. Flycatchers: eastern kingbird, great crested, eastern phoebe, willow, least flycatcher, eastern wood-pewee, horned lark. Swallows: tree, bank, rough-winged, barn, purple martin. Blue jay, crow, black-capped chickadee, tufted titmouse, white-breasted and red-breasted nuthatches, brown creeper. Wrens: house, Carolina, marsh. Mockingbird, gray catbird, brown thrasher, robin. Thrushes: wood, hermit, Swainson's. Eastern bluebird, blue-gray gnatcatcher, golden-crowned and ruby-crowned kinglets, water pipit, cedar waxwing, starling. Vireos: white-eyed, yellow-throated, solitary, red-eyed, warbling.

Warblers: black-and-white, blue-winged, Tennessee, Nashville, northern parula, yellow, magnolia, Cape May, black-throated blue, yellow-rumped, black-throated green, blackburnian, chestnut-sided, bay-breasted, blackpoll, pine, prairie, palm, ovenbird, northern waterthrush, common yellowthroat, hooded, Wilson's, Canada, American redstart.

Bobolink, eastern meadowlark, red-winged and rusty blackbirds, northern oriole, common grackle, brown-headed cowbird, eastern towhee, scarlet tanager, cardinal, rose-breasted grosbeak, indigo bunting. Finches: evening grosbeak, purple, house, pine siskin, American goldfinch. Sparrows: savannah, sharp-tailed, seaside, dark-eyed junco, tree, chipping, field, white-throated, swamp, song. Snow bunting.

Other Wildlife

The following reference provides information on the abundance, ranges, habitats, seasonality, and food habits of the region's birds, mammals, reptiles, and amphibians. (In 1996 it was out of print, but many have requested another printing.)

DeGraaf, Richard M., and Deborah D. Rudis. *New England Wildlife: Habitat, Natural History, and Distribution.* General Technical Report NE-108. Broomwall, PA: U.S. Department of Agriculture, Forest Service, Northeastern Forest Experiment Station, 1986.

Trails

An excellent system of short but pleasant trails is maintained by the state, the Appalachian Mountain Club, and Sierra Club volunteers. Trailside camping is prohibited. The following references are helpful:

AMC Massachusetts and Rhode Island Trail Guide, 7th ed. Boston: Appalachian Mountain Club, 1995.

Weber, Ken. *Walks & Rambles in Rhode Island,* 2nd ed. Woodstock, VT: Countryman Press, in press.

Camping

The state has 6 campgrounds with 1,414 sites, 755 of them at Burlingame State Park. The *Rhode Island Camping Guide* (available free from the RI Tourism Division, see State Agencies below) also lists about 24 commercial campgrounds, with over 2,500 sites, as well as 10 residential camping facilities. The American Automobile Association's *Northeastern CampBook* (free to members) also lists both public and private campgrounds.

Camping is permitted in campgrounds only, prohibited elsewhere in State Forests and Wildlife Management Areas. The 3 state camping areas for which we have entries do not accept reservations. Pets are prohibited in all state-operated campgrounds.

Fishing and Hunting

Some streams are stocked with trout, and there's action in some freshwater lakes and ponds. More anglers, though, head for salt water. The Division of Fish and Wildlife has hunting maps that name the principal game species. Hunting is not permitted in the federal refuges.

Boating, Canoeing

Saltwater opportunities are unlimited. Several lakes are large enough for powerboats. Canoeing waters include several rivers, lakes, and ponds, as well as wetlands and sheltered tidewater. The following references are helpful:

AMC River Guide: Massachusetts, Connecticut, Rhode Island, 2nd ed. Boston: Appalachian Mountain Club, 1990.

Weber, Ken. *Canoeing Massachusetts, Rhode Island, and Connecticut,* 2nd ed. Woodstock, VT: Countryman Press, in press.

State Agencies

Department of Environmental Management
235 Promenade St.
Providence, RI 02908
(401) 277-6800

All environmental matters, including wildlife, forests, and parks, are the responsibility of this department. Sites that include forests, wildlife management areas, and parks are jointly managed. Sometimes it's not clear who has primary responsibility, but it doesn't matter—the agencies work together.

Division of Fish and Wildlife
Government Center
Tower Hill Rd.
Wakefield, RI 02879
(401) 789-3094

Publications

Wildlife area maps.

Division of Forest Environment
Rt. 101
North Scituate, RI 02867
(401) 647-3367

Division of Parks and Recreation
2321 Hartford Ave.
Johnston, RI 02919-1713
(401) 277-2632

Rhode Island Tourism Division
1 W. Exchange St.
Providence, RI 02903
(401) 277-2601
(800) 556-2484

Publications

Boating and Fishing Guide.

Official state highway map. Includes information on parks, beaches, local attractions, etc.

Rhode Island Camping Guide. Information on both public and private campgrounds.

Visitors Guide (annual). Lists recreation areas, parks, beaches, wildlife sanctuaries, biking information, ferry schedules.

Private Organizations

Appalachian Mountain Club
5 Joy St.
Boston, MA 02108
(617) 523-0636

The Naragansett Chapter of AMC has major responsibility for maintaining the state's hiking trails. Contact them through the Boston office or through the RI Trails Coordinator at (401) 885-4262.

Publications

AMC Massachusetts and Rhode Island Trail Guide. 7th ed., 1995.
AMC River Guide: Massachusetts, Connecticut, Rhode Island, 2nd ed., 1990.

Audubon Society of Rhode Island
12 Sanderson Rd.
Smithfield, RI 02917
(401) 949-5454

The society owns and protects almost 7,000 acres of property in and around the state. Nine of their refuges are open to the public for hiking and nature observation.

Publications

Conway, Robert A. *Field Checklist of Rhode Island Birds.* Bird checklist, free.

Guide to Refuges (leaflet). With SASE. Properties map, 1990. $2.

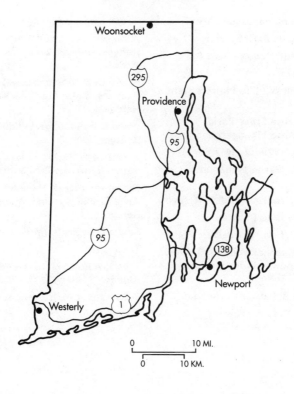

RI
R H O D E I S L A N D

Woonsocket

295

Providence

95

95

138

Newport

Westerly

1

0   10 MI.

0   10 KM.

Natural Areas in Rhode Island

An Alphabetical Listing

Arcadia Management Area

Bay Islands Park System

Black Hut Management Area

Block Island

Buck Hill Wildlife Management Area

Burlingame State Park/ Burlingame Management Area

Caratunk Wildlife Refuge

Carolina Game Management Area

Davis Memorial Wildlife Refuge

East Bay Bike Path

Ell Pond; Long Pond; Blue Pond

Emilie Ruecker Wildlife Refuge. *See* Seapower Point National Wildlife Refuge

George B. Parker Woodland

George Washington Management Area

Great Swamp Management Area

Ninigret National Wildlife Refuge/Ninigret Conservation Area

Norman Bird Sanctuary. *See* Sachuest Point National Wildlife Refuge

Powder Mill Ledges Wildlife Refuge

Sachuest Point National Wildlife Refuge/Norman Bird Sanctuary

Seapower Marsh Management Area/Emilie Ruecker Wildlife Refuge

Snake Den State Park

Trestle Trail

Trustom Pond National Wildlife Refuge

Wickaboxet Management Area

Arcadia Management Area

Rhode Island Department of Environmental Management
13,000 acres.

On both sides of Hwy 165 between the CT border and I-95.

Largest of RI's public lands, Arcadia sprawls over a 6- by 6-mi. area. It combines under integrated management what were 3 State Parks, 2 Management Areas, and a State Forest. The only campground has been eliminated.

Terrain is rolling to hilly with rock ledges and outcrops, some vertical rock walls, ponds, and streams with cascades. The 2 principal recreation areas, both at ponds, are often crowded in warm weather.

This is the state's prime hiking area. 15 of the 40 trails described in Ken Weber's *Walks & Rambles in Rhode Island* (see "Trails" in Introduction) are here, and there are links with the CT trail system. Hiking is most popular in spring and fall. On a hot summer day, we met no one during an hour's walk. About 5,000 visitors per year are hunters.

Entering from CT, we saw first the entrance to the Beach Pond Recreation Area. Its parking lot was near capacity. Next on Hwy 165, at an Arcadia sign, we turned onto a well-kept dirt road. Gated woods roads were on both sides. We stopped at a bridge, and our Labrador plunged into the stream. We passed no cars.

Plants: Except in the developed area, the site is almost entirely forested, predominantly with mixed hardwoods, mostly oaks and hickories with smaller stands of maple and beech. White pine is the principal softwood. We saw some dense thickets of laurel and rhododendron. The understory includes pin cherry, dogwood, laurel, sassafras, witch hazel, hawthorn, greenbrier, grape. Blueberries grew along the roadside. On the trails we saw many ferns, club mosses, lichens, fungi, wildflowers.

Birds: No checklist, but the Audubon publication (see Introduction) is useful. It looks like a good birding area.

Mammals: Reported species include chipmunk, gray squirrel, fox, raccoon, otter, cottontail, snowshoe hare, beaver, coyote, deer.

Features

Beach Pond Recreation Area shares a 2-mi. beach with CT's Pachaug State Forest (see entry). Fishing, swimming, boating, picnicking.

Browning Mill Recreation Area on Browning Mill Pond. Fishing, swimming, boating, picnicking.

Stepstone Falls is a cascade on Falls River. A fire tower is nearby.

Activities

Hiking: Over 65 mi. of trails, gentle to moderately steep, through varied habitats. Many are part of RI's Inter-Park Trail System, maintained by the Narragansett Chapter of the Appalachian Mountain Club. Trail links with Pachaug State Forest (see entry in CT). The major trails are marked with yellow or white blazes. Trailside camping is prohibited except at AMC shelters.

The Narragansett Chapter trails coordinator asked that we urge visitors to obtain a map of the area before hiking at Arcadia. There are many, many spur trails, he said, and it's possible to lose one's way. The most complete map is in the AMC trail guide (see "Trails" in Introduction). Call the trails coordinator at (401) 885-4262 for further assistance if necessary. (Note: Just as we were turning in our RI chapter to the publisher, we received in the mail the trails coordinator's own working map of Arcadia, which appeared to be hand-drawn. It looked like a bad day at the pretzel factory! We repeat—*do not hike any distance here without a map.*)

Hunting: In designated areas, deer, raccoon, gray squirrel, cottontail, snowshoe hare, pheasant, quail, dove, grouse, woodcock, some waterfowl.

Fishing: Trout in stocked streams. Ponds have pickerel, small- and largemouth bass.

Boating, canoeing: On ponds.

Publications

Division of Fish and Wildlife maps.

Headquarters

Arcadia Headquarters, Forest Environment Div., 260 Arcadia Rd., Hope Valley, RI 02832; (401) 539-2356.

Bay Islands Park System

Rhode Island Department of Environmental Management
2,300 acres.

Bridge access to several islands. Ferry from Colt Park in Bristol to Prudence Island. Access to others by private boat.

When gales kept sailing ships from maneuvering into the seaports of Boston and New York, Narragansett Bay offered safe haven. The 25-mi.-long estuary offered abundant supplies of fish and shellfish. Trade and fishing made the colony prosper.

Such a harbor needed defenses. The first fort, on Goat Island, was built in 1702. As recently as World War II, big guns guarded the bay's entrance. In 1973 the Navy began releasing some of its property to the state, and the Bay Island Parks system began to take shape.

The official state highway map shows a number of small State Parks in and around the bay. South Prudence is the largest of the island parks. Little information has as yet been published about the islands other than Prudence.

RI's 420-mi. shoreline and its sheltered waters offer great opportunities for sailing, cruising, fishing, and other water-based activities. The Bay Parks assure public access. However, there is no longer any camping at the island parks.

Features

Prudence Island was settled in the 1600s. The central portion of the 7-mi. long island has both permanent and seasonal residents. In 1980 the N end became the *Narragansett Bay National Estuarine Reserve* and the S end became a State Park. The island is said to have more deer per square mile than any other place in New England. Trees include red maple, gray birch, pitch pine, black oak, and red cedar. Key marine species include bluefish, striped bass, and winter flounder. Birds include osprey, blue heron, and waterfowl.

Narragansett Bay National Estuarine Research Reserve: 4,950 acres. The NERR is accessible only by ferry or private boat. The reserve includes undisturbed salt marshes, tidal flats, rock shores, eelgrass meadow, ponds, open water, upland fields, forests, and a historic farm site. It contains the major watershed of the island and also its largest stream. There are 4 mi. of hiking trails; a hiker's guide is available.

(Additional hiking, a deep-water pier, and other recreational facilities are located at the State Park at the island's south end.) Off-site estuarine education programs are conducted on the island during the summer; off- and on-site wayside exhibits inform visitors about the ecology and historic uses of the area. Research is conduced on the comparative ecology of salt marshes, weather (atmospheric chemistry), and long-term water quality.

Hiking: Nature trails, N and S ends of Prudence.

Publications

Information page.

Estuarine Reserve hiker's guide.

South Prudence nature trail guide.

Headquarters

RI Div. of Parks and Recreation, 2321 Hartford Ave., Johnston, RI 02919-1713; (401) 277-2632. RI Dept. of Environmental Management, 235 Promenade St., Providence, RI 02908; (401) 277-6800 or 683-4236 on site. Narragansett Bay National Estuarine Research Reserve, P.O. Box 151, South Park, Prudence Island, RI 02872; (401) 683-6780.

Black Hut Management Area

Rhode Island Division of Fish and Wildlife
1,290 acres.

N central RI. From Glendale on Hwy 102, left on Joslin Rd., then on Spring Lake Rd., which crosses the site. Follow signs to Spring Lake.

It's "Spring Lake Road" on the official state highway map, "Pond Road" on the map supplied by Fish and Wildlife. Both maps show the road ending at Herring Rd., with parking areas there and woods roads leading off. On the ground, we saw a few woods roads and trails leading into what we surmised was the Management Area, with little-used parking areas.

Turning back, we followed commercial signs to Spring Lake. A blacktop road passes through a shoreline resort community of modest cottages. Beyond, on the side away from the lake, is a Black Hut Management Area sign with little-used woods roads nearby. As the highway map shows, the Management Area has no lake frontage. However, a State Fishing Area is close by, providing lake access for canoes and small boats. The lake is about ¾ mi. long, with a forested shoreline and many water lilies.

What we saw of the terrain is gently rolling hardwood forest with moderate to dense understory.

Activities

Hiking: About 5 mi. of trails, plus woods roads.

Hunting: Pheasant, grouse, woodcock, dove, waterfowl, cottontail, snowshoe hare, deer.

Fishing: Trout, panfish.

Publication
Site map.

Headquarters
RI Div. of Fish and Wildlife, Government Center, Tower Hill Rd., Wakefield, RI 02879; (401) 789-3094.

Block Island

Mixed ownership.
About 7,000 acres.

12 mi. offshore in Block Island Sound, SE of Westerly. Year-round automobile ferry service from Point Judith; in summer from New London, CT. Passenger ferries in summer from Newport, Providence, and Montauk, NY. Air service is available from Westerly, Providence, and New York.

Shaped somewhat like a pork chop, this quiet, rustic island is about 7 mi. long, 3 mi. wide. Although most of the land is privately owned, commercial development is modest. Overnight accommodations are limited, so it's unwise to come without a reservation. Reservations are needed for cars on the ferries, too, but why bother? Most people walk or rent bicycles.

Much of the coast has rocky bluffs up to 160 ft. high, but there are also fine sandy beaches. The landscape includes low hills, moors, and valleys. Great Salt Pond divides the island into two. North of the pond is a pine forest with hiking trails. The Chamber of Commerce says there are "hundreds" of freshwater ponds.

Birds: Birders come here to see such oceanic species as shearwaters and storm petrels. Early Oct. is the season for migrants. An annual, organized bird count on an Oct. weekend often yields 150 species or more. Late fall and winter species include gulls, scoters, cormorant, loons, gannet, grebes.

Features

Block Island National Wildlife Refuge: 46 acres open to the public. At the NW tip of the island. Travel N or Corn Neck Rd. to its end; a sandy pathway leads to the Refuge. It has a sandy beach and dunes with such coastal vegetation as rose, beach pea, and beachgrass. Visitors are welcome daily, dawn to dusk. A checklist of over 190 bird species can be obtained from HQ: Ninigret NWR Complex, Box 307, Charlestown, RI 02813; (401) 364-9124.

Mohegan Bluffs offer a fine view with stairs down to the beach. These colorful cliffs form the island's S shore. Nature programs are given here in summer.

Popular hiking areas are *Clayhead Trails,* 2 mi. N off Corn Neck Rd. and the *Greenway Trails,* ½ mi. W off Center Rd.

Other refuges, various ownerships, are shown on an inset of the state highway map. One of the most attractive, for hiking as well as birding, is *Rodman's Hollow,* on Blackrock Rd. at the S end of the island, where trails descend below sea level.

Activities

Hiking: Walks and trails are mostly pastoral rather than wild, but many are quiet and delightful, through pine forests, across flower-dotted meadows, along seacoast bluffs.

Fishing: Commercial fishing has a long history here. Charter boats are available. Saltwater species include striped bass, bluefish, flounder. Ponds have bass, perch, pickerel.

Bicycling: With its spectacular scenery, winding roads, and invigorating air, the whole island is ideal for biking. (Block Island NWR does not permit biking, however.) *Rentals available.*

Information
Block Island Chamber of Commerce, Water St., Drawer D, Block Island, RI 02807; (401) 466-2982 or (800) 383-2474.

Buck Hill Wildlife Management Area
Rhode Island Division of Fish and Wildlife
2,090 acres.

In RI's NW corner. From Hwy 100, left on Buck Hill Rd. Look for unpaved entrance road in about 2½ mi.

CT is the site's W boundary, MA the N. Trails lead into both neighboring states. The shore of Wallum Lake is about half of the E boundary. Most of the site is hardwood forest, growing on land once cleared. Just N of the parking area is a 35-acre marsh that attracts waterfowl and shorebirds.

Birds: No checklist. Species mentioned include woodcock, ruffed grouse, wild turkey, mourning dove, black duck, wood duck, herons, northern harrier, flycatchers, hawks, owls, swallows.

Mammals: No checklist. Mentioned: deer, snowshoe hare, cottontail, gray squirrel, fox, raccoon, mink.

Hiking: 4-mi. blazed trail loop in the W half of the site, not approaching the lake.

Publication
Fish and Wildlife map.

Headquarters
RI Div. of Fish and Wildlife, Government Center, Tower Hill Rd., Wakefield, RI 02879; (401) 789-3094.

Burlingame State Park/Burlingame Management Area

Rhode Island Department of Environmental Management
2,666 acres.

SW RI. From US 1, ¼ mi. N on Cookestown Rd. or 1 mi. NW on Kings Factory Rd.

Driving the several roads that cross or penetrate this area, we found it less attractive than the Arcadia or George Washington sites. Along the roads are many private homes, summer camps, and other establishments. We couldn't tell whether these are inholdings or neighbors. We saw few woods roads.

There is a gigantic camping area with 755 sites in the State Park. That and 600-acre Watchaug Pond seem to be Burlingame's primary attractions. We saw the usual summer crowd at the lakeside recreation center.

The area is mostly forested with mixed hardwoods. Some open and marshy areas. Spring flowers and fall foliage are colorful.

The *Kimball Wildlife Refuge,* operated by the RI Audubon Society, is within the area. The society has a summer day camp here.

Activities

Camping: 755 sites; April 15–Columbus Day. No reservations.

Hiking: About 10 mi. of trails.

Hunting: In designated areas. Woodcock, grouse, waterfowl, gray squirrel, cottontail, snowshoe hare, deer.

Fishing: Trout, warmwater species.

Swimming: Beach on Watchaug Pond.

Boating: Canoes and small craft. Ramp.

Nearby

Ninigret National Wildlife Refuge (see entry) and several ocean beaches.

Publications

Fish and Wildlife maps.

Headquarters

RI Div. of Parks and Recreation, 2321 Hartford Ave., Johnston, RI 02919-1713; (401) 277-2632. On site: (401) 322-7337/7994.

Caratunk Wildlife Refuge

Audubon Society of Rhode Island
196 acres.

From I-195 in East Providence take Broadway Exit to Hwy 114. N to Hwy 152 (Newman Ave.), continuing on Hwy 152 about 3 mi. to Brown Ave. in Seekonk, MA, then left 1¼ mi.

Trails open daily from dawn to dusk.

The Refuge is in MA, but access is from RI, and the RI Audubon Society owns it. The site has ledgy hills, glacial boulders, glacial stream floodplain, small streams and ponds. This was once a farm, its past seen in open and reverting fields.

Plants: White, northern red, and black oaks, white pine, red cedar, hickories, red maple, hophornbeam, flowering dogwood. Many wildflowers.

Birds: No checklist. Spring courtship display of woodcock. Pheasant, ruffed grouse. Nesting species include meadowlark. Many songbirds.

Mammals: Red and gray foxes, skunk, raccoon, weasel, mink, red and gray squirrels, chipmunk, cottontail, woodchuck. Many mice, shrews, moles.

Interpretation

Visitor center with exhibits.

Naturalist programs and *sumer day camp.*

Hiking: 7 mi. of trails for hiking and cross-country skiing. Pets are prohibited.

Publication

Site map.

Headquarters

Caratunk Wildlife Refuge, 301 Brown Ave., Seekonk, MA 02771; (617) 761-8230 or (401) 949-5454.

Carolina Game Management Area

Rhode Island Division of Fish and Wildlife
1,563 acres.
SW RI. From I-95, Exit 3. E 2 mi. on Hwy 138, then S 2½ mi. on Hwy 112. Right on Pine Hill Rd., which crosses the middle of the site.

Carolina is in the chain of public lands in western RI, lying between Arcadia and Burlingame, W of Great Swamp (see entries). The terrain is level to rolling with a few rock outcrops and ledges. The site has ponds, Meadow Brook, and tributaries of the Pawcatuck River, which forms part of the E boundary. The site is crossed by a network of unpaved roads. The site map indicates some developed inholdings; we didn't see them.

Few visitors come here except in hunting season.

Plants: The land's history is indicated by old fruit trees among the oaks, maples, hawthorn, and pines. Among the attractions for birds are milkweed, clover, thistle, ironweed, knotweed.

Birds: Include quail, grouse, catbird, thrasher, red-winged blackbird, swallows.

Activities

Hiking: About 5 mi. of trails, plus lightly traveled roads.

Hunting: Deer, cottontail, wild turkey, pheasant, grouse, quail.

Fishing: Trout, warmwater fish in small ponds, stream, and river. Meadowbrook and Carolina Trout Pond are stocked with trout.

Canoeing: On the Pawcatuck River. A few campsites for canoeists are at the put-in.

Publication
Fish and Wildlife map.

Headquarters
RI Div. of Fish and Wildlife, Government Center, Tower Hill Rd., Wakefield, RI 02879; (401) 789-3094.

....

Davis Memorial Wildlife Refuge
Audubon Society of Rhode Island
96 acres.

In North Kingstown. From Hwy 2 at Frenchtown, E on Hwy 402 (Frenchtown Rd.). S on Davisville Rd. (Hwy 403) to entrance at Hunt River.

This site is classified as a "Unique Natural Area" because of its woodland, freshwater wetland, and bog. Flat to rolling terrain adjoins the steep banks of the Hunt River.

Plants: The woodland is mostly hardwoods: red, white, and black oaks, hickories, maples, beech, birches. Some white pine. Hemlock and Russian olive were planted for wildlife food and shelter. Understory includes sassafras, sweet pepperbush, huckleberry, shadbush, buttonbush, highbush blueberry. Swamp and bog vegetation includes red maple, sphagnum moss, pitcher plant, sundew, swamp azalea, sweet gale, leatherleaf. Flowering species include trailing arbutus, water lilies, arrow-arum, Indian pipe, starflower, rose pogonia, iris.

Birds: No checklist. Site is said to have abundant populations of many species, including wood and black ducks, sora, catbird, wood thrush, cardinal, flycatchers, woodpeckers, scarlet tanager, towhee, chickadee, nuthatch, titmouse, swallows, sparrows, finches.

Mammals: Species reported include deer, raccoon, red fox, opossum, skunk, chipmunk, gray squirrel, beaver, muskrat, occasional otter.

Activities
Hiking: Self-guiding nature trail.

Canoeing: Canoes and boats without motors are allowed on the river. We were told this offers "a nice half-day of naturalizing."

No pets are permitted.

Publication
Nature trail guide.

Headquarters
Audubon Society of RI, 12 Sanderson Rd., Smithfield, RI 02917; (401) 949-5454.

....

East Bay Bike Path

Rhode Island Division of Environmental Management
14.5 mi.

From Providence to Bristol, along or near the shoreline of Narragansett Bay. Access from India Point Park in Providence, from Squantum Woods State Park on Hwy 103 in East Providence, from Haines State Park on Washington Rd. in West Barrington, from Colt State Park on Hwy 114 in Bristol, or from any one of 49 intersections along the Path.

We include the Bike Path because it offers bicycle access from Providence and other urban areas to the Prudence Island and Bristol ferries, which transport visitors to a number of the state's natural areas. The Narragansett Bay area is ideal for recreational biking with its less severe winters than other New England areas and gentle terrain.

The paved path is 10 ft. wide and is open exclusively to walkers and bikers—*no motorized vehicles*. It's open daylight hours year-round, though not plowed in winter. The Path is clearly marked on the official state map. The RI *Visitor's Guide* offers a more detailed map.

Headquarters
RI Dept. of Environmental Management, 235 Promenade St., Providence, RI 02908; (401) 277-6800. For current information call (401) 253-7482 (at Colt State Park), (401) 277-2601 or (800) 556-2484 (RI Tourism Div.).

Ell Pond/Long Pond/Blue Pond

Audubon Society of Rhode Island; The Nature Conservancy; Rhode Island Division of Fish and Wildlife
490 acres plus recent additions

In SW RI, close to CT border. From I-95 Exit 2, NW a short distance to Hwy 3, SW a short distance to Canonchet Rd., then N about 2 mi. to parking.

The official state highway map shows 2 tracts of state land in green, 1 on Ell Pond, the other around Ashville and Blue Pond. The Fish and Wildlife map shows the Audubon and Nature Conservancy tracts, Audubon owning the land around Long Pond, TNC that on the N side of Ell Pond.

This conservation area has exceptional natural qualities. It's a National Natural Landmark. Weber's *Walks & Rambles in Rhode Island* (see "Trails" in Introduction) calls the first section of the Narragansett Trail the "magnificent mile." The trail ascends to rocky overlooks above 2 ponds, descends through a deep gorge. Along the way are forest groves and clearings, tall rhododendrons and hemlocks, carpets of sphagnum moss.

Ashville, largest of the ponds, is about 2,500 ft. long. Long Pond is longer but narrower. Ell, considerably smaller, is a glacial kettlehole lake surrounded on 3 sides by a red maple/Atlantic white cedar swamp.

Plants: The upland forest is largely oak/hickory. Other woodland species include chestnut oak, gray and yellow birches, sassafras, rhododendron, mountain laurel, sarsaparilla, trailing arbutus, teaberry. In moist areas, swamp azalea, sweet pepperbush. The sphagnum bog mat has cranberry, sundew, Virginia chain fern, pitcher plant.

Birds: No checklist. Reported: hawks, owls, whip-poor-will, woodpeckers, flycatchers, chickadee, titmouse, wood thrush, vireos, northern oriole, scarlet tanager, rose-breasted grosbeak, numerous warblers.

Mammals: Deer, snowshoe hare, gray squirrel, occasional bobcat and otter.

Activities

Hiking: The site is on the Narragansett Trail. 3 mi. of trails within the site. Some trails connect with CT trails.

Hunting: In the state-owned Rockville Management Area only.

Fishing: Ponds. Warmwater species.

Publication

Fish and Wildlife map.

Headquarters

Audubon Society of RI, 12 Sanderson Rd., Smithfield, RI 02917; (401) 949-5454. The Nature Conservancy, RI Field Office, 45 S. Angell St., Providence, RI 02906; (401) 331-7110. RI Div. of Fish and Wildlife, Government Center, Tower Hill Rd., Wakefield, RI 02879; (401) 789-3094.

Emilie Ruecker Wildlife Refuge

See Seapower Marsh Management Area.

George B. Parker Woodland

Audubon Society of Rhode Island
690 acres.

I-95 S to Hwy 102N, Exit 5B. Go 10 mi., turn E onto Maple Valley Rd. (also called Waterman Hill Rd.). Turn into second driveway on left.)

Open year-round, dawn to dusk.

A sign and trail map at the parking area explain that this is a place for "historical archeology": studies of old foundations, ruins of mills, and other artifacts. We took a trail through a pleasant woodland, rolling with some small, steep slopes and a deep gorge with pools and modest cataracts. The trees are mostly second-growth hardwoods with scattered large specimens including beech and oak. The site has a 15-acre nearly pure stand of chestnut oak.

We visited on a weekday. A nature study class was investigating stream fauna. We saw no one else.

There is a bird list, but HQ was closed and we couldn't get one. Mammals are said to include deer, bobcat, fox, red and gray squirrels, cottontail, chipmunk, skunk, mink, raccoon. Brook and floodplains here provide habitat for trout, salamanders, and wetland plants.

Hiking: 5 mi. of trails.

Pets are prohibited.

Publications

Site map.

Bird list.

Headquarters

Audubon Society of RI, 12 Sanderson Rd., Smithfield, RI 02917; (401) 949-5454. On site: (401) 397-4474.

....

George Washington Management Area

Rhode Island Division of Forest Environment
3,200 acres.

In RI's NW corner. On US 44, 2 mi. E of CT border.

Entering from CT on a summer weekend, we turned in at the first marked entrance, for Pulaski Memorial State Park, saw a great mass of parked cars, and left. The next entrance was marked "George Washington Camping Area." We paid a $2 entrance fee and drove to the beach parking area, which was far less crowded. The two are on the W and E shores of Bowdish Reservoir, an irregularly shaped impoundment about 1¼ mi. long, with private homes on much of its shoreline.

The George Washington complex is the largest of a cluster of state lands in the NW corner of RI, and one of the largest in the state. This is the state's highest land, with elevations to 770 ft. (RI's highest point is Jerimoth Hill, about 6 mi. S.) Terrain is rolling to hilly, with many rock outcrops and ledges. In addition to the reservoir, the site has streams, ponds, a white cedar swamp, and a marsh that attracts waterfowl and other wildlife.

The beach area where we stopped was only moderately crowded. A flock of Canada geese wandered about, accepting handouts. A sign at the boat-launching area announced a 10-hp limit, but this didn't apply to or was ignored by boaters launching from private land; we saw several boats towing skiers. The beach area is also a trailhead. The ranger told us camping and water-based recreation are heavy all summer, weekdays included. In spring and fall, the hiking trails are well used.

A few well-maintained unpaved roads cross the site. We drove them, seeing no other cars except at fishing ponds.

Who comes here? Cars in the parking lots were all from RI, CT, and MA. The ranger confirmed that well over 90% of the visitors come from nearby.

Plants: The site is heavily wooded, an attractive open forest with trees that looked 50 to 60 years old. A ranger told us the Civilian Conservation Corps did extensive reforestation in the late 1930s. Trees are being planted now to offset gypsy moth damage. Principal species include maple, birches, beech, ash, hickories. Some fine specimen trees, including a hemlock grove, remain from earlier times. Forest understory includes laurel, sassafras, and witch hazel, with some chestnut saplings. Wildflowers include partridgeberry, Indian pipe, wintergreen goldthread. Many ferns, lichens, and fungi. Water lilies in ponds.

Birds: No checklist. Mentioned: herons, black and wood ducks, hawks, owls, swallows, flycatchers, thrushes, warblers, quail, grouse, woodcock, dove.

Mammals: No checklist. Mentioned: deer, snowshoe hare, rabbit, muskrat, gray squirrel, raccoon.

Activities

Camping: 45 sites plus 2 shelters. Early April–Columbus Day weekend. Only the shelters may be reserved.

Hiking: 8, 6, and 2 mi. loops.

Hunting: In Management Areas. Pheasant, grouse, dove, waterfowl, woodcock, rabbit, squirrel, snowshoe hare, deer.

Fishing: Warmwater species in reservoir and ponds.

Swimming: Reservoir, Peck Pond, Wilbur Pond.

Boating: Ramps on reservoir and Clarkeville Pond; no motors on Clarkeville.

Ski touring: Loops begin at Peck Pond in Pulaski Memorial State Park.

Publications

Trail and campground maps.

Fish and Wildlife site map.

Headquarters

George Washington Management Area, 2185 Putnam Pike, Chepa-chet, RI 02814; (401) 568-2013.

Great Swamp Management Area

Rhode Island Division of Fish and Wildlife
3,011 acres.

From Kingston, W on Hwy 138 through West Kingston to Liberty Lane.
W to entrance.

The route is well signed. We drove on an unpaved road past HQ to a large parking area at a closed gate. Beyond is a jeep track bordering the swamp. To the S is a large wetland around shallow, 1,000-acre Worden Pond. Canoe access is on the S.

Plants: Upland forest of young mixed hardwoods. In better-drained areas are black and white oaks, some white pine. Understory includes dogwood, chokecherry, blackberry, huckleberry, pepperbush, blueber-ry. Dense moist wooded areas with red maple, tupelo, pin and swamp white oaks. Nearby are black cherry and holly, the latter rare in RI. Habitats include some dry and sandy areas, open grasslands, sphag-num bogs. Ferns include cinnamon, bracken, sweet, hay-scented, lady.

Birds: Migrating waterfowl include lesser and greater scaups, ruddy duck, common merganser, goldeneye, bufflehead, teals. Canada goose. Gamebirds include pheasant, quail, ruffed grouse, woodcock, snipe. Breeding species include black and wood ducks, bittern, red-tailed and broad-winged hawks, osprey, owls, woodpeckers, tree swallow, chickadee, white-breasted nuthatch, wrens, vireos, catbird, wood thrush, veery, ovenbird, waterthrust, red-winged blackbird, towhee, warblers, sparrows.

Mammals: Deer, cottontail, gray squirrel, fox, muskrat, mink, rac-coon, snowshoe hare, otter.

Activities

Hiking: The road we entered on the N is part of a 5-mi. loop, part of it on a dike. Miles of unimproved dirt roads and trails are shown on the site map, some penetrating the swamp. The observation tower shown on the map is gone.

Hunting: All legal species. This is one of RI's most popular hunting areas, best avoided by nonhunters in hunting season.

Fishing: Trout stocked in Chickasheen Brook, on the W side of the site. Warmwater species in ponds.

Canoeing: Chipuxet River access is on Hwy 138, 2 mi. W of Kington; 4-mi. paddle to Worden Pond. Usquepaug River access is 3 mi. W on Hwy 138, then 2 mi. S on Hwy 2; a 2-mi. paddle to the Charles River, then 2 mi. to Worden Pond.

Publication
Fish and Wildlife map.

Headquarters
RI Div. of Fish and Wildlife, Government Center, Tower Hill Rd., Wakefield, RI 02879; (401) 789-3094.

Ninigret National Wildlife Refuge/Ninigret Conservation Area

U.S. Fish and Wildlife Service; Rhode Island Department of Environmental Management
407 acres/174 acres.

Between US 1 and Block Island Sound, near Charlestown. Refuge is off US 1; Conservation Area via East Beach Rd. HQ is accessed from Green Hill Beach Exit to Rt. 1A; go 1 mi. to Shoreline Plaza entrance.

Dawn to dusk daily.

The Ninigret Refuge complex includes several satellite refuges in RI. (It includes units in CT as well.) Located along the Atlantic Flyway, the 5 RI refuges serve as important stopover areas during spring and fall migrations. We have separate entries for Trustrom Pond and Sachuest Point, and for Block Island, on which there is a small unit. Pettaquamscutt Cove, and important black duck habitat, is accessible only by small boat or canoe and presently has no developed trails. (It is still in the acquisition process.)

Ninigret Pond, 1,700 acres, is RI's largest salt pond, separated from Block Island Sound by a long barrier beach with sand dunes. On the inland side, the federal refuge occupies an abandoned airport, now an area of grassland, shrubland, deciduous woodland, and freshwater ponds. The federal land also includes a small tract on the barrier beach. Within this Refuge there is only foot or bicycle travel.

The Conservation Area is a barrier beach more than 2 mi. long. Like most public beaches, it attracts crowds in summer, but here there is a limitation: the parking lot is closed when it reaches its capacity of about 100 cars. The road beyond the parking lot is suitable for 4-wheel-drive vehicles only. At the E end is an area of salt marsh.

Birds: The Refuge checklist of 289 species, plus 21 accidentals, includes reports from Trustom Pond, Sachuest Point, and Block Island as well as here. It includes most of the species that occur in RI, and we have therefore used it in compiling the bird list in the state preface. Spring and fall are the best seasons for wildlife viewing in all the units. There is an observation platform overlooking Ninigret Pond.

Woodcock courtship display flights are a feature here beginning in mid-March. The warbler migration peaks in May.

Mammals: No checklist. 40 species recorded. Often or occasionally seen: red and gray foxes, chipmunk, deer. Coyotes have been seen.

Reptiles and amphibians: No checklist. Often or occasionally seen: eastern painted turtle, garter snake.

Marine life: Includes blue crab, bay scallop, winter flounder.

Interpretation

Visitor center, at Sachuest Point unit, (401) 847-5511, open year-round.

Naturalist programs are conducted by the Refuge staff and volunteers year-round at various locations.

Frosty Drew Nature Center, an independent, self-supporting project with trails and nature programs, is in Ninigret Park, off US 1 on Old Post Rd., (401) 364-1222/6244.

Activities

Camping: In the Conservation Area, 30 sites for self-contained units. April 15–Oct. 31. No pets. 4-day limit.

Hiking: Over 9 mi. of trails in the Refuge. Hiking also on Grassy Point; access through Ninigret Park. Hiking on the barrier beach is best at low tide, with firm sand underfoot.

Fishing: Surf. Permitted from Refuge Seashore in accordance with regulations, and at the Conservation Area.

Bicycling: On paved runways at the Refuge.

Publications

The National Wildlife Refuges of Rhode Island (includes Map).

Bird checklist

Headquarters

Ninigret National Wildlife Refuge, Rt. 1A, Shoreline Plaza, Box 307, Charlestown, RI 02813; (401) 364-9124. RI Div. of Parks and Recreation, 2321 Hartford Ave., Johnston, RI 02919; (401) 277-2632.

Norman Bird Sanctuary

See Sachuest Point National Wildlife Refuge.

Powder Mill Ledges Wildlife Refuge

Audubon Society of Rhode Island
100 acres.

From I-295 Exit 7B, W of Providence, 1 mi. W on US 44, then 0.1 mi. S on Hwy 5 (Sanderson Rd). Turn left at second driveway.

This small but delightful site is also the Audubon Society's state headquarters. On the coastal plain, it is upland woodland, with almost pure stands of northern red oak, white pine, and pitch pine. It includes a small pond and red maple swamp.

Pets are prohibited.

Plants: Understory includes serviceberry, sweet pepperbush, sweet fern, huckleberry, witch hazel, elderberry, highbush blueberry, northern arrowwood. Seasonal wildflowers include jack-in-the-pulpit, wild sarsaparilla, pipsissewa, downy rattlesnake plantain, pink lady's slipper, bunchberry, Indian cucumber root, yellow pond lily, false Solomon's seal, iris. Peak season is early summer.

Birds: Checklist available. More than 150 species recorded, 50 known to nest on the refuge.

Mammals: Checklist available. 14 species recorded include muskrat, opossum, gray fox, woodchuck, chipmunk, gray and red squirrels, cottontail, deer. Present but seldom seen: striped skunk.

Reptiles and amphibians: Checklist of 9 species available. Includes eastern painted turtle, northern brown snake, eastern garter snake, American toad, green frog, bullfrog, wood frog.

Interpretation
Audubon HQ has a library, gift shop, resource center, and birdfeeding station. Office open 9–5 weekdays; closed major holidays. Trails open daily dawn–dusk. 2-mi. *nature trail* begins at HQ.

Nearby
Snake Den State Park (see entry), 1 mi. away, is shown on the highway map as "under development." It's open to hiking.

Headquarters
Audubon Society of RI, 12 Sanderson Rd., Smithfield, RI 02917; (401) 949-5454.

....

Sachuest Point National Wildlife Refuge/Norman Bird Sanctuary

U.S. Fish and Wildlife Service; Independent
242 acres/250 acres.

E of Newport. *For Refuge:* From US 1 follow Hwy 138 E across the Newport Bridge to Miantonomi Ave. Continue 1.2 mi. on Green End Ave., turning right onto Paradise Ave. Go 1.3 mi., left onto Hanging Rock Rd. In less than 0.5 mi. bear right to Sachuest Point Rd., to entrance. *For Sanctuary:* From Green End Ave., go past Paradise Ave. and take a right at Third Beach Rd., S to entrance.

Refuge and visitor center open year-round. Sanctuary open daily Memorial Day–Labor Day, closed Mon. the rest of the year.

These adjoining sites are at the tip of land where the Sakonnet River enters Rhode Island Sound. The coast is rocky. The Refuge is grassland, shrubland, fresh- and saltwater marsh, sandy beaches, and dunes. It was established in 1970 to provide nesting, resting, and feeding habitat for migratory birds. The Sanctuary has rugged outcrops, ledges of pudding stone, open and reverting fields, swamp, pond, and woodland.

Three public beaches are along the access roads, so traffic in warm weather may be heavy.

Birds: Checklist available (for all units of the Ninigret Complex). This is one of RI's best birding areas. Fall and winter are best seasons. About 250 species have been recorded, 70 of them breeding here. More than 15 waterfowl species winter here. It's a good place to see the fall hawk migration. The Sanctuary has a woodcock singing ground. Refuge species of special interest include harlequin, eider, and oldsquaw ducks, snowy and short-eared owls.

Mammals: No checklist. 10 species recorded. Red fox and cottontail are often seen, striped skunk occasionally, harbor seal on rare occasions.

Interpretation

Visitor center at the Refuge is the only one for the Ninigret Complex in RI. The building is open daily, though staff and volunteer hours vary. Call (401) 847-5511 for current hours, information.

Museum at the Sanctuary has natural history exhibits.

Guided *walks* and *workshops* are offered year-round, including free Sunday morning bird walks spring and fall.

Activities

Hiking 3 mi. of trails at the Refuge; 5 mi. of trails at the Sanctuary.

Fishing: Surf. Excellent for bluefish, striped bass, tautog, in season.

Ski touring: On trails at the Sanctuary.

Headquarters

Sachuest Point National Wildlife Refuge, P.O. Box 307, Charlestown, RI 02813; (401) 364-9124. Visitor center: (401) 847-5511. Norman Bird Sanctuary, 583 Third Beach Rd., Middletown, RI 02840; (401) 846-2577.

Seapowet Marsh Management Area/Emilie Ruecker Wildlife Refuge

Rhode Island Division of Fish and Wildlife; Audubon Society of Rhode Island
296 acres/50 acres.

Eastern RI. From Tiverton, S on Hwy 77 to Seapowet Ave., then W toward Puncatest Rd. and entrances. Ruecker entrance is on Seapowet Ave.

The marsh is on the Sakonnet River, the Eastern Passage of Narragansett Bay. The marsh is dissected by a number of narrow channels and includes several salt ponds.

The Refuge, a gift of Emilie Ruecker, is on the N side of Seapowet Ave. It includes tidal flats, salt marsh, a freshwater pond, a small oak/hickory woodland, and a pine/spruce plantation. Day camps operate here in summer and programs are offered occasionally. The Refuge has blinds for nature observation and photography.

Plants: Marsh vegetation is predominantly cordgrass, with saltmeadow grass, spike grass, rushes, saltwort, seaside plantain, seaside goldenrod. On somewhat higher ground are shadbush, bayberry.

Birds: No checklist. The several habitats and viewpoints make it a fine birding site. Species reported include pheasant, ruffed grouse, screech owl, mourning dove, goldfinch, white-eyed vireo, great and little blue herons, cattle, snowy, and great egrets, glossy ibis, black-crowned night-heron, rails, waterfowl, yellow-rumped and yellow warblers, redstart, yellowthroat, osprey.

Activities

Hiking: Although it's smaller than the Management Area, the Refuge has 3 short, well-developed trails with a good trail guide. The marsh has a short trail across its midsection.

Hunting: In the Management Area only. Rails, pheasant, quail, dove, waterfowl.

Fishing: From the Management Area. Saltwater species.

Boating, canoeing: Unimproved ramp on Puncatest Neck Rd. Canoeing in marsh channels.

Publications

Management Area: map.

Refuge: trail guide with map.

Headquarters

RI Div. of Fish and Wildlife, Government Center, Tower Hill Rd., Wakefield, RI 02879; (401) 789-3094. Audubon Society of RI, 12 Sanderson Rd., Smithfield, RI 02917; (401) 949-5454.

Snake Den State Park

Rhode Island Department of Environmental Management
744 acres.

From Providence, W on US 6 to Brown Ave., beyond I-295; then right.

As of 1996 this state land was listed as "under development." 170 acres are leased to the Dame family for farming. Under the sponsorship of the RI Historical Farm Association, the farm is open to the public, with the request that visitors don't interfere with operations or trample crops.

The rest of the site, woodlands and reverting fields, is available for hiking year-round during daylight hours.

Headquarters

RI Div. of Parks and Recreation, 2321 Hartford Ave., Johnston, RI 02919-1713; (401) 277-2632.

Trestle Trail

Rhode Island Department of Environmental Management
6½ miles.

E access at Coventry Center on Hill Farm Rd. Trail extends to CT border.

This gravel trail was built on an abandoned railroad bed, so it's level, easy walking. Much of the route is on an embankment with woodlands on both sides, but there is considerable visual variety. Coventry Reservoir is at the E end. The trail passes through cuts and rock ledges, crosses highway bridges and a trestle, and ends near Carbuncle Pond at the Nicholas Farm Management Area where swimming is permitted.

Railroad rights-of-way and their adjacent banks and ditches are almost always rich in botanical variety, partly because of the effects of edges and variations in soil moisture, often because trains have transported seeds from place to place. The Trestle Trail is no exception. Species suppressed by railroad maintenance practices are now flourishing.

Since our original edition, the Narragansett Electric Company has transferred its lands on the E portion to the state, so the state now owns the entire trail. The Dept. of Environmental Management tells us that a somewhat complicated management situation has evolved subsequently, but that it looks as though the town of Coventry will assume day-to-day management responsibility for the trail.

Only hiking and bicycling are permitted—*no motors allowed.* We were asked to urge trail users to proceed with caution as the trail is now under improvement and will be for some time. Now advised, the Dept. urges people to use the trail.

Information
RI Dept. of Environmental Management, 235 Promenade St., Providence, RI 02908; (401) 277-6800. Town of Coventry: (401) 822-9170.

Trustom Pond National Wildlife Refuge
U.S. Fish and Wildlife Service
641 acres.

From US 1 near Perryville, take Moonstone Beach Exit in South Kingstown. Follow Moonstone Beach Rd. for 1 mi., turn right onto Matunuck Schoolhouse Rd., 0.7 mi. to Refuge entrance, on left.

Trustom Pond, 160 acres, is RI's only undeveloped salt pond, making it especially valuable to wildlife. The Refuge was established in 1974 to provide nesting, resting, and feeding habitat for migratory birds. Most of the site is upland habitat, once a farm, now reverting. It includes grassland, shrub, and coastal hardwood forest, fresh and brackish marsh, small freshwater ponds, and wooded swamp. Trustom Pond is separated from Block Island Sound by Moonstone Beach, a barrier beach of sand and dunes. The beach is a nesting site for 2 threatened species—least terns and piping plovers.

There is foot access only. Crowding is limited by the size of the parking lot. Moonstone Beach Rd. ends at a public beach, but there is no swimming within the Refuge. The beach is closed April 1–Sept. 15 to protect the nesting birds.

Plants: About 10% of the site is forested. Prominent woodland, understory, and brush species include serviceberry, black cherry, oaks, red maple, viburnum, blueberry, bayberry, smilax, blackberry. Beach species include beachgrass, beach pea, roses, seaside goldenrod.

Birds: Best birding is in spring and fall. There are 3 observation platforms. Checklist of the Ninigret NWR Complex (see entry) notes species occurring here. About 300 species have been recorded, including most of those listed in the Introduction. Refuge management says there is "something good in each season," noting piping plover, least tern, and osprey in spring, wintering waterfowl.

Mammals: No checklist. 40-plus species recorded. Often or occasionally seen: red and gray fox, cottontail, chipmunk, woodchuck, muskrat, deer. Coyote, mink, and otter are present but seldom seen.

Reptiles and amphibians: No checklist. 20-plus species recorded, including painted and snapping turtles, bullfrog, garter snake, brown snake, smooth green snake, northern water snake.

Interpretation

Information kiosk at trailhead.

Nature trails: 1.4 and 1.9 mi.

Fishing: Surf, chiefly for bluefish and stripers.

Headquarters

Ninigret National Wildlife Refuge Complex, Box 307, Charlestown, RI 02813; (401) 364-9124.

Wickaboxet Management Area

Rhode Island Division of Forest Environment
682 acres.

N of Arcadia Management Area. From I-95, Exit 5. NW on Hwy 102 to Plain Meeting House Rd., then N about 3 mi. to the unit.

If you happen to pass this way, as we did, here is an opportunity for a short walk in woods seldom visited except in hunting season. The sign was missing, but a locked gate painted orange marks the entrance. From here a jeep road runs N across the site. What we first saw was rather flat land with mixed hardwood forest, but there are also steep slopes, rock ledges, and a scenic knob. Features include a stream and a swampy area. Birding is reasonably good. Wildflowers in season.

Activities

Hiking: About 5 mi. of trails and woods roads.

Hunting: Grouse, raccoon, gray squirrel, snowshoe hare, deer.

Publication

Site map.

Headquarters

Wickaboxet Management Area, 260 Arcadia Rd., Hope Valley, RI 02832; (401) 539-2356.

CONNECTICUT

Only 2 states are smaller than Connecticut. Only 3 exceed its population density.

Urbanization has burgeoned along the corridor between New York City and Boston. Of the 253-mi. shoreline, only a few fragments remain in public ownership. CT has no National Park, no National Forest, 1 National Wildlife Refuge. Even so, most of the state is green, with many quiet places to enjoy.

CT measures 90 mi. W–E, 55 mi. N–S. It's hilly. The highest ground is in the NW, 1,000 to over 2,000 ft. Elevations in the SW and E are predominantly 300 to 1,000 ft. The Connecticut River bisects the state. The principal rivers flow S from MA, most often in steep-sided narrow valleys. Settlement and subsequent development followed the rivers upstream. Many dams have been built for flood control and power.

The National Climatic Center says CT's weather has more variety than monotony. "A 'normal' month, season, or year is the exception rather than the rule." On the average, the higher NW has 70 below-freezing days in a year, the central and coastal regions 25 to 30 days. Summer temperatures above 90°F occur about 10 days per year.

Average annual precipitation is 44 to 48 in., with no regular dry or wet seasons. Most snow falls in Jan. and Feb. Away from the coast, most of the state has some snow cover from late Dec. through early March.

State Lands

By the late 19th century, loggers had felled most of the primeval forest. Only one-fifth of the land remained forested. Today three-fifths of the land is tree-covered. In the new forests of mixed hardwoods with a scattering of conifers, stone walls mark the boundaries of fields once cultivated.

It was private land then and most of it is now. With no federal land to provide green space, wildlife habitat, and recreation, the state has done remarkably well on its own. Distributed over the state are more than 100 State Forests and State Parks, the largest with over 23,000 acres. The CT Audubon Society, The Nature Conservancy, and other private groups have acquired attractive preserves.

The state system has been planned to provide nearby green spaces and outdoor recreation for CT residents, and does so admirably. Outsiders who want to camp will find limited opportunities. Only 11 State Parks and 3 State Forests have campgrounds. Camping elsewhere on public land is prohibited. State and commercial campgrounds in resort areas are usually full on fine weekends. It's wise to have reservations. Distances are short, however, so any campground can be a base for exploring other sites.

State Parks without campgrounds may also be crowded, especially those offering water-based recreation. Parks in western CT tend to be less crowded than those on or near the coast.

Most developed State Parks have entrance signs. So do the 3 Forest campgrounds. Except at these developed sites, Forest roads often have no signs. Boundaries between state and private land are often unmarked. No matter—local hunters, anglers, hikers, birders, and picnickers can tell you where to go.

If you are traveling to New England for outdoor adventures, CT has few places we'd recommend over the larger and wilder natural areas farther north. If you are traveling through CT, however, there are many places worth stopping for. We never ended a day without finding a delightful marsh, pond, waterfall, hemlock grove, or hilltop. Almost every day we hiked quiet trails, usually alone. For entries we've chosen places well worth visiting for an hour or a day.

It's worth sending for the free *Connecticut Vacation Guide,* issued annually by the Tourism Division, Department of Economic Development, 865 Brook St. Rocky Hill, CT 06067-3405; (800) 282-6863 or (860) 258-4355. The guide offers useful information for those visiting the state, including a compact listing of State Parks and Forests and their facilities. It also lists private campgrounds, downhill and cross-country ski areas, fishing charters, bicycling information.

Trails

We've seen nothing like it anywhere: a statewide system of blazed trails. It's astonishing to find it in a densely populated state, the more so that the system has been planned, built, and maintained by a private organization of volunteers, the Connecticut Forest and Park Association:

Connecticut Forest and Park Association
16 Meriden Rd.
Rockfall, CT 06481
(203) 346-2372

The CFPA began this work in 1929. It has persuaded many private landowners to allow trails to cross their properties. Today it can say to CT residents, "Go a few miles away from your home, and you can soon be on a forest trail."

The CFPA trail coordinators organize volunteers to maintain the 500-mi. blue-blazed hiking trail system, which traverses most of CT. The system has 15 principal trails, including the CT section of the Appalachian Trail (maintained by the CT Chapter of the Appalachian Mountain Club), and many feeders, loops, and spurs.

We considered including brief descriptions of the principal trails and decided not to. Wherever you are in the state, trails are nearby, and there is no substitute for the trail descriptions and maps in the CFPA's *Connecticut Walk Book* (see below), itself an impressive achievement. It describes not only main trails but numerous subsidiary trails and loops. It's loose-leaf, so maps and descriptions can be detached for field use. The book was being revised in 1996; contact CFPA for information on availability.

Many trail segments are within State Parks and State Forests. Linking them is a never-ending task. The privilege of crossing private land is contingent on good behavior. It may be lost when a property changes hands. Where there's no open land, a trail may be routed along a public road, preferably a quiet way. Some trails have gaps. In general, the longest unbroken segments are in the northern half of the state.

Camping is forbidden except at designated sites. Some of these are the campgrounds of State Parks and Forests. There are a few shelters but not enough to support trips over several nights. Long-distance hikers use off-trail quarters.

The two other references listed overlap the *Connecticut Walk Book* in part, but their emphasis is on day hikes to places of special interest:

Connecticut Forest and Park Association. *Connecticut Walk Book,* 18th ed. Rockfall, CT: Author, in press.

Hardy, David, et al. *Fifty Hikes in Connecticut: From the Berkshires to the Coast,* 4th ed. Woodstock, VT: Countryman Press, in press.

Keyarts, Eugene. *60 Selected Short Nature Walks in Connecticut,* 4th ed. Old Saybrook, CT: Globe Pequot Press, 1994.

Maps

The official state highway map serves most purposes. Although it shows only the general locations of State Forests and Wildlife Areas, we could usually find the ones we sought by cruising roads and, if necessary, inquiring. The map has a long list of public boat-launching areas, a chart showing the facilities in Parks and Forests, and other information. It's available from:

Tourism Division, State of Connecticut
Department of Economic Development
865 Brook St.
Rocky Hill, CT 06067-3405
(800) 282-6863 or (860) 258-4355

The CT State Parks Division (see "State Agencies" below for address) has site maps for a few of the State Parks and State Forests. The most complete series is available from the Wildlife Division (see "State Agencies" for address). Their 98 8½-by 11-inch maps include most of the State Forest. We found them helpful, despite inaccuracies. Pathfinding is made more difficult by the lack of name signs on many local roads.

The American Automobile Association provides useful maps free to members.

Flora and Fauna

Only a few small groves of giant white pines remain. Groves of large hemlocks are somewhat more numerous. The predominant pattern of the new forest is mixed hardwoods with scattered white pines and hemlock groves. A useful 64-page pocket manual to identify these trees is *Forest Trees of Southern New England.* The manual has descriptions and line illustrations of 48 trees (available from CT Forest and Park Assoc., 16 Meriden Rd., Rockfall, CT 06481, for $2, which includes postage and handling). Most of the coastal salt marshes and freshwater wetlands have also vanished, but significant sites remain and are now protected by law.

Preserves of the CT Audubon Society, the National Audubon Society in CT, and other private groups (see "Private Organizations" below) maintain and interpret the state's ecosystems. The 2 Audubon groups (independent of one another in CT for some years) have checklists of wildflowers and of birds. More than 200 bird species have been recorded in CT.

For birds and wildflowers, these two general references are, as always, helpful:

Peterson, Roger J. *A Field Guide to Eastern Birds,* 4th ed. Boston: Houghton Mifflin, 1980.

Peterson, Roger T., and Margaret McKenny. *A Field Guide to Wildflowers of Northeastern and North-Central North America.* Boston: Houghton Mifflin, 1975.

The following two references are out of print, but we found copies:

Billard, Ruth Sawyer. *Places to Look for Birds.* Hartford: Department of Environmental Protection, 1972.

Proctor, Noble S. *25 Birding Areas in Connecticut.* Chester, CT: Globe Pequot Press, 1978.

After a drastic decline, the deer population recovered dramatically. Deer are hunted, subject to season and bag limits. The relatively abundant game mammals are gray squirrel, cottontail, snowshoe hare, raccoon, red and gray foxes, woodchuck, and opossum.

The following reference relates bird, mammal, amphibian, and reptile species to place, habitat, and season in New England.

DeGraaf, Richard M., and Deborah D. Rudis. *New England Wildlife: Habitat, Natural History, and Distribution.* General Technical Report NE-108. Broomwall, PA: U.S. Department of Agriculture Forest Service, Northeastern Forest Experiment Station, 1986. (This is out of print, but many have asked that it be reissued.)

Camping

CT provides over 1,400 campsites throughout the state. The season in state campgrounds is mid-April–Sept. 30. Limited off-season camping is permitted at some locations, but all campgrounds are closed Jan. 1–mid-April.

Reservations can be made at most state campgrounds, by mail only, during the period between Memorial Day and Labor Day. Request applications from the State Park Division:

Connecticut Department of Environmental Protection
Bureau of Outdoor Recreation
State Parks Division
79 Elm St.
Hartford, CT 06106-5127
(860) 424-3200

Pets are prohibited in State Park campgrounds, permitted on leash in State Forests.

Canoeing, Boating

Several rivers have flatwater and whitewater canoe runs. Few runs are longer than 10 mi. Some require portages around dams. Some are canoeable only during spring runoff. Three state canoe camps are on the lower Connecticut River (see entry). Our entries note canoeing and boating opportunities.

CT's coast is on Long Sound, one of the U.S.'s most popular waters for boating and fishing.

Lakes with no bordering State Park or State Forest aren't mentioned in entries. Public launch sites on lakes, rivers, and salt water are listed on the official highway map.

Helpful references include:

AMC River Guide: Massachusetts, Connecticut, Rhode Island, 2nd ed. Boston: Appalachian Mountain Club, 1990.

Borton, Mark C., et al. (eds.). *The Complete Boating Guide to the Connecticut River,* 2nd ed. Easthampton, MA: Connecticut River Watershed Council, in press. (Available from the council at 1 Ferry St., Easthampton, MA 01027.)

Canoe Camping. Hartford, CT: Dept. of Environmental Protection, State Parks Div., n.d.

Weber, Ken. *Canoeing Massachusetts, Rhode Island, and Connecticut.* Woodstock, VT: Countryman Press, in press.

Fishing

Water condition in CT rivers, where pollution had curtailed some of the state's best fishing, has improved substantially. Shad fishing has returned to the Connecticut River, and there is an annual shad derby.

Fishing is noted as an available activity in many public areas. Many streams and ponds are stocked. Most of the trout caught are from hatcheries. The Farmington and Housatonic Rivers provide some of the best trout fishing in the East. Other species include bass and pickerel.

Judging by the fleets of small boats we saw in harbors, saltwater fishing is extremely popular. Bluefish is a leading catch.

State Agencies

The Dept. of Environmental Protection has responsibility for all the state's natural resources.

Department of Environmental Protection
79 Elm St.
Hartford, CT 06106-5127

All of the numerous administrative units are at the same address. For example, the State Parks Division is responsible for recreation areas in State Parks and State Forests. It can be contacted at:

Bureau of Outdoor Recreation
State Parks Division
79 Elm St.
Hartford, CT 06106-5127
(860) 424-3200

Publications

Camping in Connecticut (leaflet).

Canoe Camping (leaflet).

Off-Season Camping (leaflet).

Mimeo information pages on State Parks, State Forests, State Reserves (undeveloped parks).

Information on hiking trails.

The Wildlife Division manages the state's wildlife resources:

Wildlife Division
79 Elm St.
Hartford, CT 06106-5127
(860) 424-3011

Publications

Hunting and Trapping Field Guide (free). No hunting is allowed on Sun. WMA maps are available on site. Contact the Div. if you need more information before visiting a particular WMA.

Fisheries Division
79 Elm St.
Hartford, CT 06106-5127
(860) 424-3474

Publication

Connecticut Angler's Guide (free).

Tourism Division
865 Brook St.
Rocky Hill, CT 06067-3405
(800) 282-6863 or (860) 258-4355

Publication

Connecticut Vacation Guide.

Private Organizations

Connecticut Audubon Society
118 Oak St.
Hartford, CT 06106
(860) 527-8737

National Audubon Society
Audubon Center of Greenwich
613 Riversville Rd.
Greenwich, CT 06831
(203) 869-5272

The Nature Conservancy
Connecticut Chapter
55 High St.
Middletown, CT 06457-3788
(860) 344-0716

Connecticut Forest and Park Association
16 Meriden Rd.
Rockfall, CT 06481
(203) 346-2372

Connecticut River Watershed Council
1 Ferry St.
Easthampton, MA 01027
(413) 529-9500

White Memorial Foundation
Rt. 202
Litchfield, CT 06759
(860) 567-0857

C O N N E C T I C U T

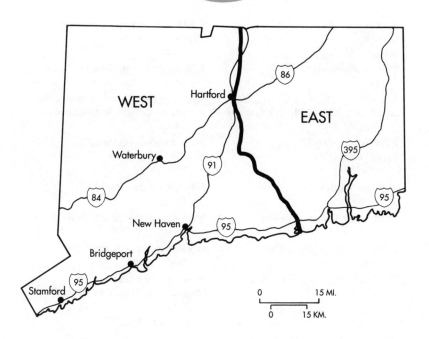

WEST

EAST

Hartford

86

Waterbury

91

395

New Haven

95

84

95

Bridgeport

Stamford

95

0   15 MI.

0   15 KM.

Natural Areas in Connecticut

An Alphabetical Listing

Algonquin State Forest
West

Assekonk Swamp Wildlife Management Area
East

Audubon Center in Geenwich and Fairchild Wildflower Garden
West

Barn Island Wildlife Management Area
East

Bigelow Hollow State Park
East

Bluff Point Coastal Reserve
East

Campbell Falls State Park
West

Chatfield Hollow State Park
West

Cockaponset State Forest
West

Connecticut Audubon Society at Fairfield (Larsen Sanctuary)
West

Connecticut River
West/East

Devil's Den Preserve
West

Devil's Hopyard State Park
East

Durham Meadows Wildlife Management Area
West

Edward Steichen Memorial Wildlife Preserve
West

Ellithorpe Flood Control Area
East

Fairchild Wildflower Garden. *See* **Audubon Center in Greenwich**
West

Franklin Swamp Wildlife Management Area
East

Gay City State Park
East

Hammonasset Beach State Park
West

Hopeville Pond State Park
East

Housatonic State Forest/ Housatonic Meadows State Park
West

Hurd State Park
East

Indian Well State Park. *See* **Kettletown State Park**
West

James L. Goodwin State Forest
East

John A. Minnetto State Park
West

Kettletown State Park/Indian Well State Park
West

Natural Areas in Connecticut

by Zones

WEST ZONE

Algonquin State Forest

Audubon Center in Greenwich and Fairchild Wildflower Garden

Campbell Falls State Park

Chatfield Hollow State Park

Cockaponset State Forest

Connecticut Audubon Society at Fairfield (Larsen Sanctuary)

Connecticut River

Devil's Den Preserve

Durham Meadows Wildlife Management Area

Edward Steichen Memorial Wildlife Preserve

Fairchild Wildflower Garden. See Audubon Center in Greenwich

Hammonasset Beach State Park

Housatonic State Forest/ Housatonic Meadows State Park

Indian Well State Park. See Kettletown State Park

John A. Minnetto State Park

Kettletown State Park/Indian Well State Park

Larsen Sanctuary. See Connecticut Audubon Society at Fairfield

Macedonia Brook State Park

Mattatuck State Forest

Mohawk State Forest

Nassahegon State Forest

Nepaug State Forest

Penwood State Park/Talcott Mountain State Park

Peoples State Forest

Salt Meadow National Wildlife Refuge. See Stewart B. McKinney National Wildlife Refuge

Shade Swamp Sanctuary

Sharon Audubon Center

Sleeping Giant State Park

Stewart B. McKinney National Wildlife Refuge

Talcott Mountain State Park. See Penwood State Park

Tunxis State Forest

White Memorial Foundation

EAST ZONE

Assekonk Swamp Wildlife Management Area

Barn Island Wildlife Management Area

Bigelow Hollow State Park

Bluff Point Coastal Reserve

Connecticut River

Devil's Hopyard State Park

Ellithorpe Flood Control Area

Franklin Swamp Wildlife Management Area

Gay City State Park

Hopeville Pond State Park

Hurd State Park

James L. Goodwin State Forest

Mansfield Hunting Area/
Mansfield Hollow State Park

Mashamoquet Brook State Park

Meshomasic State Forest

Morgan R. Chaney Sanctuary

Natchaug State Forest

Nehantic State Forest

Nipmuck State Forest

Pachaug State Forest

Quaddick State Forest and State Park

Quinebaug River Wildlife Management Area

Rocky Neck State Park

Salmon River State Forest

Shenipsit State Forest

Algonquin State Forest

Connecticut Department of Environmental Protection   West
2,947 acres.

From Winsted, N on Hwy 8. About 1.6 mi. N of Colebrook town line, turn left on Sandy Brook Rd. Look for access points on both sides.

The Forest is listed as "undeveloped," a forest reserve. No woods roads or trails are shown on Wildlife Div. maps. We found no informal trails. Bushwhacking is the way to go, or just stroll down the road.

A separate 406-acre block is on both sides of US 44 along the Mad River, NW of Winsted, just beyond the dam. It has a parking area and river trail on the S side. Reverting fields, some mixed hardwoods, a small pond.

Fishing: Trout in Sandy Brook.

Publications
Wildlife Div. maps.

Headquarters
CT Dept. of Environmental Protection, State Parks Div., 79 Elm St., Hartford, CT 06106-5127; (860) 424-3200.

Assekonk Swamp Wildlife Management Area

Connecticut Department of Environmental Protection   East
700 acres.

SW of North Stonington. From intersection with Hwy 201, NE on Hwy 184 about 2.5 mi.; 0.25 mi. E of Jeremy Hill Rd., left on dirt road. Open barway at 0.4 mi. and continue to parking area.

A wild, picturesque marsh; enough open water for canoeing; reverting fields; mixed hardwood forest. Parking area, trails, and open fields are on the W side of the site.

Activities

Hunting: Pheasant, small game only. Closed to waterfowl hunting.

Canoeing: Access is across a field behind the North Stonington fire-house, at intersection of Hwy 2 and Rocky Hollow Rd. Not much open water in summer. Best birding is by canoe.

Publication

Map.

Headquarters

CT Dept. of Environmental Protection, Wildlife Div., 79 Elm St., Hartford, CT 06106-5127; (860) 424-3011.

....

Audubon Center in Greenwich and Fairchild Wildflower Garden

National Audubon Society West
485 acres.

Exit 28 from Hwy 15, the Merritt Parkway. 8 mi. N on Riversville Rd. The Fairchild Garden is S of Center on Riversville Rd., left on N. Porchuck Rd.

Open 9–5 Tues.–Sun. except holidays and holiday weekends.

The Center includes woods, old fields, deep ponds, wet meadows, clear streams, habitats with an abundance of birds and small mammals. Nature trails throughout the site include a wetland boardwalk. Guided walks are scheduled occasionally.

The garden environment includes deciduous woodland, a small pine forest, damp meadows, a pond, and open areas. Along its trails can be seen specimens of almost all the wildflowers, shrubs, ferns, and mosses indigenous to CT. There is a honeybee exhibit too.

This is a National Audubon Nature Education Center, and during the summer months there is an adult ecology camp here.

Birds: Checklist of approximately 200 species available. Bird blinds are available on request.

Hiking: 15 mi. of trails.
Pets, picnicking, and smoking are prohibited.

Publications

Maps.

Bird checklist.

Trail guide.

Headquarters

Audubon Center of Greenwich, 613 Riversville Rd., Greenwich, CT 06831; (203) 869-5272.

....

Barn Island Wildlife Management Area

Connecticut Department of Environmental Protection   East
748 acres.

SE corner of CT. US 1 to traffic light at Greenhaven Rd. Right on Palmer Neck Rd. to parking.

On Little Narragansett Bay, between Wequetequock Cove and Paw-catuck River. Tidal and brackish marsh grades into oak forest with reverting fields. Trails and unpaved roads across the marshes and in the upland areas.

Birds: Variety of waterfowl winter in the bay. Many shorebirds in spring and fall. Grouse, pheasant, woodcock, and quail in brushy areas. Many songbirds.

Activities

Hunting: Waterfowl, other game birds, squirrel, cottontail.

Boating: Ramp at parking area. Saltwater canoeing in calm weather.

Publication

Map.

Headquarters

CT Dept. of Environmental Protection, Wildlife Div., 79 Elm St., Hartford, CT 06106-5127; (860) 424-3011.

Bigelow Hollow State Park

Connecticut Department of Environment Protection   East
513 acres.

From Union, 2 mi. E on Hwy 197.

A state pamphlet describes this as "a large picnic area in a scenic, natural setting." It's on the Nipmuck Trail, thus a convenient trailhead, and it adjoins the Nipmuck State Forest (see entry).

Rolling forest land surrounds Lake Mashapaug, 1½ mi. long, and Bigelow Pond, both good trout waters.

Activities

Fishing: Bigelow Pond and Lake Mashapaug. Trout.

Swimming: No lifeguard.

Boating: Ramp on the lake. Hand-carried craft on the pond.

Headquarters

CT Dept. of Environmental Protection, State Parks Div., 79 Elm St., Hartford, CT 06106-5127; (860) 424-3200.

Bluff Point Coastal Reserve

Connecticut Department of Environmental Protection   East
806 acres.

From I-95, Exit 88. S on Hwy 117, right on US 1, left on Depot Rd., under railroad overpass to parking.

This is the last significant fragment of undeveloped shoreline in CT. We haven't seen it on a summer weekend, but we were told the half-mile walk from the parking area to the beach and lack of a developed swimming area deter crowds.

The reserve is a bluff or headland overlooking Mumford Cove, Long Island Sound, and the Poquonock River. Highest point is 128 ft.

above sea level. The wooded highland descends to a 100-acre tidal salt marsh. A long, narrow sandspit curves westward, ending at Bushy Point, a small island. Beach vegetation includes beach plum, beach pea, red and white shore roses.

Headquarters
Connecticut Department of Environmental Protection, State Parks Div., 79 Elm St., Hartford, CT 06106-5127; (860) 424-3200.

···

Campbell Falls State Park

CT Department of Environmental Protection   West
365 acres.

On the MA border. From Torrington, N on Hwy 272. Cross US 44 and keep going on Hwy 272, past Haystack Mountain State Park on the left. Just before MA border, W on Spaulding Rd. to Park.

At this time the Park is a State Reserve and undeveloped. A short trail through a fine hemlock forest leads to a parking area in MA. At the concrete post, turn left to the short falls trail. A 50-ft. falls on Ginger Creek drops into a narrow ravine. Not much water was dropping when we visited, but it's obviously attractive in full flow.
    State literature says this is a good picnicking spot.

Headquarters
CT Department of Environmental Protection, State Parks Div., 79 Elm St., Hartford, CT 06106-5127; (860) 424-3200.

···

Chatfield Hollow State Park

Connecticut Department of Environmental Protection   West
356 acres.

From Killingworth, 1.5 mi. W on Hwy 80.

This small Park adjoins part of the very large Cockaponset State Forest (see entry) and provides access to over 18 mi. of hiking trails, including the blue-blazed Chatfield Trail. The site is a heavily wooded hollow with caves and ledges. 7-acre Schreeder Pond, built in the 1930s by the Civilian Conservation Corps, provides fishing and swimming.

Headquarters

CT Department of Environmental Protection, State Parks Div., 79 Elm St., Hartford, CT 06106-5127; (860) 424-3200.

Cockaponset State Forest

Connecticut Department of Environmental Protection   West
15,652 acres.

From Chester, 3 mi. W on Hwy 148. Or from Hwy 9, Exit 8, then 0.5 mi. E on Beaver Meadow Rd.

CT's second largest State Forest extends for about 10 mi. N–S, in several blocks, on both sides of Hwy 9 in the western Connecticut River Valley. As the state acquired the land, efforts to restore forest conditions began. The most intensive period was 1933–1941, when a large contingent of the Civilian Conservation Corps was quartered here.

Oak, hickory, and maple are now the predominant species on higher ground, with beech, birch, oak, and tulip in stream valleys. Dogwood and laurel are conspicuous in the spring.

The Forest has a well-developed trail system.

Forest HQ is on Beaver Meadow Rd., just ½ mi. E of Exit 8 from Hwy 9. From here Filley Rd. runs S through the Turkey Hill block, passing Turkey Hill Reservoir and Pataconk Reservoir, the Forest's 2 largest water bodies, each about ¾ mi. long. The area includes small streams, ponds, and marshes including a white cedar swamp. Several mi. to the SW, S of I-95 on Hwy 146, are 2 small blocks of tidal waterfowl marsh on Great Harbor.

Activities

Camping: 16 "casual sites." No reservations.

Hiking: The blue-blazed Cockaponset Trail runs N–S in the Turkey Hill block, about 7½ mi., with alternate trails permitting circuit hikes. In the Killingworth block, which includes Chatfield Hollow State Park (see entry), are the 4½ mi. Chatfield Trail and others.

Hunting: Grouse, waterfowl, cottontail, deer, squirrel, raccoon, other furbearers.

Fishing: Trout fishing is said to be fair to good.

Ski touring: Trails and unplowed roads.

Adjacent
Chatfield Hollow State Park (see entry).

Publications
Maps, 8½ × 11-inch, little detail, for the various blocks.

Headquarters
CT Department of Environmental Protection, State Parks Div., 79 Elm St., Hartford, CT 06106-5127; (860) 424-3200.

....

Connecticut Audubon Center at Fairfield (Larsen Sanctuary)

Connecticut Audubon Society   West
160 acres.

From Merritt Pkwy, Exit 44. Bear right, then immediate right turn onto Congress St. Follow Audubon signs to Fairfield Center on Burr St. (Or I-95, Exit 21 at Fairfield.)

Sanctuary: Open daily dawn–dusk. Center: Open Tues.–Sat. 9–4:30, closed holidays.

In a small tract, skillful management can increase natural diversity. 30 years ago, this site was covered with second-growth hardwoods. Now it also has ponds and open fields. Woodlands are managed. Species of plants, shrubs, and trees have been added to offer food and cover to birds and small mammals.

No pets or picnicking permitted.

Interpretation
The purpose here is environmental education.

Nature center and *library.*

6½ mi. of *boardwalk trails* with *illustrated guide.*

Trail designed for the blind, disabled, and elderly.

Nature education programs for adults and children.

Publications

Walk Guide. $2.

Trail map.

Mimeo information pages: list of common trees and shrubs, geology, cross-country ski guide.

Headquarters

CT Audubon Society, 2325 Burr St., Fairfield, CT 06430; (203) 259-6305.

....

Connecticut River

70 river mi.   West/East

MA border to Long Island Sound.

Beginning near the Canadian border and descending for more than 400 mi., the Connecticut is New England's longest river. The lower river bisects CT before entering Long Island Sound. There is development on both sides, and few long sections of shoreline at this end of the river could be called natural. On warm weekends, powerboat traffic is heavy near Hartford and other urban centers. Boating is popular in the state and many launch sites are overcrowded.

Nonetheless, quiet times and places remain. The state provides opportunities for camping along the river. Hurd State Park (see entry), 47 river mi. below the MA line, 26 river mi. S of Hartford, is the first state campsite, reserved for canoeists. Other state campsites are at Gillette Castle State Park (Mile 56) and Selden Neck State Park (Mile 58).

None of these parks currently offers swimming, and we don't recommend that activity either in the lower Connecticut, nor would we drink its water. However, anadromous fish have reappeared in the river, and great progress has been made in reducing pollution. Still, all who take part in recreation on the lower Connecticut should inquire about its condition locally.

Activities

Camping: Reservations must be made 2 weeks in advance, stating camping area, date, name and address of leader, number and ages of party members, type of boat, intended put-in and take-out points. Manager: Gillette Castle State Park, East Haddam, CT 06423; (860) 526-2336. One night only. No vehicle access to river.

Canoeing: Concession at Gillette provides outfitting and transportation. (860) 739-0791.

Boating: State launch sites at Enfield, Haddam Meadows, Old Saybrook, Salmon River, Suffield, and Windsor. Some riverside towns have ramps. (See the state map for a more complete list and more detail.)

Publications
Canoe Camping (leaflet).

Headquarters
CT Dept. of Environmental Protection, State Parks Div., 79 Elm St., Hartford, CT 06106-5127; (860) 424-3200.

....

Devil's Den Preserve

The Nature Conservancy West
1,720 acres.

N of Norwalk. From Merritt Pkwy, Exit 42. N on Hwy 57 for 5 mi. Turn E on Godfrey Rd., 0.5 mi. to Pent Rd. and right to parking.

Trails open daily sunrise–sunset.

Its formal name is Lucius Pond Ordway–Devil's Den Preserve, but we invariably heard of it as Devil's Den or "The Den." This is the largest wild area remaining in SW CT. The terrain is a series of rocky ridges rising from 260 to 610 ft., providing views of Long Island Sound. Intermittent streams flow through oak/maple woodland. Dense swamps are in the lowlands.

The Preserve contains Godfrey Pond, a millpond created in the 1700s; the Saugatuck Wildlife Refuge, an extensive shrubby marsh along the West Branch of the Saugatuck River; the Great Ledge, a high rock formation over the Saugatuck Reservoir; and Ambler Gorge, a picturesque ravine with cascade. There are prehistoric shelters built by native Americans, and sites where charcoal was made at the turn of the century.

Plants: The site is almost totally forested. Principal trees are red maple, beech, red and white oaks, hickory. Red maple dominates in wetlands, beech, birch, and maple on lower slopes. Midslopes are dominated by red and white oaks, with chestnut oak above. 500 species of flowering plants have been recorded, including pink lady's slipper, cardinal flower, and Indian pipe.

Birds: 145 species recorded. Seasonal abundance of warblers and other songbirds, pileated woodpecker, ruffed grouse, wood duck.

Mammals: 23 species reported, including most small mammals common to the region. Red fox, bobcat, coyote.

Reptiles and amphibians: 28 species reported, including wood turtle and marbled and spotted salamanders.

Interpretation
Guided hikes and nature walks for all ages are led by volunteers and are very popular. Schedule is printed in the newsletter. Reservations are required for most events.

Nearby
Katherine Ordway Preserve: 65 acres. In Weston, located at 165 Goodhill Rd. also owned and managed by TNC, this sanctuary has over 3 mi. of trails and features lush stands of mountain laurel, open fields of wildflowers, and an arboretum with specimen trees collected from around the world by the site's donor. (A map is currently in revision.)

Hiking: More than 20 mi. of well-marked trails described in Preserve trail guide.
    Pets and bicycles are prohibited.

Publications
Leaflet with map.

Interpretive Trail Guide.

The Great Ledger (semiannual newsletter).

There are also research papers and a variety of printed materials on vegetation and wildlife.

Headquarters
Lucius Pond Ordway–Devil's Den Preserve, Box 1162, Weston, CT 06833; (203) 226-4991.

Devil's Hopyard State Park

Connecticut Department of Environmental Protection   East
860 acres.

S of Colchester. From the intersection of Hwys 156 and 82, 3 mi. N.

More than 100,000 visitors come here each year, but there are quiet days. The chief attraction is Chapman Falls, where Eight Mile River plunges down a 60-ft. escarpment. Around the splash pool at the base are several kettleholes. The river continues through a handsome hemlock forest. The hillsides are steep, wooded. Small marshes are in the E and SW portions of the Park.

Activities

Camping: 21 wooded sites near the falls. (No swimming.) Reservations available.

Hiking: About 15 mi. of trails and woods roads.

Fishing: Brook trout. American and lamprey eels travel to the base of the falls each spring.

Publication
Leaflet with map.

Headquarters
Devil's Hopyard State Park, 366 Hopyard Rd., East Haddam, CT 06423; (860) 873-8566.

Durham Meadows Wildlife Management Area

Connecticut Department of Environmental Protection   West
571 acres.

S of Middletown. From Durham, S on Hwy 17. Entrance is ½ mi. beyond junction with Hwy 77. For N block, N on Hwy 17, W about 1 mi. on Hwy 147.

Most of the site is marsh along the Coginchaug River, partly over-grown in swamp maple. Also reverting fields, some old-growth hard-woods, open water. Three streams join the Coginchaug. Foot travel is difficult.

Birds: Include ducks, rail, marsh wren. Blue-winged teal nest.

Activities

Hunting: Pheasant, woodcock, waterfowl, cottontail, squirrel.

Canoeing: Best in spring when water is high and before vegetation becomes thick. Put-in is on Hwy 147, W of N block entrance.

Publication
Map.

Headquarters

CT Dept. of Environmental Protection, Wildlife Div., 79 Elm St., Hart-ford, CT 06106-5127; (860) 424-3011.

Edward Steichen Memorial Wildlife Preserve

Connecticut Audubon Society   West
54 acres.

From US 7 at Topstone (between Georgetown and Danbury), turn right on Topstone Rd. Entrance is on the left just beyond Chestnut Woods Rd.

Edward Steichen, the famous photographer, bought Huckleberry Swamp and other lands in 1928 and allowed natural succession to proceed. The Preserve includes a red maple swamp, shrubby swamp, and uplands. A boardwalk enters the swamp.

A 94-page ecological survey of the site traces its geological history and includes annotated lists of its flora and fauna.

Publications

Leaflet with map.

The following may be available for purchase: Roth, Linda, Henry Woolsey, and Ellen Baum. *Huckleberry Swamp and Adjacent Uplands.*

Headquarters
CT Audubon Society, 118 Oak St., Hartford, CT 06106-5127; (860) 527-8737.

Ellithorpe Flood Control Area

Connecticut Department of Environmental Protection   East
400 acres.

Near the MA border. From Stafford Springs, N on Hwy 32 beyond Hwy 190. Left on Crow Hill Rd. Park on near side of railroad tracks.

A quiet place for an easy walk through wetlands. Walk beside the tracks and around a barrier to a dirt road on a dike. It's straight and level, with swamp, swamp forest, and areas of open water on either side. Two local residents had carried a small boat about half a mile to one snag-dotted pond. They said the bass and pickerel fishing was fine. We had good birding.

Nearby
Shenipsit State Forest (see entry).

Publication
Map.

Headquarters
CT Dept. of Environmental Protection, Wildlife Div., 79 Elm St., Hartford, CT 06106-5127; (860) 424-3200.

Fairchild Wildflower Garden

See Audubon Center in Greenwich.

Franklin Swamp Wildlife Management Area

Connecticut Department of Environmental Protection   East
620 acres.

Between Franklin and North Franklin on Hwy 32.

Except in hunting season, if you're passing by, this is a pleasant spot for a short walk. Headquarters and parking are well marked. A dirt road between Hwy 32 and the parking leads toward HQ. Take the blacktop to the left through a closed gate. On the left is a shooting range. Down the hill are trails, chiefly jeep tracks. The site extends along Under Mountain Rd., through fields and woodlands.

The moderately hilly terrain includes mixed forest, hardwood swamp, open swale, and fields. We saw two small ponds, a great horned owl, and no other visitors.

Hunting: Pheasant, woodcock, cottontail.

Publication
Map.

Headquarters
CT Dept. of Environmental Protection, Wildlife Division, 79 Elm St., Hartford, CT 06106-5127; (860) 424-3200.

Gay City State Park East

Connecticut Department of Environmental Protection   East
1,569 acres.

From Bolton, 3 mi. S on Hwy 85.

Named for a vanished mill town, the Park is crossed by the Blackledge River, which provided water power. A small pond at the Park's center has a sand beach. The SW sector is a swamp.

Rolling and forested, the Park has 10 numbered trails, offering a variety of loop hikes. Trails connect with the Shenipsit Trail, a short distance to the W, which runs from Cobalt through the Meshomasic and Shenipsit State Forests (see entries) to the MA border.

Publication
Map with text.

Headquarters
CT Department of Environmental Protection, State Parks Div., 79 Elm St., Hartford, CT 06106-5127; (860) 424-3200.

Goodwin State Forest

See James L. Goodwin State Forest and Conservation Center.

Hammonasset Beach State Park

Connecticut Department of Environmental Protection   West
919 acres.

Between Madison and Clinton. From I-95, Exit 62, then 1 mi. S.

With 2 mi. of fine beach on Long Island Sound and CT's largest state campground, easily reached from most CT cities, this is a crowded place in summer. Birders enjoy it in spring and fall. Part of the undeveloped acreage has been designated a Natural Area Preserve.

Birds: Meigs Point has marsh and shorebirds. The extensive marsh on the Hammonasset River attracts waterfowl, herons, possibly clapper rail. The scrubby upland is habitat for thrashers, grackles, warblers.

Activities
Camping: 541 sites. Reservations available. 185 sites open off-season, to Nov. 1.
Fishing: Saltwater species.

Headquarters
Hammonasset Beach State Park, Box 271, Madison, CT 06443; (203) 245-2785 office; (203) 245-1817 campground.

Hopeville Pond State Park

Connecticut Department of Environmental Protection   East
554 acres.

From Connecticut Turnpike (Hwy 52), Exit 86. Then Hwy 201 to 3 mi. E of Jewett City.

Driving in, we passed a great number of picnic tables scattered on the wooded shoreline of a small, attractive pond. The campground is on the opposite shore. The Park has heavy weekend use in season.

We include it because it adjoins the Pachaug State Forest (see entry), largest in CT, and serves as a bedroom and trailhead.

Activities

Camping: 82 wooded sites near pond. Reservations available.

Canoeing: Rentals.

Headquarters

Hopeville Pond State Park, 193 Roode Rd., Jewett City, CT 06351; (860) 376-2920 office, (860) 376-0313 campground.

Housatonic State Forest/Housatonic Meadows State Park

Connecticut Department of Environmental Protection   West
9,543 acres/451 acres.

Several tracts on both sides of the Housatonic River, between US 44 and Cornwall Bridge. The State Park is 1 mi. N of Cornwall Bridge on Hwy 7.

The Housatonic River Valley is one of CT's most scenic areas, although US 7 and a railroad run close to the river. Rising from the river are forested hills cut by ravines and streams, with nearby swamps and beaver flowages. Portions of the river are canoeable, when there's plenty of water. Friends told us about "rump-bumping,"

floating downstream in rubber tubes. (Swimming is not permitted at the State Park.)

The State Park is a narrow strip along the W shore of the river. Campsites are under pines near the riverbank. One block of Forest land adjoins the W boundary of the Park. Another, across the river, rises more than 700 ft. to the N–S ridge of Mine Mountain. Both have trails. From the Park, Pine Knob Loop, 2½ mi., climbs to a viewpoint at 1,160 ft.

The Forest is listed as a Forest Reserve. It includes almost a dozen blocks, the largest with more than 3,000 acres. The Appalachian Trail crosses portions of the Forest. About 2,300 acres are in small blocks, not shown on available maps.

The *Cream Hill block*, 2,290 acres, is E of the river. At West Cornwall, cross the covered bridge on Hwy 128 and take Cream Hill Rd. The block is hilly, forested, with laurel thickets, some swamp. Cream Hill's elevation is 1,503 ft. The Appalachian Trail crosses Cream Hill Rd. and Yelping Hill Rd. The Pine Knoll lean-to is on Wickwire Rd. *Dean Ravine* and *Barrack Mountain* are scenic destinations for day hikers.

The *Sharon Mountain block*, 3,030 acres, lies N of West Cornwall, E of the river. Access is from US 7 on Cornwall Rd. or Pine Swamp Rd. Mixed hardwoods, beaver flowages, some swamp. Local trails cross the site.

The *Canaan Mountain block*, 1,370 acres, is farthest N, between US 7 and East Canaan. Access is from US 44 via Lower Rd. Sometimes referred to as "wilderness," the block is roadless and has no marked trails. Highest point is 1,962-ft. Bradford Mountain. Canaan Mountain, in the N sector, is 1,762 ft. The forest includes mixed hardwoods, white pine, and hemlock, with an unusual stand of red pine.

Activities

Camping: 102 sites at State Park. 25 sites open off-season; limited facilities Oct. 15–Jan. 1. Reservations available.

Hiking, backpacking: Appalachian Trail, local trails, logging roads (long unused).

Hunting: Grouse, pheasant, woodcock, wild turkey, cottontail, gray squirrel, raccoon, deer; some waterfowl in Sharon Mountain block.

Fishing: Trout, chiefly in river. A 2-mi. section at the State Park is restricted to fly fishing.

Publications

Maps, 4 sections.

Headquarters

CT Dept. of Environmental Protection, State Parks Div., 79 Elm St., Hartford, CT 06106-5127; (860) 424-3200. Housatonic Meadows State Park, Cornwall Bridge, CT 06754; (860) 927-3238 office, (860) 672-6772 campground.

Hurd State Park

Connecticut Department of Environmental Protection   East

884 acres.

On the E side of Connecticut River, 3 mi. S of Cobalt on Hwy 151.

Hurd is the most northern of 3 state-operated canoe camps on the Connecticut River (see entry), 47 river mi. S of the MA border. The bank is steep, with granite ledges, rising from about 10 ft. to 266 ft. on Split Rock and 408 ft. on White Mountain. Hurd Brook drops to the river over cascades in a hemlock gorge.

For motorists, this is a day-use park, with picnic shelter and about 2½ mi. of woodland trails in 2 loops, one riverside, the other to the Split Rock viewpoint. It has an interesting diversity of wildlife and fine display of colors in the fall.

Activities

Camping: Boat access only. Primitive sites. Permit required, requested at least 2 weeks in advance from Manager, Gillette Castle State Park, East Haddam, CT 06423; (860) 526-2336. May 1–Sept. 30.

Canoeing: This is not a put-in site; no vehicle access to the river.

Headquarters

CT Dept. of Environmental Protection, State Parks Div., 79 Elm St., Hartford, CT 06106-5127; (860) 424-3200.

Indian Well State Park

See Kettletown State Park/Indian Well State Park.

James L. Goodwin State Forest and Conservation Center

Connecticut Department of Environmental Protection   East
2,171 acres.

On US 6, 3 mi. E of South Chaplin.

Forest trails usable daily from dawn to dusk. Center has limited hours, call before visiting: (860) 455-9534.

The original forest was cut and the land farmed until about 1900. In 1913 the owner, James L. Goodwin, one of the first forestry graduates, began developing the site as a tree farm. He became a leader in promoting good forest management. In 1964 he gave the land to the state, dedicating it to conservation education. 80 acres were set aside for a conservation center. It's a fine place to learn the history of CT woodlands and see how the forest has been restored.

The site includes hardwood forest, softwood plantation, wildlife ponds, and flooded swamp.

Interpretation

Display of all forest practices common to CT.

Arboretum features woodland shrubs.

Guided walks and *field trips* available for groups, by appointment.

Activities

Hiking: Easy hiking trails and woods roads extend throughout the area. The Natchaug Trail crosses the Forest.

Horse riding: On woods roads.

Fishing: Bass, bluegill, bullheads in ponds.

Boating: Canoeing on flooded swamps. Boats with electric motors on Pine Acres Pond.

Adjacent
Natchaug State Forest (see entry).

Publication
Map.

Headquarters

CT Dept. of Environmental Protection, State Parks Div., 79 Elm St., Hartford, CT 06106-5127; (860) 424-3200. On site: (860) 455-9534.

John A. Minnetto State Park

Connecticut Department of Environmental Protection   West
678 acres.

Off Hwy 272, 6 mi. N of Torrington.

The site is a long, narrow strip of rolling, open land along Hall Brook, now a flood control area. A central portion serves the function of a municipal park with such activities as picnicking, swimming, field sports, and winter sports. The other 500 acres are mostly wetland, with trails and good waterfowl viewing.

Headquarters

CT Dept. of Environmental Protection, State Parks Div., 79 Elm St., Hartford, CT 06106-5127; (860) 424-3200.

Kettletown State Park/Indian Well State Park

Connecticut Department of Environmental Protection   West
429 acres/153 acres.

I-84, Exit 15. Then Hwy 67 E for ¼ mi. turn right onto Georges Hill Rd. 4.5 mi. to Park./2 mi. N of Shelton on Hwy 110.

These 2 Parks are linked by the Paugussett and Pomperaug Trails. Both Parks are on the Housatonic River, Kettletown bordering for 2 mi. on an impoundment called Lake Zoar.

Activities

Camping: At Kettletown. 72 sites, through Columbus Day. Reservations available. Off-season camping to Jan. 1, 30 sites, limited facilities.

Hiking: A handicapped accessible trail is now available at Kettletown.

Fishing, swimming: At both sites.

Boating: Ramp at Indian Well. State ramp a short distance upstream from Kettletown.

Headquarters
Kettletown State Park, 175 Quaker Farms Rd., Southbury, CT 06488; (203) 264-5169 office, (203) 264-5678 campground./CT Dept. of Environmental Protection, State Parks Div., 79 Elm St., Hartford, CT 06106-5127; (806) 434-3200.

....

Macedonia Brook State Park

Connecticut Department of Environmental Protection   West
2,300 acres.

From Kent, 4 mi. N on Hwy 341.

In mountainous terrain near the NY border, this is one of CT's largest and wildest State Parks, with little development other than campground and trails. It is crossed by 4 mi. of Macedonia Brook, with a deep gorge and upper and lower falls. Elevations range from 670 to 1,360 ft., with views of the Catskills and the Taconic Range from the heights.

The site is mostly forested with mixed hardwoods. Woodland bird species are abundant during migrations; birders often camp so they can be in the woods at dawn.

Activities

Camping: 80 sites.

Hiking, backpacking: The Appalachian Trail traverses the Park, crossing Cobble Mountain and Pine Hill. Two lean-tos. Other trails are color-coded.

Fishing: Stream. Said to be good. Trout are stocked.

Headquarters
Macedonia Brook State Park, 159 Macedonia Brook Rd., Kent, CT 06757; (860) 927-3238 office, (860) 927-4100 campground.

Larsen Sanctuary

See Connecticut Audubon Society at Fairfield.

Lucius Pond Ordway–Devil's Den Preserve

See Devil's Den Preserve.

Mansfield Hunting Area/Mansfield Hollow State Park

Connecticut Department of Environmental Protection   East
2,500 acres.

1 mi. E of Mansfield Center off Hwy 89.

A flood-control dam on the Natchaug River created 500-acre Mansfield Hollow Lake. The Park surrounds the N portion of the impoundment, called Naubesatuck Lake. The more extensive Hunting Area is adjacent, extending upstream along the Natchaug and Fenton Rivers.

The developed area of the Park is on a wooded bluff overlooking the lake. Swimming is not permitted because the lake is a public water supply, but picnicking, boating, and fishing are enough to attract crowds on fine weekends. The shallow lake is deep enough for boating. Water level is fairly constant in summer. We were there in a dry season, and the drawdown was less than 18 in. The area is largely mixed hardwood forest, with reverting fields, brushy marsh, and beaver flowages. Wildlife is abundant.

Activities

Hiking: Easy trails along the shoreline and through fields and forest. A spur extends to the Nipmuck Trail.

Hunting: Pheasant, grouse, quail, small game.

Fishing: Said to be one of CT's best areas for trout, smallmouth bass, bullhead, and chain pickerel.

Boating: Paved launching ramp. No hp limit.

Publications

Map of State Park.

Map of Huntington Area.

Headquarters

CT Dept. of Environmental Protection, Wildlife Div., 79 Elm St., Hartford, CT 06106-5127; (860) 424-3011. State Parks Div., same address; (860) 424-3200.

Mashamoquet Brook State Park

Connecticut Department of Environmental Protection   East
860 acres.

From Putnam, 5 mi. SW on Hwy 44.

In the eastern highlands, this attractive Park is usually at capacity on summer weekends. We drove past many picnic tables to a swimming beach on a small pond. Not far away are Natchaug and James L. Goodwin State Forests (see entries), which have fine hiking rails but no campgrounds. Before and after the swimming season, the Park is a convenient base. It includes the former Wolf Den and Saptree Run Parks.

The Park has rolling woodlands in all stages of succession: reverting fields; stands of smooth alder, juniper, and young red cedar; birch replacing cedar; oak replacing birch. Beaver-flooded swamp has a short boardwalk. Table Rock and Indian Chair are large stone formations.

Activities

Camping: 2 campgrounds, 20 and 35 sites. Reservations. Off-season camping through Nov. 3; limited facilities after Columbus Day.

Hiking: Short trails within the Park.

Headquarters

Mashamoquet Brook State Park, Pomfret Center, CT 06259; (860) 928-6121.

Mattatuck State Forest

Connecticut Department of Environmental Protection West
4,531 acres.

Several scattered tracts. The largest is N of Watertown, along the W side of Hwy 8, crossed by US 6. A second is across the river, crossed by Hwy 262. Others are E and N. Site maps are needed.

From the Naugatuck River, hills rise as much as 500 ft. The tracts of the Forest include several hills with bare granite crests, providing good vistas. Much of the area is forested, but the stands we saw were of poor quality. We wouldn't make this an entry were it not for the Mattatuck Trail, which begins near Wolcott and traverses portions of the Forest, including Mount Tobe and Cedar Mountain, as well as Black Rock State Park.

Nearby

Black Rock State Park: 439 acres. On US 6 N of Watertown. Adjoins part of the Forest. It has 90 campsites, pond fishing and swimming, and is usually crowded on warm weekends.

Publications

Maps, 5 sections.

Headquarters

CT Dept. of Environmental Protection, State Parks Div., 79 Elm St., Hartford, CT 06106-5127; (860) 424-3200.

Meshomasic State Forest

Connecticut Department of Environmental Protection East
7,886 acres

N of Hwy 66 at Cobalt.

This is one of CT's largest land areas, an undeveloped Forest Reserve, in the rolling hills E of the Connecticut River. No highway crosses its main body but it has a modest network of local roads, several of which have unmarked trailheads. Best access is by Great Hill Rd., N of Cobalt, on its S boundary. Great Hill, ascended by trail, is a bare granite outcrop with a lookout. The Shenipsit Trail begins here; another trail ascends from Great Hill Pond. Mixed hardwood and conifer forest. Witch hazel is cut commercially. Several brooks drain W to the Connecticut River. Cobalt was once mined here. The area is of interest to rockhounds.

The state agencies have no site maps. The Shenipsit Trail maps in the *Connecticut Walk Book* (see "Trails" in Introduction) are useful here.

Activities

Hiking: The Shenipsit Trail extends N through the Meshomasic and Shenipsit State Forests (see entries) to the MA border, with some gaps.

Hunting: Deer, small game.

Fishing: We've seen no indication that pond or stream fishing is great, but trout are stocked.

Ski touring: Trails and unplowed roads.

Headquarters

CT Dept. of Environmental Protection, State Parks Div., 79 Elm St., Hartford, CT 06106-5127; (860) 424-3200.

....

Mohawk State Forest

Connecticut Department of Environmental Protection   West
3,351 acres.

From Goshen, 4 mi. W on Hwy 4.

Closed at sundown.

Long ago, friends who had a summer place nearby brought us here for sightseeing and a picnic. Both are popular. A good road ascends to the observation tower atop 1,683-ft. Mohawk Mountain, where the view is splendid. One can picnic there or at intermediate stops. Hillsides are moderately sloping to steep, some boulder-strewn, cut by deep ravines. Mountain biking is popular here. Numerous fishing streams. Several glacial eskers. The oak/beech/hickory forest includes white pine and is interspersed with handsome hemlock groves. The ski area on the NW slope isn't conspicuous. It has tows, lifts.

Features
Black Spruce Bog, near Forest HQ, has a trail and boardwalk. Pitcherplant, sundew, mountain holly, other bog species.

Hiking: We hiked several short, pleasant trails. The 35-mi. Mattatuck Trail crosses the top. (So did the Appalachian Trail until it had to be relocated because a landowner blocked the route.) The Great Gulf Trail, E of the Tourney Rd. entrance, is a 1-mi. loop along a deep ravine.

Nearby
Cathedral Pines, a 42-acre property of The Nature Conservancy, is an impressive grove of huge white pines and hemlocks. From Cornwall, S on Pine St., turning or bearing left at intersections; about 1 mi.

Publication
Map.

Headquarters
CT Dept. of Environmental Protection, State Parks Div., 79 Elm St., Hartford, CT 06106-5127; (860) 424-3200.

....

Morgan R. Chaney Sanctuary
Connecticut Audubon Society   East
235 acres

From I-395, Exit 77, drive NW on Hwy 85. Beyond Konomoc Lake, turn right on Turner Rd. to entrance on left.
Open dawn–dusk.

After 3 centuries of land clearing, cultivation, and pasturing in this region, few signs remain of the primeval ecosystem. The society has used the inherent characteristics of this site to develop a diversity of natural habitats. Stone walls, foundations, and the ruins of a dam are relics of earlier uses.

At 426 ft., the site overlooks the adjacent, town-owned Great Swamp, a public water supply. A hemlock ravine near the entrance has intermittent streams.

Publications

Leaflet with site map.

Mimeo information pages on the regional setting, geology, hydrology.

Headquarters

CT Audubon Society, 118 Oak St., Hartford, CT 06106; (860) 527-8737.

Nassahegon State Forest

Connecticut Department of Environmental Protection   West
1,226 acres.

From Burlington on Hwy 4, SE on Washington Turnpike, a local road.

This irregularly shaped Forest is of interest chiefly as a link in the Tunxis Trail, with several blazed local trails permitting loop hikes. The Washington Turnpike bisects the site. Turn S on Stone Rd. to intercept the trail, which crosses near the S boundary. The site is rolling, with low hills. Cover is mixed hardwoods with spruce and pine plantations.

Headquarters

CT Dept. of Environmental Protection, State Parks Div., 79 Elm St., Hartford, CT 06106-5127; (860) 424-3200.

Natchaug State Forest

Connecticut Department of Environmental Protection   East
12,935 acres.

4 mi. S of Phoenixville on Hwy 198.

Natchaug, which means "land between the rivers," is one of the largest State Forests. It's popular for its hiking and backpacking, horse trails and horse camp, excellent fishing, and riverfront picnic sites. The land is rolling, largely covered by hardwood forest with an occasional mixture of hemlock and pines. The understory includes much laurel, spectacular in the blooming season. Habitats include numerous marshes and riparian zones.

Most of the Forest is E of the Natchaug River. The well-signed entrance road crosses the river to Forest HQ. Just beyond is a beaver pond and marsh with wildlife. Several gravel roads traverse the area. Driving in, we saw picnic tables widely spaced under trees beside the stream.

It's a hiker's forest and one of the few where backpacking is allowed, camping by permit at designated sites. The Nipmuck Trail extends about 26 mi. N from Mansfield Hollow State Park (see entry) to Hwy 171 in Union, near the Bigelow Hollow State Park (see entry) entrance; an extension to the MA border is planned. The Natchaug Trail traverses the James L. Goodwin and Natchaug State Forests (see entries). With local trails and logging roads, they form a network available to horse riders, cross-country skiers, and snowmobilers as well as hikers. Silvermine Horse Camp is 2 mi. S of Phoenixville on Hwy 198.

Activities

Hiking, backpacking: About 55 mi. of trails.

Horse riding: Trails and roads. Horse camp has 15 sites available. April 19–Thanksgiving. (First come, first served.)

Hunting: Deer, cottontail, squirrel, raccoon, grouse, woodcock, pheasant, waterfowl.

Fishing: Trout stocked. Natchaug River and streams.

Ski touring: Unplowed roads and trails.

Publications

Maps: site, backpack trails, snowmobile trails.

Adjacent

James L. Goodwin State Forest (see entry).

Nearby

Mashamoquet Brook State Park (see entry) has a campground.

Headquarters

Natchaug State Forest, Star Rt. Pilfershire Rd., Eastford, CT 06242; (860) 974-1562.

Nehantic State Forest

Connecticut Department of Environmental Protection   East
3,798 acres.

From the Connecticut Turnpike, N on Hwy 156. About 1 mi. S of Hamburg, turn right.

The directions are to the Tanney Hill block (also spelled "Tanny" and "Taney"). Other Forest acreage is to the NE. Falls Brook is on the S boundary of the Tanney Hill block, as are Uncas and Norwich Ponds.

This is a State Forest Reserve. The Forest has been recovering from heavy damage in the 1938 hurricane. Mixed hardwoods, small streams, marshes, reverting fields.

Activities

Hiking: The Wildlife Div. map shows trails throughout the area, used chiefly by hunters.

Hunting: Grouse, deer, squirrel, cottontail.

Fishing: Ponds, warmwater species.

Publication

Wildlife Div. map.

Headquarters

CT Dept. of Environmental Protection, State Parks Div., 79 Elm St., Hartford, CT 06106-5127; (860) 424-3200.

Nepaug State Forest

Connecticut Department of Environmental Protection   West
1,199 acres.

S of New Hartford on Hwy 219. Turn left at intersection with US 202. Forest is N of US 202, W of Farmington River.

We spotted the Tunxis Trail sign on the N side of US 202, at a narrow dirt road that enters the Forest. The road didn't seem suitable for cars, but there's no barrier. We found no other road leading in. Pine Hill Rd., shown on the Wildlife Div. map as traversing the Forest, is a dead-end stub.

This is another Forest Reserve. Except for hunting, the Forest is of interest chiefly as a link on the Tunxis Trail. The Trail runs W along US 202 for a short distance before turning S.

Publication
Wildlife Div. map.

Headquarters
CT Dept. of Environmental Protection, State Parks Div., 79 Elm St., Hartford, CT 06106-5127; (860) 424-3200.

....

Nipmuck State Forest

Connecticut Department of Environmental Protection   East
8,058 acres.

On the MA border, both sides of I-84.

The Wildlife Div. map shows the several Forest tracts but with little detail. We found one signed entrance about ½ mi. W of the intersection of Hwy 89 and 190. Just beyond is the signed entrance of Laurel Sanctuary. E of the intersection is the road in to Morey Pond. We had less success in finding Bear Den and Sessions Meadow marshes, but it was late in the day.

Terrain is rolling. The diverse habitats include mixed hardwood and conifer forest, evergreen plantations, wooded wetlands, marshes, ponds, brooks, beaver flowages.

Aside from trails, there's little development: a boat ramp at Morey Pond, a good road into Laurel Sanctuary. It's a hiker's forest, featuring the Nipmuck Trail, with good birding plus hunting and fishing.

Features

Bear Den Marsh and *Sessions Meadow Marsh* are waterfowl areas W of I-84. Access is by Stickney Hill Rd. to Bear Den or Skopec Rds. What we think was Bear Den Rd., unsigned, seemed too muddy for our motor home that day.

Laurel Sanctuary offers an extensive display of the state flower, blooming about the second week of June.

Morey Pond seemed isolated until we saw highway traffic on the opposite side. It's attractive, nonetheless, a forest setting, water lilies massed at one end. Parking for about 6 cars, one picnic table. We saw two children swimming while their parents fished. No sign prohibits powerboats, but the pond seemed too small for them.

Activities

Hiking: The Nipmuck Trail has 2 southern branches, both originating near Mansfield Center, soon joining, continuing N through Bigelow Hollow State Park into the Nipmuck State Forest (see entries) about 25 mi. Another trail links the Forest with the Natchaug Trail. Other trails and woods roads.

Hunting: Grouse, woodcock, squirrel, snowshoe hare, raccoon, deer.

Fishing: Trout stocked in ponds and streams.

Boating: Ramp on Morey Pond.

Ski touring: Trails and unplowed roads.

Nearby
Bigelow Hollow State Park (see entry).

Publication
Wildlife Div. map.

Headquarters
CT Dept. of Environmental Protection, State Parks Div., 79 Elm St., Hartford, CT 06106-5127; (860) 424-3200.

....

Pachaug State Forest

Connecticut Department of Environmental Protection　　　　East
22,938 acres.

Forest's several sections surround Voluntown. A principal entrance is on Hwy 49 1 mi. N of Voluntown.

Largest of CT's public land areas, this was one of the most abused—logged, burned, allowed to erode, much of it flattened by the 1938 hurricane. Most of the area is again forested, partly by natural succession, elsewhere in more than 3,000 acres of plantations. The land is gently rolling, the highest point 441 ft., exposed rocks providing evidence of past erosion. Old cellar holes and miles of stone fences record a history of cultivation and grazing.

The Pachaug River crosses the area but is largely outside Forest boundaries. The Forest has numerous streams, 7 lakes, several impoundments, open and brushy marshes, southern white cedar swamps, and a rare rhododendron sanctuary. It is crisscrossed by graded and unimproved roads. Maps show no point as much as a mile from a road. They also show 35 mi. of hiking trails.

The Pachaug is one of the few CT Forests with campgrounds and one of the rare CT areas where backpacking is permitted. Overnight hikers must have permits and use designated shelters. Contact the Forest or the Dept. of Environmental Protection for details.

Features

The *Great Meadow* complex: 70 acres. E of Hwy 49, N of the river. A wildlife marsh, oak forest, hardwood swamps, hemlock stands, white pine plantations, open and reverting fields. (Not to be confused with the Great Meadows unit of the McKinney NWR.)

Green Falls, off Hwy 138, 3 mi. E of Voluntown, has only 18 campsites. It is chiefly a day-use area, often crowded in fine weather because it offers swimming and boating as well as fishing. We saw one trailhead on the access road marked "Green Falls Trail." The trail map shows the Pachaug and Narragansett Crossover Trails at about this point but no Green Falls Trail. The Nehantic Trail is nearby.

The *H. H. Chapman Area* is about 1 mi. N of Voluntown off Hwy 49. The area includes Forest HQ, Beachdale Pond, and a boat launch site on the Pachaug River. Firetower Rd., W of Voluntown on Hwy 138, runs N to intersect Headquarters Rd., passing the parking area for Mt. Misery Overlook, highest point in the Forest. Nearby are the Mt. Misery Campground, with 20 sites, a Rhododendron Sanctuary, blooms peaking about July 4, and access to the Pachaug and Nehantic Trails.

Hell Hollow–Sue Hopkins Area, further N, off Hwy E of Ekonk, has a similar diversity of habitats.

Activities

Camping: 2 campgrounds, 40 sites. No reservations accepted. Off-season camping to Jan. 1. Primitive facilities at all times.

Hiking, backpacking: On the Nehantic, Quinebaug, and Pachaug Trails. Trailside camping zones are available. The Pachaug Trail extends for about 30 mi. from Green Falls Pond to Pachaug Pond. The Nehantic Trail, about 14 mi., runs from Green Falls Pond to Hopeville Pond. Quinebaugh is a 5½-mi. trail linked with the Pachaug.

Horse riding: Trails are open to horse travel, and woods roads are also suitable. The Frog Hollow Horse Camp has 18 sites available, first come, first served, April 19–Thanksgiving.

Hunting: Deer, squirrel, cottontail, raccoon, fox, grouse, pheasant, duck, woodcock.

Fishing: In 7 lakes, 9 impoundments.

Boating: Launch site on Pachaug River in H. H. Chapman Area.

Canoeing: Lakes, Pachaug River. Canoe rentals.

Ski touring: On trails and unplowed roads.

Publications

Maps: Green Falls Area, H. H. Chapman Area, Backpack trails, Horse trails, Wildlife Div. map, 3 sections.

Nearby

Hopeville Pond State Park (see entry).

Headquarters

Pachaug State Forest, P.O. Box 5, Voluntown, CT 06384; (860) 376-4075. Frog Hollow Horse Camp, RFD #1, Voluntown, CT 06384; (860) 376-4075.

Penwood State Park/Talcott Mountain State Park

Connecticut Department of Environmental Protection   West
787 acres/557 acres.

Penwood: 4 mi. W of Bloomfield on Hwy 185. Talcott: 3 mi. S of Simsbury on Hwy 185.

These contiguous parks, N and S of Hwy 185, attract hikers for their trails and sightseers for their fine vistas. They lie along the Talcott Mountain Range. The 45-mi. Metacomet Trail, part of CT's Blue Trail System, traverses both.

Penwood was given to the state in 1944; the donor required that it be left in natural condition. He and his wife had built many of the trails, as well as a road artfully designed to fit into the mountain contours, passing a high pond. The highest elevation is 741 ft. Both the Connecticut and Farmington River Valleys can be seen from that peak elevation.

Talcott Mountain State Park, acquired 20 years later, has a famous landmark, the Heublein Tower, built by the former owner on a 1,000-ft. promontory, overlooking most of N central CT. The tower, open seasonally, is reached by a 1.5 ridgeline foot trail. On clear days visibility can be as much as 50 mi. (It's also a good spot to watch hang gliders!)

Slopes are moderate to steep, forested, with rock outcrops. Seasonal wildflowers include Dutchman's breeches, trillium, bloodroot, hepatica, trailing arbutus, trout lily, wood anemone. Often-seen birds include turkey vulture, bald eagle, and pileated woodpecker.

Publications
Site maps

Headquarters
CT Dept. of Environmental Protection, State Parks Div., 79 Elm St., Hartford, CT 06106-5127; (860) 424-3200.

Peoples State Forest

Connecticut Department of Environmental Protection   West
2,942 acres.

From Winsted, E on US 44; turn E on Hwy 318 across the Farmington River, then N.

The Forest lies between East River Rd., beside the river, and Park Rd., about 1½ mi. E. Greenwoods Rd. runs generally N–S, bisecting the site. Beaver Brook Rd. branches off Greenwoods at Beaver Swamp, following a trout stream.

The site was acquired in 1923 thanks to the CT Forest and Park Association. We judged that nine-tenths of the visitors are from nearby. Most of them gather at two recreation areas on East River Rd. The Matthies Grove area ("Peoples Recreation Area" on the site map), about a mile N of Hwy 318, has a large parking area, ball field, many picnic tables, and other facilities. Nearby is a grove of 200-year-old white pines. The Whittemore Area, farther N, is chiefly for picnicking. Both are on the river and are convenient for trout anglers and hikers.

Access to the two recreation areas is clearly signed. On East River Rd. and Park Rd., we saw unmarked roads that enter the Forest.

No point in the Forest is more than ¼ mi. from a road, but the interior roads are lightly traveled. A network of trails offers opportunities for hikes of up to a half-day.

Elevations range from 500 ft. at the river to 1,200 ft. Most is rolling forest land, young mixed hardwoods with heavy stands of hemlock, white pine, and spruce. The trails are blazed, but not always well maintained.

It's a fine recreation resource for nearby residents. Visitors from other areas can find somewhat more attractive trails in the Tunxis State Forest (see entry) a few miles N.

Nearby

The 782-acre American Legion State Forest is just across the river. Although much smaller and with only two short trails, it has a campground.

Activities

Camping: 30 sites in American Legion SF, on West River Rd. N of Pleasant Valley. Reservations accepted: (860) 379-2469/0922. Pets are permitted in campground only. Off-season camping to Jan. 1; limited facilities after Columbus Day.

Hunting: Cottontail, snowshoe hare, squirrel, raccoon, deer, grouse, some waterfowl.

Fishing: River. Trout stocked.

Publications

Map of both State Forests.

Wildlife Div. maps.

Headquarters

CT Dept. of Environmental Protection, State Parks Div., 79 Elm St., Hartford, CT 06106-5127; (860) 424-3200.

Quaddick State Forest and State Park

Connecticut Department of Environmental Protection East
972 acres/116 acres.

NE corner of CT. From US 44 at East Putnam, 7 mi. NE on East Putnam Rd.

The chief attraction is Quaddick Reservoir, over 2 mi. long. The Park attracts visitors for water-based recreation, including swimming, sailing, and canoeing (rentals available). It's sometimes crowded, but less so than parks closer to population centers. The Forest, a State Forest Reserve, N of the Park, is available for hiking.

Nearby
Buck Hill WMA and George Washington MA, in RI (See entries in RI).

Headquarters
CT Dept. of Environmental Protection, State Parks Div., 79 Elm St., Hartford, CT 06106-5127; (860) 424-3200.

Quinebaug River Wildlife Management Area

Connecticut Department of Environmental Protection East
1,219 acres.

From I-395 N of Plainfield, Exit 89. W on Hwy 14 about 2 mi. Follow signs on N to Quinebaug Hatchery. Just beyond hatchery, left to parking.

The directions given took us to the S tip of the WMA. From here it extends N along the Quinebaug River almost to Wauregan, a narrow strip in the S, two broader areas further N. Where we saw the river it was shallow, 30 to 50 ft. wide.

The parking area where we stopped is among low hills. White pine, oak, and maple form a forest with sparse understory, open enough for easy walking. Nearby are a marsh, stream, and 2 small ponds. Next to the parking are several picnic tables, trash barrel, and latrines.

It's a quiet, pleasant spot with good birding. Other portions of the site include open fields, mixed hardwoods, pine plantations, and swamps.

Parking areas for the larger N portion of the WMA are NW of Central Village on Hwy 14. If you don't find signs, ask local advice.

Hunting: Chiefly small game and pheasant.

Publication
Map.

Headquarters
CT Dept. of Environmental Protection, Wildlife Div., 79 Elm St., Hartford, CT 06106-5127; (860) 424-3011.

Rocky Neck State Park

Connecticut Department of Environmental Protection　　　　　East
708 acres.

From Connecticut Turnpike, Exit 72, then S. Or, 3 mi. W of Niantic on Hwy 156.

Don't come in summer if you dislike crowds. This is one of CT's few state beaches, a mile of gently sloping sand on Long Island Sound. Out of season it's delightful, and its several habitats provide interest for birders.

Back of the beach is mixed hardwood maritime forest. Bride Brook flows through the site, with salt and brackish marsh. A long stony ridge juts into the Sound.

Activities
Camping: 160 sites.
Hiking: About 4 mi. of trails.
Fishing: Saltwater. Mackerel, striped bass, blackfish, flounder.

Publication
Leaflet with map.

Headquarters

Rocky Neck State Park, Box 676, Niantic, CT 06357; (860) 739-5471.

....

Salmon River State Forest

Connecticut Department of Environmental Protection   East
6,115 acres.

Several sections, W of Colchester. Forest is 2 mi. W of Hwy 149 on River Rd., along Salmon River.

The Wildlife Div. issues maps of 3 Forest tracts: Dickinson Creek and Bull Hill; Dickinson; and Larson Lot. The State Parks Div. issues a map centered on the Salmon River. Even with these we had difficulty finding and identifying Forest land. The total area shown on these maps is much less than 6,115 acres, but the DEP could supply no other maps.

What we saw of the area is moderately hilly, predominantly in mixed hardwoods with occasional openings. On Hwy 149 E of Day Pond, we drove N on Shailor Hill Rd., continued on dirt beyond the blacktop, found a hunters' parking area that showed no sign of recent use, and continued on foot. It was pleasant, quiet, woodland hiking that would be enhanced by fall colors or spring flowers. This was part of the Larson Lot which surrounds the State Park, N of Hwy 16. The Salmon River crosses the NW portion of this tract.

The Salmon River flows to the Connecticut. W of Hwy 16 it is close to Gulf Rd., E of Hwy 16 to River Rd., both on the N. Access to parking, picnic, and put-in sites are near Hwy 16.

The Dickinson Creek and Bull Run tract is 1,000 acres. From Hwy 2 at Marlborough, W on Hwy 66 about 2 mi. to Flood Rd., left 0.5 mi. to fork, left 0.2 mi. This tract has mixed hardwood forest along Dickinson Creek with some hardwood swamp.

The Dickinson tract is 600 acres. From Hwy 2 at Marlborough, E on Hwy 66 about 1.5 mi. cross the Blackledge River, then left. More upland hardwood forest with small brooks and wetlands.

Activities

Hiking: The Salmon River Trail has 2 loops, both originating at Day Pond. The *Connecticut Walk Book* (see "Trails" in Introduction) trail map also shows the Shailor Hill Rd. and an old railroad grade beside the river. The Forest also has hiking opportunities on unmapped woods roads.

Hunting: Large and small game.

Fishing: The Salmon has excellent trout fishing, including a fly-fishing-only section.

Canoeing, kayaking: In early spring; about 5 mi. to the Connecticut River. State literature says that "In early spring, this site is the gathering place for whitewater kayakers and canoers."

Nearby

Day Pond State Park: 180 acres. Hike, fish, swim.

Wopowog Management Areas: 473 acres. On the Salmon River SW of Day Pond, off Hwy 196 to Wopowog Rd. Hike, hunt.

Headquarters

CT Dept. of Environmental Protection, State Parks Div., 79 Elm St., Hartford, CT 06106-5127; (860) 424-3200.

....

Salt Meadow National Wildlife Refuge

See Stewart B. McKinney National Wildlife Refuge.

....

Shade Swamp Sanctuary

Connecticut Department of Environmental Protection   West
800 acres.

Near Farmington. W of the junction of US 6 and Hwy 10. Launch canoes at the river, or continue on US 6 to parking at HQ on right. (Park outside gate when it is closed.)

Shade Swamp is a product of glaciers, which melted to leave a large mass of ice blocking the Farmington Valley about 10,000 years ago. The impounded water formed a lake extending NW beyond the present village of Farmington. When the ice melted completely it left a broad low area, which is now the swamp. The deposits form flat-topped terraces on each side. The Pequabuck River runs through the E portion, meeting the Farmington River (whose course was redirected by glacial deposits) near the NE corner of the site.

The habitats are diverse here: open marsh, brushy marsh, hardwood swamp, mixed hardwood forest, evergreen plantations, open fields. There are many wildflowers, and excellent birding. The Farmington Garden Club works with the Dept. of Environmental Protection on projects relating to the Sanctuary.

Two self-guided nature trails are marked by white and blue blazes. The first is 2½ mi. long, in the W portion of the Sanctuary, showing various stages of woodland succession. The 1½ mi. Blue Trail runs through the E section, through wetlands, then following a glacial terrace. Both trails are accessible from the N side of US 6, E of the junction of US 6 and Hwy 177, in the vicinity of Tunxis Community College.

Since some of the vegetation is delicate, visitors are asked to stay on the trails (and to watch for poison ivy).

Pets are prohibited.

Shade Swamp can also be enjoyed by canoe, from US 6 to Meadow Rd. in Farmington.

Publications

Trail guide with map and checklists of plants, birds, mammals, reptiles and amphibians.

Information page.

Headquarters

CT Dept. of Environmental Protection, 79 Elm St., Hartford, CT 06106-5127; (860) 424-3200. On-site HQ: (860) 677-1819 (not always staffed).

....

Sharon Audubon Center

National Audubon Society   West
684 acres.

From Sharon, 2 mi. SE on Hwy 4.

Open Mon.–Sat., 9–5; Sun. 1–5. Closed holidays. Trails open daily dawn–dusk.

Charcoal mounds and old stone walls in the woodlands tell of past land clearing and forest regeneration. Present-day habitats include pond and stream, field and forest, marsh and swamp. They can be visited along 11 mi. of trails. Almost two-thirds of the site is forested with hardwoods and white pine, with groves of large hemlocks.

More than 175 bird species have been recorded. Mammals include deer, bobcat, mink, beaver, otter, red and gray foxes, squirrel, cottontail.

There are wildflower and herb gardens, an interpretive building with exhibits, and a bookstore.

This is a National Audubon Nature Education Center.

Publication
Brochure.

Headquarters
Sharon Audubon Center, 325 Cornwall Bridge Rd., Sharon, CT 06069; (203) 364-0520.

Shenipsit State Forest

Connecticut Department of Environmental Protection   East
6,126 acres.

From Stafford Springs, W about 6 mi. on Hwy 190. Left on Sodom Rd.

The Shenipsit State Forest Reserve has several blocks, generally W and N of Stafford Springs. Wildlife Div. maps cover only 3 blocks encompassing 2,650 acres. These maps do not show private inholdings. Driving on several roads that cross Forest blocks, we saw houses on both sides and no markers identifying Forest land.

Sodom Rd. is marked as a Forest entrance. This is near the N end of the 30-mi. Shenipsit Trail, which extends S to Cobalt on Hwy 66. Several little-used woods roads branch off the main road. The forest in this area includes white pine and hemlock as well as hardwoods, trees apparently 30 to 50 years old, with a moderately dense understory.

The Shenipsit Trail crosses the Forest's highest points: 1,121-ft. Bald Mountain and 1,061-ft. Soapstone Mountain.

Terrain includes moderately steep slopes, rock outcrops, ledges, small streams and ponds.

Features

Bald Mountain can be approached by Old Country Rd., N from Hwy 190 just E of Gulf Rd.

Soapstone Mountain can be reached by an unpaved road NW from Hwy 140 just W of Crystal Lake. The road continues to Hwy 190. Observation tower.

Activities

Hiking: Shenipsit Trail, other trails, woods roads.

Hunting: Grouse, woodcock, cottontail, squirrel, deer.

Ski touring: Trails and unplowed roads.

Publications

Maps of Crow Hill block, Tower and Bald Mountain blocks.

Nearby

Ellithorpe Flood Control Area (see entry). The Wildlife Div. map shows this as part of the Crow Hill block.

Headquarters

CT Dept. of Environmental Protection, State Parks Div., 79 Elm St., Hartford, CT 06106-5127; (860) 424-3200.

Sleeping Giant State Park

Connecticut Department of Environmental Protection 1,439 acres.

West

From Hamden, 2 mi. N on Hwy 10.

Seldom have we read more entertaining trail guidance: "Its white paint blazes lead over the *right lower left leg* . . . *Pass along the upper right thigh,* cross the *waist* and go up onto the rocky slabs of the *left shoulder* . . ." (*Connecticut Walk Book*).2 mi. of mountain top form the silhouette of the giant lying on his back. A 30-mi. trail network winds through mixed hardwood forest with mountain laurel, brooks, swamps. Highest point is 739 ft. Mount Carmel, accessible via a 1½ mi. trail and providing a view of Long Island Sound. Observation tower. The Park is a popular rock climbing spot.

Activities

Camping: Don't plan on camping here! One of the few campgrounds in a heavily populated region, it has only 6 sites, for tents and small vehicles.

Hiking: The Quinnipiac Trail, oldest in the blue-blazed hiking trails system, 21 mi. long, passes over the Giant.

Fishing: Stream.

Headquarters

CT Dept. of Environmental Protection, State Parks Div., 79 Elm St., Hartford, CT 06106-5127; (860) 424-3200.

....

Stewart B. McKinney National Wildlife Refuge

U.S. Fish and Wildlife Service   West
717 acres.

8 separate units located along the CT coast between Norwalk and Westbrook. HQ is SE of Exit 64 off I-95 on Old Clinton Rd. in Westbrook.

Five islands, a barrier beach, tidal salt marsh, and upland habitats make up the Refuge. Located within the Atlantic Flyway, it provides important nesting, feeding, and resting areas for many species of wading birds, waterfowl, songbirds, shorebirds, and terns, including the endangered roseate tern.

Salt Meadow: 191 acres. In Westbrook, is CT's original National Wildlife Refuge, acquired in 1971. Today it serves as HQ for the McKinney complex, which was established in 1984. (HQ and visitor center are located in a historic manor house.) In addition to the salt marsh, it has forest, grassland, and shrubland. Prominent trees include oaks, yellow poplar, and black cherry. The Menunketesuck River runs through, separating forest from marshland. 2.5 mi. of trails offer access for wildlife observation. Over 200 species of birds have been recorded here. Osprey nest on a platform in the marsh.

Chimon Island (70 acres) and *Sheffield Island* (56 acres) both in Norwalk, *Falkner Island* (5 acres) in Guilford, and *Milford Point* (22 acres) in Milford were all acquired to protect nesting habitat for piping plovers, wading birds, and terns. Chimon has supported as many as

1,200 pairs of herons, egrets, and ibises. Herring and great black-backed gulls nest along Sheffield's rocky shoreline. Falkner supports one of the few remaining nesting colonies of roseate terns in the NE, and the largest common tern colony in CT. Milford, a barrier beach peninsula, is a historic nesting area for piping plovers. An observation platform may be used here year-round. The waters surrounding these island units provide habitat for wintering waterfowl.

Goose Island (1 acre) located just east of Chimon Island, is a gravel beach and brushy upland offering nesting habitat for gulls and American oystercatchers.

Great Meadows Marsh (367 acres), added in 1994, contains the largest unditched saltwater high marsh in CT, and provides feeding and nesting habitat for over 270 species of birds; it's an important wintering area for American black ducks.

Finally, *Outer Island* (5 acres) is the southernmost island in the Thimble Island chain, and its inclusion in the Refuge last year helps assure the well-being of migratory birds that utilize the coastal areas of Long Island Sound.

Future expansion of the refuge is anticipated.

Dogs are permitted only at the Salt Meadow unit.

Publications
Trail maps.

Headquarters
Stewart B. McKinney National Wildlife Refuge, P.O. Box 1030, Westbrook, CT 06498; (860) 399-2513.

....

Tunxis State Forest

Connecticut Department of Environmental Protection   West
8,638 acres.

On the MA border. Blocks on both sides of Barkhamsted Reservoir. Crossed by Hwy 20.

The state lists this Forest as an undeveloped Reserve and provides no information other than Wildlife Div. maps. The 2 maps given us cover only part of the Forest. The *Connecticut Walk Book* (see "Trails" in

Introduction) map is a good guide to the Tunxis Trail, but it doesn't show Forest boundaries and covers little of the area E of the reservoir frontage. It adjoins the Granville State Forest in MA (see entry there), but we found no trail connection.

It's delightful hiking country, and you won't meet many people there. To explore, take the well-marked Tunxis Trail N from its crossing on Hwy 219 E of the reservoir or cruise along lightly traveled Hwy 20 and look for side roads. We found two that were paved for a short distance, then became dirt or gravel. The Tunxis Trail leaves Hwy 20 on a woods road open to vehicles, but soon breaks away from it.

The area is gently rolling, most of it between 1,000 and 1,160 ft. elevation, a few hills rising above 1,200 ft. Pine Mountain, on the Tunxis Trail, reaches 1,391 ft., sufficient in this region to make it a good observation point for the hawk migration. Roaring Brook, dropping down to the reservoir on the E side, has an attractive waterfall. On the W side, a short walk S from Hwy 20, is a waterfall on Falls Brook.

Habitats include reverting fields, ponds, brooks and swamps, beaver flowages, and forest. We hiked through an open mixed hardwood forest and, on a slight rise, entered an extensive dark grove of hemlock. On the higher ground of Pine Mountain are moosewood, hobblebush, mountain ash, wood sorrel.

Howells Pond is popular with anglers. From West Hartland, proceed NW on West St. The roads don't always match those on the Forest map, but we found the pond easily.

Activities

Hiking: The Tunxis Trail is the best-known route, but we saw many inviting woods roads and informal trails.

Hunting: Cottontail, snowshoe hare, gray squirrel, raccoon, grouse, wild turkey, some waterfowl.

Publications
Wildlife Div. maps, Howells Pond area map.

Headquarters
CT Dept. of Environmental Protection, State Parks Div., 79 Elm St., Hartford, CT 06106-5127; (860) 424-3200.

White Memorial Foundation

The White Memorial Foundation   West
4,000 acres.

From Litchfield, 2.2 mi. W on US 202.

Grounds open 24 hr. year-round.

The Foundation owns and maintains this extensive Preserve for conservation, education, recreation, and research. It has 60% of the shoreline of Bantam Lake, 2.4 mi. long, the largest natural lake in CT. In the Litchfield Hills, elevations are from 894 to 1,120 ft. Habitats include forest, hardwood swamp, brushy to open marsh, open fields, beaver flowages, Bantam River, several streams and ponds.

Plants: About 60% of the area is forested with mixed hardwoods, white pine, and spruce. The understory includes mountain laurel, azalea, shadbush. Many wildflowers, ferns, and mosses, including wetland species.

Birds: Checklist available. Waterfowl, rails, herons, gulls, terns, hawks, owls, numerous songbirds. Observation platforms.

Mammals: Common species include deer, beaver, cottontail, chipmunk, squirrel, raccoon. Less often seen: mink, weasel, bobcat, flying squirrel, fox.

Features

Four areas totaling 200 acres are essentially undisturbed, including stands of old-growth white pine, hemlock, and hardwoods.

The *Conservation Center Museum,* once a private home, has natural history, conservation, and wildlife exhibits, and a *library* of over 4,000 volumes about conservation. Open daily; closed Sun. mornings and major holidays.

Weekend programs include nature walks.

Nature trail, self-guiding. Half-mi. *boardwalk* around Little Pond.

Activities

Camping: 2 family campgrounds, 48 and 20 sites. Mid-April–mid-Oct. Reservations suggested.

Hiking: 35 mi. of trails and roads. Trails include a section of the Mattatuck Trail, a major N–S route that connects with the Appalachian Trail. Woodland roads are also used for horse riding and ski touring.

Fishing: Bantam Lake. Northern pike, bass.

Swimming: Beach on Bantam Lake.

Boating: Marina opposite the Folly Point Campground has ramp and moorings.

Ski touring: Trails and woodland roads.

Off-road vehicles, including snowmobiles, are prohibited. No motor vehicles on woods roads. Pets must be leashed.

Publications

Trail map. $2.

Guide to Birding (annotated list) 75 cents.

A Guide to the habitat Groups. 50 cents.

The Natural Areas of the White Memorial Foundation. 75 cents.

Headquarters

The White Memorial Foundation, Rt. 202, Litchfield, CT 06759; (860) 567-0857.

INDEX